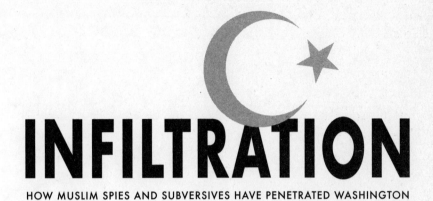

INFILTRATION

HOW MUSLIM SPIES AND SUBVERSIVES HAVE PENETRATED WASHINGTON

PAUL SPERRY

NELSON CURRENT

A Subsidiary of Thomas Nelson, Inc.

www.nelsoncurrent.com

Published in Nashville, Tennessee, by Nelson Current, a subsidiary of Thomas Nelson, Inc.

Nelson Current books may be purchased in bulk for educational, business, fundraising, or sales promotional use. For information, please e-mail SpecialMarkets@ThomasNelson.com.

Scripture quotations are from THE NEW KING JAMES VERSION. Copyright © 1979, 1980, 1982, Thomas Nelson, Inc., Publishers.

Library of Congress cataloguing-in-publication data on file with the Library of Congress.

ISBN 1-5955-5003-8

Printed in the United States of America

05 06 07 08 09 QW 5 4 3 2 1

For my two children, and their children,
in the hope that they will not have to live under terror alerts.

CONTENTS

CONTENTS

PREFACE

"It's a Muslim's duty to help another Muslim in the community. We didn't know what they were up to. It's guilt by association."

"We didn't know there were terrorists praying beside us. Mosques are big, open places where Muslims gather from all over. Membership rolls aren't kept. Attendance is fluid. Nobody knew anything about them."

"It's a Muslim's duty to give zakat donations to brothers in need. We didn't know our money was going to support terrorist activities."

"There is no room for terrorism in Islam. We condemn it outright. Islam is a religion of peace. In fact, the Quran forbids the murder of innocent civilians."

"Jihad? Jihad does not mean holy war. It means internal struggle to improve oneself, striving against sin to be the best one can be in Allah's eyes."

"The government is conducting a witch hunt. They're on a fishing expedition for terrorists in the Muslim community. It's McCarthyism all over again!"

"He is a pillar in the Muslim community, a respected leader. The charges are racist."

By now, you have no doubt heard many of these excuses in the wake of the 9/11 terrorist attacks. Against the body of evidence presented in this book, they will ring hollow. *Infiltration*, at bottom, is a story of mass deception. A disturbing tale of how the American people have been played for fools, victims of an elaborate fraud orchestrated by the "mainstream" Muslim establishment to protect a faith from due scrutiny, while concealing an underworld that secretly plots to infiltrate and overturn the American system of government.

But brace yourself.

Exposing the fraud requires revealing unpleasant truths. Not just about respected Muslim leaders who use mosques, charities, and other nonprofit groups as cover to support terrorist activities, but also popular political figures in Washington *from both parties* who protect them, even helping them place agents of influence inside the government.

It also requires revealing unpleasant truths about Islam itself—a touchy subject, to be sure, one that must be approached with cold-eyed logic and dispassion. I can honestly say that I tried to meet that standard in the instances where it was necessary to analyze the Muslim sacred scripture to deconstruct the white lies of "moderate" Muslim leaders, along with the politically correct mythology of their apologists in the media, academia, and politics. I believe I have done the requisite research to tackle this difficult exegesis accurately, fairly, and authoritatively. Not only have I read the Muslim-approved translation and interpretation of the Quran by Abudullah Yusuf Ali, as well as several textbooks on Islam, but I have also read the books on the recommended reading list of the Council on American-Islamic Relations, the major Muslim advocacy group in Washington. They include *The Islamic Threat: Myth or Reality?* and *Silent No More: Confronting America's False Images of Islam* (which, it is worth noting, lionizes several Muslim leaders now behind bars or under investigation for terrorist ties).

To further aid in demystifying Islam, I have consulted with several experts who genuinely respect Islam on a scholarly and cultural level and have years of experience interacting with both Sunni and Shia Muslims overseas. They include Ret. U.S. Army Lt. Col. Stephen Franke, a former UNSCOM arms control inspector in Baghdad who also served as a personal Arabic interpreter to Ret. Gen. Norman Schwarzkopf during the first Gulf War. Besides being fluent in Arabic, Franke studied Islam at the Islamic Center of Washington under a visiting Saudi legal scholar. He is closely tied to the Iraqi community in Southern California and teaches Arabic cultural awareness to troops deploying to Iraq.

In addition, I have put together a glossary of common Arabic terms and concepts for easy reference at www.SperryFiles.com. It is important to know the vernacular. When American imams praise modern-day *shaheeds* at Friday sermons, for example, they are talking about martyrs, who are really suicide bombers, who are really terrorists. And when Muslim scholars try to soften the meaning of *jihad* as an "internal struggle against sin"—such as trying to quit smoking—they are dissembling. For the core meaning of jihad is "fighting the unbelievers in the cause of Allah." And dying while fighting is the highest form of faith, bringing the highest rewards in Paradise.

What's more, I am physically close to the heart of the conspiracy to institutionalize Islam in America and therefore fully immersed in the story, which puts me in a unique position to capture the kind of nuance necessary to paint a full and textured picture. All paths in the terror-support syndicate lead back to northern Virginia where I live and work as an investigative journalist, part of a state with the fastest-growing Muslim population in America. It is also the U.S. headquarters of the Saudi Wahhabi lobby. Because of my proximity, I can take readers inside the underworld that is operating right in the president's backyard. It runs along an old highway I have nicknamed the "Wahhabi corridor." A chapter by that name provides a veritable road map to the conspiracy.

Muslim subversives and fellow travelers who agreed to be interviewed for this book were given ample running room to defend themselves and their positions. I am not interested in setting up straw men. And those hoping for mindless Islam-bashing or *ad hominem* attacks against sacred Muslim figures such as Muhammad will be disappointed. I use only facts to advance the argument of the book.

It has become abundantly clear in the three and a half years since 9/11, however, that even those who *thoughtfully* and *factually* criticize Muslim leaders in America can expect to be reflexively smeared as "bigots," "racists," or "Islamophobes" by these same leaders, desperate as they are to change the subject, and by their apologists in the punditry, eager as they are to claim the mantle of tolerance. This author, unfortunately, will be no exception.

But make no mistake: this book is an indictment of subversive Muslim leaders representing Saudi Wahhabi interests, a dangerous criminal syndicate that is secretly funding terrorists abroad and facilitating them at home while planting the seeds of insurrection inside America's institutions. It is *not* a general indictment of people of Islamic faith or Arabic origin. I have worked for Arab Americans and lived, roomed, and dined with immigrant Muslims, both Sunni and Shia. Today I call immigrant Muslim neighbors friends. I respect them all as individuals.

So save the smears.

Now for the facts.

INTRODUCTION

"There have been an increasing number of instances in which Wahhabists have successfully penetrated key U.S. institutions, such as the military and [the religious programs of] our prison system."
—SEN. JON L. KYL, Republican chairman of the Senate Judiciary Committee's Subcommittee on Terrorism, Technology, and Homeland Security[1]

Some of the most respected leaders of the Muslim community in America—the so-called "moderates" who have broken bread in the White House, prayed in Congress, advised the Pentagon and even lectured cadets at the FBI academy—are harboring a secret dream about the future of American culture.

Abdurahman M. Alamoudi, the influential founder of the American Muslim Council has, for example, repeatedly told Muslim audiences that the goal of Muslims in America is to turn the U.S. into an Islamic state, even if it takes "a hundred years."

"I think if we are outside this country, we can say, 'Oh, Allah, destroy America,'" says Alamoudi, who has advised the Pentagon on Islam and stocked it with Muslim chaplains. "But once we are here, our mission in this country is to change it."[2]

Imam Siraj Wahhaj, one of the most popular Muslim preachers in America, has privately told his flock, "In time, this so-called democracy will crumble, and there will be nothing. And the only thing that will remain will be Islam."[3]

Omar M. Ahmad, the chairman of the nation's leading Muslim-rights group—Washington-based Council on American-Islamic Relations, or CAIR—has asserted the following to a Muslim audience: "Islam isn't in America to be equal to any other faith, but to become dominant. The Quran should be the highest authority in America."[4]

WORDS, NOT BOMBS

Forget everything you have been told about these "moderate" and "mainstream" leaders. *Infiltration* explodes the facade of moderation and patriotism that Muslim scholars, imams, clerics, businessmen, and political leaders in the burgeoning Muslim community in America have conveyed in the wake of the 9/11 terrorist attacks. In reality, the Muslim establishment that publicly decries the radical fringe—represented by al-Qaida's brand of orthodox Islam known as Wahhabism, the official state religion of Saudi Arabia—is actually a part of it. The only difference is they use words and money instead of bombs to accomplish their goals.

Alamoudi, for one, is now in jail after pleading guilty to charges he plotted acts of terrorism—but not before he had a chance to influence the Pentagon. It was the widely respected Alamoudi, once an honored White House guest, who created the Muslim chaplain corps in the U.S. military, a program that has allowed a Saudi-based al-Qaida front called the Muslim World League to sponsor scores of American soldiers to make pilgrimages to Saudi holy sites. There are now as many as twenty thousand Muslim soldiers in the U.S. military. Some of them have been convicted of betraying their country by helping al-Qaida, America's sworn enemy. And Muslim translators and a Muslim chaplain assigned to the U.S. military base in Guantanamo Bay, Cuba, where al-Qaida suspects are under interrogation, have been accused of engaging in espionage and other suspicious activities.

Other Muslim translators and even Muslim agents working for the FBI—our first line of defense against an encore attack by al-Qaida—have also been accused of betraying the country they took an oath to protect against all enemies, foreign and domestic. And more are lying in wait to double-cross America, whose government continues to believe that Islam is compatible with traditional American values. As it continues to worship at the altar of cultural diversity, political correctness, and religious tolerance for tolerance's sake, terror-enabling Muslim subversives masquerading as "moderates" have insinuated themselves into the fabric of American society, knitting their own impressive network of support for the bad guys, targeting the U.S. government and the business sector. Taking advantage of its religious freedoms and tax-exemption laws, they have gained firm footholds in key American institutions, including:

- Public schools and universities

- The political system

- The federal and state prison system

- Law enforcement—including the Department of Homeland Security

- The military—including the nuclear weapons laboratories

- Even the White House

"There have been an increasing number of instances in which Wahhabists have successfully penetrated key U.S. institutions, such as the military and [the religious programs of] our prison system," warns Sen. Jon L. Kyl, Republican chairman of the Senate Judiciary Committee's Subcommittee on Terrorism, Technology, and Homeland Security.[5] He fears the infiltration is "part of a larger pattern" of subversion.[6]

Muslim subversives have managed to build an "impressive infrastructure of support for the bad guys" like al-Qaida terrorists, says FBI counterterrorism veteran Donald Lavey. He notes that this did not just happen overnight, nor did it slow down after September 11, 2001, astonishingly enough.

For the past thirty years, Muslim subversives have been working clandestinely to undermine America's constitutional government and the Judeo-Christian ethics on which it was built, says Lavey, who more recently served as counterterrorism chief for Interpol, the international police organization. Their goal, quite simply, is to replace the U.S. Constitution with the Quran, the Muslim sacred book, and turn America into an Islamic state. Kyl agrees, saying they "seek the ultimate overthrow of the Constitution."[7] And they plan to do this by exploiting the very rights and freedoms they intend to banish, while counting on the ever-trusting American people to remain blind to their true intentions.

In this project, they have been aided and abetted by tireless champions of spiritual and cultural relativism in the media and academia, who have mitigated the threat in the public's mind by mainstreaming Islam.

For instance, not long after the 9/11 attacks, Georgetown University professor John Esposito—a leading apologist for Islam who receives foreign funding from a wealthy Saudi-tied businessman—told CNN that Islam was tolerant of other religions, even claiming that Muslims and Christians share common beliefs. As proof, he offered that the mother Mary is mentioned more often in the Quran "than in the New Testament." While true, it is obvious from even a cursory reading of the Quran that the only reason it cites Mary so many times is to brand Jesus a mere mortal in the Muslim mind. Christ is referred to exclusively in the text of the Quran as "Jesus, son of Mary," and never "Jesus, son of God," which would be blasphemous to Allah. If anything, the literary distinction points up how *different* the two faiths are.

Either the professor had not read the Quran, or he was being disingenuous—which would not be a first for those trying to mainstream Islam. Thus another myth about Islam was planted in the minds of Americans, many of whom have never read the Bible, let alone the Quran. I only later learned that Esposito wrote one of the books that Ahmad's CAIR is stocking in some sixteen thousand public libraries across the country as part of its campaign to "educate" Americans about the allegedly non-threatening nature of Islam. In his book, he sings the praises of Hamas, even though it was designated a terrorist group by the Department of State more than three years before he wrote his book.

Enlisting the help of the cultural elite is bad enough, but Muslims who want to overthrow the American system patiently from within, with backing primarily from Saudi Arabia through its Washington-based Wahhabi lobby, have also been assisted, unwittingly, by the very government institutions now charged with winning the war on Islamic terrorism: the FBI and the Pentagon. They have also infiltrated the religious programs of American prisons, a dangerously fertile recruiting ground for al-Qaida that has already produced dirty bomb suspect Jose Padilla, among other Muslim terrorists. Prisons are a potential powder keg, and Muslim chaplains are providing the match.

There are now an estimated two hundred thousand Muslim inmates in America, with about ninety-six hundred in federal prisons alone. Most are black converts, and many are eligible for parole. As they prepare to reenter the general population, they are receiving spiritual guidance from chaplains who preach that the attacks on the World Trade Center and Pentagon were justified. In a chilling report, the Department of Justice inspector general recently found that some authorized federal prison imams have ties to terrorist groups, and at least one sympathized with the 9/11 hijackers. And what's worse, prison officials knew about it—and did nothing. The imam who defended the 9/11 attacks even received "good" and "excellent" job evaluations.[8] Most of the Muslim prison chaplains were endorsed by Saudi-backed institutes, which have been granted exclusive certification rights.

"Foreign states and movements have been financing the promotion of radical, political Islam within America's armed forces and prisons," Kyl warns. "This radical Islam preaches extreme intolerance and hatred of American society, culture, government and the principles enshrined in the U.S. Constitution. And it seeks the ultimate overthrow of the Constitution." The senator adds, "Terrorists have exploited America's religious tolerance, and the chaplain programs in particular, as key elements have infiltrated the military and the prisons."[9]

The fifth column of Muslim spies and traitors marching into their ranks has been ushered in by the spiritual and cultural relativism entrenched in their bureaucracies. Lest Washington offend a religious minority, even in this epic battle inextricably and unavoidably tied to their faith, it has nonetheless:

- trusted Muslims to hunt down Osama bin Laden in Afghanistan, only to have them deliver him to safety in Pakistan;

- trusted Muslim chaplains to counsel Muslim soldiers ordered to fight fellow Muslims, only to have them aid and abet the enemy and frag their superior officers;

- trusted Muslims to help interrogate Muslims under investigation, only to have them steal our own secrets about bin Laden's terror network at Gitmo, where they operated a veritable spy ring;

- trusted Muslim FBI agents to eavesdrop on Muslim targets, only to have them tip them off;

- trusted Muslims to translate accurately and speedily the Arabic statements of Muslim suspects in custody or under surveillance at the FBI, only to have them betray us as well.

These are the fruits of well-rooted political correctness, critics say.

"The fear of being falsely accused of prejudice, coupled with political correctness, may be part of the reason we got into the situation we're in right now," Kyl regrets.[10]

Perhaps most shocking of all, the main FBI translator program, based in the Washington field office, is a den of deceit and dual loyalties, a place where mistranslations of al-Qaida intercepts by Muslim and Arab linguists is commonplace, say agents and translators who have worked there.

Take former FBI linguist Sibel Dinez Edmonds. When she showed up for her first day of work at the field office, a week after the 9/11 attacks, she expected to find a somber atmosphere. Instead, she was offered cookies filled with dates from party bowls set out in the room where other Middle Eastern linguists with top-secret security clearance translate terror-related communications. The cause for the celebration? The 9/11 attacks. Some of her colleagues openly and loudly derided the country they are paid to protect. With her Arab supervisor looking on, another Arab translator sneered: "It's about time they got a taste of what they've been giving the Middle East."[11]

It gets worse.

The language services squad is the frontline in the FBI's war on terrorism, collecting all foreign language tips, information, and terrorist threats to homeland security. Agents act on what the squad translates and reports back to them. The sooner agents get the information, the sooner they can thwart terrorist attacks. Investigators had missed clues to both the 1993 and 2001 World Trade Center attacks because they were buried in a backlog of untranslated wiretaps and documents in Arabic, a backlog that is still growing.

Despite the mountain of untranslated material, which could hold clues to the next al-Qaida attack, Edmonds says her supervisor ordered her and other translators to just let the work pile higher. Why? To compel Congress to boost their department budget. The supervisor was promoted to running the Arabic desk, the key to intercepting the al-Qaida plots, after he threatened to sue the FBI for racial discrimination.

The bureau is extremely sensitive to such complaints. Even after the Islamic attacks on America, it instated a bureau-wide Muslim-sensitivity training program. The FBI is putting both veteran agents and new recruits through the program, which includes inviting Muslim clerics and leaders to preach about the allegedly peaceful attributes of Islam—despite the fact the FBI overlooked close ties between a Muslim cleric and two of the al-Qaida hijackers. It viewed the relationship as purely "spiritual," and therefore "innocuous."[12] (My own investigation of the imam, relying on information from his former roommate and U.S. Treasury documents, reveals he has links to terror that are far more extensive than has been reported.)

The FBI sensitivity training, denounced by some active and former agents, was mandated after 9/11 by FBI Director Robert Mueller, who agreed to speak at an American Muslim Council convention even though the organization has voiced support for terrorist groups. The FBI defended his controversial appearance by calling AMC "the most mainstream Muslim group in the United States."

Now its founder, Alamoudi, is behind bars.

Lavey tells me Mueller is so worried about offending Muslim groups that he refuses to publicly use the terms "Islamic" and "terrorism" in the same sentence. He argues the director's main objective behind his sensitivity program is political: mollifying vocal Arab-American and Muslim pressure groups like AMC and CAIR.

The FBI is not alone. *Infiltration* documents examples of stubborn post-9/11, pro-Islam PC at other institutions, corporate boardrooms, the Department of Defense, and the all-important Department of Transportation, which is slapping airlines with huge fines for allegedly discriminating against Middle Eastern passengers who pose a threat to security. The secretary of transportation has even hired an Islamic activist to coordinate policy with Congress. The welcome mat is out to militant Islamists seeking to penetrate these institutions.

Other books have examined the radicalism that is spreading from the Arab world to America's shores, but *Infiltration* will take the discussion to a new level, showing through exhaustive investigative detail how Islamists with covert agendas have permeated every layer of American society—from classrooms and military bases to city councils and Congress—and how they are slowly and assiduously manipulating an open and ever-tolerant society to try to transform the U.S. into an Islamic state. It is a well-rooted enemy with an impressive support network, something terrorism researcher Steven Emerson first examined in his bestseller *American Jihad.* But Emerson essentially stopped there. While he "was the first to explore the semi-clandestine network established by extreme Islamists on America's shores," says Khalid Duran, who helped Emerson translate Arabic materials, he "failed to expose Islamist infiltration of the armed forces and academe." Or of the FBI. Or the U.S. Bureau of Prisons. Or the Department of Homeland Security. Or most alarming, the White House itself.[13]

SHOCKING REVELATIONS

Through exclusive interviews with career FBI agents and linguists, U.S. Customs and Border Protection agents, U.S. Army intelligence officials and other intelligence and law enforcement sources—as well as through highly-sensitive government documents—readers of *Infiltration* will learn for the first time that:

- A senior White House official of Persian origin has been put in charge of government contracting and outsourcing, even though congressional lobbying records show he once lobbied on behalf of a Muslim activist who is now a confessed terrorist.

- The same official prior to 9/11 lobbied Congress and federal agencies to make it harder for federal law enforcement to deport Middle Eastern immigrants with suspected terror links.

- An Islamic activist obtained a sensitive intelligence post at the Department of Homeland Security even though he failed to disclose his past association with the same confessed terrorist—an omission overlooked by a federal personnel agency he happened to previously advise as one of its top internal lawyers.

- In their rush to recruit Arabic translators after 9/11, both the FBI and Pentagon cut corners on background checks and hired Muslim translators in spite of their ties to various foreign military and intelligence agencies in Syria, Egypt, Pakistan, and Turkey.

- Laptops with classified intelligence about al-Qaida investigations have gone missing from the translation unit in the Washington field office of the FBI.

- Over the objections of counterespionage agents, the FBI hired the daughter of a former senior Pakistani intelligence officer to translate intercepts of Pakistani targets; about six months later, a secret FBI code was compromised, falling into the hands of the Pakistani government.

- A Muslim FBI agent who refused to wear a wire to secretly record a Muslim target of a counterterrorism investigation was friends with the bookkeeper of the target.

- Alamoudi's deputy, a Palestinian activist who sponsors an orphaned child of a Palestinian suicide bomber, has nearly unfettered access to the White House through Bush political adviser Karl Rove.

- President Bush struck a deal with Muslim-rights groups to avoid describing terrorism as "Islamic."

- With the blessing of the White House, a Republican-tied Islamic institute has been running influence operations against the federal government.

- Even as it claims to be moderate, IRS financial records show that CAIR, the powerful Muslim advocacy group, has donated money to terrorist front groups such as the Holy Land Foundation, while employing three officials recently arrested for terrorist-related activities.

- Financial and land records show CAIR has received substantial foreign support for its operations, contradicting public denials by CAIR officials.

- In a campaign to Islamize the American workplace, CAIR has won with the backing of the EEOC more than two hundred cases of alleged religious discrimination against U.S. companies, some of which have agreed to put managers through Muslim-sensitivity training.

- The widely cited number for the size of the Muslim population in America—seven million—was pulled out of thin air by a CAIR board member who doubled as an "independent researcher" for the study that first published the inflated figure.

- A Muslim social studies teacher who was on the Saudi government payroll is educating your children about Islam in public schools through sugarcoated textbooks and role-playing exercises in which kids "become Muslims" for weeks.

- The large Washington-area mosque that ministered to at least two of the Saudi hijackers who attacked the Pentagon—the same mosque listed in the personal phone book of one of the 9/11 plotters in Germany—is owned and controlled by a trust tied to the Saudi Wahhabi lobby, according to local property records.

• At least four leaders of the mosque have come under federal investigation or scrutiny for terrorist ties, including a former imam who not only held closed-door meetings with two of the 9/11 hijackers but also counseled young Muslims at George Washington University located just blocks from the White House, and who continues to exhort Muslims to become martyrs by fighting and dying in the cause of Allah, according to a transcript of a recent sermon he gave in London.

• In an exclusive interview, an American Muslim who roomed with the 9/11 imam on a 2001 pilgrimage to Mecca says he voiced support for terrorism during their *hajj* trip.

• Yet, according to law-enforcement documents I obtained, the government let the imam—Sheikh Anwar N. al-Aulaqi—leave the country after 9/11 on a Saudi Arabian Airlines flight—despite a federal warrant for his arrest in connection to a terrorist-financing investigation headed by the U.S. Department of Treasury.

• The tenants of a Pentagon-area apartment building popular with diplomats working for the Saudi Embassy in Washington cheered the 9/11 attacks, according to a leasing agent and former residents.

A WORD ABOUT ORGANIZATION

Infiltration is divided into seven parts. The first exposes the deceptive methods used by Muslim leaders to conceal the dark underbelly of Islam in an effort to gain wider acceptance in Washington. Called "In Allah We Trust," the section is a critical component to the story of infiltration, because it explains how Washington's politicians and pundits can still, even after 9/11, buy into Muslim leaders' hype about the peaceful, non-threatening nature of Islam. Simply put, they have been spun by even slicker spin doctors. And in their gullibility, they have left the door open to anti-American agents and infiltrators.

A full chapter in this section will be devoted to the Muslim art of telling "white lies" to defend the faith and further the cause of Allah, as instructed in the *hadiths*, the sacred supplements to the Quran. The Muslim establishment plays an elaborate word game. It is easy to be fooled by such duplicity, so I have provided readers with the intellectual tools to easily identify it.

For example, many Muslim leaders in America when asked to condemn terrorist acts sternly argue that the Quran forbids terrorism, which they define as the "murder of innocent civilians." Such statements generally assuage skeptics. But they are disingenuous, as orthodox Muslims do not consider Jews and Christians necessarily to be "innocent." Nor do they view Israelis and Westerners necessarily as "civilians" just because they do not wear uniforms. And what the public recognizes as "murder," they may recognize as "justice." So you have to carefully parse what they say. I will quote former Muslims who say such white lies are not considered a sin in Islam. In fact, they are encouraged if they protect the faith or help fellow Muslims.

Of course, duplicity is hardly limited to Muslim leaders. Just ask Christian evangelists such as Jim Bakker or Jimmy Swaggart. But they hid personal failings that ran afoul of their preaching. Many American Muslim leaders hide not their personal failings, but what they preach in Friday sermons, which more often than not advocate violence against Jews, Christians, and the West, as I will document in a chapter on Wahhabi mosques in America. Titled "Sanctuaries of Terror," the chapter is one of many in the book dealing with the silent threat from the Muslim community in America. The section called "The Terror Support Network" sets up the rest of the book, the "infiltration" sections, which explore the major areas of American society where such Islamist moles, spies, facilitators, conduits, agents of influence, and outright traitors have penetrated. Alarmingly, they have managed to burrow not just into the nation's religious establishment, but also law enforcement agencies, the military, the business sector, and the education and political systems.

The afterword, "The Perfect Enemy," makes the case through the eyes of law enforcement and intelligence veterans that this threat in many ways is worse than the Red Menace. For almost fifty years, Americans were virtually paralyzed with fear over Communist infiltrators, only to find their numbers and influence much smaller than first believed. Many of them were Hollywood dilettantes who would not think of resorting to violence to further their cause. And in the end, though the Cold War threat was certainly real, America was never attacked. In contrast, the danger from the Green Menace (green being the color of Islam) is both clear and present.

Yet the public reaction to this threat seems milder. Why?

In a word, *religion.*

It was easy for Americans to suspect atheists. But Islam is a large and established religion protected by the First Amendment (even though that protection does not cover sedition). Americans are told even by their president to respect, not suspect, their Muslim neighbors and their faith. He never ceases to remind them that Islam is a "peaceful," "loving," even "great" religion, and that we share the same God. In effect, Muslims have both political and religious immunity, even though so many worship at Wahhabi mosques that exalt suicide bombers and preach death to the West and Israel (with some even obliterating Israel from maps and bas-reliefs while showing "Beautiful Palestine" in its place). No one wants to think places of worship would engage in such activities. But many do, and it is the perfect cover for subversion—although that is not to suggest that all Muslims in America are involved in un-American activities, or even that they all subscribe to a strict code of Islam like Wahhabism. The Muslim community is no monolith, divided as it is by Shiites and Sunnis and more moderate Sufis, and not all of them observant.

For example, Sufi Sheikh Muhammad Hisham Kabbani, who practices a form of Islamic mysticism, is a moderate voice, and an outspoken critic of Wahhabism. Saudi reformer Ali Ahmed, a Shiite Muslim who fled the Sunni-dominated Saudi kingdom, is another, along with fellow moderate Shiite Agha Jafri.

However, they are not considered part of the established Muslim leadership in America, and have only minor voices in the national debate. Why? Mainly because the vast majority of mosques in America practice Sunnism, Islam's main sect, and as many as eight out of ten are under Saudi Wahhabi control. The large Washington-area mosque tied to the 9/11 hijackers and plotters is hardly the exception. Just down the street from Dar al-Hijrah Islamic Center is a smaller mosque that encouraged young Muslim men to kill fellow Americans in Afghanistan. They trained for the jihad at the NRA's firing range before being arrested. The mosque's imam, now under indictment, even cheered the space shuttle *Columbia* disaster as a "good omen," according to court documents. The "Blind Sheikh" Omar Abdul Rahman's mosque in New Jersey, moreover, was a recruiting base for the first World Trade Center terrorists. And another Wahhabi mosque clear across the country in Santa Clara, California, raised money for bin Laden's second in command—not once, but twice. (The same mosque, tellingly enough, counts the chairman of CAIR as a longtime member.) These Saudi-controlled mosques and their related charities—such as those affiliated with the recently raided Safa group in northern Virginia—have provided spiritual and material support to terrorists hell-bent on destroying Israel and the West.

"THE GREAT SATAN"

After the 9/11 attacks, FBI Director Mueller assured Americans that the nineteen al-Qaida hijackers operated alone when they lived here, that they were relatively isolated and got no help or support from the Muslim community. According to him, 9/11 was just the result of a few bad apples.

Only, he was not leveling with the American people.

In fact, the Joint Inquiry into 9/11 by Congress found that a number of Muslims provided the hijackers with "substantial" assistance, including finding housing, opening bank accounts, obtaining driver's licenses, locating flight schools, and facilitating other transactions. What's more, some of the hijackers were in various degrees of contact with more than a dozen American Muslims who at some point had come under FBI investigation for terrorism activities. And some of the mosques the hijackers attended in California, Florida, Virginia, Arizona, and Maryland were also attended by persons of interest to the FBI. Even before al-Qaida attacked, the bureau was conducting full-field investigations of fifty-seven individuals connected to al-Qaida.[14] And they are just the tip of the iceberg.

All told, al-Qaida has trained up to one hundred and twenty thousand terrorists around the world, and as many as five thousand terrorist operatives are said to be inside the U.S., according to U.S. intelligence. That means there are potentially five thousand terrorists preparing for martyrdom operations against their host while hiding unmolested in the Muslim immigrant community—just like the nineteen hijackers.

If Director Mueller and other PC-addled bureaucrats and politicians in Washington do not understand the enemy, many of the field agents working terrorist leads in Chicago, New York, Detroit, San Diego, Minneapolis, and Phoenix understand all too well. They know firsthand that there is a network of terrorists, facilitators, and pro-terrorist Muslim organizations operating within the U.S. largely under the radar. Yet there is still a reluctance in Washington to let agents knock on doors for fear of offending religious and ethnic minorities—and triggering a CAIR media *fatwa*.

As a result, the FBI still knows alarmingly little about the growing threat inside the Muslim community in America. The former head of the FBI's Washington field office, Michael Rolince, admits the bureau's knowledge is about twenty on a scale of one to one hundred. Another career supervisor says the FBI has not adequately reached out to the Muslim community in which it should be developing sources.[15]

What is truly remarkable is that the Muslim preachers and activists quoted at the top of this introduction have been preaching anti-American hate to the Muslim community for years, yet they never raised serious red flags at FBI headquarters. And quite tellingly, they never faced recriminations or ostracism from the Muslim community. In fact, they only grew in stature.

Consider the case, too, of the former Florida professor, Sami al-Arian, now accused of running benign-sounding nonprofits like the World Islamic Studies Enterprise, or WISE, as fundraising fronts for terrorist groups. Though agents suspected he was up to no good a decade ago, he remained a respected leader in the Muslim community and an honored White House guest in both the Clinton and Bush administrations. He even posed for photographs with candidate Bush. Yet privately, he called America "the Great Satan" and argued for "the dismantling of the cultural system of the West," according to federal court documents. His Florida charities were connected to the Safa network of Muslim charities in northern Virginia, which also sounded harmless—until agents were finally authorized to take a closer look at their money trail.[16]

These religious and charitable groups have availed themselves of the advantages of exemption from federal income taxes. Call it tax-exempt terrorism. Should this be allowed to continue? The Senate Finance Committee, for one, is auditing two dozen Muslim nonprofits to learn the scope of the problem. Preliminary findings show the groups have "abused" U.S. tax laws, a committee staffer says. In the afterword, I will also explore possible remedies with lawmakers and legal scholars.

Terror-support groups posing as Islamic charities, think tanks, and other nonprofits have even discussed running infiltration operations against the U.S. government to collect intelligence. One terrorism document seized in a search of al-Arian's home is especially instructive. Written in the inscrutable language of Arabic, which functions as a secret code for Muslim militants operating in America, it was translated to English and revealed the following:

> Our presence in North America gives us a unique opportunity to monitor, explore, and follow up. We should be able to infiltrate the sensitive intelligence agencies or the embassies in order to collect information.[17]

Unfortunately, our "sensitive intelligence agencies" have not made it very hard for them to put agents in place.

Exhibit A is the FBI translator program. John M. Cole, who retired late last year from the FBI as program manager for foreign intelligence investigations covering India, Pakistan, and Afghanistan, says he observed serious security lapses involving the screening and hiring of translators.

"We have serious problems with the hiring of language specialists," he tells me. "Background investigations are not being conducted properly, and we're giving people TS/SCI (top secret/sensitive compartmented information) clearance who shouldn't have it." He says at least a dozen translators still on the job have major "red flags" in their files. "And we have espionage cases because of it," Cole adds, ominously.[18]

The internal threat is much deeper and better organized than the government is willing to admit. *Infiltration* serves as a wakeup call to the American people about this growing Islamist threat from within America's borders, not just from Osama bin Laden's gang abroad. Even if the al-Qaida leadership is decapitated, terrorism experts fear the threat is a hydra-headed phenomenon that will not go away with al-Qaida. And the reason is plain, if impolitic: its blood supply is a religion. The 9/11 Commission, to its credit, recognized this in describing the threat broadly as "Islamist terrorism." Here is its unanimous conclusion:

> Our enemy is twofold: al-Qaida, a stateless network of terrorists that struck us on 9/11; and a radical ideological movement in the Islamic world, inspired in part by al-Qaida, which has spawned terrorist groups and violence across the globe. The second enemy is gathering, and will menace Americans and American interests long after Osama bin Laden and his cohorts are killed or captured. Thus our strategy must [prevail] in the longer term over the ideology that gives rise to Islamist terrorism.[19]

But even the independent commission hedged. That so-called "radical" ideology of Islamism is simply Islam in practice. And it is being practiced every day at hundreds of mosques across America. Any strategy to prevail over it must strike at that root. And it may require, for starters, auditing Wahhabi charities and mosques for signs of financial jihad, while tightening IRS requirements for acquiring tax-exempt status to make sure no religious applicant supports violence of any kind. In addition, terrorism experts say the government would be well-advised to launch more sting operations at Wahhabi mosques to crack down on the pro-jihad preachers of hate who encourage young Muslim men to carry out acts of violence. These imams are arguably more dangerous, if more cowardly, than the terrorists themselves. One charismatic cleric who does not blow himself up can inspire dozens of acolytes who do.

Of course such measures would first require rousting officials in Washington from their politically correct sleepwalk, something that even another attack on the homeland might not accomplish, as you will see on the following pages.

As a final note, I have done a good deal of primary reporting for this book including firsthand interviews with a number of the players and participants. To avoid repetitive citations, though numerous quotes from a particular interview may be used throughout a chapter, the interview will be cited in the notes only once.

I
IN ALLAH WE TRUST

1

DON'T PICK ON MUSLIMS

Sensitivity Training for FBI Agents

"The bureau is against—has been and will be against—any form
of profiling [of Arabs or Muslims]."
—FBI DIRECTOR ROBERT S. MUELLER[1]

A year after the 9/11 terrorist attacks, the FBI invited the head of an influential
Arab-rights group to speak about Islam to about four hundred new agents in the
auditorium of the FBI Academy, the bureau's high-security training campus hid-
den in the woods of Quantico, Virginia, about an hour south of Washington.
The lecture by Dr. Ziad Asali, then-president of the American-Arab Anti-
Discrimination Committee, was mandatory and lasted about one hour. Asali, a
Palestinian refugee, "talked about how peaceful their religion is, and how not to
offend Muslims . . . showing respect for their culture, things like that," says FBI
Academy spokesman Kirk Crawford.[2]

And at least four times the following year, the FBI's New York field office held
all-day sensitivity training sessions, not far from Ground Zero, featuring Imam
Feisal Abdul Rauf of the Masjid al-Farah mosque. Speaking for about two hours
each session, "he gave an overview of Islamic culture and some of the differences
between what fundamentalist terrorist groups say are the teachings of the Quran
and what he believes, as a student of religion, the Quran actually says," says special agent James Margolin, spokesman for the FBI New York office.[3]

For example, Rauf asserted that the Quran, the sacred book of Muslims, "certainly doesn't counsel terrorism, murder, or mayhem," Margolin says. And he said
terrorists have misinterpreted the Quranic term *jihad* to mean violent, or armed,
struggle against nonbelievers. Rauf claims it means internal struggle.

The rest of the training sessions were conducted by a Muslim FBI agent born
in Pakistan. Foria Younis, who works for the Joint Terrorism Task Force, advised
fellow agents to respect Muslims by honoring their religious and cultural customs.

For instance, she said they should refrain from showing a Muslim the soles of their shoes, which is a sign of disrespect.

The Muslim-sensitivity training program, denounced by some active and former agents, was mandated by FBI Director Robert S. Mueller after the 9/11 attacks and is still in effect. Officially known within the bureau as "Enrichment Training Sessions," the program invites Muslim clerics and scholars to preach to agents about the allegedly peaceful attributes of Islam.

But critics say the Muslim leaders who have lectured to agents have an agenda of soft-peddling the violent aspects of the religion and shielding Muslims from FBI questioning.

"The Muslim and Arab leaders Mueller brought in to train us about Islam weren't interested in helping us investigate terrorism. They all have an agenda of making sure FBI agents don't discriminate against Muslims and Arabs," says recently retired FBI special agent John B. Vincent. "They even came to Quantico to lecture new agents on how not to pick on them."[4]

Mueller has met several times with Arab and Muslim groups since the 9/11 attacks. He even agreed to be the keynote speaker at an American Muslim Council luncheon in Washington[5]—a move that drew fire from AMC critics who warned the director he was legitimizing a group that has sung the praises of Hamas and Hezbollah, officially designated terrorist groups with American, as well as Israeli, blood on their hands. The annual conference also featured speakers from the PLO and government of Syria, a terrorist-sponsoring state. A Mueller spokesman at the time dismissed the concerns, calling the AMC "the most mainstream Muslim group in the United States."[6] Last year, its founder, Abdurahman M. Alamoudi, confessed to plotting acts of terrorism and is now behind bars.[7]

"Mueller should lead the FBI in this war and leave the sensitivity sessions to the human resources department or CNN," complains retired FBI special agent Donald Lavey, who served twenty years in the bureau's counterterrorism section. "Let's just hope the director is leading the charge in this war against terrorism with an equal amount of zeal that he shows for cultural sensitivities," adds Lavey, who points out that Mueller is so politically correct he refuses to use "Islamic" and "terrorism" in the same sentence.[8]

FBI headquarters defends the Muslim-sensitivity program as a way to reach out to the Muslim community in America.

"I hate the word 'sensitivity' training," says FBI spokesman Ed Cogswell. "I would call it an awareness training relative to cultural issues."[9]

Some former colleagues of the late FBI agent John O'Neill say the legendary al-Qaida hunter would probably roll over in his grave if he knew about the

Muslim sensitivity program required at his old New York office, where he headed counterterrorism operations last decade.

"This would not have been an issue high on his priority list," says Ivian C. Smith, a retired FBI manager who worked in counterintelligence at bureau headquarters.

"He would not have been interested in improving the cultural awareness of a bunch of FBI agents. He would have considered it a waste of time," Smith says. "And knowing John, he would have probably figured out a way to avoid going to the meetings."

"He was no-nonsense," Smith adds, "brutally focused on al-Qaida."[10]

Still, Smith allows that the cultural training could be beneficial to investigators if designed to help agents improve their field interviewing and interrogation techniques to gain the cooperation of Muslim witnesses and suspects.

HOLD THE BACON

Margolin says this is certainly one of the goals of the program. For example, he notes, agents also are taught to respect the dietary restrictions of devout Muslims. So-called *halal* dietary laws require their meat be butchered in a certain way. Also, they cannot eat pork or pork byproducts.

"So if you're attempting to be accommodating to a religious Muslim you're interviewing or someone you may have arrested, and you say, 'Gee, I'll run across the street and get you something to eat; you know, you haven't eaten in six hours,' you don't get them a cheeseburger—and you definitely don't get them a bacon cheeseburger," Margolin says. "That would be taken as an offense, when in fact what you're trying to do is maybe open some channels of communication," he adds. The same concerns apply to showing a Muslim witness or suspect the sole of your shoe, he says.

But Lavey insists the program's main objective is political: mollifying vocal Arab-American and Muslim interest groups. He argues that Mueller is so worried about offending American Muslims that he's loath to even describe the most serious terrorist threat against America as "Islamic."

"There's a continued reluctance on the part of the entire FBI to ever use Islamic and terrorism in the same sentence," he says.

Indeed, a search of transcripts of Mueller's congressional testimonies, press conferences, and public speeches turns up no examples of him using the phrase "Islamic terrorism," although he has used the phrase "militant Islamic groups." He typically describes terrorism in generic terms, such as "international terrorism."

It is worth noting that Margolin of the New York office also avoided using the term "Islamic terrorists" during my lengthy interview with him, opting instead for "fundamentalist terrorist groups."

Though bureau spokesman Cogswell admits political correctness "can get out of hand" in Washington, he insists there is no bureau-wide "edict" against describing terrorism or terrorists as "Islamic."

However, President Bush personally made a deal with the Muslim community to never make such a description in public, according to one Muslim activist group. "President Bush told us in a meeting with him that he will make it a point to detach the Islamic label from the word terrorism," says Salam al-Marayati, executive director of the Los Angeles-based Muslim Public Affairs Council. "So you will never see President Bush saying, 'Islamic terrorism.'"

"And in fact, this will help all of us in focusing and concentrating on the problem, and not spreading the whole issue to the religion of Islam," he says.[11]

Actually, it will only worsen the problem, Lavey argues, by distracting from the core issue in the war on terrorism, which is Islamic fundamentalism. He says it is impossible to separate religion from terrorism carried out in the name of Islam, and Washington cannot be shy about calling things by their proper name in a time of war. If it is too "culturally sensitive" to even define the enemy, he argues, it cannot effectively protect the country from it.

"As someone who worked Middle East terrorism for nearly twenty years, I am bothered by the fact that so many influential government leaders and religious leaders who represent Islam see only one side of the sensitivity coin," Lavey says.

"Director Mueller will ensure that all FBI personnel are culturally sensitive to the tenets of Islam," he explains. "But who will ensure that responsible Islamic leaders will be culturally sensitive to the citizens of the United Sates who saw and continue to see their country attacked and innocent countrymen murdered in the name of Islam?"[12]

SUGARCOATING JIHAD

Lavey and others fear Muslim leaders are teaching FBI agents the PC, sanitized version of the Quran in the interest of mainstreaming Islam. The message agents are hearing is that Muslim terrorists like Osama bin Laden have misinterpreted the Quran, and that devout Muslims in America do not sympathize with them, even though the Quran is replete with instructions exhorting the Muslim faithful to fight, even slay, the "unbelievers" in the cause of Allah. Unbelievers include Christians and Jews.

They cite, for example, Muslim clerics' campaign to spin jihad as nonviolent and nonthreatening to people outside the faith. "They're sugarcoating jihad as an internal struggle by Muslims to improve themselves," Vincent says. "But there is also, without a doubt, a violent component to jihad as taught by the Quran, which is when they kill other people who don't subscribe to their religion—and not just non-Muslims, but also hypocrites," or Muslims who do not follow the Quran.[13]

If agents go into investigations with the assumption that American Muslims do not believe what al-Qaida or Hamas terrorists believe and do not sympathize with their cause, agents argue they may be easily snowed by Muslim suspects, witnesses, and informants. They may also be less inclined to investigate Muslim clerics and scholars themselves, even though some who have preached in this country have been tied to Islamic terrorists.

For example, the nine-hundred-page report on 9/11 intelligence failures released by Congress took the FBI to task for failing to pursue leads back to a local imam involved with two of the al-Qaida hijackers who helped crash an American Airlines jumbo jet into the Pentagon. Khalid al-Mihdhar and Nawaf al-Hazmi were close to the imam, Anwar Aulaqi. He and the hijackers moved from San Diego to Falls Church, Virginia, where they joined the Dar al-Hijrah mosque, which will be covered in-depth in another chapter. A phone number for the mosque was found in the German apartment of Ramzi Binalshibh, roommate of hijacking ringleader Mohamed Atta.

Margolin, for his part, says he is inclined to accept the New York imam's interpretation of the Quran, even though he admits he has not read any of it himself.

"I haven't read the text," he says. "But even in Judaism and Christianity, there are portions of the Old and New Testament that are open to interpretation, and people who are politically left or politically right use the Bible as the authority for their positions."

And besides, he adds, the bureau's job is to investigate criminal acts of violence that have been committed, not instructions for violence that may or may not be directed by a religion against those who do not believe in that religion.

"While what the Quran actually says is not insignificant, what we're ultimately concerned with is criminality," Margolin says—which is exactly the kind of tunnel vision that critics say blinded the FBI to the 9/11 cells operating inside America. Before 9/11, supervisors and agents accustomed to solving bank robberies and other black-and-white crimes had little interest in collecting intelligence and analyzing it to prevent terrorism before it happens, a subject I will expand on in the section on law enforcement.

THE PHOENIX MEMO

But bureaucracy was only part of the reason the FBI missed the hijackers' plot. Minority politics also played a role. It turns out that the Phoenix memo—a pre-9/11 proposal by an FBI agent in Arizona to check Middle Eastern students in flight schools—was shelved at headquarters in part because it would have violated bureau guidelines against racial profiling.[14]

Could it happen again? You bet.

"The bureau is against—has been and will be against—any form of profiling," Mueller has testified in response to questions about investigating terrorist leads based on ethnicity or religion.[15] He even reassured the Muslim Public Affairs Council that he does not view the Muslim community as any more suspect than other communities in America. "None of our agents focus on the fact that somebody looks Muslim or not," he said in an April 24, 2003, interview with an MPAC official in his Washington office, while noting the bureau's efforts to train agents to be more sensitive to Muslims. The official, in turn, complimented him: "I think you have been very supportive of the Muslim community."[16]

Career agents worry that Mueller is forcing counterterrorism squads to work at cross-purposes. On one hand, they are under pressure to aggressively flush out terrorist cells inside the Muslim community. But on the other hand, they are told to bend over backwards to avoid offending individuals in that clearly hard target group. They say headquarters' obsession with minority politics is handcuffing field agents trying to work the Muslim community for leads—particularly when they try to question worshippers at American mosques, a shocking number of which have been discovered to be sanctuaries for terrorist activities, as I will document in a coming chapter.

Less than four months before Alamoudi was arrested, Mueller dispatched the head of his civil-rights shop to another AMC conference in Alexandria, Virginia, to tell some three hundred good and decent Muslim leaders and imams gathered there that protecting their civil rights was his "number one priority." FBI official Tom Reynolds assured them that the bureau does not target or even suspect Muslims. "The director has said from the beginning that Islam is good," he said. "The problem is not the [Muslim] community; the problem is a handful of terrorists." With that, an AMC board member stood up to say he has heard "horror stories of how people were investigated" as terrorists. Jamal Barzinji complained that charities to which American Muslims have donated have been raided and shut down. And Barzinji should know: he and a network of charities he and other Washington-area Muslims run are under investigation for funding terrorism. "You didn't shut down the United Way," he fumed at

Reynolds, referring to embezzlement scandals brought on that giant charity by its former president.

Reynolds responded by saying the bureau would not tolerate any Muslim harassment: "When FBI agents overstate their grounds, call me." He noted that the bureau has an Office of Professional Responsibility that investigates agents' conduct, and that federal law enforcement officers have been held accountable in the past for religious harassment. For example, Reynolds reminded the audience of the Secret Service agent who was suspended for scrawling "ISLAM IS EVIL" on the prayer calendar of a Muslim accused of having connections to terrorism during a 2002 federal raid of his Detroit home. In addition, he said the bureau would continue its Muslim-sensitivity training of agents at Quantico.[17]

CHOKING BACK TEARS

According to an AMC press release at the time, Reynolds reportedly "choked back tears while talking about the internment of the Japanese Americans during World War II. He promised that it would never happen again." The FBI official closed his talk by underscoring the fact the bureau views their mosques as partners in the war on terrorism, not targets of investigation. And he expressed his wish that more Muslims would themselves become FBI agents.

AMC's Barzinji thanked Reynolds for his compassion but advised that more U.S. officials like him would need to "come forward to us and build bridges" before Muslims would be comfortable cooperating with the FBI.[18] Apparently it is not enough that Reynolds's boss regularly meets with Muslim leaders as part of permanent working groups between law enforcement and the Muslim community. In fact, Mueller still allows Alamoudi's former deputy at the AMC—Khaled Saffuri—to lecture him about civil rights every six months.[19]

Robert Swan Mueller III is a lawyer by training with no crime-fighting experience as a cop. The career bureaucrat is widely praised inside the Beltway as a genuinely nice man, and that conciliatory nature has taken him far in Washington. Before Bush appointed him to the helm of the FBI for a ten-year term, he worked for Bush's father as a top official in the Department of Justice.

But case agents dismayed by his sensitivity classes and reliance on hardcore Islamist groups for cooperation are not impressed that a *gemutlichkeit* (a German term for yes-man commonly used in D.C. circles) is leading the core agency responsible for fighting terrorism at home. "The bureau is already risk averse," said an FBI counterterrorism agent in Washington. "We don't need a yes-man right now."[20]

Lavey, who also served as INTERPOL's anti-terrorism chief, agrees: "Director

Mueller's decision to placate and bow down to perceived slights against the Muslim community, and the continued reluctance on the part of the FBI to ever use Islamic and terrorism in the same sentence, are not particularly reassuring signs in a time of war."

He says law enforcement should make no apologies for aggressively protecting Americans—including patriotic Muslims—from the Islamist threat, even if other Muslims are offended. Hurt feelings mend with time, he says. Charred bodies do not.

"Most people of common sense during World War II were aware that not all Germans, Italians, and Japanese were evil people," Lavey says, "but we won the war with apologies to no one."[21]

Of course that was sixty years ago. Washington now worships at the altar of diversity, a ritual uninterrupted by even a foreign attack on the homeland. "Political correctness is too broad and deep institutionally to be overridden," laments terrorism expert Thor E. Ronay, president of International Assessment and Strategy Center Inc. in Washington. "It arises from years of inculcation in the agencies, and more generally in the culture that we all operate in."

"The main fool in this picture is the FBI," he adds.[22]

But it is hardly alone. Several other agencies on the front line of the war on terrorism have also sacrificed security on the altar of diversity.

2

POLITICALLY CORRECT SUICIDE

Still Bowing to Islam in Washington

"Allah is the greatest! Allah is the greatest!"
—last words of hijacker pilot ZIAD JARRAH as he crashed
United Airlines Flight 93 into an empty field in
Shanksville, Pennsylvania, killing all aboard

In dealing with the Soviet threat, President Reagan said America should trust, but verify. Well, leaders today have not verified what Muslim activists and scholars have told them about Islam, the new threat. They have not looked at its sacred book for themselves. They have merely taken the word of its apologists and dissemblers that it is a "peaceful" and "tolerant" religion that forbids violence against non-Muslims and is compatible with fundamental American values.

Consumed by an almost pathological fear of being labeled religious bigots, politicians in Washington refuse to engage the nation in an honest, intelligent religious debate, even though religion is at the core of the threat. They are content to use pleasant platitudes like "Islam is a religion of peace" to deal with a serious, long-term threat to American values, culture, and security.

Incredibly, and in spite of all reason, such political correctness was not extinguished with the last flames at Ground Zero. Even many of the federal agencies on the front line in the war on terror are stubbornly hewing to pre-9/11 norms. What follows is a story of political correctness run amok at a time when America can least afford it.

STATE DEPARTMENT

The agency responsible for designating foreign terrorist organizations still calls Chechen terrorists "rebels" and "separatists," and not Islamic terrorists, which is what they are.

And in another example of politically correct language, to say nothing of revisionist history, the former secretary of state practically redefined American heritage as Judeo-Christian-Islamic. In a nationally televised interview in 2003, Colin Powell described Iraq as "an Islamic country by faith, just as we are Judeo-Christian." But then out of deference to Muslim activists who do not like the phrase, he quickly corrected himself, saying "we are a country of many faiths now."[1]

A few months earlier, Agha Saeed of the American Muslim Alliance had demanded that the new language of "Judeo-Christian-Islamic" be used "in all venues where we normally talk about Judeo-Christian values, starting with the media, academia, statements by politicians, and comments made in churches, synagogues, and other places."[2] Then, just prior to Powell's TV appearance, Muslim scholar Mohammed al-Hanooti reiterated the Muslim community's desire to expand the term to Judeo-Christian-Islamic. "The Islamic contribution to [American] society is mounting," he said, "and we need to recognize this."[3]

While it is true that America is a nation of many faiths, the ideas that underpin the civil liberties embodied in the U.S. Constitution come from Judeo-Christian culture, not Islam. No offense, but Muslims were not a part of the framing of the American system of government. James Madison did not exactly have a copy of the Quran at his elbow when he penned the Bill of Rights.

Unless the Constitution is replaced, no one in Washington should hesitate to define American values as anything other than Judeo-Christian, some historians assert, particularly when Islamic values run counter to them.

"It is not without reason that many U.S. citizens sense that Islam's goals run counter to national and personal interest," says former New York University professor Gilbert T. Sewall. "Concern about the ability and willingness of many domestic Muslims to assimilate—that is, to put American constitutional values in front of their religion—is not unfounded."[4]

HOMELAND SECURITY DEPARTMENT

Bowing to pressure from the American Arab Anti-Discrimination Committee, as well as the Saudi Embassy, the department has agreed to stop conducting special security checks on visitors entering the U.S. from some twenty-five Muslim countries. Following 9/11, border authorities had targeted young males from Saudi Arabia, Pakistan, and other high-risk countries for special screening. But no more.[5]

Homeland Security officials are so nervous about Arab profiling, in fact, that many Arabs on the terrorist watchlist are not even listed as Arabs in the database, I have learned. In the race field, they are identified as "White" or "Hispanic."

And get this: U.S. border authorities are advised when interviewing visitors from Muslim countries that few Muslims believe violence is justified under Islam. "The majority of Muslims believe violence is against the teachings of the Quran," cautions a recent department briefing paper I obtained.[6] The statement is demonstrably false. If Muslims believe that, they cannot believe their Quran (which means they would not be Muslims). It not only condones violence, but commands it, as documented in a coming chapter.

Meanwhile, the Transportation Security Administration, which is part of Homeland Security, still refuses to profile passengers who fit the terrorist profile of young, male, and Muslim. Like all passengers, they are subjected to special screening only if they are randomly selected by computer, or if they meet sterile criteria that have nothing to do with ethnicity or creed.

Also, Transportation Secretary Norman Mineta, perhaps the most politically correct member of the Cabinet, has slapped airlines with huge fines for removing suspicious Arab and Muslim passengers who pose a threat to passenger safety, as detailed in another chapter.

JUSTICE DEPARTMENT

Prosecutors are kowtowing to the demands of Muslim-rights groups in monthly outreach meetings, allowing them to in effect dictate the terms of investigations of Islamic terrorists. Even former Attorney General John Ashcroft last year assured them that law enforcement does not have "any interest" in the Muslim community, as if it were not the best place to look for terrorists.[7]

Meanwhile, the FBI director, besides putting his agents through sensitivity training, has formed permanent working groups with the American Muslim Council, the Council on American-Islamic Relations, and the Islamic Society of North America—even though associates of each have been the object of law enforcement action. Talk about unilateral disarmament.

Over at the Federal Bureau of Prisons, a former social worker is naively giving militant Islamists free reign. Chaplain administrator Sue VanBaalen, a nun who studied at a Berkeley seminary, has allowed the Islamic Society of North America, or ISNA, and the Graduate School of Islamic and Social Sciences, or GSISS, to control Islamic worship services at federal prisons. As I point out in a coming chapter, the federal pen has become a recruiting ground for al-Qaida. She thinks the groups, which have endorsed Muslim prison chaplains for the past decade, are "moderate" organizations that do not support Saudi Wahhabism and have not "demonstrated any tendency toward extremism." How does she know? She has their word. They did, after all, attend interfaith prayer services following the 9/11 attacks.[8]

Yet if Sister Sue, as she is known, had checked with counterterrorism agents, she would have found that both ISNA and GSISS have been under the law enforcement microscope for years. About a dozen charities, organizations, or individuals under federal scrutiny for possible ties to terrorism are linked in some way to ISNA, which, through a subsidiary, controls most of the Wahhabi mosques and schools in America. One of its directors is Imam Siraj Wahhaj, an unindicted co-conspirator in the first World Trade Center attack. He has urged his followers to overturn the U.S. system of government and set up an Islamic dictatorship. Others have raised the banner of jihad against Israel and America. They are the "moderate" Muslim leaders Sister Sue relies on to pick the Muslim chaplains counseling violent offenders in the nation's prisons.

The Wahhabi-influenced GSISS, moreover, is under investigation for supporting terrorism. Its offices outside Washington were raided by federal agents after 9/11. Its president is close to Sami al-Arian, the accused terrorist fundraiser, and has sent him fat checks, making him an unindicted co-conspirator in the terror-financing case.[9] His "moderate" group teaches the Muslim chaplains who preach in prisons.

No matter, Sister Sue trusts her Muslim inmates are practicing a "disciplined religion that helps them to lead good lives."[10] Bless her heart, she also believes the best way to correct bad behavior is "through restorative rather than punitive treatments."[11]

TREASURY DEPARTMENT

The head of the office charged with cracking down on Muslim charities that finance terrorism practically blew kisses to ISNA officials at an outreach event last year. Juan Zarate, deputy assistant secretary of the treasury, invited officials to be a part of the department's standing advisory group on charities. *"Assalumu alaikum,"* Zarate said in his opening remarks. "I have been fortunate enough to speak and work with ISNA. Our ongoing cooperation bears testimony to our sustained efforts and shared commitment" to end terrorist financing.[12]

Cooperation? ISNA officials rejected his suggested anti-terrorist accounting guidelines for Muslim charities as an "impracticability." They told him, in essence, that charities cannot be bothered screening the foreigners they aid for connections to terrorist groups. Nor can they be bothered with Zarate's other recommendations, including maintaining contact information for foreign recipients of donations and records of their activities.[13] Treasury investigators have traced millions of dollars from Muslim charities to al-Qaida and Hamas terrorists, funds that were supposedly intended for relief workers in places like Bosnia, Chechnya, and the West Bank.

THE PENTAGON

Last year, in yet another outreach meeting with ISNA (and yet another sign that diversity is trumping security), the deputy chief of the Navy's chaplain services expressed concern that military personnel "lack clear understanding of Islam and Muslims" and have developed a prejudice against them. And the head of the Army's chaplain services promised to provide "cultural sensitivity courses" to American soldiers, which of course was music to ISNA officials' ears.[14]

THE CIA

The former head of the CIA unit that tracks Osama bin Laden claims the agency under longtime Director George Tenet devoted more resources to dealing with diversity and multicultural issues than fighting al-Qaida. Tenet, who stepped down last year, "starved the bin Laden unit of officers while finding plenty of officers to staff his personal public relations office, as well as the staffs that handled diversity, multiculturalism, and employee newsletters," says former senior CIA officer Michael Scheuer.[15]

CONGRESS

In 2003, members of the American Muslim Council, whose terrorist founder is now behind bars, got a tutorial on lobbying and then visited their congressional delegations to talk about protecting Muslim-rights during a trip to Capitol Hill. Representatives from the AMC have lobbied to weaken U.S. counterterrorism laws, and slaves to PC on both sides of the aisle have gladly done their bidding, a subject I return to at length in a later chapter.

THE WHITE HOUSE

The president sets the tone throughout the government. The message regarding Islam has been clear: trust and respect the faith, and do not associate Muslims with terrorism. And the message has been consistent, starting with President Clinton, who after the first Trade Center attack complained about "so many people" unfairly identifying "the forces of radicalism and terrorism with Islam."[16] He said the American people need to know that terrorism is not a Muslim thing:

I tried to do a lot as I have traveled the world—and I did this when I was in Jordan speaking to the Jordanian parliament—to say to the American people and to the West generally that even though we have had problems with terrorism coming out of the Middle East, it is not inherently related to Islam—not to the religion, not to the culture. And the tradition of Islam in Indonesia, I think, makes that point very graphically. It's something our people in America need to know, it's something people in the West—throughout the West—need to know.[17]

President Bush, who considers Islam a "great religion," has carried on the tradition, and then some. Here are some highlights:

- He was the first president to mention mosques in an inaugural address. And whenever he mentions "churches and synagogues" in any speech, he is quick to add "mosques."

- He has promised Muslim leaders he will refrain from using the word Islamic to describe terrorism, as in "Islamic terrorism."

- A week after 9/11, Bush visited a mosque in Washington, removing his shoes according to Muslim custom. He met there for an hour with Muslim leaders, who presented him with a copy of the Quran. Outside at a press conference, he pleaded for Americans to "respect" Muslims and Islam's teachings of "peace." Bush stood next to Council on American-Islamic Relations president Nihad Awad, who is on record supporting terrorism. He even invited Awad to sit near the first lady during his 9/11 speech to Congress a few days later, in which he insisted that Islam's "teachings are good and peaceful."

- A week later, Bush met again with Muslim leaders, this time at the White House. (Reappearing was Khaled Saffuri, who works at the Islamic Free Market Institute with GOP powerbroker Grover Norquist, who is best friends with Bush political adviser Karl Rove.) At the close of a prayer led by a Wahhabi imam, Bush offered the words *"Ameen,"* Arabic for "Amen," not realizing he was praying to a different God.

- Two months after the attacks, during Ramadan, the president made history by hosting the first-ever *iftaar* dinner at the White House. He bowed his head during a prayer offered by an imam who asked Allah to "make us true believers." The next month, he did one better by inviting Muslims over to the White House to celebrate *Eid.* (Both events were organized by Saffuri, a character examined in-depth in a later chapter.)

- Then on the eve of the first anniversary of 9/11, he praised Islam as a loving faith that no American should fear. "All Americans must recognize that the face of terror is not the true face of Islam," he said. "Islam is a faith based upon love, not hate."[18]

- A month later, he out-did himself by proclaiming, "Islam is a vibrant faith. We respect the faith. We honor its traditions. Our enemy does not. Our enemy don't[sic] follow the great traditions of Islam. They've hijacked a great religion. . . . Islam is a faith that brings comfort to people. It inspires them to lead lives based on honesty, and justice, and compassion."[19]

- Visiting the resort island of Bali a year after Islamic terrorists tied to al-Qaida blew up two nightclubs there packed with American and other foreign tourists, the president had more praise for Islam, gushing, "Islam is fully compatible with liberty and tolerance."[20]

Many conservatives are annoyed by Bush's nonstop defense of Islam. They say they understood the need for such rhetoric right after the attacks to quell bias against Muslims and prevent vigilantism. But they say it is sounding more and more like boosterism, which could lead Americans into a false sense of security about the threat.

Some say it shows Bush does not fully understand the enemy and is not serious about defeating it. National-security expert Michael Waller, for one, thinks the president is putting a fig leaf over the problem. "It's despicable. It's disgusting," says Waller, a professor at the Institute of World Politics in Washington. "It shows he's not serious about winning the war on Islamic terrorism."[21]

In part, Bush is currying favor with Muslim groups at the request of Rove, who has worked with Norquist over the years to cultivate Muslims as a new voter base for the GOP, a highly controversial issue I explore in a later chapter.

But Bush also believes his pro-Islamic rhetoric. His adviser on Islam is a law professor who thinks that Osama bin Laden and his ilk are not real Muslims but impostors who have distorted a great religion. David Forte of Cleveland State University is a religious pluralist who believes nothing as evil as 9/11 could come from a religion. It is from Forte that Bush got his lines about bin Laden "hijacking" and "perverting" a peaceful religion. "The key thing we have to do," Forte advised, "is say these guys are attempting to undermine Islam."[22]

Even though Forte has been anointed in the press as an authority on Islam, it is not really his, well, forte. He does not speak Arabic and merely dabbles in Quranic law. It is not clear if Bush, for his part, has even read the Quran, let alone studied it. The White House is not saying.

But Forte has led him to believe that the leaders in the Muslim establishment who gave him the Quran are no less patriotic than him. "They're outraged, they're sad," Bush said at the mosque after the terrorist attacks. "They love America just as much as I do."[23]

That may be what they have told him. But that is not what many of them have told their Muslim brothers privately.

3

FROM THE WHITE HOUSE
TO THE BIG HOUSE

The Two Faces of America's 'Moderate' Muslim Leaders

"I'm proud of the Muslim leaders across America."
—PRESIDENT GEORGE W. BUSH[1]

The most prominent national leaders of the Muslim faith say they represent a mainstream agenda, but in fact they represent the whole anti-Western ideology behind the 9/11 terrorist attacks, and their allegiance is with Islam, not the United States.

These crypto-Islamists have a secret agenda of Islamizing America while making it harder for authorities to investigate the bad guys. They cannot speak candidly about their true intentions and still remain players in the political arena. That would only arouse suspicion and fear, and lead to their isolation. The last thing they want is to marginalize Islam in America. They want to advance it. So they save their true feelings for Muslim audiences, and Washington isn't the wiser.

The eight Muslim leaders you will read about below are not fringe players in American Muslim politics. They are the blue chips, the best the Muslim community has to offer. Some of these paragons of virtue have recently gone from the White House to the big house, while others are still playing their Washington hosts for fools.

IMAM SIRAJ WAHHAJ

A black convert to Islam, Wahhaj is one of the most recognized leaders in the American Muslim community, serving on the boards of no less than five major Muslim organizations. He also garners respect in Washington, where he holds the honor of being the first Muslim to give the opening prayer in Congress. He has even dined with former Secretary of State Madeleine Albright.

Wahhaj leads a mosque in Brooklyn, where he can often be seen preaching in white robes. He is known locally as a gentle man, always smiling, and is said to routinely denounce terrorism in sermons. He has also received commendations from police organizations for helping to drive out crime in the neighborhood. In 2003, a Brooklyn borough president proclaimed a day in Wahhaj's name to honor what the official called a "lifetime of outstanding and meaningful achievement."

The imam may convincingly play the role of good American citizen in public. But privately he talks treason. In fact, he secretly despises the American system of government and wishes to transform it into an Islamic state.

"In time, this so-called democracy will crumble, and there will be nothing," Wahhaj seethes in one of his sermons available on audiotape. "And the only thing that will remain will be Islam."[2]

It's not the first time he has preached insurrection. In 1991, the same year he gave the invocation to Congress, he delivered a speech to Muslims in Texas titled, "The Muslim Agenda in the New World Order," in which he warned that America would fall like the Soviet Union unless it accepts the Islamic agenda.[3]

Then the next year, Wahhaj suggested to a Muslim audience in New Jersey that Muslims had the numbers to take control of the United States in a political coup. "If we were united and strong, we'd elect our own emir [leader] and give allegiance to him," he said. "Take my word for it, if six to eight million Muslims united in America, the country will come to us."[4]

And while Wahhaj may denounce terrorism, he hosted the Blind Sheikh Omar Abdel-Rahman at his Brooklyn mosque, and later went to court to defend him as a character witness in his terrorism trial. The "respected scholar," as he described Abdel-Rahman, was nonetheless sentenced to life in prison for conspiring to bomb New York landmarks. A longtime member of Wahhaj's mosque also was convicted in the plot. And the imam himself was named as an unindicted co-conspirator.

MUZAMMIL H. SIDDIQI

With his silver beard and glasses, the Harvard-educated Siddiqi is the picture of scholarship. A highly regarded imam like Wahhaj, he is also considered one of the foremost authorities on Islamic law and serves on the boards of several national Muslim groups, including the country's largest, the Islamic Society of North America. As then-ISNA president, Siddiqi had the solemn honor after 9/11 to represent the Muslim faith during the prayer service for victims at the National

Cathedral in Washington. "But those that lay the plots of evil, for them is a terrible penalty," he said, quoting from the Quran (while leaving some to wonder if he was referring to the terrorists or their infidel target).

Later that month, he was invited to meet with the president at the White House. In a ceremony in the Roosevelt Room, Siddiqi presented Bush with a copy of the Quran. Bush thanked him and praised his participation in the memorial service at the cathedral. "He did a heck of a job," the president gushed, "and we are proud to have him here." Siddiqi assured Bush that the Muslim community had "unanimously condemned" the terrorist acts of 9/11.

Just a year earlier, however, the imam gave another message to a different president.

At an anti-Israel rally across from the White House in October 2000, he and other Muslim leaders praised Palestinian terrorists and implored President Clinton to end support for America's ally Israel. Then he issued a stern warning to Americans to side with Palestinian Muslims against the Jews, or face Allah's punishment—a warning that called into doubt not only the sincerity of his shock and disgust over the 9/11 attacks but also his public reputation for moderation.

"America has to learn," Siddiqi said to the crowd of cheering Muslims. "If you remain on the side of injustice, the wrath of God will come. Please all Americans, do remember that, that Allah is watching everyone. If you continue doing injustice and tolerating injustice, the wrath of God will come."[5]

As director of the Fiqh Council of North America, a group that dispenses Islamic jurisprudence, Siddiqi has advised American Muslims to participate in the political system—but only in order to change America into a Muslim country. "I believe that as Muslims, we should participate in the system to safeguard our interests and try to bring gradual change," said the mufti, as Siddiqi is called, in a 2003 *fatwa*, or religious decree. "We must not forget that Allah's rules have to be established in all lands, and all our efforts should lead to that direction."[6]

In private, Siddiqi sounds more like an insurgent than a cleric. He also acts differently. Often described as soft-spoken and mild-mannered, he was involved in an altercation at the mosque he leads in Southern California. Police last decade were called to the Islamic Society of Orange County, one of the largest mosques in the country, to calm a melee involving about two hundred members and officials of the mosque. The confrontation erupted into a scuffle, and Siddiqi had to be removed from the premises by police, according to local press accounts at the time.[7]

Last year, the FBI showed up at the mosque to question Siddiqi about an al-Qaida suspect he helped convert there, a subject that will be explored in greater detail in the chapter on mosques, "Sanctuaries of Terror."

SHEIKH HAMZA YUSUF

Yusuf, a Muslim convert, teaches Arabic and Islamic affairs in northern California. Known as a charismatic speaker, he routinely addresses conventions held by groups within the Muslim establishment. Cultivating a moderate image, he advised the president on Islamic issues after 9/11. On September 20, 2001, Yusuf met with Bush at the White House—the only Muslim in a group of religious leaders invited to pray with him. After praying, the group broke into a chorus of "God Bless America."

"Hate knows no religion. Hate knows no country," Yusuf intoned outside the White House that day. "Islam was hijacked on that September 11, 2001, on that plane as an innocent victim."

But while the imam was preaching peace and understanding to the American public at the White House, FBI agents were looking for him back at his home in California. Authorities had shown up at his doorstep to question him about an eerily prophetic speech he had given two days before the attacks. "He's not at home," his wife told the agents. "He's with the president."[8]

Oops.

On September 9, 2001, Yusuf had told a gathering of Muslims in Irvine, California, that America "stands condemned" to suffer "a very terrible fate."

"This country is facing a very terrible fate," he said ominously in the speech, which he gave to support a Muslim cleric arrested for fatally shooting an Atlanta cop. "The reason for that is that this country stands condemned. It stands condemned like Europe stood condemned because of what it did. And lest people forget, Europe suffered two world wars after conquering the Muslim lands."

"Europe's countries were devastated; they were completely destroyed," Yusuf added. "Their young people were killed."[9]

Perhaps he was just having a bad day. Surely a California-born U.S. citizen raised by a Catholic father and Greek Orthodox mother would never wish such a fate on America. But don't count on it. Listen to what Yusuf confided to another Muslim audience assembled at the Islamic Circle of North America's annual convention in 1996:

> I am a citizen of this country not by choice but by birth. I reside in this country not by choice but by conviction in attempting to spread the message of Islam in this country. I became Muslim in part because I did not believe in the false gods of this society, whether we call them Jesus or democracy or the Bill of Rights or any other element of this society that

is held sacrosanct by the ill-informed peoples that make up this charade of a society.[10]

Only in America can Muslim leaders who represent the anti-American dogma behind the 9/11 attacks on America be invited by the president of the United States to come to the White House and pray with him for the survival of America. Only in America can they go on television and lead prayers at a national memorial for America. Only in America.

IHSAN BAGBY

A prominent black convert to Islam, Bagby has taught Islamic studies at American universities for more than a decade and is a respected member of the Muslim establishment, serving on the boards of the Islamic Society of North American and the Council on American-Islamic Relations. He is sought out by the media as an expert on Islamic issues and has been described as "one of the nation's leading scholars of Islam"—an "instant authority," no less.

Bagby, who cuts a distinguished figure with his business suits and salt-and-pepper hair, can appear perfectly reasonable in his discussions of Islam and comes across as a patriotic Muslim. But in a moment of candor in the late 1980s, Bagby revealed what many skeptics say is the true sentiment of devout Muslims in America. "Ultimately we can never be full citizens of this country," he said, "because there is no way we can be fully committed to the institutions and ideologies of this country."[11]

OMAR M. AHMAD

A Silicon Valley executive, Ahmad founded the Council on American-Islamic Relations, a Muslim-rights lobbying group based in Washington. He is a key player in the Muslim establishment and an honored guest at the White House. He was one of the Muslim leaders invited by the president to the National Cathedral to join the nation in mourning the 9/11 tragedy. Shortly after the attacks, he proclaimed that Muslims condemn "terrorism in all its forms."[12] Portraying himself as a moderate, he is also widely accepted in the local community and serves on the Santa Clara County public library board.

However, librarians might be interested to know that Ahmad does not think much of their book selection, particularly when it comes to books referencing the U.S. Constitution or religions other than Islam. Here is what he confided to a Muslim audience at a 1998 Islamic conference in nearby Fremont, California:

"Islam isn't in America to be equal to any other faith but to become dominant. The Quran should be the highest authority in America, and Islam the only accepted religion on Earth."[13]

IBRAHIM HOOPER

Hooper is the public face of CAIR. A Muslim convert from Canada, he has served as its national communications director since the group's founding in 1994. A regular on TV, he is easily recognized by his white skull cap. Hooper, who has a masters degree in journalism, is a forceful and disciplined spokesman for the entire Muslim establishment, never deviating from the message that Islam is a religion of peace. And he never lets a charge against Islam—or CAIR—go unanswered.

After the 9/11 attacks, CAIR fended off allegations it supported terrorists. Hooper immediately issued a press release stressing that CAIR represents the "mainstream" views of the Muslim community. The statement read, in part, "In all its actions and statements, CAIR seeks to reflect the mainstream beliefs and views of the Muslim community in North America."[14] The following year, Hooper showed up on the White House guest list along with other CAIR officials.

But Hooper's own views are anything but "mainstream."

In 1993, before he was a hard-boiled flack for CAIR, Hooper revealed more than he should have in an interview with a Minneapolis reporter. Then a local Muslim activist, he said he wanted to see the United States become an Islamic nation. He made the remarks just five weeks after Islamic terrorists car-bombed the Twin Towers, killing six and injuring more than a thousand in New York.

"I wouldn't want to create the impression that I wouldn't like the government of the United States to be Islamic sometime in the future," Hooper says. "But I'm not going to do anything violent to promote that. I'm going to do it through education."[15]

Of course by "education," he really means agitprop, which he and CAIR have been alarmingly effective in using against politicians, media figures, and CEOs to get what they want, as my groundbreaking investigation of CAIR will reveal in coming chapters.

SAMI AL-ARIAN

As a tenured Florida university professor, al-Arian made an impression on Clinton and was invited to the White House at least once during his administration. He also curried favor with George W. Bush, even helping to get out Florida's Muslim vote for him in 2000, which some say provided Bush with the margin of victory in that hotly contested state. During the campaign, al-Arian and his family posed for snapshots with Bush and his wife, Laura, at the Florida Strawberry Festival. Bush even gave their tall son, Abdullah, the nickname "Big Dude."

In turn, al-Arian accepted an invitation to the White House in the summer of 2001, where he took a front-row seat in a briefing on Bush's faith-based initiative. Six days later, Big Dude, who was working in Washington as a congressional aide, also visited the White House.

Al-Arian, a Palestinian, is widely respected among national Muslim leaders who praise his activism for Muslim causes. But he is also admired in the local Muslim community in Tampa, where he helped establish a local mosque and school. He also started a local coalition for national "peace" and was one of the first Muslim leaders to strike a patriotic tone and condemn the 9/11 attacks, while expressing grief for fellow American victims.

"I am a very moderate Muslim person," insists al-Arian, who in public has lauded the many freedoms America offers.[16]

However, in private talks with Muslim audiences about America, the balding, bespectacled professor has taken on a completely different persona and tone. In a speech last decade at a Cleveland mosque, for example, he thundered, "Let's damn America, let's damn Israel, let's damn their allies until death."[17]

In addition, al-Arian once demonized America as the "Great Satan, which makes the wrong right and the right wrong," in a forty-page manifesto he once drafted advocating violent jihad.[18]

And in a speech to another Muslim audience, he described a mortal struggle between Islam and the West. "We are in a battle of life and death, in a battle of fate and future against the Western hegemony and tyranny wanting to control the capabilities of the [Muslim] nations in order to enslave, steal, and control them," he said. "What is needed is the dismantling of the cultural system of the West."[19]

Now the professor is behind bars awaiting trial on charges he led the U.S. operations of the Palestinian Islamic Jihad terrorist group and conspired to aid suicide bombings against Israel. The federal case against him finally broke free of years of political gridlock in Washington after Fox News Channel host Bill O'Reilly drew national attention to it after 9/11 by grilling al-Arian on his top-rated show.

ABDURAHMAN M. ALAMOUDI

A tireless organizer and promoter, Alamoudi is by far the most politically connected activist in the Muslim establishment, serving at one time or another as an officer in more than a dozen national Islamic groups, including some he founded, such as the American Muslim Council. He has been welcomed at the White House by both Clinton and Bush for his work on behalf of Muslim causes. He was a goodwill ambassador for the Department of State, which sent him to Muslim countries at least half a dozen times last decade to speak about Muslim life in America. In 1993, he even created the Muslim chaplain corps for the Pentagon.

In 1996, also during the Clinton administration, he organized the first Ramadan dinner for government officials. The bearded, lanky Alamoudi met in the White House with both Clinton and Vice President Al Gore that year, as well as the prior year, to discuss Muslim concerns. All the while he contributed tens of thousands of dollars to political candidates from both parties.

During the 2000 race, he caught the attention of the Bush campaign. Then-Gov. Bush invited Alamoudi and other Muslim leaders to his Austin mansion for a powwow. The next year he met with Bush officials in the White House to discuss their faith-based agenda and subsequently was invited to Ramadan events there. And of course, the FBI director gave his personal blessing to Alamoudi's operations after 9/11 by headlining the AMC's convention and calling the group "the most mainstream Muslim group" in the country.

The son of a Yemeni businessman, Alamoudi is a pillar of the local Muslim community in Washington, his hometown, where he is admired for reaching out to Muslims in need. The American Muslim community considers him a moderate, and his photo even graces the cover of a popular book lionizing mainstream Muslim leaders titled, *Silent No More: Confronting America's False Images of Islam.*

But there is nothing more false than Alamoudi's image of moderation. His private words and deeds betray the public reputation he's cultivated. Alamoudi is not only an extremist, he's a bona fide *terrorist* who endorses al-Qaida's killing of non-Muslims[20]—including Americans—and wants to conquer America in the name of Allah.

First, his words.

At the Islamic Association for Palestine's 1996 annual convention in Illinois, Alamoudi told his brothers in faith:

> Muslims sooner or later will be the moral leadership of America. It depends on me and you. Either we do it now or we do it after a hundred years, but this country will become a Muslim country. And I think if we are outside this country, we can say, "Oh, Allah, destroy America." But once we are here, our mission in this country is to change it.[21]

He went on to describe Muslim activism in America as "an investment," adding that "we all are in this together." So it would seem, so it would seem.

Go back to the White House rally at which Siddiqi marked America for punishment. Alamoudi was there with him, shouting from the park across from the White House. And in a fit of candor, he blurted out his support for the terrorist groups Hamas and Hezbollah.[22] Eight months later he was escorted into the White House as an honored guest.

Now for his deeds.

In 2003, British authorities busted Alamoudi as he planned to smuggle $340,000 in sequentially numbered $100 bills from a Libyan-tied charity into the U.S. Back in the states, Alamoudi eventually pleaded guilty to plotting terrorist acts with Libya. Prosecutors also connected him to Hamas, not surprisingly, but also to al-Qaida and seven known terrorists whose identities were found in his confiscated Palm Pilot. Prosecutors also alleged in court that Alamoudi explicitly endorsed a terrorist act, citing a 1999 conversation he had with an unidentified person during one of Alamoudi's State Department-sponsored trips to the Middle East. According to a transcript, Alamoudi complained that the 1998 al-Qaida attacks on the U.S. Embassies in Africa were not all that effective because they killed only Africans and not any Americans.

Now Alamoudi has traded his business suits for a jumpsuit and clearly will not be going on any more goodwill tours for the State Department. Nor will he be going to another White House *iftar* dinner.

But other crypto-Islamists are still welcome there—including Alamoudi's former deputy, Khaled Saffuri, who meets regularly with top U.S. officials to lecture them about spying on Muslims. And just last year, the secretary of state agreed to sit down with Muslim leaders—including CAIR executive director Nihad Awad, who also has declared support for Hamas—to hear them gripe about America's role in the Middle East and overall image problem in the Muslim world.

Yet their own image remains largely untarnished in the eyes of the Washington establishment. "Sadly, some individuals in this country have questioned the loyalty of some Muslim Americans to this country just because of their religion," bemoans the FBI's Mueller, the head of the one agency that's supposed to know better.[23] The validation of Muslim leaders with exactly that—questionable loyalties—has not missed a beat in Washington. Their charade of presenting a benign face to the general public while spewing treasonous venom in the safe company of fellow Muslims is still paying dividends in the form of political credibility and clout.

How can men of such deep faith be so two-faced? Isn't dishonesty forbidden in Islam? Not if it advances the faith.

4

WHITE LIES

The Islamic Art of Deception

"We are against all forms of terrorism. Our religion is against terrorism."
—ABDURAHMAN ALAMOUDI, after 1998's U.S. embassies attacks[1]

A popular *hadith* or story is told of Ali, the cousin of the Muslim prophet Muhammad. One day a man came running by while Ali sat on a chair. After the man ran past him, Ali moved to another chair. Right away, a group of people came searching for the man who had just rushed past Ali. When his pursuers asked Ali if he had seen the man, he replied, "Since I have sat on this chair, I have not seen anyone."

This story is admired by Muslims. "They count it as a 'white lie' which was told in wisdom," says Reza F. Safa, a former Muslim who converted to Christianity. "In their opinion, white lies are the lies that help people." And as long as a lie helps or protects a fellow Muslim or the Islamic faith, he says, it is not considered a sin.[2]

In fact, a Muslim can profess the faith in total insincerity if necessary to avoid persecution. "Whereas the Bible says you die if you're persecuted, the Quran says no, you can lie to get out of persecution," says former Muslim Hale Smith.[3] Lying about religion to avoid persecution is actually an Islamic doctrine called *taqiya*, or "dodging the threat," which is accepted by both Shia and Sunni Muslims.

In practice, Muslims have applied the concept of expedient duplicity more broadly over time, say historians. When Muslims were a minority community in parts of the Middle East, it encouraged them to temporarily adopt a peaceful attitude to deceive their non-Muslim neighbors, while secretly planning subversion. As Islam advanced on the battlefield, it was used as subterfuge to convince targeted enemies that jihad, or holy war, was not aimed at them, scholars say. It was also used as propaganda to seed discord among the ranks of the enemy.

Historically, "*al-taqiya* was a formidable weapon," says Walid Phares, a Lebanese-American political professor at Florida Atlantic University in Boca Raton, Florida. "Today, scholars may identify it as deception."[4]

The Arab media often uses *taqiya* to cast Islam in the best light and the West in the worst light, severely distorting facts in the process, admits the editor of the London-based daily *Al-Sharq Al-Awsat*. Arab reporters believe "that lying for the sake of the cause is moral and honorable," says Abd al-Rahman al-Rashed.[5]

In Washington, Muslim activists and lobbyists use lies as a legitimate means of gaining political clout. They pass themselves and their agendas off as peace-loving and patriotic. They cannot frankly discuss their views and still maintain their viability in the political arena. That would only arouse suspicion and lead to their isolation. So they and the organizations they represent usually couch their true beliefs about things like Jews and jihad in moderate language while addressing the non-Muslim public. Only before Muslims audiences do they speak openly of their true feelings, as secretly taped recordings have revealed to their chagrin.

"*Taqiya* in our own time is reflected in the attempts by Muslim activists in the West to present Islam favorably, replete with tolerance and peace, faith and charity, equality and brotherhood," says historian Serge Trifkovic, author of *The Sword and the Prophet: History, Theology, Impact on the World*. "The 'misunderstood Muslims' tell us that jihad is really the 'striving for Allah' and 'inner struggle.'" And they selectively quote from the Quran to support their spin, he says.[6]

"FANCY DANCE OF EVASION"

Irshad Manji, a Muslim, agrees. She says Muslim scholars and clerics performed a "fancy dance of evasion" after the 9/11 terrorist attacks when they maintained that nothing in the Quran authorizes killing people.

"Post-September 11, I repeatedly heard this mantra from Muslims: the Quran makes it absolutely clear when jihad can and can't be pursued, and the terrorists unquestionably broke the rules," says Manji, author of *The Trouble with Islam: A Muslim's Call for Reform in Her Faith*. "To quote one such voice, Allah 'says in unequivocal terms that to kill an innocent being is like killing entire humanity.'"

But that is "wishful whitewashing," she says. "You know the chapter and verse that's cited as 'unequivocal'? It actually bestows some wiggle room. Here's how it reads: 'We laid it down for the Israelites that whoever killed a human being, except as punishment for murder or other villainy in the land, shall be regarded as having killed all mankind.' Sadly, the clause starting with 'except' can be deployed by militant Muslims to fuel their jihads."[7]

Whenever Muslim leaders are asked to condemn violent attacks on non-Muslims, they sternly denounce "all forms of terrorism," while pointing out that Islam forbids terrorism and any violence against "innocent" people or "civilians." "We are against all forms of terrorism," Alamoudi said after 1998's U.S. embassy bombings. "Our religion is against terrorism." Technically, they are right. Such statements are accurate.

But like Ali's response to his inquisitors, they are cleverly worded dodges. You see, Islamists do not consider all non-Muslims as "innocent" or "civilians." And what the West defines as "terrorism," they may define as "legitimate resistance" or "justice." What the West defines as "terrorists," they may define as Israeli and American "occupiers" or "oppressors." So their statements against terrorism and terrorists are really nothing more than legal lies. It all depends on what their meaning is. (Imagine if Bill Clinton were Muslim!) At the same time Alamoudi publicly condemned the embassy "terrorism" in Africa, he privately expressed disappointment in the low American death toll.

Rarely, if ever, will you hear a Muslim activist group simply state: we condemn this horrible act of violence against non-Muslims. Instead, their condemnations are loaded with qualifiers, and non-Muslims go right on assuming they mean the best.

Left unquestioned and unparsed, such circumlocution has helped Muslim leaders de-link terror from their faith in the mind of the American public. They also count on no one cracking open the Quran to verify their denials about violent Islam.

Take the recent statements made by prominent Muslim clerics in Washington regarding the rash of beheadings of American hostages in Iraq. Imam Mohamad Adam el-Sheikh of the Dar al-Hijrah mosque told *USA Today* that "beheadings are not mentioned in the Quran at all."[8] Another Muslim scholar, Yvonne Haddad of the Center for Muslim-Christian Understanding at Georgetown University, agreed, telling *New York Newsday*, "There is absolutely nothing in Islam that justifies cutting off a person's head."[9]

They both claimed that such atrocities were falsely attributed to the teachings of Islam, and the politically correct media bought their claims.

"SMITE AT THEIR NECKS"

But had reporters bothered to open up a copy of the Quran, they would have found that their trusted Muslim sources were simply wrong to say that it does not mention beheadings, or that there is "absolutely nothing" in Islam that justifies decapitation. Here are just a couple of relevant verses in the Quran:

> Remember thy Lord inspired the angels (with the message): "I am with you. Give firmness to the Believers. I will instill terror into the hearts of the Unbelievers. Smite ye above their necks and smite all their finger tips off them.
> —Surah 8:12 (The interpreter Abdullah Yusuf Ali's footnote to the violent passage makes no mistake about what it means. He explains: "The vulnerable parts of an armed man are above the neck. A blow on the neck, face, or head, finishes him off.")

> Therefore, when ye meet the Unbelievers (in fight), smite at their necks.
> —Surah 47:4 (The footnote explains: "When once the fight (Jihad) is entered upon, carry it out with the utmost vigor, and strike home your blows at the most vital points ('smite at their necks'), both literally and figuratively. You cannot wage war with kid gloves.")

Either these prominent Muslim scholars are not familiar with the Islamic scripture, which would be odd, or they are misleading the public.

"In dealing with non-Muslims, lying and deceit is permissible" under the Islamic doctrine of *taqiya,* Smith emphasizes. "It's okay to feed them a moderate version of Islam. Any lie that promotes or advances Islam is good, and you don't advance Islam [in non-Muslim countries] by showing its warts."

But would respected Islamic scholars and clerics really try to deceive the American public? Yes, and here are just a few examples of their duplicity.

- New York state's chief Muslim prison chaplain, Warith Deen Umar spent years convincing prison officials of his moderate views. Then after 9/11, he revealed his true feelings and "defended the September 11 terrorist attacks and supported terrorism in statements he made at an event outside a prison," according to a recent federal report.[10]

- The head of one of the nation's most prestigious Islamic institutions, the Graduate School of Islamic and Social Sciences, took steps to conceal alleged payments to Palestinian terrorists. In a letter seized by investigators, Taha al-Alwani, a respected Muslim scholar and spiritual leader, advised his pal Sami al-Arian, a suspected Islamic Jihad leader, to construct a "facade" to disguise a fifty-thousand-dollar donation to his alleged terrorist front.[11]

- Likewise, leaders of the largest and most venerable Muslim charity in America, the Holy Land Foundation, took several steps to conceal from federal authorities their alleged conspiracy to fund Palestinian terrorists. They hired a security firm to sweep their offices for listening devices. They took training in detection of wiretaps. They shredded documents after board meetings. And they hid "incriminating documents" at off-site locations, investigators say. Some of the leaders were imams in their local communities.[12]

- The popular imam Ali al-Timimi insisted in the press that "my position against terrorism and Muslim-inspired violence against innocent people is well known by Muslims."[13] But privately, he was encouraging eleven jihadists in Virginia to go to Afghanistan and kill Americans. And now he is behind bars for inciting the very violence he claimed to oppose.

Such dissembling has kept a number of myths about Islam alive.

5

TOP TEN MYTHS OF ISLAM

*Everything You Ever Wanted To Know about Islam
but Were Afraid To Ask*

"Allah said to them: Die."
—THE QURAN, Surah 2:243

It is the duty of every Muslim—man, woman, and child—to read the Quran, which is Arabic for "recitation." And they are encouraged to memorize it. The book is so sacred to Muslims that they believe they must keep it in a place of prominence in their home—and above all other books. In fact, no other book can rest atop it. Because of the intense focus on their scripture, the term fundamentalism is foreign to Muslims. They are all fundamentalists, or they are not Muslims. "Muslim fundamentalist" is a redundancy of terms.

The Quran contains 114 chapters called *surahs*, and 6,666 verses called *ayahs*. It is shorter than the New Testament, I was pleased to learn after 9/11, for I had decided to read it and see for myself whether the Muslim terrorists were getting their ideas from it, or whether, as was the conventional wisdom, they were just heretics using it as an excuse to murder innocent people.

So I went to a local bookstore and picked up a little red paperback copy, which seemed to be the Gideon's version of the Quran. I set about reading it with an open mind and heart, looking for the good in it—the peaceful message, the poetry and permissive spirit the president and pundits had assured us it contained. Instead, I was assaulted, page after page, by venomous and violent passages. It read more like a manual of war than any religious tract. The spleenful tenor alone made me physically ill.

But wouldn't you know, I had read the wrong version.

After quoting from it in columns, I was informed by angry and offended Muslims that the original English translation by J.M. Rodwell is not accurate because it was written by a "bigoted" Englishman. You silly *kaffir*, they chided me, you must read Abdullah Yusuf Ali's translation, which is the most widely respected version of the Quran and approved by the Council on American-Islamic Relations. So I traipsed back to the bookstore and purchased Ali's *Meaning of the Holy Quran*, which to my annoyance was so thick I practically got a hernia lugging it back to my car. Because it contains Ali's commentary, the thing runs a whopping 1,759 pages long.

Bound in a handsome, green-and-gold cover, it is published by Amana Publications, whose president happens to be the brother of Jamal Barzinji, one of the leaders of a Virginia group suspected of aiding terrorists. And it is edited by the International Institute of Islamic Thought, a suspected terror-financing front raided by federal agents after 9/11.

But compared to Rodwell's version of the Quran, it is surprisingly watered-down. How do I know? Because where Rodwell says "infidels," Ali says "unbelievers" or "People of the Book," a decidedly more respectful title given to Jews and Christians. And Rodwell makes grim reading as far as the status of women is concerned in Islam. Not so much with Ali. For instance, Rodwell quotes the Quran authorizing Muslim men to "scourge," or whip, their disobedient wives, while Ali glosses over that disturbing part. According to his interpretation, the Quran says to merely "spank them," and then only "lightly"—an adverb not even found in the original Arabic text.

While the overall tone of Ali's version is much softer, or at least not as nakedly hateful, I discovered that the meaning is nonetheless the same. And Ali's commentary only confirmed much of my earlier revulsion.

After finishing his tome, I concluded that Islam's boosters, propagandists, and apologists were fibbing about the true nature of Islam, and getting away with it—big time. They had created a politically correct mythology around an inherently violent and intolerant faith. There are many myths about Islam and the Quran worth debunking, but here are what I believe to be the top ten myths that directly impact America's security, which is the main point of this book.

NO. 1: ISLAM IS A RELIGION OF PEACE

Islam *is* a peaceful religion—for devout Muslims. Everyone else is marked for punishment, or "severe penalty," as the Quran puts it. Peace exists only insofar as non-Muslims submit to the word, or sword, of Islam. Until then, there is no peace. Just fighting, endless fighting. True believers fight for the cause of Allah. The Quran exhorts the faithful to "fight"—even "slay"—non-Muslims "in the cause of Allah."

Put another way, Muslims *do* desire world peace but only after the entire world is conquered in the name of Allah. Peace is reserved for them, while others pay for protection. This is their great commission, which can be summed up with this salient passage from the Quran:

> Fight those who believe not in Allah nor the Last Day, nor hold that forbidden which hath been forbidden by Allah and His Messenger, nor acknowledge the religion of Truth, from among the People of the Book, until they pay the *jizyah* [poll tax] with willing submission, and feel themselves subdued.
>
> —Surah 9:29

Ali explains in his introduction to this chapter—called *Al Tawbah*—that Jews and Christians stand in the way of Allah's glory and must be fought. "The People of the Book have obscured the light of Allah, but the Truth of Allah must prevail over all," he says. "We must be ready to fight for the Faith that is in us; otherwise we shall be unworthy to uphold Allah's banner."[1]

Islam does not mean "peace" as some maintain. It means "submission," a very different matter. And the core function of Muslims is to obtain submission from all for Allah, if necessary by force. Muslims are commanded to "fight" so the word of Allah can become supreme. It is just that simple. And the Quran clearly advocates violence against Christians and Jews. Wahhabism or Islamism is just Islam put into practice because it really does not advocate anything the Quran does not advocate itself.

This of course is what the Muslim establishment is denying and is not what you are hearing from the president or pundits.

"Islam means peace," claims CNN's Christiane Amanpour, who is of Persian descent. And "the Quran makes it clear that killing is always wrong."[2]

But that beards the truth. The only killing forbidden in the Quran is the killing of fellow Muslims—"Never should a Believer kill a Believer" (4:92)—and innocent souls. Unbelievers who get in the way of pan-Islam do not fall under that protective umbrella.

People do a lot of things in the name of religion that their religion does not really call for. Unfortunately, most Muslim terrorists are not guilty of this, and they can quote extensively from their scripture to support their actions. References to violence are replete throughout the Quran, which contains no fewer than fifty verses referring specifically to "fighting unbelievers in the cause of Allah," "warfare," and "jihad." In fact, "fighting is prescribed upon" Muslims (2:216).

Am I taking these violent passages out of context? That would be hard to do, when the context itself is unambiguously violent. "Some argue that a true Muslim is not militant," says Reza Safa, a former Muslim. "On the contrary, this is the very nature and teaching of Islam."[3]

NO. 2: JIHAD MEANS INNER STRUGGLE AGAINST SIN

Whenever jihad is mentioned in the Muslim holy book, it means the obligation to fight. Not just with the pen or placards or ballots, but with instruments of war.

But do not take my word for it. Ali calls jihad "warfare," and says, "Believers will either conquer or die as martyrs in the cause. Believers expect punishment for the Unbelievers for their infidelity, either through their own instrumentality or in some other way in Allah's Plan."[4]

The violent jihad is not for everyone, he allows. "It is not everyone—least of all poltroons and fainthearted persons—who is fit to fight the cause of Allah," for once you commit to jihad, there is no half-stepping. Allah expects you to either successfully destroy the infidel enemy or die trying (or at least get hurt in the process).[5]

And Allah frowns on those Muslims too wimpy or lazy to fight, Ali says. He offers them no guarantee he will forgive them of their sins, or see them in Paradise.

> Not equal are those Believers who sit (at home) and receive no hurt, and those who strive and fight in the cause of Allah with their goods and their persons. Allah hath granted a grade higher to those who strive and fight with their goods and persons than to those who sit (at home).
> —Surah 4:95

"In a time of jihad, when people give their all, and even their lives, for the common cause, they must be accounted more glorious than those who sit at home," Ali explains. "The special reward of such self-sacrifice is high spiritual rank, and special forgiveness and mercy, as proceeding from the direct approbation and love of Allah."[6]

The physically disabled are offered an exemption from the jihad. And those too old or ill to participate can still help by giving "asylum and aid" (8:74) to the jihadi fighters—or as may be the case, terrorists.

Those Islamic apologists who acknowledge that violence is a part of jihad, rationalize it by arguing it is confined to defense against oppressors. They insist Muslims are forbidden from any broader use of jihad.

Actually, that is not true, either. As noted above, the Quran expressly sanctions, in the context of violent jihad, a broader purpose of fighting Jews and

Christians either until they submit spiritually to Islam and convert or submit as a kept people who pay for protection against violence.

But again, do not take my word for it. Listen to author Dr. Ali Sina:

> What is the difference between a moderate Muslim and a terrorist Muslim? As a former Muslim myself, my long and careful analysis leads me to the conclusion that the only difference is the latter wants to start the jihad against the infidels now, while the former thinks it is better to wait until the Muslims are strong and then attack. The difference is in the form not in substance. Their only disagreement is when and how the jihad against the infidels should take place. Otherwise all the Muslims, whether moderate or extremists, believe in the same book. That book calls for waging war against the non-Muslims until they are subdued and humiliated.[7]

Another chapter of the Quran instructs Muslims to fight unbelievers until "there prevails justice and faith in Allah altogether and everywhere" (8:39). That is a pretty broad mandate.

So-called moderate American Muslim leaders such as Muzzamil Siddiqi say these violent passages are taken out of context. Sorry, that dog won't hunt either. Ali has put them into context for anyone who wants to take the time to read his notes. And so does one of Islam's top apologists, John Esposito. Remarkably, the Georgetown University professor admits deep inside his book that jihad means to fight to spread Islam, not just to defend it, and to "wage war against [Jews and Christians] who refuse Muslim rule":

> The mission of the Islamic community is to spread the rule or abode of Islam globally, much as Muhammad and his followers expanded Islamic rule through preaching, diplomacy, and warfare, and to 'defend' it. Islamic law stipulates that it is a Muslim's duty to wage war against poly-theists, apostates, and People of the Book (Jews and Christians) who refuse Muslim rule, and those who attack Muslim territory. To die in battle is the highest form of witness to God and to one's faith. The very Arabic word for martyr (*shaheed*) comes from the same root as the pro-fession of faith (*shahada*).[8]

NO. 3: TERRORISM DOES NOT COME FROM ISLAM

When the hijackers slit the throats of some of the flight attendants, they were simply following directives from the Quran—as were those who beheaded *Wall*

Street Journal correspondent Daniel Pearl in Pakistan, and those in Iraq who have decapitated Americans on videotape.

The Quran orders Muslims to "instill terror into the hearts of the unbelievers" and to "smite above their necks" (8:12), which Ali agrees is the most effective and humane way to finish the enemy off. Mohamed Atta counseled his 9/11 confederates to sharpen their knives so as not to "discomfort your animal during the slaughter." Then he quoted in his four-page letter from the same passage (8:12) of the Quran:

> When the confrontation begins, strike like champions who do not want
> to go back to this world. Shout, *"Allahu Akbar,"* because this strikes fear
> in the hearts of the non-believers. God said: "Strike above the neck, and
> strike at all of their extremities."[9]

The Quran, which instructs Muslims to "cast terror" or "instill terror" in several spots in the text, authorizes terrorist tactics, even kidnappings (which we have seen in Iraq), and frowns on "mealy-mouthed compromises" with the enemy, Ali says. It tells Muslims to fight and slay the unbelievers "wherever ye find them, and seize them, beleaguer them, and lie in wait for them in every stratagem (of war)." (9:5) According to Ali, "the fighting may take the form of slaughter, or capture, or siege, or ambush and other stratagems."[10]

NO. 4: ALLAH IS THE SAME GOD OF THE BIBLE

Some national polls show that as many as four out of five Americans agree that Muslims worship the same god as Christians and Jews.[11] It is a popular notion cultivated by years of interfaith propaganda about alleged shared religious values and themes. And it is nonsense on stilts.

Those trying to mainstream Islam are quick to highlight all the common figures cited in the Quran and the Bible—from Moses, Noah, and Abraham to Jesus Christ and the mother Mary. Catholics in particular are impressed with the attention Mary seems to get in the Quran. She is mentioned thirty-four times, which is more citations than she gets in the New Testament. (Christ, meanwhile, is mentioned by name thirty-three times.) "The virgin Mary is mentioned more in the Quran than in the New Testament," chirps Esposito, an Italian Catholic.[12]

But what they do not say is that the Quran cites Mary—the only woman mentioned by name in the Quran, fittingly—primarily to denigrate Christ. The two are usually mentioned together. Over and over, Christ is called "Jesus, the son of Mary," as opposed to "Jesus, the son of God," to emphasize that Allah has no partners—no son, no Holy Ghost. (Muslims believe Christ was born only a man and died a man—and not on a cross. They do not believe he was crucified.)

Here is an example of its usage: "Christ, the son of Mary, was no more than a Messenger" (5:75). This is hardly a unifying theme. If anything, it shows that Muslims and Christians worship completely different gods. In fact, the biggest sin in Islam is *shirk:* associating partners like Christ with Allah. In the Quran, Christ is demoted to prophet status, and is viewed as a good Muslim but not as great as Muhammad.

The Quran uses the phrase "son of Mary" as a "curse" on Christians, not a compliment. "And (they take as their Lord) Christ, the son of Mary," it says in Surah 9:31. "Yet they were commanded to worship but one God." To which Ali adds with derision, "The deification of the son of Mary is put here in a special clause by itself, as it held (and still holds) in its thrall a large portion of civilized humanity."[13]

Islam's boosters also argue that we are all children of Abraham. But even that points up a difference. Muslims believe they are descendants—physically and spiritually—of Ishmael and Esau, while Jews and Christians see themselves as the spiritual descendants of Abraham, Isaac, and Jacob.

And whereas the Quran contains references to these and other biblical characters, the Bible makes no mention of Muhammad. Its forty authors told a consistent story over the course of centuries, even prophesying Christ and his crucifixion. Yet oddly, none foretold of this extraordinary last messenger of Allah. You will not find Muhammad's name—or that of Allah or Mecca or the Quran—anywhere among the 774,746 words of the Bible.

"It is a grave mistake to believe that the God of the Quran is the same God of the Bible," Safa says.[14]

He says the key difference between the faiths is love. He notes that God's love is universal. He loves all his creation, including Muslims. Yet Allah does not love the unbelievers (3:32) and has only conditional love for believers (3:57), Safa says.

What's more, God's love is a sacrificial love. "For God so loved the world that He gave His only begotten Son, that whoever believes in Him should not perish but have everlasting life" (John 3:16 NKJV).

Of course, this is seen as blasphemous by Muslims, who believe a real god like Allah would never lower himself. According to Ali, the Quran says Christians have "corrupted" the meaning of redemption. Muslims are encouraged to sacrifice their blood for Allah, not the other way around, he says.

> We offer our whole selves to Allah, and Allah gives us salvation. This is the
> true doctrine of redemption. Any other view of redemption is rejected by

Islam, especially that of corrupted Christianity, which thinks that some other person suffered for our sins and we are redeemed by his blood. It is our self-surrender that counts. Our complete surrender may include fighting for the cause, both spiritually and physically.[15]

One day, I decided to look up the number of references to love in the Bible versus the Quran. What I found convinced me above all that Christians and Jews do not worship the same god as Muslims. Citations of love in the Quran total ten, and six relate to love of Allah (as opposed to, say, your neighbor). Whereas citations of love in the Bible total 395, with thirteen in the context of love of God. It is clear from the Bible that love is more important than anything; that it conquers all fear and evil; that God is love; that love flows from him; and that he commands us to love one another, even our enemies—which are concepts not found in the Quran. Here are some examples from both the New and Old Testaments:

This is My commandment, that you love one another as I have loved you.
—John 15:12 NKJV

Beloved, let us love one another, for love is of God; and everyone who loves is born of God and knows God.
—1 John 4:7 NKJV

. . . God is love . . .
—1 John 4:16 NKJV

Love does not rejoice in iniquity, but rejoices in the truth. Bears all things, believes all things, hopes all things, endures all things. . . . And now abide faith, hope, love, these three; but the greatest of these is love.
—1 Corinthians 13:6, 7, 13 NKJV

. . . the Lord God, merciful and gracious, longsuffering, and abounding in goodness and truth, keeping mercy for thousands, forgiving iniquity and transgression and sin . . .
—Exodus 34:6, 7 NKJV

. . . Love your enemies, do good to those who hate you, bless those who curse you, and pray for those who spitefully use you. To him who strikes you on the cheek, offer the other also. . . .
—Luke 6:27–29 NKJV

Christ, known as the Prince of Peace and the Lamb, was the world's greatest pacifist and peacemaker. According to the Bible, he commanded his followers to never even hold anger in their heart toward their enemies, least of all kill them. In his Sermon on the Mount, Christ said, "You have heard that it was said, 'You shall love your neighbor and hate your enemy.' But I say to you, love your enemies, bless those who curse you, do good to those who hate you, and pray for those who spitefully use you and persecute you"(Matthew 5:43, 44 NKJV).

But the god of the Quran flat-out orders Muslims to kill their enemies. "Fight in the cause of Allah those who fight you," the book says. "And slay them wherever ye catch them" (2:190, 191).

"The prophet himself played an important part in fighting," even condoning political assassinations, according to Middle East historian James A. Bill of the College of William and Mary in Virginia.[16] Compare that to Christ rebuking Peter for drawing his sword and cutting off the ear of a soldier of one of the Pharisees who had come to take him away. He even healed the man's injured ear. As the Old Testament prophesied, Christ had done no violence.

Turning the other cheek is looked upon as a sign of weakness in Islam, which "demands justice and vengeance, an eye for an eye and a tooth for a tooth," Safa says.[17]

But Muslims defending the violent nature of Islam contend that Christ actually advocated violence. Imam Siddiqi, for one, points to two biblical passages to support their case. In the first, Christ says he has "not come to bring peace but a sword" (Matthew 10:34 NKJV). Siddiqi says this shows he was for bloodshed.

But as subsequent passages reveal, he was not exhorting his followers to take up arms but instead telling them that a sword would come against them. His controversial message would and did stir up conflict, even between members of the same family. The sword was a figure of speech—symbolism that apparently is lost on Siddiqi. In fact, Christ did not care for such weapons. When he rebuked Peter, he said, "Put your sword in its place, for all who take the sword will perish by the sword" (Matthew 26:52 NKJV). In other words, violence only begets violence.

Still, Siddiqi further argues that in the book of Luke, "Jesus says enemies who do not accept his reign should be slain in his presence."[18] In this case, Siddiqi is referring to a parable involving a nobleman. The reference, made through the voice of the nobleman, is to the judgment day, not a literal order by Christ. Apparently Siddiqi is not used to parables, given the literalness of the Quran.

In any case, he and other Muslim leaders argue that the God of the Old Testament is at least as violent as Allah. Yes, he was a jealous, angry, and violent God. But unlike Allah, his wrath targeted ancient tribes that went astray. He did not make the same sweeping commands against all unbelievers as Allah, who most of the time orders Muslims on earth to fight and punish and slay unbelievers not by his hand but "by your hands" (9:14).

Drawing more contrast, even the abodes of the gods are different in the Bible and Quran.

In the Quran, heaven is a very physical, even sensual place, where carnal appetites are satisfied. Men are supplied young maidens, chaste and pure. They drink from rivers filled with wine that does not produce hangovers. They dwell with their companions in beautiful mansions furnished with plush cushions and rich carpets. There, they recline in jewel-encrusted thrones, while served fruit and wine in shiny goblets by nubile servants with big, lustrous eyes.

The biblical heaven, in contrast, is a metaphysical place devoid of lust, power, riches, and other carnal pleasures. The risen dead neither marry nor are given in marriage, but are like angels.

It cannot be the same God if heaven is different.

By all objective measures, the god of the Quran is a fundamentally different deity than the god of the Bible. One final point: Christ, who died broken on the cross so Man could live, said his power is made perfect in weakness. His spirit can be summed up in a two-word verse: "Jesus wept" (John 11:35 NKJV). This is the reverse concept of the Quran, where weakness is an abomination. The Muslim god, in stark contrast, can be summed up in a five-word verse: "Allah said to them: Die" (2:243).

NO. 5: THE QURAN TEACHES TOLERANCE OF OTHER RELIGIONS

"Constantly Muslims are enjoined to respect Jews and Christians, the 'People of the Book,' who worship the same God," claims scholar Karen Armstrong, author of *Islam: A Short History.*[19] She adds, "Muslims have no tradition of anti-Semitism, no tradition of hating Jewish people."[20]

Coming from a historian, this is nothing short of intellectual malpractice. The Quran rails against the "inequity of the Jews" (4:160) and compares them to "apes and swine" (5:60) and "donkeys" (62:5). It says Jews are "evil" (62:5), and the enemy of Muslims: "Strongest among men in enmity to the Believers wilt though find the Jews" (5:82).

Ali puts a finer point on the anti-Semitic text, supplying his own derogatory remarks. He says Jews are "beasts of burden" who have "corrupted" the message of Allah.[21] He also calls them, in so many words, men without faith, who are arrogant, illiterate, treacherous, and full of tricks.

Tolerance? Respect? If anything, Muslims are taught to hate Jews—as well as

Christians. "O ye who believe!" the Quran enjoins Muslims. "Take not the Jews and Christians for your friends" (5:50).

Perhaps I am misinterpreting something. No, "They are more likely to combine against you than to help you," Ali confirms in his commentary. Don't even think about befriending them, he warns. "He who associates with them and shares their counsels must be counted as of them." Such Muslims are considered "hypocrites" in league with the enemy, which brings an even harsher doom.[22]

The Quran heaps scorn on Christians, too.

The Muslim profession of faith, or *shahada*, says, "There is no God but Allah, and Muhammad is his prophet." So Muslims believe Christians, who believe in the Father, Son, and Holy Ghost, are polytheists who worship false gods—that is, they are no better than idolaters. And they consider the Christian profession of faith—that Christ is the son of God—to be blasphemous to Allah. And those who blaspheme Allah, well, watch out.

> They do blaspheme who say: Allah is one of three in a Trinity. For there is no god except One God. If they desist not from their word (of blasphemy), verily a grievous penalty will befall the blasphemers among them.
> —Surah 5:73

> They do blaspheme who say: Allah is Christ the son of Mary.
> —Surah 5:72

Ali contends that the Quran repudiates the Christian "dogma that he was Allah, or the son of Allah, or anything more than a man."[23]

Those trying to mainstream Islam ignore these passages, while zeroing in on the only one in the Quran that shows any semblance of tolerance: "Let there be no compulsion in religion" (2:256). However, even that passage is abrogated by the one that orders Muslims to "seize and slay wherever ye find" any Muslims who "reject Faith" (4:89). Such "hypocrites" are "worse than the enemy," Ali says.[24] So much for no compulsion.

NO. 6: OSAMA BIN LADEN HIJACKED ISLAM AND DISTORTS ITS TEACHINGS

This is a fundamental misunderstanding of both the faith and the enemy. Bin Laden has not betrayed his faith. Quite the contrary, he has honored it like few other Muslims have over the past fourteen hundred years of Islam. He is driven by a purist vision of Islam, not a corrupted or perverted one. To try to minimize

him as an oddball, while absolving his violent faith of all complicity, is to mini-
mize the threat America faces. He is a deeply religious man *and* a mass murderer.
Of course, these two things are hard to reconcile if you do not understand true
Islam.

Many of the leaders in al-Qaida have very sophisticated educations. They do
not believe what they believe out of illiteracy or ignorance. We forget that bin
Laden's deputy Ayman al-Zawahiri is a medical doctor, a surgeon no less. Above
all, they are students of the Quran. When bin Laden formulates his declarations
of war, he makes every effort to justify them through Quranic law.

"There is much consciously Islamic content to both Osama's acts and the
widespread—I must say widespread—Muslim affirmation of his acts," says professor Frank Vogel, director of the Islamic legal studies program at Harvard Law
School.[25]

Bin Laden's anti-U.S. position is not inconsistent with Quranic law, although
even some orthodox clerics have frowned on his methods (at least publicly).
Conventional wisdom may say bin Laden has perverted the teachings of the
Quran, but conventional wisdom has not read the Quran. Here are some of bin
Laden's religious justifications for his terrorism:

- In his December 2001 videotape, bin Laden quoted the Quran in saying
  he was ordered to "fight the people until they say there is no God but Allah,
  and his prophet Muhammad."

- Years before the 9/11 attacks (which bin Laden called "Operation Holy
  Tuesday"), when he declared war on Americans, bin Laden again quoted
  the Quran, saying it is permissible to spill even the blood of American
  civilians, after getting approval from *fatwas,* or religious decrees, issued by
  Saudi clerics. He called on every Muslim who believes in Allah and wishes
  to be rewarded to obey Allah's "order to kill Americans and plunder their
  money whenever and wherever they find them." He called it a "religious
  duty for each and every Muslim to be carried out in whichever country
  they are until al-Aqsa mosque [in Jerusalem] is liberated from their grasp
  and until their armies have left Muslim lands," including the holy soil of
  Saudi Arabia.

- To justify the indiscriminate World Trader Center slaughter, bin Laden
  again turned to the Quran, which permits Muslims to assault whoever
  assaults them in eye-for-an-eye fashion. He argued that he was merely
  responding in kind to the American embargo and periodic bombing of
  Iraq, which had killed women and children and other noncombatants. He

explained that any Muslims working in the "false gods" of the Twin Towers with the infidels were traitors and deserved to die even more, and that if an innocent Muslim child in or near the buildings were killed, the child died a martyr (if an involuntary one).

- He further justified attacking civilians by citing U.S. support for the state of Israel, which he calls an occupying force in Muslim holy land. Since U.S. taxpayers help finance Israel's military force, he considers them fair game under the rules of the Quran. And now more than ever, he views American civilians as guilty of "murder" and "villainy in the land."

- Just before the Iraq war, he warned Arab nations not to ally themselves with America and again quoted from the Quran: "O ye who believe! Take not the Jews and the Christians for your friends and protectors: they are but friends and protectors to each other."

- In addition, the official al-Qaida manual that British authorities seized in May 2000 in a raid of an al-Qaida member's flat in England is laced with verses from the Quran that are used to buttress the terror network's philosophical positions and tactics.

Not following Islam? Unfortunately, bin Laden is following it all too well. He is a living testament to Quranic teachings, right down to living in caves, where Muhammad was known to meditate and, according to Muslims, had his vision from the angel Gabriel. The terrorist leader is a millionaire who has nonetheless lived a pious life, shunning the palaces of the "whiskey Wahhabists" back in Saudi. And he has spent his fortune and risked his own life fighting the "enemies of Islam."

Islam's apologists allege that Muslims are baffled by bin Laden's holy war. He is "a man, who to the dismay of millions of Muslims around the world, uses the Quran to justify his call to arms against the United States," claims CNN's Amanpour.[26]

In fact, devout Muslims around the world who have dutifully read their Quran know bin Laden is a "lion of Allah," as they say. That is why so many of them in Pakistan and throughout Asia and the Middle East have named their newborn boys after Osama—"the warrior." Like it or not, many Muslims look upon 9/11 as a miracle of faith and bin Laden as a blessed servant with divine protection. Calling on Allah, he was able to hobble the Great Satan in the course of breakfast—and live to brag about it, going on four years now, while threatening to do it again! We see a murderer, while they see a holy man—and a hero.

"They call him a terrorist, but in reality he is a true Muslim hero who deserves to be backed by all Muslims throughout the world," says Saudi businessman Saad al-Shahrani.[27] Prominent Saudi clerics like Suleiman Alwan praised bin Laden in sermons after 9/11, saying what he did was jihad, and that those killed were not innocent. Nearly two-thirds of Pakistanis, meanwhile, hold bin Laden in high regard, according to a Pew Research Center poll taken last year. And nearly half say suicide attacks against Americans and other Westerners are justified. He even has fans in South Africa. "Bin Laden is a hero," agrees Muslim activist Moain Achmad, who sells T-shirts in Cape Town glorifying the U.S. enemy No. 1. The front of his shirts read: "Long Live Bin Laden."[28]

The admiration is not limited to Muslims abroad or ultra-orthodox Muslims. Bin Laden represents what most devout Muslims stand for in their faith, say U.S. intelligence officials, while not necessarily what they are willing to exercise. "Even among the more moderate elements [of the Muslim community], I think you will find sympathy for what he stands for, and what he's trying to do. Maybe not his tactics, but certainly for his vision of unifying all Muslims under one caliphate," or global Islamic theocracy, says a CIA officer, who last year testified anonymously as "Dr. K" before the 9/11 Commission. "I think you probably have a great deal of support for that vision."[29]

The reason so many Muslim leaders even in America have not done a better job of denouncing the "distortions" in bin Laden's interpretation of their shared faith is because they are not altogether distortions. And like bin Laden, they believe America is "on the side of injustice," as Siddiqi said before 9/11, and deserves Allah's "wrath."

And listen to the head of the National Association of Muslim Chaplains in America.

"Osama bin Laden probably will go down in history as a hero to Muslims," says Warith Deen Umar, former chief Muslim chaplain for New York state prisons.

"You will probably find people—not just in prisons—who cheered" the 9/11 attacks, says Deen, who himself defends the attacks as scriptural. "You will find people all over the world who cheered at the black eye that America got."[30]

Muslims who have read their Quran know that bin Laden has not strayed from its teachings but has fought in the path of Allah.

"So many times I have been asked if Osama bin Laden is a Muslim, and I have refused to go for the easy option," says Farid Esack, author of *Quran, Liberation and Pluralism*. "Appending a *kaffir* label to Osama will only allow me to walk away comfortable in my lies that there is nothing in my sacred text that inspires him, that my theology is not filled with well-documented argument for his terror, and that the vast majority of Muslims in the world do not support him and al-Qaida."

"I may denounce them," he adds. "I cannot, however, disown them."[31]

Bin Laden did not "hijack" a "great religion," as the president would have you believe. He embraced it. He is not a "radical" or "extremist" or "crazy" Muslim. The horrible truth is, he is a good Muslim, and a model one at that.

NO. 7: ISLAM IS COMPATIBLE WITH
WESTERN-STYLE DEMOCRACY

President Bush maintains that Iraqis yearn for Western-style democracy—and, by golly, he is going to give it to them. "The nation of Iraq is fully capable of moving toward democracy and living in freedom," he insists.

But Western-style democracy—with individualism and secularism as its hallmarks—is incompatible with Islam.

Even under Saddam Hussein's more secular regime, Iraq was demonstrably an Islamic nation. And it still is. In between the Baghdad bombings, you can hear the calls to prayer, and whenever the smoke clears, you can see the minarets. In the countryside, women wear head-to-toe black *abayas*. And suicide bombers kiss the Quran before they kill American troops.

For Muslims in the Middle East, Islam is a complete system of religion and government, ethics and the law, military and jihad, as well as worship. And the Quran is their constitution. There is no room for Western values. They do not draw the line between mosque and state, or between military and civilian. And they do not afford equal rights for all citizens. Men and women are not treated alike, and certainly not Jews and Muslims. It is a theocracy of Muslims, by Muslims, and for Muslims.

The inclination of the secular West is to separate the religious and the political in analyzing the enemy. Politicians try to distinguish between the terrorists who they think use Islam for political aims, and spiritual Islam. But this ignores reality. They are one and the same. Islam is an all-embracing ideology for individual and corporate life, and not just for religious life. The Quran is the law for state and society.

"The goal of Islam is to produce a theocracy with Allah as the ruler of society, a society with no separation between religion and the state," Safa says. "This society would have no democracy, no free will, and no freedom of expression."

Thus in Islamic countries, opposition to Islam and its leaders—those believed to be appointed by Allah—is prohibited. So, too, are individual lifestyles that take away from Allah. You cannot be a slave to Allah if you are a slave to the almighty dollar, for instance. The Quran calls for collective submission to Allah under a worldwide *ummah*.

"While the West gazes into the 'Windows of Microsoft,' Islam gazes into the 'Windows of Heaven,'" opines Islamic scholar Dr. Mohamed Khodr of Virginia.[32]

This is a departure from Christianity, which instructs followers to respect secular leaders while living godly lives within secular societies. As Christ said, "give to Caesar what is Caesar's, and to God what is God's."

"Islam to a Muslim is more than a religion, more than daily rituals. Islam is a way of living, thinking, and reasoning," Safa adds. "Knowing this will help you understand why Muslims think and reason so unlike people in Western societies. Islam obliges its followers to follow Muhammad's way of thinking," as espoused in the Quran and the traditions, or *hadiths*, of the Muslim prophet.

The Quran is an all-purpose instruction manual for life, regulating everything from diet to home finance to divorce to even bathing. To devout Muslims, it is a living document and a detailed blueprint for government. In short, it is the Islamic code of life, rendering all secular codes meaningless.

Even Muslims in America are reminded of this. "We must not forget that Allah's rules have to be established in all lands," imam Siddiqi recently decreed.[33]

Expecting devout Muslims to yearn for Western-style democracy is the folly of Western apologists who have not read the Quran and want to read Western values into a religion that simply are not there. Bush says militant Muslims abroad (not to mention at home) "hate us because they hate freedom." No, Mr. President, they hate us because we are not Muslim. Period.

NO. 8: THOSE VIRGINS? THEY ARE REALLY RAISINS

The multiculturalists in the Ivory Tower, who have never studied a culture or religion they did not like, are disturbed by the rash of Muslim suicide attackers killing non-Muslims in the name of their religion and for the company of the blessed dark-eyed virgins of Paradise. And so they are desperately looking for ways to rehabilitate the repeat violent offender called Islam. And they think they have finally found the solution.

Scholars have put forth the theory that the references to virgins in the Quran have somehow been misinterpreted over the centuries by Islamic scholars like Yusuf Ali. The virgins who are awaiting the good Muslim martyrs as their reward in Paradise are in reality raisins, they posit. Those nubile companions with swelling breasts are really nothing more than plump little fruits.

Alas, the theory does not hold up to closer scrutiny. Yes, the text of the Quran talks about the abundance of fruit awaiting martyrs in Paradise, a delicacy in the arid desert. And it describes gardens with grapevines. But any grapes or raisins promised certainly cannot be confused for:

- the "companions with beautiful, big, and lustrous eyes" (56:22)

- or the "chaste women restraining their glances" (38:51)

- or the maidens "whom no man before them has touched" (55:56)

- or the "fair" and "beautiful" companions "reclining on green cushions and rich carpets of beauty" (55:76)

Raisins that recline on couches and glance at you? Perhaps the historian who pioneered the raisin theory—which has so enraged orthodox Muslims that he has to use a pseudonym—has been watching too many California Raisins commercials. Ali in his footnotes says all of these descriptions refer, in fact, to "maidens or virgins."[34] He adds, "It is made clear that these Companions for heavenly society will be of special creation—of virginal purity, grace, and beauty inspiring and inspired by love."[35]

Even Irshad Manji, the feminist Muslim author, says the professor's theory is laughable. "Raisins instead of virgins? Please," she says. "How can the Quran be so mistaken?"[36]

Atta certainly was not confused about his reward. In preparation for his honeymoon in heaven, he made sure he looked and smelled nice and advised the other hijackers under his command to do the same. "The time between you and your marriage [in heaven] is very short," he advised them in a four-page letter titled "THE LAST NIGHT," which was handwritten in Arabic and later translated by the FBI. "Shave excess hair from the body and wear cologne. Shower. Do not leave your apartment unless you have performed ablution," or cleansing.

"Know that the gardens of Paradise are waiting for you in all their beauty, and the women of Paradise are waiting, calling out, 'Come hither, friend of God,'" Atta added. "They have dressed in their most beautiful clothing."

Then he packed his wedding suit. The clothing found in one of Atta's bags was not a pilot's uniform, as first reported, but his Paradise wedding suit, says an American Airlines employee who was with authorities when they first opened his luggage at Logan International Airport in Boston. It had not made his connecting flight.

Alongside the navy suit—which was eerily laid out as if Atta were in it, with a sapphire-blue necktie neatly knotted and looped under a crisp dress-shirt collar—was a bottle of flower water, or cologne. At the foot of the bag, which had been locked, was a fancy leather-bound Quran in gold leaf.

"It was like opening a casket," the American Airlines employee tells me.

"All the pieces came together when we saw that suit," he says. "This was his suitcase he thought he was going to get into Paradise with."[37]

Ironically, Atta was the only passenger among the eighty-one aboard American Flight 11 whose luggage did not make the flight. As a result, the thirty-three-year-old Egyptian native, who was single, was denied his ceremonial groom's outfit. Because of an American Airlines policy instated just before 9/11 to curb baggage-related flight delays, Atta's two checked bags—which had been held up from an earlier flight from Maine—were left behind in Boston, says the employee, who requested anonymity for fear of reprisal from the Dallas-based carrier, which continues to gag all employees from talking about the 9/11 hijackings. Two of the hijacked flights were American. Atta piloted the one that hit the first World Trade Center tower.

NO. 9: POVERTY AND OPPRESSION MOTIVATE THE TERRORISTS

Bin Laden says the hijackers were following the teachings of the Quran, not just his orders, and that they knew they were enlisting in martyrdom operations. Some doubt that. They say the hijackers were tricked into doing what they did.

But this is more politically correct mythology. They made out wills and video testaments. They performed ablution the night before their death runs. At flight schools, they only wanted to learn how to steer jumbo jets toward targets and had no interest in practicing takeoffs and landings. And they praised Allah as they crashed them. They knew what they were doing.

Others say they were not really devout Muslims and did what they did for the thrill or the fame. Or out of sheer lunacy. They point to reports of them patronizing bars, for example.

But the hijackers followed orders to blend into the American scene so as not to appear serious about their religion and raise suspicions. Privately, they were so pious they put towels over Florida hotel room pictures showing women in beach clothing. They worshipped at orthodox mosques. And they ate *halal* meals. In fact, Atta was so careful not to eat pork fat that he scraped the frosting from his cakes.

The night before the attacks, Atta advised his brothers to "continue to pray through this night. Continue to recite the Quran." He told them to read the chapters of the Quran dealing with jihad, such as Tawba and Anfal. And he quoted scripture promising their rewards. "You will be entering Paradise," he said. "You will be entering the happiest life, everlasting life."[38]

Islam's apologists insist the Quran does not make Muslim suicide attackers tick. They say many are ignorant and driven by poverty and oppression, not religion.

But that certainly cannot be said for the 9/11 hijackers, who were both well-off and educated. Atta, whose affluent family had a vacation home on the Mediterranean, studied at one of the most prestigious colleges in Egypt. Several others were college students and sons of imams and other influential members of Middle Eastern society.

Likewise, the apologists are quick to romanticize Palestinian attacks on kids in pizza parlors as the desperate struggle of the downtrodden against an oppressive Israeli military. Some like *Boston Globe* columnist Ellen Goodman still like to pretend Palestinians are freedom fighters and are only using suicide as a "cheap defense weapon," deluded by the "despair" of their impoverished existence.[39]

But if Palestinians are deluded into carrying out such wicked acts, it is not a function of their social or economic condition. It is a function of their faith. In fact, studies show most of the suicide bombers over the past several years were educated and came from middle-class families. And all knew the Quran backwards and forwards, reciting verses from several of its chapters that feature such relevant themes as jihad, martyrdom, the rewards of Paradise, and the importance of faith. In fact, Palestinian *shaheeds*, or martyrs, are known to keep a small copy of the sacred book in their left breast pocket, above the heart, as they blow themselves and their victims up.[40]

NO. 10: THE QURAN DOES NOT ENCOURAGE SELF-IMMOLATION

The most damaging image to Islam on the world stage is that of the suicide bomber and, in the wake of 9/11, the suicide pilot and hijacker. They strike terror in the hearts of Westerners and cause them to fear the whole faith, which marginalizes Islam politically. Those who seek to put a happy face on Islam—the subversives and their friends in the media and academia—want to erase this image by claiming the suicidal terrorists are betraying their faith. They argue Islam forbids suicide, and so far it has been an effective argument because technically they are right.

But don't be fooled. It's another smokescreen hiding another unpleasant truth about Islam.

Selfish suicide may be a one-way ticket to hell, but suicide while fighting in the name of Allah is a one-way ticket to heaven. Muslims call it "self-sacrifice." And it is the most important test of faith in Islam.

The "test" of loyalty to Allah is not good acts or faith in general but martyrdom that results from fighting unbelievers. It is the only assurance of salvation in Islam. And the reward for death in the cause of Allah is greater than the reward for good works or faith. Warrior martyrs automatically pass the Paradise entrance "test" and go to the head of the class, according to the Quran.

> When ye meet the Unbelievers (in fight), smite at their necks. . . . [I]f it had been Allah's Will, he could certainly have exacted retribution from them (Himself). But (He lets you fight) in order to test you. . . . [T]hose who are slain in the way of Allah—He will never let their deeds be lost. Soon will He guide them and improve their condition, and admit them to the Garden which He has announced for them.
>
> —Surah 47:4

So, battling non-Muslims is a loyalty "test." The true test of faith in Allah is a Muslim's willingness to kill and be killed fighting for his cause.

This concept of a loyalty "test"—a death pact, if you will—is corroborated in a passage in a previous chapter titled Al Imran. It reveals that Allah uses self-sacrifice in holy war as a way to weed out the truly faithful from those who "flinch" from death.

> If a wound hath touched you, be sure a similar wound hath touched the others. Such days (of varying fortunes) we give to men and men by turns: that Allah may know those that believe, and that He may take to Himself from your ranks Martyr-witnesses (to Truth). . . . Allah's object also is to purge those that are true in Faith and to deprive of blessing those that resist Faith. Did ye think that ye would enter Heaven without Allah testing those of you who fought hard (in His Cause) and remained steadfast? Ye did indeed wish for Death before ye met it: Now ye have seen it with your own eyes (and ye flinch!)
>
> —Surah 3:140-143

Do you think the suicide hijackers took this "test" seriously? You bet they did. Listen to what Atta told his fellow hijackers the night before their suicide mission, keeping in mind the verses above, in particular the phrases "remained steadfast" and "test."

> If you fall into hardship, how will you act and how will you remain steadfast and remember that you will return to God. This test from Almighty God is to raise your level and erase your sins.[41]

Erase sins? That's right. The Muslim warrior who dies while fighting in Allah's cause receives a special "forgiveness" of sins from Allah (4:96). "Martyrdom is the sacrifice of life in the service of Allah. Its reward is therefore even greater than that of an ordinarily good life," Ali explains. "The martyr's sins are forgiven by the very act of martyrdom."[42] The martyr also receives the direct approval and love of Allah (in addition to his harem of virgins in the gardens of perpetual delight). This greeting from the divine—which Ali calls "the final bliss, the sight of Allah Himself"—is not afforded normal fighters—only the ones who spill their own blood while spilling that of the enemy.[43]

It is tantamount to a lifelong groupie who finally gets a backstage pass. He is in the VIP lounge, surrounded by fawning virgins, and the big guy is about to make a cameo. He has truly died and gone to heaven. Now you know why so many Muslim men blow themselves up. These ideas are not fantasies in their heads. They are in the Quran.

Ali says that, unlike the Bible, the Quran encourages "self-sacrifice" in jihad for Allah and rejects the "monkish morality" practiced by Paul and other apostles who allowed themselves to be locked up and beaten for their beliefs. It lacks "common sense to ignore lust of blood in man which has to be combated," Ali says.[44]

Under Islamic law, such martyrdom operations are not considered a form of suicide and should not be deemed unjustifiable means of endangering one's life, says Sheikh Faysal Mawlawi, deputy chairman of the European Council for Fatwa and Research.

"Prophet Muhammad strictly forbade suicide and made it clear that anyone who commits suicide would be cast into hell," he says. "But in such cases, suicide means a Muslim killing himself without any lawfully accepted reason, or killing himself to escape pain or social problems.

"On the other hand, in martyr operations, the Muslim sacrifices his own life for the sake of performing a religious duty, which is Jihad against the enemy," Mawlawi adds. "Accordingly, a Muslim's intention when committing suicide is certainly different from his intention when performing a military operation and dying in the cause of almighty Allah."[45]

Dying while fighting unbelievers for Allah is not viewed as a selfish waste of life. And far from being a sin, it is the highest honor a Muslim can attain. "To a Muslim, dying and killing for the cause of Islam is not only an honor but also a way of pleasing Allah," Safa says. *Shaheeds*, as Muslim martyrs are called, are head and shoulders above every other Muslim, he says. They have a great edge in the afterlife. Self-sacrifice for the cause of Allah guarantees an eternal life of pleasure and honor in the hereafter. It reserves Muslims a first-class ticket to Paradise. "The only way Muslims can have assurance of salvation and eternal life is by becoming a martyr for the cause of Islam," Safa says.[46]

He says local Muslim clerics recite to young men the verses from the Quran that promise the reward of Paradise, and all its oddly non-spiritual perks, if they die while fighting the "unbelievers"—Jews and Christians—in the name of Allah. "Are you ready for martyrdom?" the young man is asked. "Yes, yes," he repeats. "He is then given the oath on the Quran," Safa says, explaining the ritual. "These young men leave the meeting with one determination: to kill."

Palestinian suicide bombers, for one, do not refer to their deeds as "suicide" but as "sacred explosions."

But what of the mothers and fathers left sonless by these young men of fanatical faith, these duty-bound suicide bombers, these glorified martyrs? They have cause only to rejoice, says the Quran. Citing Surah 3:170, which says Allah's martyrs do not really die, Ali offers comfort: "The dear ones have no cause to grieve at the death of the martyrs. Rather have they cause to rejoice."[47]

That explains how, not long ago, a Palestinian grandmother could proudly pose with her beaming teenage grandson for a final photograph knowing that just hours later he would strap himself with explosives and eviscerate Israeli "infidels"—and himself—in the name of Allah. This adoring old woman was actually celebrating the boy's imminent death, as if he were about to cross the stage at his high-school graduation ceremony.

But to her, a death certificate sealed by Allah meant more than any diploma. She said she was happy—overjoyed that her grandson would soon disembowel himself—because she knew he would be instantly transported to a better place. Meanwhile, the pubescent grandson dreamed of the carnal pleasures awaiting him in Paradise—the "virgin-pure" maidens that his teachers highlighted in the Quran.

Palestinian mothers of martyrs, moreover, are known to ululate in joy over the honor that Allah has bestowed upon their families. Funeral announcements of suicide bombers in the Palestinian press often read more like wedding announcements. Families talk of their martyred sons marrying the "black-eyed in heaven."

And such Quranic promises explain how the father of another young Palestinian, who recently set off a bomb on a crowded commuter bus, could gush, "My son will go to heaven"—as if he had just scored the winning touchdown at the homecoming game in front of Ivy League scouts. Most fathers would be bawling their eyes out over such a senseless loss.[48]

Where do they get such abiding faith? From the Quran.

Over and over, their sacred book teaches them to love death more than life. The Muslim Brotherhood in Egypt and Syria, which according to Safa has helped the Palestinians against the Israelis, has this as its slogan: "The Quran is our constitution, the prophet is our guide; Death for the glory of Allah is our greatest ambition." Greater than land or voting rights. Greater than family or love. Above all, death. This is the enemy Israel faces. This, sadly, is now America's enemy, too.

Ali confirms that true Muslim warriors for Allah hold life cheap. He says they "eagerly desire death" because it will "bring them nearer to Allah."[49] He adds that "dying in doing your duty is the best means of reaching Allah's mercy."[50]

But moderate Muslims argue that Islam's culture of death is misunderstood. They say it is meant to encourage Muslims to live pious lives on earth so they will be rewarded in the afterlife.

"The heavy focus on death and afterlife in Islam is so that the believer can live the best possible life on this earth here and now," says Hesham A. Hassaballa, an American Muslim. "For example, when someone is acutely aware of the hereafter, he would go to great lengths to treat others kindly and justly on earth. He would not harm his fellow human beings, for he knows that he will be accountable to God for how he treated his fellow man. He would not strap a bomb on his body, walk into a pizza parlor during the lunchtime rush, and blow himself up. He would not commandeer a plane and fly it into the World Trade Center. For the score will be settled by God on Judgment Day."[51]

You would hope. Only, that is not the message his scripture is sending. It tells him he can bypass good works on earth and go straight to the Paradise penthouse if he martyrs himself fighting infidels. Sure, no one really knows if the god of the Quran views blowing up infidels in pizza parlors and office towers as over the top.

But there is little doubt from the Quran that he rewards Muslim martyrs who fight and carry out acts of "terror" against "unbelievers" in jihadi warfare. There is little doubt that it describes in great detail a special rank, place, and privilege for such loyal foot soldiers in the afterlife. If you are not convinced, check out this passage:

> Allah hath purchased of the Believers their persons and their goods. For theirs (in return) is the Garden (of Paradise). They fight in His cause, and slay and are slain.
>
> —Surah 9:111

Or look at Surah 4:74:

> To him who fighteth in the cause of Allah—whether he is slain or gets victory—soon shall we give him a reward of great (value).

No matter how you spin it, this is why so many Muslims answer the call to suicidal violence against non-Muslims. "Defeat them through suicide attacks so that you may be successful before Allah," says bin Laden, in a recent call to the Muslim faithful to kill more Americans.[52] And right now in America, investigators fear another Mohamed Atta is busy packing another Paradise wedding suit in preparation for another martyrdom attack.

II
THE TERROR NETWORK

6

THE THREAT STILL AMONG US

Draining the Terrorist Swamp in Our Own Backyard

"Our greatest threat is from al-Qaida cells in the United States that we have not yet been able to identify."
—FBI DIRECTOR ROBERT MUELLER[1]

Exit polls taken after the last presidential election show that three out of four voters worry that America will be attacked again by terrorists.[2] Their fears are not unfounded.

Despite what some would still like to believe, whether for peace of mind or out of a kind of patriotic defiance, the 9/11 attacks were not a fluke carried out by nineteen lucky ne'er-do-wells. They were the successful follow-up to a flubbed earlier strike. It took them eight years, but the terrorists came back and finished off the World Trade Center. The harsh truth is, al-Qaida has not peaked, and its leaders have not retired. They are as patient and determined as ever to kill Americans. And there are many more trained terrorists with death wishes—some already in place inside America—who are just waiting for the orders to launch an encore attack.

One of the most chilling parts of the 567-page 9/11 Commission Report is buried in a footnote, albeit a long one running three pages. It names al-Qaida operatives who were sitting on the bench on 9/11, held in reserve for a larger, more deadly operation. They include:

Ali Abd al Rahman al-Faqasi al-Ghamdi: Originally a candidate for the 9/11 operation, he "was held in reserve by bin Laden for a later, even larger operation," the report says. He was recently given amnesty by the Saudi government.

Saud al-Rashid: He also trained for the suicide mission. Saudi authorities released him from custody in 2002. "He has no credible explanation why photos of him were found with those of three other hijackers, or why others identified him as a candidate hijacker," according to the report.

Abderraouf Jdey: Also known as Faruq al-Tunisi, he is a trained pilot who was slated for a "second wave" of suicide attacks after 9/11. He has a Canadian passport and is still at large.[3]

These are just a few of the known players on al-Qaida's new first team. Another, Adnan al-Shukrijumah, is considered by investigators to be "the next Mohamed Atta." He has lived in Florida and was last spotted in Central America. Al-Shukrijumah allegedly conspired with al-Qaida agent Jose Padilla to blow up several New York high-rise apartment buildings simultaneously. In a fiendishly clever plot, they planned to rent apartments inside the buildings, hermetically seal them off, turn on the natural gas, leave a timer-controlled spark-gap switch in the kitchen, and beat it out of the city before the explosions. Padilla, now in U.S. custody, had perfected the technique in the Afghan outback. Al-Shukrijumah, also known as "Jafar the Pilot," is still at large.

Then there is Adam Gadahn, the "American al-Qaida," who grew up in California before converting to Islam and shipping off to Afghanistan to train for suicide missions. He is suspected of conspiring to blow up gas stations and underground fueling facilities in the Washington area. Al-Qaida is trying to recruit more non-Arab converts like him because they are less suspicious. Gadahn is still at large.

The FBI is hunting for them, in addition to Jdey and others. Their whereabouts are unknown. They could be trying to get into the United States, or they could already be inside the country, using a Muslim community for cover.

But these are just the al-Qaida operatives that investigators know about. There are many more like them who have not been identified and who may be hiding somewhere inside America. Which leads to another chilling part of the 9/11 Commission Report that has gone largely unreported in the national media.

It deals with interrogations of the captured mastermind of the 9/11 plot, Khalid Sheikh Mohammed, known inside U.S. intelligence and law enforcement simply as "KSM." He has been cooperative, even talkative, when asked to describe details of the planning, organization, and decision-making that went into the attacks of more than three years ago. He has even revealed information about Osama bin Laden and the command structure of the al-Qaida terrorist network. But Mohammed falls silent whenever investigators try to learn about al-Qaida cells inside America.

"In an assessment of KSM's reporting, the CIA concluded that protecting operatives in the United States appeared to be a 'major part' of KSM's resistance efforts," says the 9/11 report in another footnote. "For example, in response to questions about U.S. zip codes found in his notebooks, KSM provided the less-than-satisfactory explanation that he was planning to use the zip codes to open new e-mail accounts."[4]

When it comes to revealing the names and locations of al-Qaida operatives in the country who might be preparing to launch future attacks, Mohammed remains mum. And the FBI could desperately use his help. Although investigators since 9/11 have been able to ferret out cells in Lackawanna, New York, and Portland, Oregon, they are a long way from identifying all of them.

"Our greatest threat is from al-Qaida cells in the United States that we have not yet been able to identify," says FBI Director Robert Mueller. "Finding and rooting out al-Qaida members once [they are] in the United States and have had time to establish themselves is the most serious intelligence and law enforcement challenge."[5]

That's not to say the FBI does not have its eye on suspected cells. It clearly does, as evidenced by the record number of surveillance warrants it has requested since 9/11. Question is, exactly how many cells are there? What is al-Qaida's strength inside America? The month before 9/11, the FBI was conducting fifty-seven full-field investigations throughout the U.S. that were related to al-Qaida. The individuals under surveillance were either suspected operatives or sympathizers who could graduate to become operatives.[6]

But that is just a small sample of al-Qaida's presence inside America. U.S. intelligence says the organization has trained up to one hundred and twenty thousand terrorists around the world, and as many as five thousand of them may be inside the U.S.[7] And al-Qaida is organizing them into larger cells for at least future suicide hijacking operations, a U.S. intelligence official tells me. "Al-Qaida is planning to use more people for a hijacking than were used before. After 9/11, they learned that they may need more people to subdue crew and passengers," he says, explaining that "they still like the idea of planes as weapons."[8] The four hijackers aboard United Airlines Flight 93 had to abort their mission apparently after brave passengers rushed the cockpit. The plane crashed into a Pennsylvania field, far short of its intended target—the U.S. Capitol.

Bigger operations require more logistical support. In a typical al-Qaida operation, there are operational terror cells, and then there are independent cells assigned small tasks to aid the operational cells in pulling off major acts of terrorism. Such cells, called logistical cells, often are unaware of the members or even the full plans of the other cells. The compartmentalization of information protects the integrity of the mission should the members of the support cells be questioned by authorities.

Reconnaissance, or spying, is the chief job of al-Qaida's logistical cells. Al-Qaida spies in recent years have taken photographs of major financial buildings in New York, Washington, and Newark, New Jersey, to help terrorists prepare for possible strikes against these economic targets. Documents describing surveillance at the buildings were discovered last year in Pakistan, written in perfect English. Investigators say Mohammed sent a British man known as Issa al-Britani to America to conduct the surveillance and write the report. He may have had two collaborators helping him case the buildings, and investigators are looking at associates of his living in New Jersey and California.

Separately, authorities are looking for a Pakistani woman who has lived in Boston and the Washington area, as well as Houston. Aafia Siddiqui, who has studied at MIT, is said to be close to al-Shukrijumah. Because of her knowledge of the United States, investigators suspect she is a "fixer" for al-Qaida—someone who can support and help get things done for operatives.

Another Pakistani named Kamran Akhtar was caught last year videotaping skyscrapers in six U.S. cities—Atlanta, Austin, Houston, Dallas, New Orleans, and Charlotte, North Carolina—as well as a dam in Texas, and metro rail and trolley systems in Atlanta, Houston, Dallas, and New Orleans. One of the tall buildings in Charlotte he filmed houses the local FBI office. He was in the country illegally, as are thousands of other Pakistanis, and was convicted of violating immigration laws and making false statements. Akhtar, who claims he shot the footage as a tourist, received a short jail sentence and will soon be released. Meanwhile, authorities continue to investigate his activities for possible ties to terrorism.

FBI special agent Gary Harter of the Washington field office says al-Qaida operatives are highly trained in what is known as "prolonged static surveillance" methods, ranging from using hidden cameras to posing as tourists or even street-corner panhandlers to case a target for terrorism.

"Al-Qaida operations have been characterized by meticulous planning, a focus on inflicting mass casualties, and multiple, simultaneous suicide attacks," he said in a recent FBI bulletin circulated among law enforcement agencies. "Operatives are highly trained in basic and sophisticated surveillance techniques, posing challenges for counterterrorism and security forces in identifying terrorist surveillance."[7]

He has advised police around the country to be on the lookout for the following possible indicators of terrorist surveillance:

- Discreet use of still cameras, video-recorders, or note-taking at non-tourist type locations.

- Prolonged static surveillance, using operatives disguised as panhandlers, demonstrators, shoe-shiners, food or flower vendors, news agents, or street sweepers not previously seen in the area.

- Unusual or prolonged interest in security measures or personnel, entry points and access controls, or perimeter barriers such as fences or walls.

- Unusual behavior such as starting or quickly looking away from personnel or vehicles entering or leaving designated facilities or parking areas.

- Observation of security reaction drills or procedures.

- Increase in anonymous telephone or e-mail threats to facilities in conjunction with suspected surveillance incidents, indicating possible surveillance of threat-reaction procedures.

- Foot surveillance involving two or three individuals working together.

- Mobile surveillance using bicycles, scooters, motorcycles, cars, trucks, sport-utility vehicles, boats, or small aircraft.

- Use of multiple sets of clothing, identifications, or the use of sketching materials (paper, pencils, etc).

- Questioning of security or facility personnel.[10]

Al-Qaida operatives are also very methodical and patient in preparing for attacks. Ohio truck driver Iyman Faris, for example, spent nearly a year researching the kinds of gas torches that might be used to cut the suspension cables of the Brooklyn Bridge. He finally reported back to his al-Qaida handlers that none of the gas cutters would work. He is now in prison along with a confederate who plotted to blow up an Ohio shopping mall.

As they go about their normal business, the American people really have no idea how active and determined these terrorist operatives are each and every day around the country. Although the homeland has not been struck again in three years, the terrorists operating inside America have been very busy, according to federal law enforcement documents. For example, an internal Department of Homeland Security report I obtained shows that law enforcement responded to nearly thirty incidents of terrorism-related activities *just during a two-week period in 2002*. Among other incidents, police reported that Middle Eastern suspects:

- took surveillance photographs of cruise ships in Los Angeles

- purchased kayaks near the port of Los Angeles

- stole explosives devices from the University of Colorado

- applied to drive fuel trucks in Port Everglades, Florida

- took surveillance photos of bridges and buildings in St. Louis

- inquired about ambulance services along the East Coast

- stole large volumes of potentially harmful chemicals in Ocala, Florida

- tried to purchase a fuel truck in Waverly, Nebraska[11]

Where are the terrorists most active? Law enforcement has identified active terror cells and groups, including ones affiliated with al-Qaida, operating in a number of cities across America. Top areas of concern, according to a related Homeland Security report, include:

- Dallas and Arlington, Texas

- Denver

- Tucson, Arizona

- San Diego

- Los Angeles

- San Francisco and Santa Clara, California

- Seattle

- Detroit

- Chicago metro area

- Plainfield, Indiana

- Kansas City, Missouri

- Oklahoma City, Oklahoma

- Boston

- New York metro area

- Philadelphia

- Washington D.C. and the Maryland and Virginia suburbs

- Raleigh, North Carolina

- Orlando, Florida

- Tampa, Florida

- Boca Raton and Fort Lauderdale, Florida[12]

Not coincidentally, most of these terror hot spots boast among the nation's largest populations of Arabs and Muslims. But they cover large areas. Broken down by small towns and suburbs, the terrorist connection is even more striking. The Census Bureau recently put together a table for the Department of Homeland Security that lists all the places across the nation with populations of ten thousand or more and one thousand or more people of Arab ancestry. They represent the largest and closest-knit Arab and Muslim communities in America. The list reveals a strong correlation between these Arabic-speaking communities and terrorist cells, providing U.S. intelligence and law enforcement with a valuable roadmap to terrorist breeding grounds. Here are a few choice examples:

Falls Church, Virginia: The Washington suburb, where one in every ten residents is Arab, provided refuge to the hijackers who attacked the Pentagon (an issue I explore in detail in a coming chapter).

El Cajon, California: Two of the 9/11 hijackers received aid and comfort in the San Diego suburb, which has a 3 percent Arab population.

Bridgeview, Illinois: Known as the "American West Bank," the Chicago suburb is home to a huge population of Palestinian refugees, as well as several Hamas terrorist fronts under investigation.

Lackawanna, New York: The al-Qaida cell known as the "Lackawanna Six" was based out of this Buffalo suburb, which has a 6 percent Arab population.

Jersey City, New Jersey: Nearly 3 percent of the population is Arab in this city next door to New York, where Blind Sheikh Omar Abdul Rhaman led a mosque and plotted to wage urban warfare against America by blowing up New York buildings and landmarks.

Dearborn, Michigan: This Detroit suburb, where Arabs account for one of every three residents, has become a prime target of FBI counterterrorism investigations.

Hollywood, Florida: This suburb of Fort Lauderdale—where Padilla and al-Shukrijumah lived, along with one of the al-Qaida hijackers—also has a high concentration of Arabs and Muslims, according to the Census Bureau table.[13]

Al-Qaida sleeper cells use Arab and Muslim communities as cover to blend in and live low-profile lives, undetected by authorities until they are activated by al-Qaida leaders. These ethnic communities are also places to raise cash and recruit sympathizers and facilitators like those who assisted the hijackers in a number of different ways.

7

THE FACILITATORS

Giving Aid and Comfort to the Terrorists

"Those who fight for the Faith in the cause of Allah—as well as those who give them asylum and aid—these are all in very truth the Believers. For them is the forgiveness of sins and a provision most generous."

—THE QURAN, Surah 8:74

In the summer of 2002, the director of the FBI went to Capitol Hill and told a fib. Bob Mueller maintained in interviews with congressional investigators looking into the 9/11 attacks that the Muslim hijackers largely avoided mosques and got no help from terrorist sympathizers or facilitators in the Muslim community. To hear the director, they operated in isolation while in America, like visitors from outer space.

"As far as we know, they contacted no known terrorist sympathizers in the United States," Mueller insisted in June 2002.[1]

But it wasn't true. And congressional investigators found out the FBI knew better from its own documents. The hijackers maintained "a web of contacts" with a number of other Muslims during their stay in the U.S., they found. While they prepared for the attacks, they got "substantial assistance" from their Muslim brothers in finding housing, opening back accounts, obtaining driver's licenses, locating flight schools, and facilitating other transactions.[2]

Their review of FBI case files further showed that at least fourteen of the facilitators had come to the bureau's attention during counterterrorism investigations *before* 9/11. In fact, four of them were the focus of active FBI probes at the same time they were helping the hijackers! In a draft analysis of the hijackers' activities based on information available November 2001—several months before Mueller testified—the FBI's Investigative Services Division concluded:

In addition to frequent and sustained interaction between and among the hijackers of the various flights before September 11, the group maintained a web of contacts both in the United States and abroad. These associates, ranging in degrees of closeness, include friends and associates from universities and flight schools, former roommates, people they knew through mosques and religious activities, and employment contacts. Other contacts provided legal, logistical, or financial assistance, facilitated U.S. entry and flight school enrollment, or were known from [Osama bin Laden]-related activities or training.[3]

And far from staying away from mosques, the hijackers flocked to them, attending no less than seven mosques in California, Florida, Virginia, Arizona, and Maryland. Some of them were also attended by terrorist suspects under FBI investigation.

No one in Washington wants to heap scorn on the Muslim community. But the unpleasant truth is, the hijackers received aid and comfort from numerous facilitators in Muslim communities from coast to coast. Many cheered their success on 9/11, and some even had advance knowledge of their plans. Retracing the steps of just two of the hijackers, Hani Hanjour and Nawaf al-Hazmi, illustrates just how much help they got.

In January 2000, cell leader Hazmi arrived with muscle hijacker Khalid al-Mihdhar in Los Angeles, where they remained for nearly three weeks before traveling south to San Diego. Hanjour, the pilot of the Pentagon flight, joined them there later. Practically from the moment they stepped off the plane at Los Angeles International Airport, they were treated like celebrities. The Saudi consulate dispatched an agent to meet with them over lunch. They were driven to San Diego and feted at a welcoming party there. They were given money to rent an apartment. An imam famous for counseling martyrs ministered to them in private, closed-door sessions. In short, they got the royal treatment.

Let's look at a few of their known contacts in the Muslim community and the roles they played in facilitating their plans.

Fahad al-Thumairy: A former Saudi diplomat and hard-line Muslim cleric in Los Angeles, he assigned a Saudi government agent to do advance work for the hijackers in anticipation of their arrival. Phone records show he spoke with the agent, Omar al-Bayoumi, numerous times before and after the hijackers entered the U.S.[4]

Omar al-Bayoumi: He acted as the advance man. Also on the Saudi government payroll, he was summoned to the Saudi Consulate in Los Angeles shortly after the hijackers arrived. Following a closed-door meeting there with Thumairy,

Bayoumi met hours later with Hazmi and Mihdhar at a *halal* food restaurant in Culver City, a few blocks from a Saudi-controlled mosque where Thumairy was known to preach anti-Western sermons, promote violent jihad, and meet with young jihadists—including a known al-Qaida operative earlier in 2000. The hijackers also spent time at his mosque. At their lunch, Bayoumi arranged for them to move to San Diego, where he lived.

After returning to San Diego, Bayoumi let the hijackers crash at his place for a couple of weeks, and use his cell phone. Then he helped them find an apartment, securing it with a check drawn from his bank account. He even co-signed their lease. Bayoumi then threw a party for the hijackers, attended by twenty male members of the local Muslim community, as well as an unidentified visiting sheikh. What they were celebrating is unclear, but Bayoumi videotaped the occasion, indicating it had special significance.

Bayoumi is a suspected Saudi spy. Officially, he worked for a Saudi aviation contractor in San Diego, but investigators believe he was a "ghost employee," who was on the government payroll but not required to work. As he was settling the hijackers in, he suddenly got a huge raise, including a $4,000-a-month stipend for expenses. His pay stayed at that level until he left the U.S. in August 2001—the month before the attacks.

What's more, Bayoumi was the subject of a previous FBI anti-terror probe, which found he has ties to al-Qaida as well as the Saudi government, investigators say. In fact, he was one of the fourteen people whom congressional investigators had linked to terrorist inquiries before 9/11. An FBI report written after a search of Bayoumi's residence asserted that an "exhaustive translation of his documents made it clear that he is providing guidance to young Muslims, and some of his writings can be interpreted as jihadist."[5] Additionally, he was close to bin Laden supporter Osama Bassnan, another Saudi national who lived in San Diego at the time, and who also reported to Saudi officials.[6]

Both Thumairy and Bayoumi are back in Saudi Arabia now. Despite their suspicious connections to the hijackers, neither was charged in the 9/11 conspiracy. And the videotape of the hijackers' party was never seized for analysis.

Mohdar Abdullah: A close associate of both Bayoumi and Thumairy, he was tasked with shuttling the hijackers back and forth between Los Angeles and San Diego. Fluent in both Arabic and English, Abdullah was perfectly suited to assist the hijackers in pursuing their mission. He also helped them obtain California driver's licenses and apply for flight schools.

What's more, Abdullah, a twenty-something student from Yemen, shared the hijackers' hatred for the U.S. government and knew about the 9/11 plot in advance, according to informants as well as phone records that show he stopped using his cell phone after receiving a call from Hazmi about three weeks before the attacks. And during a search of his possessions after the attacks, FBI agents found a notebook with references to planes falling from the sky, mass killing, and hijacking. In interviews, he expressed sympathy for the hijackers, saying the U.S. had the attacks coming. He worked with Hazmi at a Texaco gas station owned by a Palestinian who cheered upon learning of the 9/11 attacks.[7] (Another associate referred to Hazmi and the other hijackers after the attacks as "more than heroes."[8])

In the U.S. illegally, Abdullah was deported back to Yemen without being charged in the 9/11 conspiracy—a decision that still has investigators shaking their heads.

The 9/11 Commission speculates Abdullah might have been an agent in place. "We believe it is unlikely that Hazmi and Mihdhar—neither of whom had any prior exposure to life in the West—would have come to the United States without arranging to receive assistance from one or more individuals informed in advance of their arrival," they conclude in the 9/11 Commission Report.[9]

Osama Awadallah: A friend of Abdullah from Yemen, he also helped Hazmi and Mihdhar adjust to life in San Diego. After investigators found his phone number in Hazmi's abandoned Toyota at Washington Dulles International Airport, they searched his belongings and found photos, videos, and articles related to Osama bin Laden.

Anwar Aulaqi: Also from Yemen, the Wahhabi preacher had closed-door meetings with the hijackers at the hardcore mosque he ran at the time in San Diego. He, too, was allowed to return to Yemen, even though he had been the subject of earlier counterterrorism investigations, a controversy I investigate in-depth in a coming chapter, revealing shocking new details gleaned from law enforcement documents.

Yazeed al-Salmi: He moved in with Hazmi when Mihdhar left the U.S. temporarily to visit family members in Yemen, which borders Saudi. About a year before the attacks, Hazmi deposited into his San Diego bank account nearly two thousand dollars in traveler's checks Salmi had purchased at a bank in Saudi. Salmi, a friend of Abdullah, had previously known Hani Hanjour from Saudi.

In December 2000, Hanjour arrived in San Diego and rendezvoused with Hazmi to start their trek across the country to Washington, where they would hijack the flight out of Dulles airport. First they stopped in Arizona, where Hanjour brushed up on his flight training. He was familiar with the state, having studied English years earlier at the University of Arizona in Tucson. He had also taken flying lessons there. A number of important al-Qaida figures had set up shop in the area—including bin Laden's personal secretary and his top procurement agent for weapons of mass destruction—and some of their associates had trained with Hanjour to be pilots.

Investigators believe Hanjour's old roommate and training partner, Rayed Abdullah, may have assisted him during his visit. At the time, Abdullah was one of ten young Muslim men that FBI field agents in Arizona were watching due to their interest in aviation and militant Islam. In fact, Phoenix-based counter-terrorism agent Kenneth Williams worried about an "inordinate number of individuals of investigative interest" taking flight training in Arizona. He had a hunch it was part of a coordinated effort by bin Laden to establish a cadre of pilots to conduct terrorism. His fears were confirmed when he found posters of bin Laden in the apartment of the primary subject of his investigation. Normally young subjects of interviews tend to be somewhat intimidated in their first contact with the FBI. But this one was cocky. He told the agent that he considered the U.S. government and military legitimate targets of Islam.[10]

Williams became increasingly alarmed by what he learned, so two months before 9/11 he proposed FBI headquarters systematically check Middle Eastern students in flight schools. But his proposal was turned down because it would have violated bureau guidelines against racial profiling.

The bin Laden support network in Arizona is still in place, according to Williams.

"As al-Qaida formed and took off and became operational, we've seen these people travel back into the state of Arizona. We've seen Osama bin Laden send people to Tucson to purchase an airplane for him [and] it's my opinion that's not a coincidence," he says. "These people don't continue to come back to Arizona because they like the sunshine or they like the state. I believe that something was established there, and I think it's been there for a long time. We're working very hard to try to identify that structure."[11]

A FAMILIAR FACE IN WASHINGTON

Then in March 2001, Hanjour and Hazmi drove east to Washington, settling in Falls Church, Virginia, a suburb just outside the capital. Through the Dar al-Hijrah mosque there, they met a Jordanian man named Eyad al-Rababah (who has since been deported). Investigators believe he was tasked to help the hijackers by the mosque's imam, who was a familiar face. He was none other than Anwar Aulaqi, the same hard-line cleric who had counseled Hazmi in private sessions at his former mosque in San Diego. Investigators doubt their reunion three thousand miles away was a coincidence. Hazmi was the second in command for the entire operation and therefore an important figure in the mission. Rababah helped him and Hanjour find a room in an apartment nearby in Alexandria, Virginia. He also helped them get Virginia driver's licenses.

But if that were not enough, he also came by several weeks later and picked up the hijackers for a trip to Connecticut, where they made some seventy-five calls from their hotel room to area flight schools and realtors. They also used it as a base to scout out the New York City area. After a short stay there, Rababah drove them to Paterson, New Jersey, to have dinner and show them around the Muslim community there. A few weeks later, Hazmi, Hanjour, and several other hijackers moved to New Jersey and rented an apartment there.

Rababah, like the other facilitators, claims he was just helping out Muslim brothers. But investigators have questioned other parts of his story.[12]

The Quran provides an option for those Muslims who do not want to, or cannot for physical reasons, join the violent jihad to prove their faith. They can support the jihadists by raising money for them, for example, or by helping them book flying lessons or obtain driver's licenses and housing. And giving them such aid and comfort puts them in good standing with Allah. Call it terrorism by proxy.

Consider this verse from the Quran, Surah 8:74: "Those who fight for the Faith in the cause of Allah—as well as those who give them asylum and aid—these are all in very truth the Believers. For them is the forgiveness of sins and a provision most generous."

Devout Muslims like Abdullah or Rababah may not be members of al-Qaida, but they are members of an *ummah* underworld that secretly supports its aims and activities. The sympathetic network includes thousands in this country who may not participate in the planning or execution of terrorism but are nonetheless part of its infrastructure of support. This is a reality to which the political establishment in Washington is just now starting to wake up.

Even FBI Director Mueller recently acknowledged the growing threat from facilitators in the Muslim community. "The threat from single individuals sympathetic or affiliated with al-Qaida, acting without external support or surrounding conspiracies, is increasing," he says.[13]

Still, he estimates their numbers range in the hundreds, which many field agents say is far too conservative. The British government estimates that as many as fifteen thousand British Muslims support al-Qaida and other terrorist groups, and Britain has only a quarter of America's population.[14]

Also, al-Qaida leaders have drafted plans for "using multiple cells operating independently in the United States that could execute ten operations simultaneously or in sequence that would produce a big impact on the United States," according to an al-Qaida informant. He has told the FBI that the terror group has the necessary people positioned inside America to carry out such a plan of attack, noting that leaders still have many contacts here.[15] And those are just the terrorist operatives. Al-Qaida planners must also be confident they have a sufficient number of sympathizers and facilitators within the Muslim community to successfully support and protect ten terrorist cells in ten different locations around the country for such a large, coordinated attack.

This all suggests the existence of a far greater al-Qaida support network within the United States than Washington is willing to publicly admit.

Yet one of the most active hubs in the network is in Washington's own backyard.

8

THE WAHHABI CORRIDOR

Exposing the Washington Nerve Center

"The truth is, the residents of Skyline Towers cheered that very day
as the Trade Center fell. The people in these buildings are animals."
—former tenant of Pentagon-area apartments
popular with Saudi diplomats and Muslim immigrants[1]

One of the many remaining mysteries of the 9/11 tragedy is where the hijackers
who attacked the Pentagon stayed while they lived in Virginia. Many in the media
have cited an address in Falls Church. But that apartment building at 5913
Leesburg Pike was a fake address the hijackers used to obtain their Virginia state
driver's licenses. They did not actually stay in the apartments, which are popular
with Hispanic immigrants in the area.

The media remain curiously incurious. Who else lived at the apartments with
the hijackers? Who was the landlord?

The 9/11 Commission Report is not much help. It says only that four of the
hijackers lived together with at least two other Middle Eastern immigrants in
unidentified apartments "in Alexandria," which borders Falls Church. I tracked
down a lawyer for one of the immigrants who roomed with the hijackers and
asked him for the address. He says it was a three-bedroom apartment they all
shared but could not locate a street address from case files he pulled from storage.
He vaguely recalls from memory that it was "somewhere off of Route 1" in
Alexandria. His Jordanian client, Rasmi al-Shannaq, was deported for visa violations after being cleared in the 9/11 case. The lawyer, Frank Draper of the
Baltimore office of the public defender, says his client's uncle suggested he stay at
the apartment building, where he was doing renovation work at the time. This
was in the summer before the attacks.

In the absence of an exact address, rumors abound.

One sunny day last fall while interviewing a reliable Middle Eastern source at a Starbucks on Leesburg Pike in Falls Church, I brought up the hijackers. On most afternoons, that Starbucks location—just a short drive from Route 1 and the Pentagon—looks more like a cafe in Cairo than a hip coffeehouse in America. Dark, lanky men wearing *kufis*, the white skullcaps commonly worn by Muslim men abroad, gather around the tiny tables inside and outside the shop sipping strong blends and speaking loudly in Arabic. Some get very animated, gesturing wildly at each other as if in the throes of a heated political debate. Many are cabbies, judging from the inordinate number of taxis in the parking lot.

My source and I were sitting at a table next to a window facing Leesburg Pike, an old highway that runs through Northern Virginia. He motioned to twin highrise apartment buildings looming across the highway, also known as Route 7.

"They stayed there, you know," he said of the hijackers who rammed the American Airlines jumbo jet into U.S. military headquarters.

A chill ran down my spine. I imagined they might have patronized the same Starbucks, chatting safely in Arabic about their wicked project among the many other Muslim immigrants there. Perhaps they even sat at our table.

I decided to run the rumor to ground. I first checked online apartment reviews posted by tenants of the high-rise apartments, which are known as the Skyline Towers. Some former tenants said the hijackers stayed there. So I paid a visit to the apartments. The manager declined an interview, but a leasing agent confirmed that most everyone there had heard the same rumor when they took over management from the previous firm not long after the attacks.

The Skyline Towers, built in 1969 as luxury units, were recently renovated, a project that began around the time the hijackers moved in. There is a north and a south tower, like the World Trade Center, each climbing twenty-six stories tall, which is high for the area, now governed by height limits. The view from one of the top-floor penthouses is breathtaking. There you can clearly see Columbia Pike, a major commuter thoroughfare that leads straight to the Pentagon, and the Washington Monument beyond it. From the air, the towers are an area landmark for pilots, and on a map you can practically draw a straight line from them to the Pentagon along Columbia Pike. Hani Hanjour, the Saudi national who piloted Flight 77, may have tried to spot the towers as he closed in on his target.

Hanjour stayed in a three-bedroom apartment with three other Saudi hijackers: Nawaf al-Hazmi, Majed Moqed, and Ahmed al-Ghamdi. They moved out shortly before the terrorist attacks. Skyline rents three-bedroom units. And residents say FBI investigators visited the towers after 9/11 and conducted interviews.

"Four Arab Muslim young males who moved out of Skyline Towers just before 9/11 were involved with the terrorism," said one former resident who lived at the apartments from 1999 to 2003.[2]

A leasing agent for the towers says she also heard that the hijackers stayed there, though she could not say which unit they occupied. "That's what we all heard when we came here" in 2001, she says, the year the company she works for took over leasing and management of the building. Again, the site manager did not respond to requests for comment.

The leasing agent, whose identity must remain anonymous, said Skyline Towers is home to a large number of Saudi and Yemeni diplomats who work at their countries' embassies in Washington. It is not clear if the Saudi hijackers had any contact with them. She says a number of Arab male residents left soon after the 9/11 attacks, which brought increased FBI scrutiny to the complex, but she says many have slowly returned over the past couple of years.

The apartments are very popular with Middle Eastern immigrants, which has turned off some white American tenants since 9/11. "If you're a white American, prepare to be a tiny minority," a tenant who left last year warns applicants in an online customer review. Renters at the luxury towers are "mostly Arab [and] African."[3] "I hope you like Arabs because there are a lot of them," says another former resident.[4]

Women in head-to-toe *abayas* are a common sight in the halls and on the elevators during the day. In the convenience store, located in the basement of the north tower, scarf-wearing Arab women holding infants browse aisles stocked with Middle Eastern spices and teas, pita bread, and other foods favored in the region. In fact, the little shop carries more packages of pita bread than loaves of sliced bread. Pork products, forbidden in Islam, are also in short supply. A former resident, a non-Muslim who moved out in 2003, says she felt out of place amid all the covered Muslim women: "I felt that I might have to start covering myself to fit in."[5] Another calls the apartments "little Afghanistan," where *burqa*-clad women are still a common sight, post-Taliban.[6] Even orthodox Muslim women get their hair done, however; and for that, there is an Islamic parlor called Ahmet's in the same basement.

Some apartment employees who worked there on the morning of 9/11 say they felt the high-rise quiver from the shock of Hanjour smashing the hijacked Boeing 757 into the side of the nearby Pentagon at about 345 mph, killing nearly two hundred people. "I was working on the ninth floor . . . when I heard the third plane hit the Pentagon," said a Skyline Towers employee named Joye. "It was horrifying. It scared me half to death and shook our building. I was so frightened by the sound that I could not talk."[7]

Not everyone in the apartment building was overwhelmed by fear. Some apparently were overcome by joy. As the World Trade Center in New York collapsed from the earlier attacks by Hanjour's confederates, residents could be heard rejoicing throughout the complex, according to one resident who was there. "The truth is, the residents of Skyline Towers cheered that very day as the Trade Center fell," the former tenant says. "The people in these buildings are animals."[8]

Some of the cars in the parking lots of both towers sport pro-Islam bumper stickers. One in green, the religion's color, proclaims, "ISLAM IS THE WAY."

AL-JAZEERA RESTAURANT

Of large states, studies show Virginia has the fastest-growing population of Middle Eastern immigrants.[9] Though the Census Bureau does not collect statistics on religious affiliation, estimates put the number of Muslims in the Washington metropolitan area at more than two hundred and fifty thousand.[10]

Baileys Crossroads is the heart of the Arab-Muslim community in the nation's capital. The area, which includes parts of the Washington suburbs of Falls Church and Alexandria, has the second-highest concentration of people of Arab descent in America, according to Census data. Number one is Dearborn, Michigan.[11] Baileys is in Fairfax County, where there are so many Arabic- and Farsi-speaking families that the public school system has designated two days each week to local TV programming in those native tongues. High schools have set up designated prayer rooms for Muslim students to go and bow toward Mecca. And school lunch calendars carry a pork warning symbolized by a little pink pig on days when hotdogs and other foods forbidden by Islam are served.

About a block away from Skyline Towers is a shopping plaza called Build America. It is an odd name for any shopping center but especially so for this development, which has virtually no shops that can be considered even remotely American. Almost all are Middle Eastern-owned and operated, and many of their storefront signs are in Arabic. Driving through the parking lot is a cultural experience, to say the least. You will find no less than ten *halal* butcher shops and meat markets. Under Muslim law, animals raised for meat must be slaughtered using a *halal*, or permitted, method by which their throats are slit and the blood is allowed to drain freely from their bodies. During the process, special prayers praising Allah are said over the beasts. Large meat wagons, filled with skinned goats and other carcasses hanging from meat hooks, make afternoon deliveries to the Skyline Butcher Shop, the Al-Amal Market and Butcher, the Al-Amanah Halal Meat Market, the Abay Market, the Awash Market and Butchery, the Tenadam International Market and Butcher Shop, and on and on.

There are several Middle Eastern food joints to choose from, including one called, believe it or not, Al-Jazeera Restaurant. It advertises in its window, "We

Serve Halal Food." There is an Oasis Cafe on the opposite side of the shopping strip, its sign adorned with camels and palm trees.

Then there is the Prince Cafe, no doubt a favorite of the sons of Saudi diplomats staying at Skyline Towers. In fact, a recently deported young Saudi national tied to terrorist activities used it as a den of iniquity before 9/11, as I will detail further on. The dimly lit cafe features an "Internet cafe" and "Shisha bar," where you can smoke pomegranate-flavored tobacco from a hookah, a traditional Arab water-filled pipe that looks like a large, ornate bong.

A few storefronts down is the Beder Discount Store, which sells Islamic books and *hijabs*, the head scarves worn by Muslim women. It competes with the Mughal Bazaar, which caters to Pakistani nationals. Falika's Fashions, meanwhile, sells African clothes. Also in the plaza: Islamic hair salons, travel agencies, holistic spas, and bakeries such as Al-Sham Original Sweets.

The architectural features of the Middle Eastern shopping center resemble those of an office park located a few blocks away in Alexandria, also on Leesburg Pike. Called the Skyline Court Professional Park, it was built with a similar color and style of brick. And its storefront signs have the same bright orange lettering against a dark brown background.

BIN LADEN'S NEPHEW

One of its more notorious tenants is the World Assembly of Muslim Youth, or WAMY, which is based in Saudi Arabia's capital city of Riyadh. The tax-exempt charity's purpose (at least what it publicly states to be its purpose) is to spread the good word about Islam—or more precisely, the orthodox version of Islam called Wahhabism, which is the official state religion of the Saudi kingdom.

However, there may be a darker purpose. WAMY's U.S. branch, tucked in the back of the office park, recently was raided by some fifty federal agents acting on information the group may be fronting for terrorists. The group lauds suicide bombers as "heroes" in its literature,[12] and until recently, it was run by Abdullah bin Laden, a nephew of Osama bin Laden, who fled back home to Saudi Arabia after 9/11. Though the Saudi-controlled enterprise is still under FBI investigation, the administration has been reluctant to freeze its assets and designate it as a terrorist entity, a move that would upset the powerful and well-connected head of the Saudi Embassy. The sensitive case is under court seal.[13]

Just around the corner from WAMY—in the same Skyline office park—is the main office of the American Muslim Foundation, founded by confessed terrorist Abdurahman Alamoudi as an offshoot to his supposedly "mainstream" American Muslim Council. A random visitor would never know it was there, since his second-floor office has no sign on the outside of the building (although it has a NO SOLICITORS sign on its interior door). Alamoudi and his erstwhile office-park neighbor, Abdullah bin Laden, served together on the board of nearby Taibah International Aid Association, which the U.S. government has blacklisted as a front for al-Qaida.

Next door to the American Muslim Foundation, funded primarily by Alamoudi's wealthy family in Saudi Arabia, resides the national headquarters of the Muslim American Society, which also has no sign on the outside of its building. The group has strong ties to the Muslim Brotherhood, a banned Egyptian terrorist group that gave rise to the Palestinian Islamic Jihad, Hamas, and al-Qaida. Alamoudi, who has made several trips to Egypt, is a member of the Brotherhood. Its U.S. front, the society, has about ten thousand members and fifty-three chapters nationwide.[14]

The clustering of dubious Muslim groups along Leesburg Pike does not stop there. The old highway might as well be called the Wahhabi corridor.

WAMY used to be headquartered back up the road in Falls Church in the basement of a generic-looking two-story office building on Leesburg Pike just north of the Skyline Towers. Tucked away there in the same building in a cramped office on the first floor is the national headquarters of another Saudi-backed youth organization—the Muslim Student Association of the U.S. & Canada. One of Alamoudi's lawyers, Kamal Nawash, is listed as a tenant in the same building.

Heading deeper into Falls Church on Leesburg Pike for about another mile takes you to the next place of interest on the Wahhabi corridor: Dar al-Hijrah, the hard-line Wahhabi mosque where Hazmi and other hijackers from the Pentagon cell worshipped and received aid and comfort. He and other hijackers were ministered to there by an imam who encourages violent jihad and martyrdom. The large mosque and its minaret are hidden behind rows of tall evergreens, making it invisible from the highway it fronts.

MUSLIM WORLD LEAGUE

They are not the only notorious members of Saudi-controlled Dar al-Hijrah, which is less than five minutes away from the Home Depot where two Muslims, a year after 9/11, fatally shot an FBI analyst in the head as she and her husband loaded supplies for their new home into their car. Alamoudi, bin Laden's nephew, and even Hamas leader and terrorist fugitive Mousa Abu Marzook have all worshipped at the mosque. They lived nearby in Falls Church. Marzook was deported last decade. Alamoudi is in prison. And Abdullah bin Laden sold his contemporary-style home, located on a cul-de-sac, in 2001 before hoofing it back to Saudi after the attacks. (Fairfax county property records show a sales price of $442,000. His attorney in the transaction is listed as Muhammad Quadir Harunani.[15])

Last year, a leader of Dar al-Hijrah put up his own house, located across the street from the Skyline Towers, as bond collateral to spring a prominent member of the mosque from jail after he and his wife were caught videotaping the Chesapeake Bay Bridge in what Maryland authorities suspect was reconnaissance for a terrorist act—one of many ignominious events tied to the mosque that will be explored in greater detail in a later chapter.

Traveling another two miles northwest on Leesburg Pike brings you to Washington Street, in the heart of the quaint and leafy city of Falls Church. At 360 South Washington Street stands a nondescript three-story office building that the average passerby would never suspect to be a front for terrorist-related activities.

But it is.

Federal agents raided the building after 9/11, the second time in five years. Inside are the U.S. offices of the Saudi-based Muslim World League and its spin-off, the International Islamic Relief Organization,[16] two al-Qaida-connected groups.[17] It is also the main office of the Success Foundation, a suspected Hamas front. On tax records, International Relief Organization president Mohamed S. Omeish lists Alamoudi's Skyline office park address—3606 Forest Drive in Alexandria—as his personal address.[18] Alamoudi and Omeish served as directors of Success Foundation. Omeish's brother, Esam Omeish, is the Dar al-Hijrah member who put up his house for the jailed mosque member suspected of casing the bridge.

The front doors of the building on Washington Street open to a cramped lobby. On the right is a travel agency, which before 9/11 had booked the Dar-al-Hijrah imam, who counseled the hijackers, as a tour guide for Saudi-sponsored pilgrimages to Mecca. He too has fled the country and is said to now be in Yemen. Inside the travel agency are several posters in Arabic and a prayer rug rolled up in a corner.

One Friday afternoon, I took the lobby elevator to the third floor to see the offices that were raided, but the doors outside Suite 300 were locked. I was able to enter instead from a back door accessible from the stairwell. Someone had stuck a piece of cardboard in the emergency exit door to prevent it from locking shut, so I opened the door and climbed up the flights of stairs. All the lights were out as I stepped into the office lobby, which was empty. Even the furniture was gone. It was dark and, frankly, a little spooky in there. It appeared that I was all alone.

But suddenly, I heard the sound of men chanting in Arabic. It seemed to be coming from around the corner and down a hallway. The chanting grew louder and louder as the men apparently were entranced in prayer and praise for Allah. Best not to disturb them, I thought. Heading back out, I spied colorful-looking, glossy guides to Islam on the counter of the lobby, stacked in front of a large crystal globe bearing the words, "Muslim World League." I grabbed one, and discovered while thumbing through it back at my car that it was co-edited by Ali al-Timimi, the Saudi-trained imam who was indicted in the fall of 2004 for encouraging eleven young Muslim men from the area to wage violent jihad in Afghanistan and Pakistan. The same cleric rejoiced in the crash of the space shuttle *Columbia*. Chillingly, the guide he helped edit includes a photo of the space shuttle. The Saudi-published booklet touts the Alharamain Islamic Foundation of Saudi Arabia, which has been blacklisted by the U.S. Treasury Department as a specially designated terrorist group.

It turns out that Timimi preached on the first floor of the same building in a small, discreet mosque called Dar Al-Arqam, the name of which is stenciled in green letters on glass doors facing the parking lot. The large, single room inside is divided by a curtain that forms a private prayer area apparently for women. On the other side of it, on a back wall above a long bookstand filled with tracts on Islam, hangs a banner: "Center for Islamic Information and Education." The mosque doubles as a think tank. I tried to go in to read some of the literature, but the doors were locked. Disappointed, I headed back to my car, at which point a young Arab-looking man walked up behind me to investigate what I was doing. I told him I would like to visit the mosque, and he motioned to a large store across the street, saying the proprietor there has the key. So I ventured across the street.

Not surprisingly, the store is a Muslim supermarket called Halalco, which includes a long and busy meat counter. It is an impressive operation, if all a bit surreal. For as *halal* butchers in white coats hacked loudly at carcasses with their meat cleavers, women with their heads shrouded in veils quietly browsed books on Islam in a makeshift bookstore set up less than ten feet away from the butchery. On the other side of the bookshelves are racks of *hijabs, abayas,* and sandals for sale. I decided to buy an English-Arabic dictionary, and only much later, back at home, discovered that I had been ripped off, literally. Someone had torn out the page with the citation for "Jew," which is *Yahoudi* in Arabic. No other page but that one had been ripped out of the book.

While at the register, I learned the owner was not on site. Leaving, I noticed a sign at the supermarket's exit, framed in a clear plastic stand. It lists the hours for the Dar Al-Arqam mosque back across Washington Street, along with an address for the Web site of its sister operation, the Center for Islamic Information and Education. I imagined the Virginia jihadists picked up some groceries at the supermarket after sitting at their guru al-Timimi's feet.

PHOTOGRAPHS OF OSAMA

Continuing along the Wahhabi corridor through Falls Church takes you to the neighboring Tysons Corner area, which has the fifth-highest concentration of residents of Arab ancestry in the country.[19] The next stop on the terror trail through the nation's capital is an apartment just off Leesburg Pike that was rented before 9/11 by a Saudi national named Saleh Ali Almari. He came to America on a student visa to go to a college in Virginia, but he never attended classes there. Instead, he signed up for flying lessons.

Then came the strikes on the Twin Towers and Pentagon. And eleven days later, Almari hightailed it back to Saudi Arabia. In December 2001, federal investigators searched his apartment and found a number of items that they believed were "possibly related to planned acts of terrorism," according to an affidavit filed in U.S. District Court. The inventory of items included:

- An FAA flight manual

- A book identifying commercial airliners

- Photographs of Almari and other Middle Eastern men posing inside and outside the World Trade Center

- A hand-drawn sketch of a plane striking the World Trade Center

- A postcard with an aerial view of the Pentagon

- A videotape titled, "Incredible Air Disasters"

- Another video titled, "Incredible Water Disasters"

- Photocopies of numerous passports that were not Almari's

- Airline tickets to Boston, New York, Washington, Los Angeles, and London

- A book about biological and chemical weapons and their use in the Persian Gulf

- Addresses of twelve oil refineries across America

- Photographs of Osama bin Laden

But perhaps the must disturbing item seized from Almari's apartment was a date book with a single entry on September 11, 2001, referencing the World Trade Center and Pentagon. The entry reads, "Trachd The World Traed Cente or the Pentegon Tracd for the Plaen" (sic).[20]

Authorities arrested Almari the next month as he tried to reenter the U.S. They charged him with visa fraud. Almari was a ringleader in a scheme that helped get a hundred and thirty other Middle Easterners into the country illegally, many of whom had also taken flight lessons. He and another ringleader from Alexandria hatched their plot during at least one meeting at the Prince Cafe near the Skyline Towers.[21]

The plot thickened when the FBI investigated another Arab man from Virginia involved in the same visa fraud ring. Agents traced transactions on a credit card owned by the suspect, Fahad A. Alhajri, who at one time had lived at the same unit near Tysons Corner where the suspicious items were found. And the information led them to a Los Angeles hotel room where his brother and two friends had stayed before the attacks. They checked out of the hotel on September 10, 2001, leaving behind clothing that looked like pilots' uniforms. The three Middle Eastern men were booked that day to fly to Washington on the same American Airlines jet that crashed into the Pentagon. They never boarded the flight, however, taking other flights back to the Middle East instead. Alhajri pleaded guilty to fraud and was ordered deported in 2003.[22]

Almari, for his part, pleaded guilty to fraud, served time, and was deported back to Saudi Arabia. Government suspicions that he may have links to al-Qaida and terrorism remain unresolved. Authorities still have not received a satisfactory explanation about the items found in his Virginia apartment.[23]

THE SAFEHOUSE

Across Leesburg Pike from the apartment where Almari stayed is the safehouse where at least one of the fifteen Saudi hijackers bunked for a spell before 9/11. Waleed M. al-Shehri, who was part of the attack on the World Trade Center, lived in a small rambler on Orrin Street in the leafy Washington suburb of Vienna, next door to Tysons Corner. Neighbors on the otherwise quiet street told me that the rental house where he boarded had a high turnover of tenants, who upset residents by parking their luxury cars up and down the street.

"We thought it was a drug house," says one neighbor, who wished to have her name withheld. "All the cars parked on the street were new BMWs, new Mercedes. People were always walking around out front with cell phones."

She says as many as eight people, mostly "Arab-looking" men, lived at one time in the house, which has been chopped up into six tiny bedrooms. The house also has four bathrooms and two kitchens, one in the basement. So many cars were parked out front on the street that neighbors complained to the local police. The neighbor says she noticed most of the cars had out-of-state tags.

Fed up with the parking problem and suspicious of activities at the house, the neighbor across the street, John E. Albritton, called federal authorities, according to his wife, Diane. She says they observed a van parked outside the home at all hours of the day and night. A Middle Eastern man appeared to be monitoring a scanner or radio inside the van, she says.

Next-door neighbors Mary Ann Neupert, 77, and Stanley E. Neupert, 79, recall at least one occasion when tenants there fired pistols in the air as they often do in Middle Eastern countries to celebrate holidays and events such as weddings. Mrs. Neupert says she found it somewhat suspicious that tenants seldom entered the house through the front door and instead "went from the street straight to the gate and entered the house from the backyard." The couple says the FBI interviewed them two days after the attacks.[24]

But they were two days too late. Other neighbors say they began calling the FBI to complain of suspicious behavior at the house, located not far from CIA headquarters, two years before the attacks. But the FBI did not investigate. And local police also shrugged off complaints. "Over the years, there have been questions about how many people the owner actually has living there, but those are zoning issues, not police issues," Vienna police Capt. John Cheyne explained to me in an interview.[25]

Federal and local investigators now suspect the home may have been used as a safehouse for terrorists. Another Saudi hijacker, in addition to al-Shehri, may have lived there. And local detectives after the attacks took a closer look at another suspicious tenant, a Pakistani national, who traveled back and forth from Vienna to Pakistan before 9/11.[26] Tellingly, there is no history of any rental listings for the home, meaning the owners have been able to rent it to apparently scores of Arab tenants without the help of leasing agents, relying apparently on word of mouth within the Muslim community.[27]

Real estate records show Iranian native Hamid Keshavarznia has owned the home for more than a decade. His brother, Saeed Keshavarznia, who has lived at the Vienna house with the tenants, is listed as a co-owner. The brothers also own homes in the nearby Virginia suburbs of Alexandria and Fairfax.[28]

THE SAFA GROUP

If you continue several miles farther northwest on Leesburg Pike, you will enter Herndon, Virginia, home to another large Muslim community where al-Qaida and Palestinian terror groups operate. It is listed among areas of terrorist activities targeted by the FBI.[29]

Just off the old highway is a cul-de-sac called Safa Court near a wooded subdivision called Mena Estates. As if the cul-de-sac were not secluded enough, three Muslim activists have built large houses on generous lots on a private drive, known as a pipe-stem, off of Safa. The close-knit neighbors—Jamal Barzinji, Yacub Mirza, and Taha al-Alwani—serve together as officers in at least nine overlapping Islamic charities, think tanks, and companies. Borrowing from their surroundings, they named one of the entities Safa Trust, and another Mena Investments.

Federal authorities charge that the "Safa group," as they have dubbed the conglomerate, runs a terror-support network using the legitimate-sounding entities as cover. They have traced some of the group's funds to wealthy Saudis with connections to Osama bin Laden, according to court records.[30]

Most of the entities list their office address at a location not far from the three activists' homes. The maze of phantom firms and charities are headquartered in two nondescript office buildings across the street from each other in downtown Herndon. Guns drawn, federal agents in 2002 raided the buildings after finally getting the greenlight, in the wake of 9/11, to ramp up their investigation of the group, which had been stalled by politics for several years. They are still running down leads from the documents and computer disks they seized in the raids. Although the Safa group's leaders have not been charged with crimes in connection with the raids, they are still the main subjects of the ever-widening probe. They strongly deny wrongdoing.

A key conduit in the alleged terror-financing network, a think tank called the International Institute of Islamic Thought, or IIIT, is headquartered in a three-story brick office building at 500 Grove Street. Investigators traced funds from IIIT to Tampa professor Sami al-Arian, a founder of the Palestinian Islamic Jihad recently jailed on related terrorism charges.[31] Al-Alwani, an Islamic scholar at IIIT, is an unindicted co-conspirator in the Tampa indictment.[32] Despite the government clamp-down, IIIT is still in business, still listed on the second floor in the lobby directory.[33]

On the first floor is a small Middle Eastern grocery store with a *halal* meat counter. On the day I visited, two skinned goats were on display in a glass case, their tongues hanging out, teeth bared. I grabbed a copy of the *Arab-American Directory*, the yellow pages for Muslims in Washington, on my way out the door, and walked toward the other end of the building, where I found a Muslim thrift shop. It is managed by an Arab woman, dressed in a flowing black gown, and her son, who likes to play rap-style Arabic music on a stereo in the store. Among items on sale: the Quran on audiotape, *hijabs,* and posters in Arabic.

The building across the street at 555 Grove Street, also three stories, originally served as the U.S. offices of the Muslim World League, the group that was raided in Falls Church. Alamoudi started out working for the league, as well as the related SAAR Foundation, which was the hub of the sprawling Muslim network based in Herndon until it began attracting bad press in 2001. Then it was morphed into the Sterling and Humana charities. SAAR was named for Sulaiman Abdul Aziz al-Rajhi, the head of the wealthy al-Rajhi banking family in Saudi Arabia whom the federal government is investigating for allegedly supporting bin Laden and his terror network.[34]

A top religious minister of the Saudi government was a director of the SAAR Foundation. The official, Saleh Ibn Abdul Rahman Hussayen, happened to check into the same Herndon hotel, the Marriott Residence Inn, on the same night—September 10, 2001—as Hani Hanjour, Nawaf al-Hazmi, and another hijacker in the Pentagon cell. Herndon is about ten minutes from Washington Dulles International Airport. The hijackers boarded Flight 77 there the next morning. After the attacks, Hussayen feigned a seizure during an FBI interview. Though doctors found nothing wrong with him, he was allowed to return to Saudi Arabia without further questioning.

During his pre-9/11 trip to the U.S., the Saudi official also paid visits to Timimi, the imam for the "Virginia jihad network" in Falls Church, and officials from WAMY's office in Alexandria, just across the Potomac River from D.C.[35] The Saudi honcho obviously knew his way around, touching as he did key nodes in the nerve center that controls the terror-support network across America. This vast network, which for years has operated under the radar, is organized like a mob syndicate, prosecutors have come to realize.

9

THE MUSLIM MAFIA

Anatomy of a Religious Crime Syndicate

"You could tie every one of these organizations into at least Palestinian terrorism—Hamas, Hezbollah, Palestinian Islamic Jihad. Every one of them. And you could tie many of them to al-Qaida, too."

—former FBI agent JOHN VINCENT,
speaking of the major Muslim groups in America[1]

In the winter of 1998, Abdurahman Alamoudi summoned the heads of the four most powerful Muslim lobbying groups for a meeting. It was time to join forces against the pro-Israel and anti-terrorism factions in Washington, he said. It was time to unite Muslims to vote as a bloc for political candidates who would adopt their agenda. Four months later, the heads of the four groups—the American Muslim Alliance, Council on American-Muslim Relations, Muslim Public Affairs Council, and American Muslim Council, which Alamoudi founded—formed the American Muslim Political Coordination Council.

Then in 1999, the national Muslim network joined with the national Arab network to hammer out a joint agreement. Alamoudi reached beyond the Muslim community by meeting with the Council of Presidents of Arab American Organizations. In addition to the heads of the four Muslim groups, the summit included the heads of the American Arab Anti-Discrimination Committee, Arab American Institute, the National Association of Arab Americans, and the Association of Arab University Graduates.

The historic summit resulted in full agreement and long-term cooperation over two main political goals: rolling back U.S. support for Israel and weakening U.S. anti-terrorism laws.[2]

In late October 2000, just days before the national election, seventeen national Muslim and Arab groups marched on Washington to protest support for

Israel. The rally across from the White House attracted more than ten thousand Muslims, who denounced the Jews and, for the first time, openly voiced support for the terrorist groups Hamas and Hezbollah. Some of their leaders ominously warned America it would suffer a terrible fate if it did not divorce Israel. It was the largest and most enthusiastic rally ever staged by Muslims, a stunning show of solidarity—and hate.

Meanwhile, Alamoudi entered into talks to merge his American Muslim Council, the central clearinghouse for Muslims in Washington, with the California-based American Muslim Alliance and its national membership of seven thousand Muslim activists. It was a natural alliance. AMA's chairman, Agha Saeed, had already agreed to lead the political coordinating council Alamoudi had started.

These were heady days for the Wahhabi lobby. Militant Islamists backed by the Saudi government controlled every major Muslim organization in America. And now they were consolidating their power and pressing Washington to adopt their agenda with a brazenness that had not been seen before.

FBI counterterrorism agents in New York, Chicago, Detroit, and other cities with large Muslim populations could only watch in frustration. They understood best of all that the Muslim groups were part of a network supporting a global jihad movement, and that a number of them appeared to have some connection to either al-Qaida or Osama bin Laden.

The CIA knew it too. In fact, analysts for the intelligence agency had just a few years earlier concluded in an internal report that at least one-third of the fifty Islamic nongovernmental organizations in existence "support terrorist groups or employ individuals who are suspected of having terrorist connections."[3]

And much of the terrorist support was coming from fundraisers held at Islamic conferences in America. In short, Islamic organizations in America were waging financial jihad. They were not just helping needy Muslims or protecting Muslim rights or whatever other cover story they offered. They were subsidizing bombs and bloodshed.

Yet they operated with virtual impunity. There was no political will in Washington to prosecute the groups, some of which were headquartered in Saudi Arabia. FBI agents simply kept tabs on their fundraisers, even as millions of dollars flowed to terrorists.

The political atmosphere changed dramatically after America was attacked, however. Washington told agents to start connecting the dots, and they began to see a lot of overlap in the operations of the Muslim groups and their leaders, confirming the hunches of veteran counterterrorism investigators. "I always believed that much of the leadership of the Islamists had the ability to interact," says former FBI special agent Robert Blitzer.[4] Although the groups appear independent of one another, many of them co-mingle funds and even share the same staff and office space. For example, some forty active Muslim charities and businesses operate out of the same office building in Herndon, Virginia.[5]

And investigators discovered the groups have interlocking boards of directors. Alamoudi, for one, sat on the boards of no fewer than sixteen Islamic organizations. "They're all connected," says former FBI agent John Vincent, who investigated Islamic groups and mosques tied to Hamas in Chicago.

Investigators also confirmed that many of the groups were laundering terrorist-bound funds through a maze of shell companies and fronts. They even used religious charities and think tanks as cover to carry out their illicit activities.

Soon, federal prosecutors realized they were dealing with a vast criminal conspiracy. And last year, the Department of Justice adopted a bold new strategy to target Muslim groups and leaders raising money for terrorist groups. In indicting three Muslim leaders for laundering money used to pay for Hamas terrorist attacks, prosecutors filed the charges under racketeering conspiracy laws. It was unusual because prosecutors for the first time treated Hamas as a "criminal enterprise" as much as a terrorist organization. Such federal racketeering and conspiracy laws are more commonly applied to Mafia figures.

The indictment followed the arrest of several leaders of the Dallas-based Holy Land Foundation, the largest Muslim charity in America. They were indicted on related conspiracy charges of illegally funneling money to Hamas. It turns out that some were related by marriage to Hamas leaders, including one on the lam in Syria. And besides running the Muslim charity, they ran a shady computer firm located across the street. InfoCom Corp.'s chairman, in fact, sat on the board of the Holy Land Foundation. Prosecutors allege they used the firm to illegally ship high-tech goods to Syria, a state sponsor of terrorism.[6]

What's more, investigators found that InfoCom hosted Internet servers for the Holy Land Foundation, as well as for several major Muslim organizations. They included the Islamic Society of North America and its affiliate, the Muslim Students Association, or MSA; and the Council on American-Islamic Relations, or CAIR, and its affiliate, the Islamic Association for Palestine.[7]

With each new indictment, the Muslim establishment in America looks more and more like a religious crime syndicate. So far, federal prosecutors have brought a variety of charges against more than two dozen of its leaders, and more than a third have pleaded guilty. And several Muslim groups with moderate public faces are now under federal investigation for terrorist ties. Here are a few examples:

- The godfather of the syndicate, AMC's Alamoudi, is serving a long prison sentence after prosecutors connected him to Hamas, al-Qaida, and seven known terrorists. They also recorded him endorsing the al-Qaida attacks on the U.S. embassies in Africa.

- Another respected Muslim leader, Sami al-Arian, is also behind bars, accused of fronting for the Palestinian Islamic Jihad and conspiring to finance terrorist attacks that killed more than a hundred people, including two Americans.

- The Islamic Society of North America, the oldest and largest Muslim organization representing some six hundred local groups, has been suspended from endorsing Muslim chaplains assigned to federal prisons, pending the results of an FBI investigation into the group's activities. The Senate Finance Committee also is investigating the group.

- Meanwhile, an Islamic school in Florida underwritten by an ISNA subsidiary has been shut down in connection with the al-Arian terrorism case.

- The leader of the Islamic Assembly of North America, Bassem K. Khafagi, has been deported after pleading guilty to charges of bank and visa fraud stemming from a federal counterterror probe of his role in the large Detroit-based group, which remains under investigation for ties to al-Qaida.

- Another umbrella group, the Islamic Circle of North America, is also under federal investigation for ties to a violent Pakistani group linked to al-Qaida.

- The U.S. offices of the Saudi-based World Muslim League, International Islamic Relief Organization, and World Assembly of Muslim Youth, or WAMY, have been raided by federal authorities.

- Prestigious Islamic think tanks—such as the Graduate School of Islamic and Social Sciences, International Institute of Islamic Thought, and United Association of Studies and Research—have also been raided.

- The Muslim community's largest charity, the Holy Land Foundation, has been linked to Hamas and shut down.

- Two other popular Muslim charities—Benevolence International Foundation and Global Relief Foundation—have been linked to al-Qaida and blacklisted by the U.S. Department of Treasury as terrorist fronts.

These organizations make up the core of the Muslim establishment in America. They are not part of the fringe but the mainstream—the best the Muslim community has to offer. And hard as it is to believe, they are also part of the infrastructure of support for the enemy.

"You could tie every one of these organizations into at least Palestinian terrorism—Hamas, Hezbollah, Palestinian Islamic Jihad. Every one of them," Vincent says. "And you could tie many of them to al-Qaida, too."

And they all, in turn, can be tied to a broader Islamic movement driven by a secret international society that helped create al-Qaida, Hamas, and Islamic Jihad, Vincent and other investigators say. It is called the Muslim Brotherhood. Founded in Egypt in 1928, the organization is committed to the globalization of Islam through social engineering and violent jihad. Alamoudi and many other leaders of the terror-support syndicate in America are members of the Muslim Brotherhood (which operates in the U.S. under the front Muslim American Society).

Investigators compare it to the Mafia, the secret Sicilian terrorist society. In fact, *mafia* comes from the Arabic word *maehfil*, meaning union. Like mobsters, the Muslim Brothers operate a secret underworld of illegal activities conducted under the cover of fronts with legitimate-sounding names. They launder money through construction companies like BMI Inc. and tax-exempt charities like Happy Hearts Trust.

Theirs is a highly organized and self-contained world, or underworld, according to investigators. The brothers have their own AFL-CIO; it's called ISNA. They have their own American Bar Association; it's called the Fiqh Council. They have their own VFW; it's called the American Muslim Armed Forces and Veterans Affairs Council. They have their own NAACP; it's called CAIR. Their FCA, moreover, is the MSA (the original U.S. chapter of the Muslim Brotherhood). Their United Way is (or was) the Holy Land Foundation. Their NEA is the Council on Islamic Education, or CIE. And their YMCA is WAMY—except, instead of holding basketball camps, it holds jihad camps.[8]

But the *ummah* underworld is harder to penetrate, investigators says, because it is shrouded by a major religion. Fearing accusations of religious bigotry, Washington is still reluctant to aggressively prosecute it. "Unfortunately, headquarters keeps dropping the ball on gathering the evidence that will tie all these groups to terrorism," Vincent says.

Meanwhile, besieged groups are fighting back, retaining crackerjack lawyers and suing the government for racial and religious discrimination. And hoping to win in the court of public opinion, they are effectively using the national media to countercharge the government with carrying out a "witch hunt" against Arabs and Muslims and using "McCarthyite" tactics to smear the entire Muslim community.

In the Muslim media, supporters for jailed leaders have blamed a Zionist conspiracy, which has helped them raise even more money in the community.

Alamoudi and al-Arian "are among the prominent Muslim leaders known for their openness, moderation, and remarkable efforts to build bridges between the Muslim world and the U.S.," claims Ahmed Yousef, executive director of the Washington-based United Association of Studies and Research, an alleged Hamas front Alamoudi helped found. "They are currently incarcerated in American prisons in order to serve the interest of Israel, which opposes any voice demanding justice for the Palestinians." Yousef adds, "The pro-Zionist loyalists in the U.S. opted to use such tactics to eliminate their roles in the Muslim community and on the American scene at large."[9]

The Christian Right also is behind the recent charges against Muslim leaders, contends Mahdi Bray, another prominent Muslim leader, who heads the Muslim Public Affairs Council. The current witch hunt, as he calls it, is the work of the pro-Israeli lobby *and* the Christian Right, both of whom he says have conspired to keep Muslims on the sidelines and exploit a post-9/11 anti-Muslim bias.

"I like to call this 'psychological terrorism,'" he says. "These arrests are an attempt to marginalize the tremendous potential the Muslim community has, especially since we're growing every day in this country."[10]

The Islamic terror-support syndicate does not appear to be very fazed by the increased scrutiny from law enforcement, measured as it is. Most of its groups are more active than ever. They still are allowed to raise tax-free donations, maintain Web sites promoting conferences, conventions, and rallies, and even lobby Congress and federal agencies, where they have been able to place agents sympathetic to their cause. In fact, they are routinely invited by politically sensitive FBI and Justice Department officials to negotiate the terms of an investigation that is supposed to be targeting the very terror-support syndicate of which they are a part.

And more and more, their activism—including the defense of key activists caught up in the investigation—is being done in close coordination with neighborhood mosques, which federal authorities are still loath to infiltrate for fear of a political backlash from Muslim-rights groups.

III
RELIGIOUS INFILTRATION

10

INTERFAITH PHONINESS

Breaking Bread with Radicals

"Islam is part of a Judeo-Christian-Islamic tradition."
—JOHN L. ESPOSITO, director of the
Center for Muslim-Christian Understanding in Washington[1]

Perhaps no one in Washington has done more to bring Islam out of the cultural shadows than professor John L. Esposito. He is director of the Center for Muslim-Christian Understanding at Georgetown University, a well-respected Catholic institution in the nation's capital. His center tirelessly promotes interfaith dialogue between Muslims and Christians. And thanks in large part to his efforts, Islam is now considered by many clergy to be a legitimate member of the religious establishment of America.

Of course, it was not easy. Esposito, who is widely quoted in the media, spent most of the last two decades pooh-poohing the widely held belief that Islam is a threat to the West and its Judeo-Christian tradition. He even attempted to dispel the notion in a recent book, *The Islamic Threat: Myth or Reality?* In it, he concludes that Islam is associated with terrorism only because Christians and Jews do not understand its true meaning. In short, Islam is a victim of "ignorance." If priests and rabbis could just establish ongoing dialogue with Muslim leaders, he argues, they would discover that Islam is a religion of peace, love, and understanding. "Contemporary Islam is more a challenge than a threat," Esposito says. "It challenges the West to know and understand the diversity of the Muslim experience."[2]

He says that Christians have more in common with Muslims than they know. So do Jews. The kinship is so close, he maintains, that Muslims should be considered as American as Jews. And he argues American heritage can be more accurately defined as "Judeo-Christian-Islamic." After all, Jews, Christians, and Muslims are all children of Abraham, he says, and believe in prophethood and divine revelation, for example.

"Muslims in the West at first seem to differ from other immigrants or indigenous converts who, however ethnically diverse, possessed a shared Judeo-Christian culture," Esposito says. "This is caused not only by ignorance of Islam or by equating it with extremism and terrorism but also by the failing to recognize the extent to which Islam is part of a Judeo-Christian-Islamic tradition."[3]

Do not believe those who say there are no Islamic moderates, Esposito says. Or that all Islamic activists and organizations are a threat, whether overt or covert. As long as they are nonviolent, Islamists deserve a seat at the table, he argues.

And he has made plenty of room for them.

One is Muzammil Siddiqi of the Islamic Society of North America, or ISNA. He is frequently invited to participate in interfaith summits and talks a good game. "We Muslims and Christians together make up more than half of the world population today. Better understanding, communication, and peaceful relations between our communities are not only good, but they are essential," Siddiqi recently intoned. "We have much more in common that we think."[4]

He has spoken at seminars held by the World Council of Churches, the National Council of Churches, the National Council of Christians and Jews in the USA, and the Interfaith Council of South Orange County in California. He is vice president of the Academy of Judaic-Christian and Islamic Studies in California.

Siddiqi is also one of the organizers of the hate-filled rally against Israel held in Washington in 2000, where his fellow Islamists raised the banner of jihad and praised Palestinian terrorists. Siddiqi sternly warned America that Allah would punish it if it continued to side with Israel.

And despite Esposito's attempts to mainstream him, Siddiqi remains a Wahhabi preacher, who thinks Allah's rules must be established in America and that Muslims should not serve in the U.S. military until that happens. And he condemns the government for using the Patriot Act and other law enforcement tools to crack down on Muslim groups suspected of supporting terrorism, including some of the groups Siddiqi has led, such as the Saudi-based Muslim World League.[5]

Esposito agrees and advises Muslims to fight back. At a recent ISNA conference, he said, "It is incumbent upon Muslims to create a strategic response."[6]

Esposito has also helped legitimize the militant Council on American-Islamic Relations, or CAIR, whose leaders have been invited to White House interfaith meetings. In a well-publicized gesture of tolerance, its executive director, Nihad Awad, organized an interfaith memorial vigil in Washington on the second anniversary of 9/11. And in another strategic post-9/11 move, he has run advertisements in newspapers across the country designed to present a kinder, gentler image of American Muslims by noting that they believe Jesus Christ was a prophet (though not God) and "strive to live by Jesus' teaching of love, peace, and forgiveness." His teachings, the CAIR ads say, "remind us that all of us, Christians, Muslims, Jews, and all others have more in common than we think."

It all sounds good. But Awad is on record supporting Hamas, a terrorist group that blows up Jews, something he does not mention in his *New York Times* ad campaign. And some of CAIR's leaders are behind bars for terrorism-related crimes, including training to blow up American soldiers in Afghanistan, as I detail in the chapter, "The Dark Lair of CAIR."

Belying Christ's passive nature, CAIR's leaders have earned a reputation for viciously attacking critics of Islam. And Esposito has egged them on. "Don't let anyone who belittles or smears Islam off the hook," he asserted at a CAIR fundraising banquet held in the wake of the 9/11 attacks.[7]

Then there is Abdurahman Alamoudi, founder of the American Muslim Council, or AMC, who has promoted interfaith activities with Catholic, Protestant, and Jewish leaders. During the Clinton administration, he served as a goodwill ambassador for Islam at the Department of State, where Esposito worked at the time as an influential Middle Eastern affairs analyst.

Of course, his respect and tolerance for other faiths left something to be desired. Before sending Alamoudi to the big house for terrorism-related crimes, prosecutors last year read a transcript of a 1999 conversation between him and an unidentified person during one of Alamoudi's State Department-sponsored trips to the Middle East. In it, Alamoudi remarked that the 1998 al-Qaida attacks on the U.S. Embassies in Africa were not effective because they killed hundreds of Africans but no Americans. He said he would have preferred instead the selection of "strategic" targets like the Jewish Community Center in Buenos Aires, where a 1994 bombing killed eighty-six people, according to the transcript. Alamoudi described the terrorist attack as "a worthy operation."[8]

ESPOSITO'S PALESTINIAN SUGAR DADDY

After 9/11, fellow AMC board member, Madhi Bray, became the first Muslim named to the Interfaith Alliance, a leading Washington voice for religious pluralism. Last year, the group, which includes priests and rabbis, rallied behind Bray and other Islamists in protesting the government's surveillance and questioning of terrorist suspects in the Muslim community.

"Official interviews about religious practices held by the government in houses of worship or in private homes are egregious breaches of the constitutional guarantee of religious freedom," the Interfaith Alliance said last fall in a press release. "The federal policy is flawed, so we ask the FBI to cease their surveillance and questioning of Muslims."[9]

Meanwhile, a group founded by Alamoudi's former deputy has received the imprimatur of the National Association of Evangelicals. The Christian group now participates in an annual conference in Qatar organized by the Islamic Institute allegedly to promote interfaith dialogue and understanding.

Critics argue that Muslim leaders are participating in such interfaith activities as a ploy to gain greater acceptance for the Islamic faith and not to gain greater understanding of, and tolerance for, other faiths. In other words, they have no intention of returning the respect and tolerance they receive.

There is no doubt that many Islamists secretly want to Islamize America, turning everyone, including Uncle Sam, into a Muslim. But that requires first infiltrating the religious establishment. To do that, they must be recognized and accepted by the national clergy. And critics point out that the only way they can do that is by posing as moderates and pluralists. *Posing* is the right word. A closer look at Esposito's book on Islam shows he lionizes Palestinian terrorists as leaders of a "political movement," and the late PLO chief Yasir Arafat as a "statesman." And he urges Washington to distance itself from Israel.[10]

That also happens to match the agenda of his backers. Georgetown University has declined to discuss the source of funding for Esposito's center for Muslim-Christian harmony. But IRS tax records I obtained show it is supported almost exclusively by a foundation headed by a Palestinian businessman with hostile views toward Israel. The Washington-based Foundation for Muslim-Christian Understanding awards annual grants in excess of $1.1 million to Esposito's center. The president of the foundation is Hasib Sabbagh, a Palestinian refugee and one-time adviser and confidant of Arafat. He is also close to the Saudi royal family.[11]

What's more, Sabbagh's daughter contributed one million dollars for the Hasib Sabbagh wing of the Georgetown center, which was built in 1995 and houses Esposito's offices. "Americans should not think 'terrorism' when they think of the Muslim world," Sana Sabbagh said in explaining the purpose of her gift and the center. (Inspired by the Sabbaghs' generosity, wealthy Malaysian Muslims are now pumping millions of dollars into Georgetown, making the Catholic college a Mecca for Islamic studies, oddly enough.)[12]

Judging from Esposito's wealthy Palestinian benefactor and their mutual pro-Palestinian bias, it appears he believes Christians (and Jews) need the "understanding" his center purports to provide more than Muslims.

But some of the most intolerant and closed-minded places in America are the places where Muslims worship. Esposito and other paid apologists for Islam do not dare tell you that. They paint mosques as models of openness, tolerance, and community dialogue. The media for the most part have gone along with the hype, describing mosques in glowing terms.

But the facts cast a great many of them in far harsher light.

11

SANCTUARIES OF TERROR

The Most Dangerous Mosques in America

"Our enemy until the day of judgment is the Christians, what we call the westerners or Europeans."
— ALI AL-TIMIMI, imam of the Dar al-Arqam mosque
just outside the nation's capital[1]

Every time you fill up your tank, you may be helping to finance a mosque in America that preaches hard-line, anti-Western Wahhabism, the official religion of Saudi Arabia. If that sounds farfetched, consider this: some of the largest mosques and Islamic centers in America are funded by the Saudi royal government, which gets most of its revenues from oil exports. And America is its biggest customer. With the exception of Sunoco, every major American gas retailer refines at least some of their gas from Saudi crude.[2]

Just as it cornered the oil market with American help, the kingdom has cornered the market for Muslim souls in America with American help. The Saudis have spent tens of millions of dollars over the past few decades to spread Wahhabism in America, and it has led to an explosion in the number of mosques. In 1980, there were 481 officially recognized mosques in the country. Now there are 1,209—and an estimated 80 percent of them are controlled by Saudi Arabia. That means control of property, buildings, appointments of imams, training of imams, and content of preaching. It even means control of literature distributed in mosques and mosque bookstores, including notices posted on bulletin boards.[3]

Some say the Saudis, who also control the mandatory pilgrimages to Islam's holiest shrines, the fifth pillar of Islam, are just satisfying a growing desire among American Muslims to purify the faith by practicing a stricter code of Islam, one that does not deviate from the word of the Quran. They say Wahhabism is popular because it provides an authentic interpretation of their sacred book, which happens to be inherently hostile toward Jews, Christians, and Western values in general. A survey by the Council on American-Islamic Relations, or CAIR, in April 2001 found that 69 percent of Muslims in America think it is "absolutely fundamental" or "very important" to have Wahhabi teachings in their mosques—with nearly the same share also agreeing that American society is corrupt and immoral.

Having said that, however, the Muslim community in America is no monolith. Almost half of Muslims are black converts who were not raised in Saudi or other Middle Eastern countries. And there are observant Muslims and nonobservant Muslims. Of observant Muslims, there are those who are orthodox and those who are not-so-orthodox. And even among orthodox Muslims, there are activists, such as the jihadists, and there are quietists. Even among Wahhabists there are those, such as Saudi Prince Bandar, known as "Whiskey Wahhabists," who promulgate a strict code of Islam but do not always follow it.

But virtually all Muslims in America are united in their opposition to Israel and U.S. foreign policy. An overwhelming majority of them believe Washington is blindly supporting Israel and ignoring the plight of the Palestinian people. According to a Zogby International poll taken right after the 9/11 attacks, 84 percent of Muslims agree that the U.S. should support a Palestinian state, and fully 70 percent think it should cut aid to Israel.[4]

And they are not afraid to make those views known at mosque. Unlike churches, mosques welcome overt political expression, in large part because the majority of their worshippers demand it, according to the same Zogby survey.[5] Friday sermons are often more political theater than worship. In fact, Washington-based CAIR's political bulletins, which go out to mosques each week, often form the theme of sermons. Topic A is almost always the Middle East, and that usually means bashing Israel and Jews, along with the American government which supports them.

Some American mosques have even performed skits and songs advocating the destruction of the state of Israel and glorifying the killing of Jewish people, according to federal investigators. And they have openly praised the suicide bombings carried out by Hamas, which has called for the annihilation of the state of Israel and the establishment of an Islamic Palestinian state in its place.[6]

The Congressional Research Service reported last decade that as much as 40 percent of Hamas's budget comes from private fundraising in the U.S. and Britain. Saudi Arabia, which holds telethons for families of Palestinian suicide bombers, provides the lion's share of the terrorist group's funding.[7]

Much of the American fundraising occurs at mosques, investigators say. "The Palestinian jihad is a huge issue with all Muslims. At the mosques, they do the *zakat* [tithing] for Palestinian martyrs," says former FBI special agent John Vincent, who spent several years investigating Hamas fronts and mosques in Chicago. It's

Vincent's conclusion that "virtually every Muslim in America supports terrorism in one way or another. They know exactly where their money is going."[8]

By and large, American Muslims do not view Palestinian suicide bombers as terrorists, says Robert Blitzer, who was the assistant section chief of the FBI's counterterrorism section last decade. "The Muslim community was penetrated with many supporters of Hamas and the [Palestinian] Islamic Jihad, and they were contributing large sums of money to these groups thinking they were helping the widows and orphans of 'freedom fighters,' who they did not view as terrorists then or now," he tells me. They believe they are involved in "humanitarian work" on behalf of the "occupied people of the Holy Land."[9]

Since 9/11, many imams of Saudi-controlled mosques in America have toned down their anti-Israeli and anti-American rhetoric during sermons because they are aware that reporters and FBI agents may be present.

But those are the English-language sermons, points out Hale Smith, a reformed Muslim formerly known as Abdul Haleem. He says clerics often reserve their hate-filled rhetoric for the sermons delivered in Arabic. He says the imam at the mosque he used to attend in San Francisco called for jihad against the Jews in Arabic.

"When he got into the incendiary parts, like calling for jihad against the Jews, he did it in Arabic. He did sermons in all Arabic with no translations. Even if you don't speak fluent Arabic, you could tell in the parts where he started talking angrily about *Yahoudi, Yahoudi, Yahoudi!*" which is Arabic for Jew, Smith says. "So if any reporters or non-Muslims were there, they wouldn't know what's going on."

THE SECOND ISRAEL

Smith, a lawyer, says he left the faith not long after 9/11 because he was disgusted with the support for terrorism he witnessed at the mosque, which he says at one time was visited by John Walker Lindh, the American Taliban. "After 9/11, I ran into so many folks charging that the Israelis did it and that this was a frame job by America. When they saw the bin Laden tape, they said it was probably a Hollywood fake, but if bin Laden did it, bin Laden was right," Smith intimated in a recent phone interview. "It was sickening. Sickening!"[10]

He says Muslims view Israel as the main target of jihad. But they see America as a derivative target because of its alliance with Israel against the Palestinian terrorists. To them, America is a "Second Israel," Smith says, and Washington is a second Knesset.

The U.S. invasion of Baghdad, the former seat of the Islamic caliphate, has created even more bitterness among American Muslims, he notes.

And it has made it easier for al-Qaida to recruit operatives at mosques. FBI investigators says the terror network is actively seeking American converts, who it believes would attract less scrutiny from authorities while conducting terrorist operations.

Investigators say the al-Qaida recruiting strategy, according to seized training manuals and detainee interviews, typically involves:

- selecting a Wahhabi mosque
- identifying young men who appear to be true believers
- developing a friendship with them over time
- learning their interests and emotional state
- and measuring their strengths and weaknesses

Al-Qaida recruiting agents then engage the promising terrorist prospects in discussions about Muslim conflicts, focusing on the invasion and occupation of Muslim lands, such as Iraq and Afghanistan, and the persecution, torture, and rape of Muslims. The targeted members of the mosque are then approached about fighting to defend their Muslim brothers in jihad.

Several mosques in America have been used as recruiting stations for terrorists. For example, the Blind Sheikh Abdul Rahman, convicted after the 1993 World Trade Center attack, used Wahhabi mosques in Brooklyn and Jersey City to build his anti-American following. The leaders of the 9/11 hijacking ring attended at least seven mosques in five states while in America.

Some mosques are also used to procure weapons. For instance, the imam of a small Wahhabi mosque in Albany, New York, called Masjid As-Salam (Mosque of Peace), was arrested last year for trying to buy a shoulder-fired missile to use in a planned terrorist act. A Saudi-tied trust holds the mosque's deed.

The unpleasant truth is that some mosques in America are being used as sanctuaries for terrorist activities. Some may be in your neighborhood. Here are ten that federal investigators are closely monitoring, counting down from the No. 10 to the No. 1 mosque of concern.

NO. 10: THE ADAMS CENTER

The All Dulles Area Muslim Society, better known as the ADAMS Center, is another Saudi-controlled Wahhabi mosque. It is located just outside the nation's capital in Sterling, Virginia, and not far from the notorious Safa group headquarters that were raided after 9/11 by federal counterterrorism agents.

Not surprisingly, the two are connected. In fact, some of the key leaders of the suspected terror front, including Ahmad Totonji, serve as directors of the mosque, which operates out of a relatively new building. And investigators found a Safa check for $250,000 endorsed to ADAMS in 1997.[11] One of the mosque's more prominent members is Ibrahim "Dougie" Hooper of CAIR.

Another member, a Pakistani immigrant, confides that leaders, quoting from the Quran, teach worshippers to hate Christians and Jews, "but Jews more." He also says that their *zakat* donations are distributed to Palestinians widowed or orphaned by anti-Israeli "martyrs." Sermons, moreover, are framed in terms of "us" and "them." America and Americans are referred to as "them," even though many congregants, including the Pakistani, are U.S. citizens.

But here is the most chilling part of what he revealed in our recent conversation. He says mosque leaders say they will work peacefully within the political system to change U.S. policy supporting Israel and to withdraw American troops from Iraq, Afghanistan, and other Muslim countries. But if the U.S. attacks Iran or Syria, the gloves will come off.

"There will be suicide bombers blowing up buses in this country, just like in Israel," he warns, even if the U.S. military does not target Muslims in America. And if mosques are shut down and Muslims' right to freely worship where they want is infringed, he says, Washington and other American cities will erupt into the kind of violence seen in the streets around Baghdad.[12]

The ADAMS Center member, who works for a Beltway contractor, explains that all Muslims are united in a kind of blood pact under the *ummah*, the worldwide Muslim brotherhood. "If you hurt one Muslim anywhere in the world," he says, "it's like hurting all Muslims." And the brothers will respond in kind, even if that means self-immolation on the streets of America.

"Muslims are not afraid to die, you know," he adds, ominously. "We are not afraid to die."

Asked if the Muslim community in America reveres Osama bin Laden as much as Muslims abroad, he replied, "I don't know about revere, but we do respect him." Why? Because he stands up against "injustice and oppression," he explains. And even though he is a rich man, he shuns palaces and walks the true walk of Islam, unlike the Saudi monarchs and Saddam Hussein, whom he referred to as "hypocrites."

NO. 9: BRIDGEVIEW MOSQUE

Also known as the Mosque Foundation, Bridgeview mosque preaches Wahhabi dogma and is controlled by the Saudis. In fact, the kingdom partially pays the salary of its charismatic prayer leader Sheik Jamal Said, a Saudi-educated Palestinian who preaches in Arabic and believes true Muslims should not celebrate Thanksgiving and other American holidays.

The Chicago-area mosque, which attracts some two thousand worshippers, most of whom are Palestinian Americans, has been under FBI scrutiny for the past several years, according to Vincent, who has personally interviewed its leaders and members. It has contributed hundreds of thousands of dollars to three terrorist front groups—Benevolence International Foundation (tied to al-Qaida), Global Relief Foundation (al-Qaida), and the Holy Land Foundation (Hamas). All three maintain offices near the mosque, and two of them have employed mosque officials.[13]

Investigators believe the Muslim Brotherhood, an Egypt-based group with a violent past, has an undue influence over the mosque. The Brotherhood gave birth to Hamas, the Palestinian Islamic Jihad, and the Egyptian Islamic Jihad, which merged with al-Qaida several years ago.

Like most of the Wahhabi mosques in America, Bridgeview's deed is held by the North American Islamic Trust, a Saudi-rooted group whose chairman is linked to Sami al-Arian, an alleged founder of Islamic Jihad now under indictment. One of the mosque's leaders, Muhammad Salah, is a suspected member of the Muslim Brotherhood and Hamas. He was arrested last year for suspicion of funneling millions of dollars to Hamas. Salah is close to Hamas political leader Mousa Abu Marzook and other suspected Hamas operatives who have worshipped at a large mosque in the Washington area. Bridgeview members have offered to put up their homes as bond collateral to spring Salah from jail as he awaits trial.[14]

One of the mosque's most honored guests was Osama bin Laden's spiritual mentor, the late Palestinian cleric Abdullah Azzam. Some of Azzam's relatives are members of Bridgeview.

NO. 8: ISLAMIC SOCIETY OF ORANGE COUNTY

The spiritual leader of the Saudi-controlled mosque is Muzammil Siddiqi, former president of the powerful and controversial Islamic Society of North America, or ISNA, which has recently come under both FBI and congressional scrutiny. He helped convert a twenty-five-year-old Californian to Islam who is now the subject of a worldwide FBI manhunt. Adam Gadahn traveled to Pakistan and Afghanistan to train at al-Qaida camps following his counseling at the Islamic Society in Garden Grove, California, in the late 1990s.

The FBI has questioned Siddiqi—reared in Pakistani religious politics and schooled in Islam at a Saudi university—about his former protégé, prompting the imam last year to make a public appeal for Gadahn, also known as the "American al-Qaida," to turn himself in to authorities.

Siddiqi serves on ISNA's board with controversial New York imam Siraj Wahhaj named as an unindicted co-conspirator in the federal case last decade against terrorist Abdul Rahman, also known as the Blind Sheikh. Siddiqi and Wahhaj spoke at the Pakistani-tied Islamic Circle of North America's 2001 convention in Cleveland together with Saudi Shaikh Abdur Rahman al-Sudais, senior imam at the Grand Mosque in Mecca, who has been quoted vilifying Jews as the "scum of humanity" and "the grandsons of monkeys and pigs." The three were billed to speak again in 2003 at an Islamic conference in Kissimmee, Florida.[15]

Siddiqi, who writes a weekly column for a Pakistani publication, has spoken at pro-Hezbollah and pro-Hamas rallies and has supported an Islamic state in the U.S., while glorifying martyrdom for the Islamic cause. The FBI fears al-Qaida is recruiting American converts like Gadahn to blend in to American society and not raise security suspicions before carrying out suicide attacks in America. Agents are searching for him and six other al-Qaida suspects in an attempt to disrupt a possible al-Qaida plot to attack America again.

Siddiqi served as a key American official for the Saudi-based Muslim World League in the 1970s and 1980s. The offices of its U.S. branch in Washington were raided by federal counterterrorism agents after 9/11. Investigators suspect the league helped bankroll bin Laden's operations.

Smith, the former Muslim from San Francisco, says the Orange County mosque recently hired a cleric he knew in San Francisco who admired Hitler for the Holocaust. "He considered Hitler most blessed by Allah," he says, "and said the only thing he did wrong was not killing enough Jews."

NO. 7: THE ISLAMIC CENTER OF SAN DIEGO

The Saudi-controlled Wahhabi mosque gave aid and comfort to two of the Saudi hijackers, Khalid al-Mihdhar and Nawaf al-Hazmi. In fact, the administrator of the mosque let Hazmi use his bank account to receive a five-thousand-dollar wire transfer from an al-Qaida operative in Dubai in the United Arab Emirates.[16] The imam at the center is a close associate of a known member of the Muslim Brotherhood connected to Zacarias Moussaoui, the alleged twentieth hijacker, as well as the former imam of another San Diego mosque who counseled the hijackers in closed-door meetings. Also, a suspected Saudi intelligence agent who acted as an advance man for the hijackers attended the Islamic Center.

NO. 6: DAR AL-ARQAM ISLAMIC CENTER

After 9/11, members of the so-called Virginia jihad network went to the Washington-area mosque to hear lectures from a popular Wahhabi preacher on the righteousness of waging violent jihad in Afghanistan, Kashmir, and Chechnya. They also watched videotapes of terrorists engaged in jihad at the small Saudi-controlled mosque. Its imam, Ali al-Timimi, told the eleven young Muslim men—nearly all of whom are U.S. citizens—that American troops are "legitimate targets" of jihad because America is the "greatest enemy of Muslims." Before they were arrested, some of the jihadists planned to die martyrs and left wills with Timimi, who celebrated the 9/11 attacks as the beginning of the "final battle" between Islam and the infidels. One of his acolytes was found with photographs of the FBI headquarters building on his computer. Another possessed a document titled, "The Terrorist's Handbook," containing instructions on manufacturing and using explosives and chemicals as weapons.[17]

The traitorous Timimi also cheered the explosion of the space shuttle *Columbia* in 2003, saying "the heart of every believer leaped with joy at the disaster of his greatest enemy." He added that it was a "good omen." The tragedy took the lives of six American astronauts and one Israeli.[18]

In addition, the spiritual leader once said in a speech: "Our enemy until the day of judgment is the Christians, what we call the westerners or Europeans."[19] Timimi, a U.S. citizen, was indicted last year on charges he aided and abetted terrorists.

A Saudi diplomat named Jaafar Idris was known to lecture at Dar al-Arqam, which shares its building with the Saudi-based Muslim World League, before the U.S. revoked his visa last year. The mosque, located on the first floor of the nondescript office building in Falls Church, Virginia, is still open and still preaching poison.

NO. 5: AYAH DAWAH PRAYER CENTER

Several of the hijackers spent their last days in heavily Pakistani Laurel, Maryland, about twenty miles outside Washington. They visited a small, hard-line mosque not far from their hotel room called the Ayah Dawah Prayer Center, which was started by a fiery young imam from Somalia named Said Rageah. The morning of 9/11, the hijackers dropped a duffel bag at the mosque's door. Taped to the mysterious bag was a note that read: "FOR THE BROTHERS." After the attacks, FBI agents questioned some members of the mosque on information they may have had prior knowledge of the plot.[20]

Maryland is also home to a large number of supporters of the Taliban, a movement that started in Pakistan and was exported to Afghanistan. Ironically, a number of them are related to Afghan president Hamid Karzai, a U.S. ally.

"A lot of people, even though they may have the Karzai name, a lot of them are not pro-current regime," says Pat Karzai, sister-in-law of the Afghan president who runs an Afghan restaurant called the Helmand in Maryland. "A lot of them have not and will not return to the country. Many of them are still Taliban supporters."[21] She claims some of Karzai's relatives in the area have even hosted Taliban leaders at their Maryland homes. Taliban leader Mullah Omar, thought to be hiding in Afghanistan, is still a fugitive.

NO. 4: MASJID AL-NOOR

Another Saudi-controlled Wahhabi mosque, it has a disturbing al-Qaida influence. Ali Mohamed, a top al-Qaida lieutenant tied to the 1998 U.S. Embassy bombings in Africa, was a central figure there. In fact, he helped Osama bin Laden's second-in-command raise money at the mosque in Santa Clara, California. Masjid al-Noor is also known as MCA, which stands for Muslim Community Association, the mosque's governing body. CAIR's founder and chairman is a member of the mosque and has given lectures there.

NO. 3: AL-FAROUQ MOSQUE

The Brooklyn mosque was linked to the 1993 World Trade Center bombing. A central figure there was Blind Sheikh Abdul Rahman, who served briefly as its imam before his conviction in the plot to blow up New York landmarks. He preached that the United States was the oppressor of Muslims worldwide and asserted that it was the religious duty of Muslims to fight the "great enemy" of Allah.

Several members with direct links to al-Qaida worshipped there, including El-Sayyid Nosair, who organized the assassination of Rabbi Meir Kahane. Another al-Qaida fighter recruited through the al-Farouq mosque was Jamal Ahmed al-Fadl. Federal investigators recently traced money raised for al-Qaida back to the al-Farouq mosque.

Another former al-Farouq imam is Fawaz Abu Damra, a suspected member of the Palestinian Islamic Jihad who has urged attacks on Jews. Muslims should be "directing all rifles at the first and last enemy of the Islamic nation, and this is the sons of monkeys and pigs, the Jews," he told a Muslim audience last decade. He is now head of the Islamic Center of Greater Cleveland, Ohio's largest mosque, where he has hosted another suspected Islamic Jihad leader—Sami al-Arian. After al-Arian spoke at a 1991 fundraiser at the Cleveland mosque, Damra told his congregation that anyone who donates money to the Islamic jihad is like the martyrs waging holy war on behalf of Allah. He asked for money for the terrorist group, whose martyr "Nidal Zaloom went out with a dagger and stabbed four Jews in Jerusalem."[22] The mosque has decided to keep Damra on as imam after he serves a short federal prison term for lying to authorities about his ties to terrorist groups. His supporters have even asked the court to allow him to preach while under home confinement in the post-prison term of his sentence.

NO. 2: MASJID AL-HIJRAH

The hard-line Wahhabi mosque in the Fort Lauderdale, Florida, area was founded by the father of Adnan el-Shukrijumah, a suspected al-Qaida operative who investigators are calling the "next Mohamed Atta." As a preacher there, Gulshair el-Shukrijumah personally counseled al-Qaida dirty bomb suspect Jose Padilla and his wife.

He was also the imam of a Brooklyn mosque connected to a terrorist plot to blow up major New York buildings and tunnels. Gulshair, who died last year, first caught the FBI's attention when he testified on behalf of convicted terrorist Clement Hampton-El, one of two members of the Brooklyn mosque tied to the plot. Masjid al-Taqwa is now run by Wahhaj, the unindicted co-conspirator in the 1993 World Trade Center bombing case.

Saudi-born Adnan el-Shukrijumah, also known as "Jafar the Pilot," is currently the subject of worldwide FBI manhunt. His late father and his mosque received checks for tens of thousands of dollars directly from the Saudi Embassy through 2003.[23]

El-Shukrijumah and Padilla also patronized Masjid al-Iman, another Fort Lauderdale-area mosque that has drawn FBI interest.

NO. 1 . . .

This hard-line Wahhabi mosque, one of the nation's largest, is a Saudi-sponsored hub of terrorist activities, a platform for hate-filled rhetoric, a fundraising house for Hamas and a magnet for Islamic militants and terrorists—including some of the 9/11 hijackers, who received aid and comfort there. It has had more of its leaders and members come under federal counterterrorism investigation than any other mosque in America. It is also right in President Bush's backyard . . .

12

THE 9/11 MOSQUE

Dar al-Hijrah

"There's always anxiety. You never know if there's an insurgent over there."

—CHARLOTTE S. NEEDHAM, who lives across the street
from the Dar al-Hijrah Islamic Center[1]

Every Friday, Charlotte S. Needham makes herself scarce. Friday is the day when prayer services are held at the large mosque across the street from her old white colonial home nestled in the leafy Washington suburb of Falls Church, Virginia. The worship service attracts some three thousand Muslims, many of whom trample her yard and leave behind trash as they come and go. Some have even parked in her driveway, before she strung a chain across it. They still block traffic on her narrow street. The elderly widow has given up complaining about the rude congregants. She finds it is better for her blood pressure if she just leaves her house on those afternoons. Essentially, Needham has been run off from the charming home her father, William Mason Smith, built in 1929, decades before the mosque appeared across the street.

In 1983, officials from a Saudi-backed group that holds the deeds to a great many of the mosques in America courted Needham's neighbor, also a widow, who lived on the large lot across from her on Row Street. "They wined and dined her," she says of her neighbor, eventually talking her into selling her property. The group, called the North American Islamic Trust, subdivided the property in 1986, according to county land records, and built yet another American mosque controlled by the kingdom, ensuring that it too preaches hard-line Wahhabism. Dubbed Dar al-Hijrah Islamic Center, the new six-million-dollar mosque, complete with minaret, opened its doors in 1991.[2]

At the time, it was the only mosque in the area, and it quickly attracted throngs of Muslim worshippers. The traffic congestion disturbed residents, and they complained to county zoning authorities. "We've all had to go to court," Needham says of herself and her neighbors, to fight what she calls the mosque's encroachment on the quiet residential neighborhood, which in the spring bursts with color from pink and purple azalea bushes. Dar al-Hijrah was outgrowing its parking lot and violating the county's requirement that all mosque parking be on-site. Worshippers were parking on people's lawns, in front of their driveways, and even in front of fire hydrants.

To alleviate the problem, the mosque's Saudi-backed founders bought a one-acre lot behind Needham's property and applied for a special permit to use it as a parking lot. "They had it all drawn up—101 slots. They were going to use the back of our property as a right-of-way to walk to the mosque," she says. "But they didn't even approach us to ask permission. It was very underhanded."

So she and several neighbors "organized petitions, and we blocked it," she adds. "No one wanted them there."[3]

Needham says the county meetings she attended were heated. "Everyone from the mosque was very hostile toward us," she recalls. "Police were there. There were altercations between some of those present." One four-hour hearing in 1993 turned into an ugly confrontation between neighbors and Muslims, who punctuated the proceedings with catcalls, jeers, and charges of religious bigotry.

In the end, an unlikely source came to the mosque's rescue. Two neighboring conservative churches—the First Christian Church and the Church of Christ—offered their large parking lots on Fridays, the Muslim Sabbath.[4] They also agreed to accommodate overflow parking during the busy Muslim holy month of Ramadan. Thanks to their kind gestures, the mosque continued to grow.

"If we chained off our churches, they'd be out of business," says Bill LaLiberte, an elder at the First Christian Church who deals with the mosque. He says it is the duty of Christians to help their neighbors.[5]

Needham says she has learned to live with the traffic and congestion, which is still so "horrendous" that a funeral home operator almost a block away has to cancel services on Fridays. She even puts up with the littering.

But it is the mosque's questionable loyalties that make her resentful. "One thing that really disturbs me is they have never, ever put out an American flag, even after September 11," Needham tells me during a recent interview in her living room. "And that would have been so reassuring to everybody around here."

She says neighbors are suspicious of the mosque's activities. "There's always anxiety," she says. "You never know if there's an insurgent over there," a term she uses to describe terrorists.

After the 1993 World Trade Center bombing, she says FBI agents visited her house several times. One day, they asked if they could park in her driveway to conduct surveillance on one of the members of the mosque. "They didn't want to park on the service road [along Route 7] because it was too visible," Needham recalls. Not long after, she says, the FBI arrested the member, who lived in a nearby subdivision in Falls Church. Agents told her he was connected to the World Trade Center case.

I asked if the FBI has been out to talk to her since the 9/11 attacks, and she shook her head. But they have questioned leaders of the mosque. And for good reason.

Dar al-Hijrah is a veritable magnet for militant Islamists. Over the years, it has attracted an alarming number of terrorist supporters, terrorist facilitators, terrorist fundraisers, terrorist co-conspirators, and actual terrorists—including at least two of the 9/11 hijackers who crashed the plane into the Pentagon. These are not just random members who come and go. Many are the very leaders and founders of the mosque.

Jamal al-Barzinji: Records show he is the trustee who signed the county land documents authorizing development of the mosque for the North American Islamic Trust.[6] According to Department of Homeland Security investigator David Kane, he is also under investigation for providing material support to terrorists. "Barzinji is not only closely associated with PIJ [Palestinian Islamic Jihad], but also with Hamas," Kane said in recently unsealed court papers.[7]

Mohamed Hadid: A construction contractor, he built Dar al-Hijrah, according to property records filed in Fairfax County.[8] His partner at the time was the SAAR Foundation, a charitable trust funded by a wealthy Saudi who was a member of a group of early Osama bin Laden supporters called the "Golden Chain." (Barzinji was an officer in the SAAR group, as well as several other Muslims now under federal investigation.) Another longtime partner of Hadid, a devout Muslim Palestinian, was Abdul Aziz al-Ibrahim, a Saudi sheik whose charitable foundation has been linked to bin Laden and the U.S. Embassy bombings in Africa.[9] Investigators note that some of the businesses Islamists set up to provide profits to terrorists include construction companies.

Samir Salah: A founder and president of Dar al-Hijrah, he too is tied to groups suspected of aiding al-Qaida and has long been under the scrutiny of U.S. authorities. He helped found the Safa Trust, SAAR's successor, which federal agents raided after 9/11. He also helped establish Bank al-Taqwa, which the U.S. government has banned as a conduit for al-Qaida and Hamas funds. What's more, Salah ran the Taibah International Aid Association, another banned al-Qaida charity, which was incorporated in Virginia by bin Laden's nephew, Abdullah. The Egyptian-born Salah allegedly is a member of the notorious Muslim Brotherhood.[10]

Sheikh Mohammed al-Hanooti: He was once the imam at Dar al-Hijrah and still leads Friday prayers at the mosque—even though he was named as an unindicted co-conspirator in the 1993 World Trade Center bombing.[11] Back then, al-Hanooti led a mosque in New Jersey that hosted Blind Sheikh Omar Abdul Rahman and some of his followers, including one of the Trade Center bombers. Al-Hanooti invited the Blind Sheikh, now in prison for conspiring to blow up New York landmarks, to deliver hate-filled speeches at his former mosque. He also had repeated contacts with the young Muslim man who murdered Rabbi Meir Kahane in New York.

Al-Hanooti, a Palestinian who admits being "anti-Israel," has told Muslim crowds that "Jews are the enemy of Allah."[12] He is known to have given disturbing lectures at Dar al-Hijrah that condemned both Israel and America. He has spoken at Jew-bashing rallies held by the Islamic Association for Palestine, a known Hamas front, where he was once a top-ranking official. In fact, the FBI says al-Hanooti is a "big supporter" of Hamas who raised more than six million dollars for the group in 1993 alone. That year, he attended a summit in Philadelphia with Hamas leaders, according to a forty-nine-page FBI memorandum written after 9/11 by former FBI counterterrorism chief Dale L. Watson.[13]

Of course, this is not the scholarly and moderate face that the silver-bearded al-Hanooti wears in public. His speeches for the Department of State have been featured overseas on the Voice of America network as an example of Arab moderation. The mayor of D.C. recently honored him as one of the top clergy in the area. And he currently serves as the Grand Mufti of the greater Washington area. His office happens to be located next door to the U.S. branch of the Saudi-based World Assembly of Muslim Youth, which was run by Abdullah bin Laden and recently raided by federal authorities. Convicted terrorist Abdurahman Alamoudi ran his operations out of the same office complex. As Mufti, al-Hanooti answers questions related to Islamic law, including ones concerning legitimate targets of jihad.

Johari Abdul-Malik: A black convert, he heads Dar al-Hijrah's outreach program. He is also a director for the National Association of Muslim Chaplains, whose founder and president has praised the 9/11 hijackers and called their attacks justified under Islam, as I will detail in a coming chapter on prison chaplains. Abdul-Malik hails from Brooklyn, home to Imam Siraj Wahhaj, another unindicted co-conspirator in the 1993 Trade Center bombing—and a frequent guest speaker at Dar al-Hijrah.

Abdul-Malik also acts as a spokesman for the mosque. After 9/11, I asked him about a recent former imam there who has been known in sermons to raise the banner of jihad and encourage Muslims to become martyrs. Abdul-Malik sees nothing wrong with such sermons and suggested that all Muslims are like U.S. Marines, comprising a spiritual army against those who are not faithful to the cause of Allah. "Telling people to give their all for their faith is not an unusual idea," he says. "That's the same thing as telling Marines in this country *semper fidelis*."[14]

I also asked Abdul-Malik about the parking situation at Dar al-Hijrah, now one of the largest mosques in the nation. He says the neighboring churches were still absorbing the overflow from its three Friday prayer services, but he did not seem very grateful for their enduring cooperation. "If Islam really catches on in the area, maybe the neighborhood churches will come over lock, stock, and barrel, and we can all share our parking lots," he remarked, cheekily.[15]

The mosque recently asked the Church of Christ, which is the larger of the two churches, if it could use its grounds for a fundraising event. The church respectfully declined.[16]

Abdurahman Alamoudi: A fixture at the mosque, he is now behind bars for plotting terrorist acts. An officer with Salah in the al-Qaida-linked Taibah group, he was a prominent Muslim activist in Washington, and an avowed supporter of anti-Israeli terror groups.

Abdullah bin Laden: Another worshipper, he lived in Falls Church until 2001, when he sold his home and fled to Saudi Arabia. He helped direct Taibah, in addition to running WAMY's recently raided offices in nearby Alexandria. He is on the U.S. anti-terrorist watchlist, according to investigators.

Mousa Abu Marzook: He was a prominent member of Dar al-Hijrah until he was kicked out of the country several years ago after the U.S. declared him a specially designated terrorist. An acknowledged political leader of Hamas, the Palestinian was indicted last year with two other longtime Dar al-Hijrah members for conspiring to funnel millions of dollars to Hamas to carry out kidnappings, bombings, and other attacks on Israel. Believed to be hiding in Syria, he remains a fugitive.

Ismail Elbarasse: He is a longtime friend and business partner of Marzook and a revered figure at Dar al-Hijrah. Investigators have traced hundreds of thousands of dollars from an account the two men jointly held at a bank in nearby McLean to a suspected Hamas operation in Chicago.[17] Like al-Hanooti, one of the mosque's spiritual leaders, Elbarasse is a Palestinian and a former board member of the Hamas front Islamic Association for Palestine. In fact, he attended the Hamas summit in Philadelphia with al-Hanooti in 1993. In his day job, Elbarasse worked as the finance officer for the Islamic Saudi Academy, a Saudi-financed school in Alexandria attended by older children of Dar al-Hijrah members, including those of the Marzooks.

Last year, Elbarasse was arrested in Maryland after authorities spotted his wife videotaping the Chesapeake Bay Bridge from an SUV he was driving. After authorities pulled him over, they discovered that a federal material-witness warrant had been issued for him the same day in Chicago in a Hamas terrorist fundraising case in which he is an unindicted co-conspirator. Authorities viewed the tape in his videocamera and found the images included closeups of cables and supports integral to the structural integrity of the bridge. They locked him up in a Baltimore jail after finding six other videotapes in his car containing footage of the Bay Bridge and other structures or potential targets. They believed the footage of the bridge to be reconnaissance and surveillance for a possible terrorist attack.

Elbarasse was released on one million dollars bond after Dar al-Hijrah members put up their homes as collateral. One of them, according to court documents I obtained, was Esam S. Omeish, a mosque board member and brother of Mohamed S. Omeish.[18] Mohamed Omeish is the president of the U.S. branch of the Saudi-financed International Islamic Relief Organization, a major contributor to Osama bin Laden's operations—as well as to Dar al-Hijrah, according to tax records I obtained. In 1998, for example, the organization listed Dar al-Hijrah as one of its top recipients of emergency relief aid in its filing to the IRS. The mosque and its weekend school received nearly fifteen thousand dollars that year. (The school includes a playground built by Nike after the shoemaker agreed to make amends for marketing a sneaker emblazoned with the word "Air" written in flames. Muslim activists took offense, arguing the squiggly lines made the word look like Arabic script for the word Allah and were therefore blasphemous.)

Other tax records show the relief organization has bankrolled Alamoudi's American Muslim Foundation, as well. And tax records filed by the foundation, meanwhile, list Mohamed Omeish as a vice president. Interestingly, Alamoudi's old office is located in the same office park with Abdullah bin Laden's old office and al-Hanooti's Grand Mufti office.

It gets even cozier. Right next door to Alamoudi's old office is the main office of the Muslim American Society, where Esam Omeish serves as president. He sits on the society's board with four other Dar al-Hijrah directors. The society has strong ties to the Muslim Brotherhood, considered by investigators to be a terrorist organization. In fact, it was founded by Brotherhood members.[19] Dar al-Hijrah imam Mohamad Adam el-Sheikh, in fact, is a Brotherhood member. It is one big happy family at Dar al-Hijrah. Esam Omeish lives in a new brick house on a pipe-stem road in Falls Church across the street from the Skyline Towers popular with Saudi diplomats. Interestingly, a neighbor of his is Abbas Ebrahim, the former bookkeeper for terrorist supporter Soliman Biheiri. He started an Islamic investment bank that included Marzook and Abdullah bin Laden as major investors. Biheiri, a member of the Muslim Brotherhood, was recently convicted of lying about his connections to Marzook in an investigation into his terrorist ties.

It was not the first time that the Dar al-Hijrah congregation had rallied around Elbarasse. In 1998, he was sent to a federal prison in New York after refusing to testify in a Hamas case. But the mosque raised tens of thousands of dollars for a campaign to pressure the Clinton administration into releasing him. And it worked. Then-Attorney General Janet Reno freed him several months later.

Abdelhaleem Ashqar: Ashqar also became a hero in the Dar al-Hijrah community when he, too, refused to testify against accused fellow Muslims in the same Hamas case. He even went on a hunger strike. Reno released him, as well, not long after he was jailed for contempt. More than three hundred well-wishers turned out at Dar al-Hijrah for his homecoming in October 1998.[20]

But it turned out to be premature. After 9/11, Ashqar found himself back in jail on new contempt charges after refusing to answer grand jury questions about Hamas and whether he was a member of the terror group. But Dar al-Hijrah came to his rescue again. He was released on one million dollars bond after members of the mosque—including no less than its administrative director, Samir Abo-Issa—put up their homes as collateral, according to court records I obtained.[21]

Last year, however, U.S. prosecutors indicted Ashqar along with Marzook for raising millions of dollars for Hamas terrorism, landing him back in the slammer. The Palestinian activist founded the al-Aqsa Educational Fund, "another fundraising organization acting as a Hamas front," according to investigator Kane of Homeland Security. It is also part of the Safa group run by Barzinji, one of the founders of Dar al-Hijrah.[22] Also, Ashqar is said to have organized the 1993 Hamas summit in Philly.

Ashqar's day job was teaching at Howard University, a predominantly black school in Washington where Abdul-Malik has also worked, as the campus Muslim chaplain.

Ashqar's wife says the Jews are behind her husband's prosecution. "This is an Israeli witch hunt," Asma Ashqar claims.[23]

She teaches at a nearby Islamic school affiliated with Dar al-Hijrah, which was denied county permission to operate a fulltime school on its property. Called the Washington Islamic Academy, the K–6 school does not exactly have a reputation for teaching tolerance. It uses Saudi and Pakistani textbooks that call Christian beliefs "nonsense" and portray Jews as treacherous people who "oppress" others. Its young Muslim students are discouraged from accepting American culture. "We want it to be a place where they don't have to assimilate, where they can practice their religion," says Majida Zeiter, the academy's Islamic studies teacher. "We teach them what it takes to be a good Muslim." On world maps hanging in the classrooms, Israel is missing. References to Israel in education materials are blackened out with markers, with "Palestine" written in Israel's place.[24]

The anti-Israeli bias can also be seen in the bookstore that Dar al-Hijrah operates behind its mosque, which is favored by Washington's Palestinian community. The store is in the basement of the original stone ranch house where the widow who sold the property lived. On sale inside are bas reliefs of the Holy Land embossed with the words "beautiful Palestine," with no signs of Israel in the picture. Many of the members of Dar al-Hijrah—which means "Land of Migration"—are Palestinian refugees who object to U.S. foreign policy and sympathize with Hamas's stated goal of establishing an Islamic Palestinian state in place of Israel.

There is also a gender bias at Dar al-Hijrah. While walking to the bookstore, I noticed a sign in the back of the mosque near a dumpster that says, "Women's Entrance." It turns out female worshippers have to enter the building through a separate rear door. And they cannot worship with the men in the large prayer room, decorated with ornate red rugs, dark-wood pillars, and domed skylights. They have to worship apart from the men in an upstairs balcony. "Their culture is so much different than ours," laments Needham, the neighbor across the street.

Ahmed Abu Ali: He attended Dar al-Hijrah while growing up in Falls Church, before recently moving to Saudi to study Islam. In 2003, he was imprisoned on suspicions he was involved in the so-called Virginia jihad network. The FBI has argued in court that Abu Ali received terrorist training at an al-Qaida camp and aspired to be a planner of terrorist attacks against America. He is considered a player in the terror game with significant ties to al-Qaida.[25]

Nawaf al-Hazmi and *Hani Hanjour:* They both worshipped at Dar al-Hijrah for several weeks in the spring of 2001 (at the same time the White House was

117

inviting Dar al-Hijrah officials to interfaith meetings). Hanjour was the al-Qaida hijacker who flew the jumbo jet into the Pentagon. Hazmi was the second in command behind hijacking ringleader Mohamed Atta, and he joined Hanjour on the Pentagon flight. At least one member of the mosque helped them obtain driver's licenses and housing before the hijacking.

Other 9/11 hijackers more than likely attended the mosque, as well. Ahmed al-Ghamdi and Majed Moqed roomed with Hazmi and Hanjour in an apartment not far from the mosque. Moreover, Salem al-Hazmi, who was part of the Pentagon cell, listed an address on Row Street similar to that of the mosque when he applied for a bank account. Investigators suspect he also worshipped there.

Ramzi Bin al-Shibh: He did not attend Dar al-Hijrah, but the phone number to the mosque was found in his apartment in Germany, where he roomed with Atta. Bin al-Shibh, now in U.S. custody, was a key planner of the 9/11 attacks.

Then there is the former Dar al-Hijrah imam who privately ministered to some of the 9/11 hijackers. He deserves special attention.

13

THE 9/11 IMAM

Letting a "Terrorist" Go Free

"*Terrorist* is defined as any person who is known to have engaged in terrorist activities, is suspected of engaging in terrorist activities, intends to engage in terrorist activities, or is an associate of someone known or suspected to have engaged, or who is intending to engage, in terrorist activities; to include any level of planning, supporting, recruiting, or funding for the activity or terrorist organization."

—from list of official definitions distributed to
U.S. border authorities by Department of Homeland Security[1]

Hale Smith converted to Islam after marrying a Muslim. The San Francisco attorney changed his name to Abdul Haleem, studied the Quran, and regularly attended mosque. The new Muslim continued to ask questions about his adopted faith, often plying his Muslim boss with them at work. But the questions began to annoy his employer, who suspected Smith might be inclined toward heresy. "He thought I was too heterodox," Smith tells me, "so he arranged for me to go on *hajj* and see the real Islam."

His boss, who owns an airport limousine service, spared no expense in arranging the pilgrimage to Saudi Arabia for his general counsel. He even made sure Smith roomed with the imam assigned to the trip, a well-respected, English-speaking cleric who had official connections with the Saudi custodians of Islam's holiest shrines in Mecca and Medina.

In late February 2001, Smith joined about thirty other pilgrims, some also from the Bay Area, at a convening point in Washington D.C. where they picked up their *hajj* visas from the Saudi Embassy. The group, which included a podiatrist, a computer programmer, and a cardiologist, boarded a flight to Frankfurt, Germany, where it met the trip imam. He was the picture of piety with his dark bushy beard, oval-shaped glasses, and long green robe. Smith introduced himself to his new roommate, and the two quickly bonded. Lufthansa had lost Smith's luggage in the transfer to the connecting flight to Medina, so the imam took him to a bazaar there to buy some clothes, helping him negotiate prices in Arabic.

At their Sheraton hotel room, however, the cleric turned all business. "He just talked Islam, Islam, Islam," Smith, 49, recalls. "He was very orthodox, very by-the-book." He told his pupil he had been raised in Yemen, an al-Qaida hotbed and home to the port where the USS *Cole* was attacked, and studied at a madrassa there. "He received his training as a sheikh in Yemen and was a very hard-line Sunni," Smith learned.

But he did not understand the full extremes of his roommate's views until he saw him interact with other clerics on the tour. "He and the other imams were very intolerant of non-Muslims—especially Jews," Smith says. During a tour of a plant in Medina where the Quran is printed, and where women are not allowed beyond a waiting room, their anti-Semitic passions boiled over. "Any time the subject of Israel came up, these guys got hot, real hot," Smith says. "They said we should be waging holy war against the Jews. They praised the Palestinian suicide bombers as martyrs and talked about raising money for them." He says the head of the printing plant joined them in the Jew-bashing.

"They believe even partitioning is wrong; they want the whole thing—all of Israel," he adds. "They really want to slay Israel."

One of the other imams, a heavy-set, bearded man, made fundraising appeals for Palestinians on the West Bank and boasted that a charitable group he helps run in America called the Holy Land Foundation was giving aid to families of Hamas suicide bombers, Smith says.

The talk only grew more belligerent as their Saudi trip extended into March. After visiting Medina, the group traveled by private, air-conditioned buses to Mecca, where Smith and his pious bunkmate checked into a room at the luxurious Ajyad Makkah Hotel.

It was not until long after the 9/11 attacks that Smith realized, to his shock, that the spiritual guide he shared a double occupancy room with in Mecca and Medina was also the spiritual adviser to some of the al-Qaida hijackers. His name: Anwar N. Aulaqi.

"I went on *hajj* with this terrorist!" Smith exclaimed in a recent exclusive interview with me. He says the experience turned him off to Islam, and he left the faith after 9/11.

It turns out that his "executive-package" trip to the Saudi holy land was arranged through a travel agency in Falls Church, Virginia, just down the road from the Dar al-Hijrah Islamic Center where Aulaqi preached and helped the hijackers. The Dar El-Eiman travel agency, which books "Sheikh" Aulaqi for special tours, is located in the same building as the U.S. branch of the Saudi-based Muslim World League, a suspected charitable front for al-Qaida. Right next door to the agency's office on the first floor of the building is the small Dar al-Arqam mosque that featured the Saudi-tied imam now under federal indictment for encouraging several young Muslims from the area to wage holy war against America.

Smith's itinerary from Dar El-Eiman lists Aulaqi as the "Imam on Trip."[2] Listed directly under him is a trip adviser named Mohammed El-Mezain of San Diego, who happens to be the co-founder of the Holy Land Foundation arrested last year on charges of funneling millions of dollars to Hamas.[3] El-Mezain and Aulaqi knew each other from San Diego. Before going to jail, El-Mezain headed Holy Land Foundation's San Diego office and, like Aulaqi, served as a leader in local mosques there. Aulaqi preached in a San Diego mosque for four years before moving in January 2001 to Falls Church to lead prayers at Dar al-Hijrah.

There is more to the connection. El-Mezain is a cousin of Mousa Abu Marzook, the political leader of Hamas and a terrorist fugitive. Before Marzook fled the United States, he lived in Falls Church and attended Dar al-Hijrah. Smith says El-Mezain acted as a trip scholar answering *fiqh* questions about Islamic law and did not actually go on the group tour of Saudi. (He is separate from the burly imam who during the tour acknowledged financing Hamas through the Holy Land Foundation, which is on the U.S. Department of Treasury's blacklist of specially designated terrorist entities. That imam, also a major player in the illegal Muslim charity, was known simply as "Sheikh Ibrahim," says Smith).

SHOCKED, SHOCKED!

In early April 2001, after Aulaqi returned from the Saudi trip, two young Saudi men showed up at his Falls Church mosque. One was Nawaf al-Hazmi, the second in command behind the *emir* or leader of the 9/11 operation, Mohamed Atta. The other was Hani Hanjour, the pilot of the plane that hit the Pentagon. Both had made their way across the United States from San Diego, where Aulaqi had previously ministered to Hazmi and another Saudi hijacker in closed-door meetings at his former mosque. Investigators believe their reunion in Falls Church was not coincidental, given the remarkable coincidence of Aulaqi's prior close relationship with Hazmi.

In fact, they suspect Aulaqi tasked a member of the Falls Church mosque to help Hazmi and Hanjour find an apartment. The member, Eyad al-Rababah, dutifully had them over for tea and set them up with a friend who had an apartment to rent nearby.[4] (Interestingly, Hazmi listed on bank account applications an apparently false address similar to the 3159 Row Street address of the mosque. Law enforcement records show Aulaqi lived at the mosque, which keeps apartments in an old stone house on the property.)

A week after the strike on the Pentagon, FBI agents paid a visit to the imam to find out more about Hazmi and Hanjour. Aulaqi expressed shock that terrorists attended both of the mosques he led, and he claimed to be unaware of even any zealotry among his worshippers. Agents showed Aulaqi a photograph of Hazmi, and he recognized his face but claimed not to know his name, even though he admitted to meeting with Hazmi several times in San Diego. He also claimed not to recall any specifics of what they discussed. What's more, he denied having any contact with Hazmi or Hanjour while they were in Virginia.[5]

But it would not be the first time the thirty-three-year-old Aulaqi has made claims that do not hold up under closer scrutiny. For example, he has repeatedly claimed New Mexico as his birthplace. It is even the first highlight listed in his biographical sketches posted on Islamic Web sites. But federal law enforcement records I have obtained indicate he was born in Aden, Yemen, on April 21, 1971, and first came to the U.S. as a Yemeni citizen on a J-1 research-scholar visa on June 5, 1990.[6] Also, a search of state vital records in New Mexico turns up no birth certificate for Aulaqi. No matches were found for Las Cruces, Santa Fe, or any other city in New Mexico by using Anwar Nasser Aulaqi or his aliases, al-Awlaki or al-Awlakhi, with his date of birth.[7] His story is contradicted even by Islamic Web sites. A biographical sketch posted on the Islamic Society of North America's Islamic media store says he was "born and raised in the U.S.," yet a bio posted by the Muslim Community Association of the San Francisco Bay Area describes him as living with his parents for "eleven years" in Yemen, where he "received his early Islamic education."

"THERE'S A LOT OF SMOKE THERE"

Still, the FBI bought his stories. It believed his relationship with the hijackers "appeared innocuous" and concluded that he was merely a "spiritual leader" to many in the community and therefore blameless.

The bureau believed this even though the FBI agent responsible for the 9/11 investigation told congressional investigators "there's a lot of smoke there" with regard to the imam's connection to the hijackers. Several individuals informed the FBI after 9/11 that Aulaqi had closed-door meetings in San Diego with Hazmi, as well as with Hazmi's roommate there at the time, Khalid al-Mihdhar, a muscle hijacker from Saudi who left the country briefly to visit family in Yemen and did not travel with Hazmi and Hanjour across the country to Virginia. One witness remembered meeting Hazmi through Aulaqi and Mohdar Abdullah—a facilitator who reportedly knew of the hijackers' evil plans—and later meeting Mihdhar at Aulaqi's mosque. This same source recalled seeing Hazmi and Mihdhar in the guest room on the second floor of Aulaqi's San Diego mosque. And on one occasion, he recalled the two leaving the room just after Aulaqi at the end of a meeting.[8]

That was in 2000. By January 2001, Aulaqi had moved to Falls Church to take over pulpit duties at the Dar al-Hijrah mosque. Within just three months of his arrival there, he was back attending to Hazmi, the leader of the Pentagon cell who had followed him there with Hanjour, the pilot.

At the same time, a key planner of the 9/11 attacks, Ramzi Bin al-Shibh, who lived clear across the Atlantic in Germany, kept the phone number of Aulaqi's new mosque among his personal contact information. Bin al-Shibh shared an apartment with Atta, the hijacking ringleader, before Atta entered the U.S. to begin taking flying lessons. (There is no evidence to suggest that Aulaqi was in contact with Bin al-Shibh or Atta prior to the attacks, but investigators consider the discovery of the phone number intriguing. Aulaqi was known to store phone numbers in a Palm Pilot. Investigators found data for seven known terrorists on the Palm Pilot they confiscated from confessed terrorist Abdurahman Alamoudi, another Dar al-Hijrah member.)

That the FBI would accept Aulaqi's story that his relationship with the hijackers was just coincidental to his job as a spiritual leader in the community is even more vexing when you consider that FBI agents in the San Diego field office had suspected the imam was up to no good before the hijackers even showed up at his mosque there. In fact, agents believed he had ties with terrorists who had tried to blow up New York landmarks last decade.

Field agents opened a counterterrorism investigation on Aulaqi in June 1999. During the probe, they discovered that he may have contacted a number of other persons of investigative interest—including a possible procurement agent for Osama bin Laden, according to FBI special agent Wade Ammerman.[9] In early 2000, Aulaqi met with an ally of Blind Sheik Omar Abdel Rahman, the spiritual leader of the terrorists who bombed the World Trade Center in 1993. Just before the Egyptian cleric was convicted of conspiring to blow up New York City tunnels and the United Nations building in 1995, his group had moved its operations from the East Coast to San Diego.

There is more to the blind cleric connection. Osama Bassnan, a bin Laden supporter from Saudi, also befriended the hijackers in San Diego and mixed in the same local circles with Aulaqi. He too came under FBI scrutiny at one point last decade for hosting a party in Washington for the Blind Sheikh. Bassnan and his family, coincidentally, received substantial financial assistance from the Saudi ambassador to Washington prior to 9/11. What's more, Aulaqi spoke at a joint Islamic Circle of North America-Muslim American Society convention in Baltimore in July 2002 with Siraj Wahhaj, the Brooklyn imam who defended the Blind Sheikh. Wahhaj was named as an unindicted co-conspirator in the 1993 World Trade Center bombing case. So was Muhammad al-Hanooti, who handed over the pulpit to Aulaqi at Dar al-Hijrah. As discussed in the previous chapter, Hanooti was close to the Blind Sheikh.

Hanooti, moreover, was the subject of a separate FBI counterterrorism investigation involving fundraising for Hamas suicide bombers through the Holy Land Foundation. Likewise, the FBI learned during its probe of Aulaqi that he knew individuals from the Holy Land Foundation, such as El-Mezain, and others involved in raising cash for Hamas.

Even so, the FBI did not consider any of the information it gathered on Aulaqi strong enough to support a criminal prosecution, and it dropped the case in early 2000—just as the hijackers began meeting with the imam behind closed doors in San Diego.[10] And nothing came of the follow-up by the bureau's Washington field office after 9/11.

"MY MUSLIM BROTHERS"

With the heat off him, Aulaqi brazenly made unsympathetic comments about 9/11 in the press, his words dripping with contempt for America and its alliance with Israel.

- For instance, he said during the last week of September 2001, as bodies were still being pulled from Ground Zero, that "these ideas of terrorists might come out of a place where the U.S. has messed up" in foreign policy.[11]

- He expounded in a separate interview that same week that America had brought on Muslim hatred mainly by supporting Israel. "The feeling that America is against us, I would say, is a majority," he said. "The people feel that America is against us because of the support of Israel, and the embargo on Iraq. The embargo on Iraq had a devastating effect on the people."[12]

- In the same interview, Aulaqi cautioned America against provoking more Muslims in its retaliation for the attacks. "The U.S. needs to be very careful and not have itself perceived as an enemy of Islam," he warned.[13]

- As U.S. forces struck Afghanistan in early October, the Muslim preacher implied they were wasting their time, because Osama bin Laden and his jihadists could not be intimidated. He even seemed to harbor respect for the hijackers. "People were willing to kill themselves on September 11, and a few missiles won't intimidate them," Aulaqi said.[14]

- Asked if he would help America fight terrorism, Aulaqi said he would call for peace and justice instead. By justice, he meant ending the West's alleged ill-treatment of Muslims around the world—including occupation of their lands—that gives rise to terrorism. "I believe force can suppress terrorism," Aulaqi said. "But only justice can erase it."[15]

- In mid-November 2001, he defended the Taliban as former freedom fighters who brought peace to the areas where they lived. And he criticized the Bush administration's targeting of them. "The Taliban repeatedly said: show us the evidence and we will turn over whoever is guilty with the crime. The U.S. should have given them the benefit of the doubt," he argued. Instead, it is "killing my Muslim brothers and sisters in Afghanistan."[16]

- In a separate interview around the same time, he argued that instead of bombing Muslim countries, the U.S. should be rethinking the foreign policies that stir up resentment in those countries. Aulaqi says 9/11 created an opportunity for change. "In the past, Muslims have been raising concerns regarding the U.S. foreign policy," he said. "I think now that not only should we be talking about these legitimate issues, but also how they should be acted upon."[17]

- In the same interview, Aulaqi decried what he characterized as America's harsh treatment of Muslims after 9/11 and suggested that they were the real victims. "There has been a rise in negative reporting on Islam in the media since the events happened. There have been 1,100 Muslims detained in the U.S. There's a bombing going on over a Muslim country, Afghanistan," he complained. "So there are some reasons that make the Muslims feel that it is the Muslims who are being hurt."[18]

- Even after the December 2001 release of a videotape of bin Laden asserting his advance knowledge of the attacks, the imam seemed to take delight in a conspiracy theory still bandied about by members of his Dar al-Hijrah flock that Israelis, not Muslims, perpetrated the attacks on America to tar Muslims. How could they cling to such notions after watching the video on TV? "There isn't a lot of trust in the U.S. media, or U.S. officials' position on anything," Aulaqi explained.[19]

• When asked to condemn the 9/11 terrorism, Aulaqi was coy. He vaguely denounced the killing of "civilians," while slipping in more elbows at America for its Middle East policies. "Even if someone has disagreement with U.S. policy, even if someone feels personally hurt by people dying in Iraq and Palestine, we don't take revenge by killing civilians," he said.[20]

Smith says that although his soft-spoken ex-roommate may at times appear to strike a moderate tone, he is not moderate at all, but a skilled dissembler. "Any lie that advances Islam is good, and this guy by personality could practice that and get away with it," he tells me. "He doesn't get angry like other imams. He has a very low-key personality. He is very smart. The raging imams wouldn't be able to get away with it like him."

Yet like those fiery types, "Aulaqi is deep into hardcore militant Islam," he adds. "He is not a cleric who just says prayers and counsels people as some of his supporters have suggested."

At the time of the attacks, Aulaqi also served as the official Muslim chaplain to the throngs of young Muslim men enrolled at George Washington University just a few blocks from the White House. He himself was enrolled at the university as a doctoral candidate.[21] He also counseled young Muslims as an imam in Fort Collins, Colorado, where he studied engineering at Colorado State University and lived on the edge of campus in the early 1990s. Aulaqi has bounced around a lot since then, coming into contact with untold numbers of Hazmi wannabes.[22]

ON THE TERRORIST WATCHLIST

Unlike their counterparts in the FBI, U.S. Customs investigators were not so quick to let Aulaqi off the hook. They have been looking at him for possible terrorist fundraising since 9/11.

According to information in government documents disclosed publicly here for the first time, Customs agents had opened three separate investigations of Aulaqi in the so-called Green Quest operation initially led by the Department of Treasury to dry up funding for terrorists.

One of the investigations—filed as Case Number: HO02PI02HO0005—involves Aulaqi's connection to the subject of a Joint Terrorism Task Force investigation that originated with the Customs office in Houston. "RADWAN

ABU-ISSA—SUBJECT OF HOUSTON JTTF INVESTIGATION—SENT MONEY TO AULAQI," states a document from the federal database called the Treasury Enforcement Communications System, or TECS II for short.[23] Abu-Issa is a forty-one-year-old Syrian national who has been in the U.S. since at least 1997. A research scholar and Muslim activist, he has taken Saudi flights in and out of the country since 9/11. He now lives in Houston. Attempts to reach him at his Houston residence were unsuccessful.

The law enforcement document lists the lead investigator in the case as Pamela L. Rhames, an FBI agent who was detailed over to Customs after 9/11 and now works in the Houston office of the Joint Terrorism Task Force. Contacted at her office, Rhames refused to talk about the investigation.

Aulaqi also was the subject of a Green Quest investigation in Washington led by Michael S. Tutko, a senior special agent with Customs. The case—Number DC02PU02DC0014—apparently has been closed.[24] The U.S. Customs Service, and with it Operation Green Quest, have been transferred to the Bureau of Immigration and Customs Enforcement—better known as ICE—within the Department of Homeland Security, which has renamed the terrorism-financing operation and shared some of its portfolio with the FBI.

Separately, Aulaqi is the subject of a "current" terror-finance investigation led by senior ICE agent David C. Kane, who has been following the financial trail of the leaders of a Virginia group suspected of aiding Islamic terrorists. The Safa group, as it is called, is funded by wealthy Saudis. One of its leaders, Jamal Barzinji, signed the deed for the Dar al-Hijrah mosque where Aulaqi preached. The document describing the Kane case says Aulaqi is the "SUBJECT OF CURRENT INVESTIGATION," listing the case under the category "FINANCIAL." It describes him as the "FORMER IMAM OF DAR AL-HIJRAH MOSQUE IN FALLS CHURCH, VIRGINIA."[25]

Because of the investigations, Aulaqi was added to the terrorist watchlist maintained by federal law enforcement. In late 2002, customs agents in New York thought they had their man when he tried to reenter the U.S. after a trip to the Middle East.

On October 10, 2002, Anwar Nasser Aulaqi arrived at John F. Kennedy International Airport on Saudi Arabian Airlines Flight 35. He gave an address of 3159 Row Street, Falls Church, Virginia—the Dar al-Hijrah mosque. An immigration inspector processing his paperwork noticed he was a match on the terrorist lookout list, according to the results of the primary inspection, a copy of which I obtained. The inspector immediately referred Aulaqi to secondary for questioning. "REASON FOR REFERRAL: ANTI-TERRORIST PASSENGER," states the secondary inspection report. The lanky Aulaqi—described as 6 feet 1 inch, 160 pounds, with black hair and black eyes—was hustled off to the customs inspections area where his bags were searched.

Next, agents escorted Aulaqi and his family to the customs detention area, according to the incident log I obtained. A supervisor was called in as agents realized they had a big fish in their net. Then, a flurry of calls was made to Washington to notify officials there that they had the subject of multiple counterterrorism investigations in custody.

One of the first calls went out to Kane, the special agent at Customs, who informed the authorities at JFK that he would consult with headquarters and also "reach out" to FBI special agent Wade Ammerman, who previously had followed Aulaqi out of the bureau's Washington field office. About an hour later, Kane called back the supervisor at the airport with some disappointing news—they would have to release the imam from custody for diplomatic reasons. "RECEIVED A CALL FROM S/A KANE NOTIFYING US THE WARRANT ISSUED BY THE STATE DEPT. HAD BEEN PULLED BACK," the incident log says. FBI special agent Nick Pindulic called from the Washington field office to confirm that "THE WARRANT HAD BEEN REMOVED ON 10/9."[26]

THE ALL-SAUDI CELL

So there was a U.S. warrant outstanding for the imam's arrest. Yet it was withdrawn on October 9—the day before he arrived. It looks as if someone pulled some diplomatic strings for Aulaqi in Washington, indicating he perhaps has some powerful patrons.

The supervisor ordered the agents to release Aulaqi, and they in effect were forced to apologize to him and his family for detaining them for what lasted a full three hours. "PASSENGERS RELEASED WITH THANKS FOR THEIR PATIENS [sic] AND GIVEN THE COMMENT CARD," the incident log says. And with that, a "Saudi representative" escorted Aulaqi to his connecting flight to Washington, where he stayed for a short while "to close out his business," an associate tells me, before hightailing it back to Yemen.

It would not be the first time Washington let potential terror suspects with Saudi connections leave the country without thoroughly investigating them.

Immediately after 9/11, the Saudi Embassy appealed to the Department of State and White House to help protect Saudi nationals from possible retaliation by spiriting them out of the country. Within days, nine flights were specially chartered for the evacuation of 142 well-connected Saudis. The 9/11 Commission revealed in a footnote that the FBI in fact did *not* interview "most of the passengers" before they departed[27]—even though the bureau knew at the time that three-fourths of the 9/11 hijackers were Saudi nationals, some of whom the CIA says received support from the Saudi government while they were living in the U.S. And it gave them a pass even though wealthy Saudis, including members of the royal family, have underwritten Saudi native Osama bin Laden's operations for years.[28]

Aulaqi's connections to the Saudi hijackers and their connections to Saudi officials are noteworthy.

Hazmi headed the only all-Saudi cell involved in the 9/11 plot. He and the other four members—Hanjour, Mihdhar, Majed Moqed, and Salem al-Hazmi—were all Saudi nationals, while some of the operatives in the three other cells involved in 9/11 were from Egypt or the United Arab Emirates or Lebanon. All five hijackers aboard the flight that hit the Pentagon were Saudi citizens, while the other three suicide flights each had at least one non-Saudi on board. And the Pentagon operation was the one that bin Laden saved his most experienced pilot (Hanjour) for. He also singled out leader Hazmi for praise in recorded messages released after 9/11. For whatever reason, this cell and its target were special.

And the cell appeared to attract the attention of Saudi government officials. On the front end of the operation, Hazmi got support through the Saudi consulate in Los Angeles, which seemed to be expecting his arrival, and directly from a suspected Saudi government agent in San Diego. The alleged intelligence agent, Omar al-Bayoumi, threw a welcoming party for Hazmi and Mihdhar as if they were celebrities or heroes. And on the eve of the Pentagon attack, Hazmi and the other members of his cell stayed in the same Washington-area hotel as the Saudi minister of mosques.

At the same time, Hazmi hooked up with a spiritual handler who appeared to be tight with the Saudi government, which officially sponsored him to take American Muslims on pilgrimages to the country's two great mosques. "To get recognized as a *hajj* tour guide by the Saudis, you have to have connections over there," Haleem says, noting that all of their travel documents were processed in one day by the Saudi Embassy. "You don't just get permission to lead tours. You have to be in with the Saudis."

They also gave the cleric their blessing to lecture at the Institute for Islamic and Arabic Sciences in America, an arm of the Saudi government. And of course, the Saudis had a say in his appointment as imam of the Dar al-Hijrah mosque they controlled through the North American Islamic Trust. In fact, Ali al-Ahmed of the reformist Saudi Institute says he assumed Aulaqi was a Saudi when he met the imam there during the funeral of a friend's wife just prior to 9/11. "He spoke like a Saudi," Ahmed tells me. "I found out later he was born in Yemen."[29] There at Dar al-Hijrah, Aulaqi maintained the close contact he had established with

Hazmi in San Diego. Their relationship continued, remarkably, from one coast to the other, as if a third party had assigned one to the other.

The Saudi-backed cleric is also tied to the suspected Saudi agent Bayoumi through four phone calls placed between Aulaqi's phone and Bayoumi's phone on the day Bayoumi helped Hazmi and Mihdhar find an apartment in San Diego.[30]

Aulaqi's long, full beard belies his youth. He was just twenty-nine at the time he was ministering to the hijackers. He was young like them and could relate to them. And investigators say the hijackers in turn revered him as a religious figure and developed a close relationship with him.

While Aulaqi is unfamiliar to non-Muslims, he is wildly popular among young Muslims, particularly jihadists, and somewhat of a celebrity in the Muslim underworld. He is a highly sought-after lecturer who has put out several CDs on martyrdom and the rewards bestowed upon them in Paradise. If you want to know more about the "seven badges of honor" awarded the martyr in *akhirah* or the hereafter, or about the women of Paradise, or how to prepare yourself to be a martyr, Aulaqi is the dean with all the answers. For example, his forty-dollar CD, "The Hereafter," takes young male listeners on a tour of Paradise that includes "riveting" descriptions of "the mansions of Paradise," "the women of Paradise," and "the greatest of the pleasures of Paradise."[31]

"THE GREAT EDGE"

After he departed the U.S. for good, Aulaqi slipped into a Muslim community in London where he encouraged other young Muslim men to be *shaheeds*, or martyrs, while giving a series of lectures in December 2002 and January 2003 at a mosque there called Masjid at-Tawhid. In the lectures—sponsored by the registered U.K. charity Jam'iat Ihyaa' Minhaaj al-Sunnah, or JIMAS—Aulaqi argued that the rewards offered to martyrs in *Jennah*, or Paradise, give them a "great edge" over ordinary believers and should make every Muslim "eager" to give his life in fighting the unbelievers in the cause of Allah. Here is the relevant portion of a transcript I obtained of his hour-long sermon titled, "Paradise":

> Don't think that the ones that die in the sake of Allah are dead—they are alive, and Allah is providing for them. So the shaheed is alive in the sense that his soul is in Jennah, and his soul is alive in Jennah. Really the shaheed is way up of everyone else. What the shaheed is given are things that are unique that nobody else gets. When it comes to shahada, you could say that they are head and shoulders above everyone else. A crown will be placed upon his head. The shaheed will not suffer the pain of death and

will not have to go through the horror and terror of the day of judgment. It is enough that he had to go through seeing the glittering of the swords before his eyes. So this should make every one of you the more eager to be a shaheed, when you see the great edge that is given to the shaheeds.

While Aulaqi appears to be more a man of the sword than a man of the cloth, he is only being true to the Quran, which preaches the same militant message to the faithful, as demonstrated in earlier chapters. The imam is a true believer who believes that militancy and martyrdom are integral to advancing Islam. When you combine those militant beliefs with his established ties to Muslim militants closely associated with the Blind Sheikh and other terrorists involved in plots to blow up New York buildings, it is not an unrealistic notion that he would sympathize with members of his flock who had the same ambitions. And considering he may be tied to an al-Qaida procurement agent, it is not implausible that he would sympathize with al-Qaida terrorists under his counsel.

Sympathizing is one thing. Question is, did he encourage them?

Smith, for one, says he would not be surprised if his former roommate and *hajj* guru prepared the hijackers for martyrdom knowing full well what they were about to do. "This guy could be a soldier," he says of Aulaqi. "He could very soberly carry out whatever advances Islam with absolute dispassion and coldness. He is very focused, very committed to the cause."

After his stay in London, Aulaqi returned to Yemen where sources say he is studying *sharia* law with prominent sheikhs. A former associate of his at Dar al-Hijrah tells me Aulaqi has entertained job offers from the Saudi government to preach and teach Islam in the kingdom.[32]

Congress released the findings of its 9/11 investigation in December 2002. The final report scolded the FBI for failing to adequately investigate Aulaqi. "The investigation was closed despite the imam's contacts with other subjects of counterterrorism investigations and reports concerning the imam's connection to suspect organizations," said the report, which censored Aulaqi's name in addition to the Saudi material.[33] A publicly embarrassed FBI brass subsequently reopened their investigation of Aulaqi and his activities at the mosques in San Diego and outside the nation's capital.

But first they had to find him. They had let him go *just two months earlier* after having him in custody in New York.

Smith around this time offered to tell the FBI all he knew about his *hajj* roommate. But he says the bureau was not interested. "I called the FBI and told them I roomed with this guy for two weeks on *hajj*, and they weren't even interested enough to take my name or number," he says. Smith also e-mailed a tip to the Department of Homeland Security, but he says he never received a response.

Last year, the independent 9/11 Commission agreed with the findings of congressional investigators and expressed further concerns about the cleric. "The circumstances surrounding his relationship with the hijackers remain suspicious," commission investigators said.[34] Did Aulaqi know what the hijackers were up to? Did he prepare them spiritually for their suicide mission? The investigators wanted to ask him but could not find him after he fled the country with the help of higher-ups in the U.S. government.

"By the time we sought to interview him in 2003, he had left the United States, reportedly returning to Yemen," the commission said in its final report. "We attempted to locate and interview him in Yemen, working with U.S. agencies and the Yemeni government, as well as other governments that might have knowledge of his whereabouts." However, "Those attempts were unsuccessful," the panel said.[35]

Aulaqi's whereabouts are still unknown, and Yemeni government officials have not been very helpful, even though the government originally sponsored his studies in America. He came here on a Yemeni government scholarship.

It is anyone's guess how many other young Muslims the 9/11 imam is preparing for martyrdom.

IV
LAW ENFORCEMENT
INFILTRATION

14

CONGRESS AND THE FBI

Playing Politics with Security

"There were a few members on the Hill that were outraged that we would ask for help from the Arab-American community. And this outrage was mainly from members who had Arab-American voters in their districts."

—former FBI special agent ROBERT M. BLITZER, assistant chief of the bureau's counterterrorism section[1]

The FBI has taken a lot of heat for missing the 9/11 plot, especially from Congress. But Congress did not exactly help the bureau catch terrorists before 9/11. In fact, just a year before the attacks, some members effectively blocked reforms that would have made it easier for agents to monitor terrorist suspects. Why? They did not want them "spying" on the Muslim community.

Rewind to 1999. That year, Congress commissioned a nearly two-million-dollar study to determine the best ways to fight terrorism in the wake of the al-Qaida bombings of U.S. embassies in Africa. The National Commission on Terrorism delivered its findings to Congress the following year. Its conclusions about the terror threat and its recommendations for protecting America, as it turns out, were amazingly farsighted.

The bipartisan panel, led by Ambassador L. Paul Bremer, warned that religiously motivated groups, namely al-Qaida, were hell-bent on inflicting "mass casualties on American soil." They "represent a growing trend toward hatred of the United States," it said, and "may lack a concrete political goal other than to punish their enemies by killing as many of them as possible."[2] The sixty-four-page report even cited the risk of such Islamic terrorists slipping into the U.S. as foreign students and then launching attacks here.

All told, the panel made more than forty specific recommendations to Congress, including:

- Letting the CIA recruit "unsavory sources" to infiltrate and spy on terrorist cells.

- Establishing at the FBI a "cadre of reports officers to distill and disseminate terrorism-related information, once it is collected," to the CIA and other agencies, since "intelligence is the best weapon against terrorism."

- Making it easier for FBI agents to get authority from the Justice Department to conduct electronic surveillance on terrorist suspects in the Muslim community.

- Adding Afghanistan to the U.S. list of state sponsors of terrorism, cutting off aid and subjecting it to full sanctions.

- Creating a joint task force including Treasury, IRS, and U.S. Customs to track terrorist fundraising in the U.S. and freeze bank accounts of suspected charities and nonprofits.

- Creating a national computer database to track the visa status of foreign students on campuses across the country.

- Considering designating Pakistan among foreign governments "not cooperating fully" with U.S. counterterrorism efforts.[3]

Even though "Pakistan has cooperated on counterterrorism at times," the report said it "provides safe haven, transit, and moral, political, and diplomatic support to several groups engaged in terrorism." As it happened, much of the 9/11 plot was hatched in Pakistan.

Copies of the report—which got surprisingly little media coverage, even to this day—went out to members of Congress, as well as President Clinton and his national security team, and former CIA Director George Tenet and former FBI Director Louis Freeh.

Yet none of the prescient recommendations were implemented. Powerful members of Congress bristled at many of the key proposals, which they viewed as too intrusive and discriminatory toward Middle Easterners. And the entire final report, titled "Countering the Changing Threat of International Terrorism," collected dust on Capitol office shelves.

"It was frustrating," says Suzanne E. Spaulding, executive director of the National Commission on Terrorism. "We were disappointed."[4]

She told me that panel members were particularly surprised that officials did not at least adopt their idea to form a task force to crack down on terrorist fundraising, which seemed like an obvious countermeasure. And monitoring the immigration status of foreign students seemed a logical and relatively easy step, since a pilot computer program had already been started in 1996.

"We couldn't imagine them not doing such a recommendation," says former CIA Director James Woolsey, one of the commissioners.[5]

Not all members of Congress sneezed at the report.

Sen. Jon Kyl of Arizona, where al-Qaida first set up shop in the early 1990s, made "a heroic effort" to pass the reforms, Woolsey says. The Republican called commission members before his Technology, Terrorism, and Government Information Subcommittee to testify on their proposals. And he introduced with Democratic Sen. Dianne Feinstein of California a counterterrorism bill that incorporated many of them.

But Hill sources say the measure was blocked primarily by Democrats led by Sen. Patrick Leahy of Vermont, who at the time was the ranking Democrat on the Senate Judiciary Committee.

Leahy objected to, among other things, recommendations making it easier for the FBI to obtain warrants to search suspected terrorists' computers and sniff their e-mail.

"Leahy objected to key provisions in the bill and held it up," a Senate aide told me.[6]

"When it finally passed [the Senate] at the end of 2000, it was too watered down and diluted to have much effect," the aide said. "And coming as it did so late in the year, the House didn't really want to take it up."

Leahy says through a spokesman that then-Attorney General Janet Reno's office agreed with some of his objections, and that he supported the bill after controversial provisions were stripped from it.

"At the time, Sen. Leahy was the ranking member of the committee, and just as it's [GOP] Sen. [Orrin] Hatch's role now, he was taking into consideration concerns by the Department of Justice about this bill," argues Leahy aide David Carle.[7]

"Once the Department of Justice's issues were resolved, the senator worked with the bill's sponsors—Sen. Kyl and Sen. Feinstein—to help get it passed," he says.

"It died in the House," Carle adds, emphasizing that the House was controlled by Republicans.

Spaulding, who also praised Kyl's efforts, says Democrats were also swayed by media reports that "mischaracterized" the tracking of foreign students as "spying" on Middle Easterners.

The report explained that "thousands of people from countries officially designated as state sponsors of terrorism currently study in the United States," and though many enter on valid visas, many overstay their visas and remain here to live.

"Seven years ago," the report continued, "investigators discovered that one of the terrorists involved in bombing the World Trade Center had entered the United States on a student visa, dropped out, and remained illegally."

"Today, there is no mechanism for ensuring the same thing won't happen again," it said. Three of the 9/11 hijackers were in the U.S. on student visas, one illegally.

Woolsey says universities also fought the proposal. "From the uproar from university lobbyists, you would have thought we had proposed jackbooted SS agents following foreigners around on campus," he says.

Democratic Sen. Paul Sarbanes of Maryland also frowned on the report, taking exception in particular to its proposal to consider listing Greece along with Pakistan as a country not fully cooperating in U.S. counterterrorism efforts, says Spaulding, chairwoman of the American Bar Association's standing committee on law and national security. Sarbanes is the son of a Greek immigrant.

Some commissioners cannot help but wonder if the reforms, many of which were adopted after the 9/11 terrorism, could have headed off the tragedy had they been adopted in 2000. Many of the same proposals have been incorporated in anti-terrorism legislation such as the USA Patriot Act passed since the attacks.

"Taken as a whole, perhaps" the report's proposals could have headed off the attacks if implemented, said Maurice Sonnenberg, vice chairman of the commission.[8]

Sonnenberg, Woolsey, and the eight other commission members, along with their staff, spent about six months in 1999 and 2000 conducting some hundred and twenty interviews with counterterrorism experts inside and outside government. They also met with officials in Israel and other countries.

Commissioners did not let the FBI off the hook, criticizing its "risk-averse" culture and political correctness. They blamed the core agency responsible for investigating terrorism for throwing "bureaucratic and cultural obstacles" in the way of field agents trying to open probes of terrorist suspects. "A full investigation may be opened where there is a reasonable indication of a criminal violation, which is described as a standard 'substantially lower than probable cause,'" the report advised.

Just weeks before 9/11, supervisors at FBI headquarters fought Minneapolis agents seeking a warrant to search alleged twentieth hijacker Zacarias Moussaoui's apartment and computer, claiming they did not have enough cause, even though agents cited two criminal violations in their request. And they frowned on a proposal by an agent in Phoenix to question Middle Eastern men enrolled at flight schools across the country, because it might look racist.

The commission report, written more than a year before, said FBI guidelines contribute to "a risk-averse culture that causes some agents to refrain from taking prompt action against suspected terrorists." It urged the FBI to ease rules for opening such investigations and "direct agents in the field to investigate terrorist activity vigorously, using the full extent of their authority."

A full decade earlier, in wartime, some enterprising agents tried to do just that, and once again, Congress blocked the anti-terror efforts.

BACKING DOWN IN DETROIT

During the first Gulf war, Bill Baker had what many in law enforcement thought was a good, proactive idea to defend the homefront. The former senior FBI official launched from Washington an operation to gather information in the nation's major Arab and Muslim communities. The internal program was aimed at deterring terrorism.

FBI agents tried to cultivate Arab sources and informants who could lead them to terrorists and help them foil their plots. They questioned Arab-American leaders in Detroit and other areas with heavy concentrations of people of Arab descent about their political views. They also asked if they knew any terrorists and advised them to contact FBI field offices if they learned of planned acts of terror.

But instead of cooperating, leaders howled discrimination, even firing off a letter to then-FBI Director William Sessions. And members of Congress went to the media to complain. Before the operation could get much traction, the FBI backed off.

One member of Congress at the time, former Democratic Rep. David Bonior, whose old district is in the Detroit area, heard about the FBI interviews and cried racism. "Many Arab Americans are today living in fear that hostilities against them will increase as a result of events in the Middle East," he said. "Now they have a new fear—that the FBI initiative is increasing the climate for a backlash" against them. He and other Detroit-area Democrats like John Conyers and John Dingell threatened to hold hearings unless the FBI stopped the counterterrorism interviews. Baker, the FBI official who devised the program, met with them privately to explain the national-security benefits of it but could not allay their concerns.

"After a few weeks and many interviews, we backed off," laments former FBI special agent Robert M. Blitzer, who was assistant chief of the bureau's counterterrorism section. More than a decade later, Hamas, Hezbollah, the al-Qaida-tied Muslim Brotherhood, and other terrorist groups are still active in the Detroit area.

"There were a few members on the Hill that were outraged that we would ask for help from the Arab-American community," adds Blitzer, who says some of the small number of Arab Americans they were able to interview were "very negative and hostile."

"And this outrage was mainly from members who had Arab-American voters in their districts."[9]

FBI counterintelligence veteran I.C. Smith singled out Bonior for rebuke. "He led a hue and cry on the Hill about the good and decent Arab citizens being singled out," he says, "and the FBI pulled in its horns and dropped the program instead of explaining why they were doing it."[10] Bonior, who received thousands of dollars in donations from suspect Muslim leaders, went on to fight a number of other counterterrorism measures, including airport profiling. He even gave the son of donor Sami al-Arian, now in jail on terrorism charges, a job in his Washington office.[11]

At the same time, however, Smith points out that the "politically correct FBI" caved easily to the congressman's demands. Then as now, he says, headquarters would rather throttle an investigation than inflame the Muslim community. In fact, political correctness in the bureau has become "institutionalized," he says.

15

INSTITUTIONALIZED PC

Still Chasing the Angry "White Guy"

"The FBI has never really profiled potential foreign terrorists."
—I.C. SMITH, former head of the analysis, budget, and
training section of the FBI's National Security Division[1]

Louis Freeh took over the reins of the FBI in 1993, the year Muslim terrorists first attacked the World Trade Center. By the time he left, just before the terrorists came back and finished the Twin Towers off, he had taken the bureau's counterterrorism efforts in a new direction. Even as the threat from Islamic terrorists grew exponentially throughout the 1990s, Freeh shifted the focus from fighting such foreign-based groups to fighting so-called "domestic" terrorists—militias, white-separatist groups, anti-abortion bombers, and other "rightwing extremists."

The shift was so dramatic at the FBI that dozens of boxes of evidence that agents gathered in the 1993 Trade Center bombing case, as well as the 1995 investigation into the so-called *Bojinka* plot that included crashing a plane into CIA headquarters, were never properly analyzed—until it was too late. The evidence held valuable clues to al-Qaida's network and operations and could have assigned more meaning to Arab nationals flocking to U.S. flight schools before 9/11, veteran agents say.

"When I left the bureau in 1998, rightwing domestic terrorism was the number one priority. And it was still a higher priority than foreign terrorism and al-Qaida and that bunch on September 11," says retired FBI agent I.C. Smith, former head of the analysis, budget, and training section of the bureau's National Security Division.[2]

Pressure to change priorities came from the White House. After the bombing of the Oklahoma City federal building in 1995, President Clinton made great political hay of the tragedy by drawing parallels between the anti-government extremists behind the plot and the small-government Republican revolution that had swept Congress. The FBI reassigned agents and analysts to track rightwing domestic groups, as well as assist in investigations of traditional federal crimes such as drug trafficking, kidnappings, and bank robberies.

"Prior to 9/11, field agents often were diverted from counterterrorism or other intelligence work in order to cover major criminal cases," the 9/11 Commission found.[3] By 2001, only a handful of analysts—and about thirteen hundred agents, or just 6 percent of the FBI's total manpower—were assigned to counterterrorism, with just one analyst assigned full-time to al-Qaida. And they were often misused, says retired FBI special agent Donald Lavey, who worked Middle Eastern terrorism investigations for nearly twenty years.

"I remember one very competent Middle East analyst at headquarters who instead of being used wisely was constantly being called on to prepare reports for the director and the headquarters bureaucracy," Lavey says. "He was being stretched beyond his capabilities with tasks which in essence were CYA reports to be given to Congress."[4]

Those were the competent ones. Fully two-thirds of the bureau's analysts overall were not even qualified to perform analytical duties, according to 9/11 Commission investigators. In fact, poorly qualified administrative personnel, including secretaries and receptionists, were promoted to analyst positions in part as a reward for good performance in their clerical jobs. Agents had a name for them: "uber-secretaries."[5]

Intelligence-gathering on foreign threats suffered as a result, even though intelligence is the best weapon against terrorism.

"Operations agents working on terrorism leads need predictive, forward-looking analysis," Smith says, "but they weren't getting that kind of raw data from analysts." Assigned to headquarters, he says he saw intelligence play "second fiddle" to criminal investigations, leading to "a systemic failure of our national security that undermined our ability to anticipate the September 11 attacks."

Before the attacks, many FBI field offices did not even have surveillance squads, he says, let alone Arabic linguists to translate wire recordings.

"They treated terrorism like they would a bank robbery. They looked at everything from a standpoint of collecting black-and-white evidence for prosecution," rather than also collecting raw intelligence to help flush out al-Qaida cells and facilitators inside America, Smith says. "And domestic terrorism like the abortion-clinic bombings and [Unabomber] letter bombs were a more comfortable fit with that mentality," he adds. "There's a lot of gray area in intelligence, and they weren't comfortable with it."

Meanwhile, the late, great al-Qaida hunter John O'Neill, the FBI's lead investigator in the USS *Cole* bombing case in Yemen, was nearly fired by Deputy FBI Director Thomas Pickard for pressing Yemeni officials too hard to cooperate. Pickard, who initially headed the 9/11 probe before retiring two months later, was uneasy with agents questioning Muslims in America after the attacks. "I don't want to see them feeling intimidated by us," he said. "Nobody feels good when an FBI agent knocks on the door."[6] Pickard, like many of the executives under Freeh who missed the al-Qaida threat, was rewarded for his pre-9/11 service with fat bonus checks.[7]

By 1999, as the government braced for security threats related to the new millennium, dedicated FBI agents like O'Neill knew the threat of homegrown terrorism from militias and other groups was not as serious as the growing threat of Islamic terrorism. Yet Freeh, under the direction of then-Attorney General Janet Reno, made "rightwing" domestic terrorism the centerpiece of the FBI's strategy to combat Y2K security threats in 1999. The strategy, called "Project Megiddo," zeroed in on white supremacists, militias, and Christian "extremists." The project was outlined in a thirty-two-page report that the FBI removed from its Web site after 9/11.[8]

Of course, it was the wrong strategy, something that was obvious even before 9/11. The only real Y2K threat came from an al-Qaida operative who luckily was stopped by an alert U.S. Customs inspector before he could carry out his plans to blow up the Los Angeles International Airport. The white "lone offenders" and "rightwing groups" Freeh and Reno were so worried about were quiet that New Year's Eve, and have been ever since.

Unlike FBI leaders, the White House counterterror czar at the time, Richard A. Clarke, a career bureaucrat, was not misled. Obsessed with al-Qaida, he paced the floor of a secure communications facility in Washington that night, monitoring intelligence traffic for any sign of activity by terrorists tied to Osama bin Laden until the threat passed on the West Coast. It was not until 3:00 A.M.—midnight in California—that he allowed himself a sip of champagne to celebrate the New Year.[9]

In fact, Clarke was so frustrated by the FBI's shallow analysis and understanding of the threat from Islamic terrorists that he turned to private terrorism researchers for regular briefings, including one he got from Steve Emerson on December 28, 1999, that traced Saudi links to possible al-Qaida agents in the America. They "told me more than the FBI ever had about radical Islamic groups in the U.S.," says Clarke, adding that the FBI at one point even insisted to him that there were no Web sites inside America that were recruiting jihadists for training in al-Qaida camps overseas or raising money for them through charitable fronts. Within days, Emerson had provided him with a long list of such

Web sites sitting on servers in America. Clarke shared the list with the FBI, but he says officials there were not interested in it.[10]

This was the counterterrorism system in place on September 10, 2001.

About three weeks later, FBI Director Robert Mueller reorganized operations to focus on Islamic terrorism. The bureau now has a formal analyst training program and its first director of intelligence. It also has increased its surveillance of Islamic terrorism suspects.

But old habits die hard.

THE AMERITHRAX CASE

Even though the fear of more Timothy McVeighs has proved overwrought, the FBI still considers "attacks by rightwing groups" to be a "serious threat," according to a six-page briefing it helped prepare last year for the Department of Homeland Security.[11] Clinging to that old terrorist profile may be hurting post-9/11 terrorism investigations. For example, the same Homeland Security document classifies the anthrax attacks as a case of "domestic terrorism" by a lone American extremist, rather than foreign-based terrorism by Islamic militants—despite little evidence to support the theory, which many in the national media have nonetheless reported uncritically.[12] FBI investigators have run into a series of dead-ends chasing that angle.

The anthrax terrorism followed quickly on the heels of the Islamic terrorism in Washington and New York. In nine separate incidents between September 2001 and November 2001, forty-five people were diagnosed with exposure to deadly anthrax spores mailed through or to their offices, primarily media outlets. Five people died. Other targets included the offices of U.S. Senate leaders and postal facilities in Washington, Florida, and Trenton, New Jersey. More than three years after the anthrax mailings, the individual or individuals responsible have never been identified, despite a $2.5 million reward for information leading to their arrest.

Investigators initially fingered former government scientist Steven Hatfill. But they have been unable to rebut his alibi that he has never been to Trenton or Princeton, New Jersey, where the anthrax letters to the Senators were mailed. And they have come up empty searching for traces of anthrax at Hatfill's apartment, his girlfriend's home, his cars, or several other places he is known to have visited.

As part of its so-called Amerithrax investigation, the FBI also sent a team of investigators to Iraq to see if the bioterrorism may have been state-sponsored. It came up empty there too.

Oddly, the bureau from the start ruled out associates of the hijackers or al-Qaida sympathizers in the Muslim community as suspects. It is odd for several reasons, including:

1. The letters end with the phrases: "DEATH TO AMERICA. DEATH TO ISRAEL. ALLAH IS GREAT." In a cynical warning to take antibiotics, the writer of the letters to *NBC News* and the *New York Post* mangled the spelling of penicillin as "penacilin," a clue that English may not be the author's first language. And the numeral "1" in the date, "09-11-01," written at the top of the page of the letters was penned with a descender instead of simply a straight line, another sign the writer might be foreign, as the stylized version is common overseas. (Interestingly, the government shows only the fronts of the envelopes in its reward poster, not the contents of the letters praising Allah.)[13]

2. The locations of most of the victims and affected postal facilities—Florida, Washington, and New Jersey—are all places the hijackers stayed and had numerous contacts with fellow Muslims who not only aided them but may have known of their plans, as documented earlier.

3. Whoever mailed the letters has a high level of comfort in and around the Trenton area, particularly in Princeton, where letters were traced back to a standard blue public drop-box near Princeton University. According to the Census Bureau, New Jersey has seven of the nation's top Arab-Muslim enclaves, including Edison and East Brunswick, which is less than fifteen miles from Princeton. Some of the hijackers had stayed in New Jersey.

4. Several of the 9/11 hijackers had at one point rented an apartment from Florida realtor Gloria Irish, who is married to the editor of the supermarket tabloid *Sun*, which is published by American Media Inc. in Boca Raton, Florida. The anthrax attacks began when a *Sun* photo editor opened a contaminated letter sent to the AMI building.[14]

5. Ahmed al-Haznawi—one of the hijackers of United Airlines Flight 93, which crashed into a Pennsylvania field—was treated for an infected black lesion on his left calf in Fort Lauderdale the June before the attacks. The emergency room doctor who treated him with antibiotics, Christos Tsonas, later diagnosed the lesion as cutaneous anthrax after consulting with experts. Al-Haznawi lived near the Boca Raton headquarters of AMI. Additionally, hijacker ringleader Mohamed Atta in late August came into a pharmacy in Delray Beach, Florida, looking for medication to treat irritations on his hands, both of which were red from the wrist down, according to a pharmacist at the store. His symptoms were also consistent with external exposure to anthrax.[15] The incidents suggest the hijackers may have prepared the anthrax-laced letters and handed them off to a mailer or mailers, who sent them after the hijackers died in the plane attacks.

These possible accomplices are still at large, possibly living in New Jersey or Florida, or both states.

6. The method and means of the anthrax attacks have an al-Qaida signature. Using the U.S. Postal Service as the delivery system for the attacks was as simple, cheap, and resourceful as the hijackers using the U.S. aviation system to attack the World Trade Center and Pentagon. And turning otherwise benign business envelopes into weapons of mass panic was just as wickedly clever as turning passenger jets into weapons of mass destruction.

7. What's more, al-Qaida was known to be developing anthrax. Although the 9/11 Commission did not investigate the anthrax terror, it did mention in its final report that al-Qaida had put a U.S.-educated biochemist to work growing anthrax in Afghanistan. In 2001, Yazid Sufaat "would spend several months attempting to cultivate anthrax for al-Qaida in a laboratory he helped set up near the Kandahar airport."[16]

The FBI argues that the exceptionally high quality of the anthrax strain found in the letters—which had been "weaponized," or refined, into an easy-to-inhale powder—makes it unlikely that al-Qaida could have produced it on its own. And it dismisses the medical leads in Florida, arguing investigators tested the places where the hijackers stayed for traces of anthrax spores, and the results came back negative.[17]

The bureau is sticking to its theory that the mailer is a disgruntled American scientist who capitalized on the 9/11 terrorism to carry out his own attacks, using the references to Allah as a ruse to throw off investigators and wrongly cast suspicion on Muslims.

But if it were an opportunistic attack, the FBI has yet to explain how the perpetrator was able to mobilize within just seven days. The first letters were postmarked September 18, 2001. It would have required, for starters, immediate access to the lethal batch of spores. Nor has the FBI explained the motive behind targeting apparently random victims up and down the East Coast. That looks more like terrorism than revenge by a disgruntled former employee.

But not to the FBI, which relies on old psychological profiles of serial murderers that do not include such a motive. Spreading mass terror does not fit the profile on the shelf, so it was ruled it out. Astoundingly, the bureau has little or no experience in profiling Islamic terrorists, and it reverted to its stock profile of a lone, unstable individual to solve the anthrax letters case. In fact, it simply dusted off the old case file on serial letter bomber Ted Kaczynski. FBI profilers are trained at Quantico to help identify potential homegrown mass murderers, Smith says, not foreign-tied terrorists operating inside America. In helping to investigate suspects in spree shootings or serial murders, profilers even follow a formula known as "RWG"—or Regular White Guys.

"They figure about 85 percent of all shooters are white guys. They back out the guys who are happily married—the regular white guys. That leaves the introspective loner types. So you end up with a pretty small part of the population" to investigate, Smith says.

THE D.C. SNIPER CASE

Unfortunately, that formula was also used to profile and catch the D.C. snipers, who in October 2002 shot thirteen people, killing ten. Two black Muslim converts managed to terrorize the nation's capital for more than three weeks while an FBI-led task force searched in vain for a lone white gun nut. The task force ignored clue after clue that the snipers were black, and that the random shootings—which started just after the first anniversary of 9/11— were acts of terrorism.

In fact, investigators knew from day one the suspects were likely black.

Witness Steve Cribbin, a U.S. Army veteran, says he spotted the Beltway snipers on the first day of their bloody rampage, laughing and hitting high-fives as they sped away from a shopping center where they had fired their first shot. He told police later that day what he had seen, but his statement was buried. "I saw the criminals before anybody," he told me.[18]

At around 5:20 P.M. on October 2, 2002, Cribbin was startled by what he told police at the time was the distinct sound of a rifle shot. He was in his car in the parking lot outside the Papa John's Pizza store in Aspen Hill, Maryland, where he moonlights delivering pizzas. He says he was resting there before his shift started when a loud bang went off.

"I was in my car waiting to go to work, just resting, and I heard a gunshot. And being I was in the military, I knew it was a rifle. It didn't sound like backfire" from a car, the thirty-seven-year-old Cribbin recalls. "And I looked around and said, man, where in the hell did that come from?"

"The next thing I know I see a car driving out" of the parking lot, he continues. "And it was like a dark blue Thunderbird or an old cop car, with a couple of black guys giving high-fives and driving away. I said, What the hell? And I didn't think nothing of it. Next thing I know, a guy tells me that there was a shot at the Michaels," a crafts store two doors down from Papa John's where the snipers shot out a window. Cribbin did not know it at the time, but the two black men he saw speed off in a dark, older-model sedan were John Allen Muhammad and Lee Boyd Malvo.

After they shot and killed a man at a nearby grocery about forty-five minutes later, a Montgomery County police detective canvassed witnesses at the Michaels shopping center and took a statement from Cribbin, who was still shaken by the events. Cribbin told the detective, Chris Homrock, that he could not be certain of the model of the car, but he was sure about the race of the men in it, noting it was still light out when they motored out of the parking lot. Homrock filed his witness statement that night with police headquarters in Rockville, Maryland, which became the command post for the multi-agency sniper task force fronted by Montgomery County Police Chief Charles Moose.[19]

Cribbin says he was surprised to learn later that police were looking for a white guy in a white truck. "I said two black guys. Turns out I was right, and they were wrong," he says. "I feel bad for the families of the victims who were killed."

The next night the snipers claimed their sixth victim: an elderly man killed while standing on a downtown Washington street. Witnesses reported seeing a dark-colored Chevy Caprice leaving the scene. From the description, D.C. police detectives thought it might be a "hoopty"—an old unmarked police car popular with young blacks in the area. It was the task force's second clue the suspect was likely black, yet it too was ignored.

Over the next two weeks, police pulled over the snipers' Chevy Caprice several times in routine traffic stops. But Muhammad and Malvo, an illegal immigrant from Jamaica, were released each time, because they were not the white suspect in a white box truck police were told to look for by the task force. They did not fit the FBI's stock profile. Time and again, the snipers were stopped and released so they could go kill more people.

"It was so frustrating, because we kept getting forced off the path, even though we had clues that they were black and driving a dark-colored sedan," says a Montgomery County police sergeant.[20]

Around the end of the first week of shootings, after a boy was shot in Maryland, investigators actually spoke by phone with Malvo, who had left a note at the scene. Detectives who worked on the case say his accent and dialect were easily recognized as Jamaican. "If you've ever read anything written by someone from Jamaica, or if you've ever talked to someone from Jamaica, you can tell right away they're Jamaican," says a Montgomery County police detective who dealt with Jamaican drug dealers as an undercover narcotics officer.[21] There was little doubt at that point they were dealing with a black immigrant, he says. Yet the task force ordered police to keep questioning white suspects.

Two weeks into the sniper nightmare, after reports tied a dark-skinned suspect to another fatal shooting at a Home Depot in Virginia, some in the media demanded to know if the task force would release a composite sketch of a possible suspect. Chief Moose, who is black, quickly poured cold water on the idea, suggesting they did not want to offend minorities.

"We want to be very careful with partial information," he asserted. "If it somehow paints some group or causes people to be misidentified and causes them hardship, that is a dilemma we want to stay away from."[22] Yet all the while, he and the FBI were advising patrolmen to stop Caucasians.

Moose was particularly sensitive to the race issue. He took the top cop job in late 1999 vowing to end racial profiling in Montgomery County, a bedroom community to Washington. Since then, the county has been under federal orders not to profile black suspects, an agreement Moose struck with then-Attorney General Janet Reno, who was a big fan of his.

Two days after Moose's unhelpful press conference, the task force received a tip from a witness in Tacoma, Washington, who suggested police check out a man he served with in the military named John Muhammad. It was their first clue they may be dealing not only with a black, but a Muslim. (The same day, Malvo essentially gave himself up by phoning his own tip into the task force about a related shooting in Montgomery, Alabama.) Still, patrolmen were ordered to stay on the lookout for a white guy.

The clues did not stop there.

Two days before Muhammad and Malvo were caught, the task force assigned an investigative team that included an FBI sharpshooter to stake out the home of Muhammad's ex-wife in Clinton, Maryland, based on the tip they had received from the Tacoma source. Mildred Muhammad is a practicing Muslim who wears traditional head garb. The task force had the snipers cold—their names, race, and even religion—but still held off issuing a lookout for them. "We were sworn to secrecy," says one of the undercover agents on the stakeout, who says he was shown photographs of both Muhammad and Malvo that night.[23]

Yet that same day, detectives with the sniper task force were still interrogating white guys in the area and confiscating their rifles.[24]

Also on that day, bus driver Conrad Johnson was fatally wounded in Aspen Hill, Maryland, three days after the snipers wounded another man in southern Virginia. The snipers had come full circle, managing to return to the original crime scene, while the task force stubbornly stuck to the old FBI profile of a lone white gun nut. "Historically, cases similar to this series [of murders] have been perpetrated primarily by white males," Moose wrote in his 2003 autobiography, citing the FBI profile.[25]

Late in the evening on October 23, 2002, Moose revealed in a terse statement that the task force was no longer looking for a white guy in a white vehicle and provided a physical description of Muhammad and his dark blue 1990 Chevy

Caprice, the same hoopty witnesses saw from the start. Photos of Malvo also went out. About three hours later, a trucker who had heard the descriptions spotted the snipers at a rest stop, blocked their car with his truck, and called the cops. After three full weeks of ignoring clues and stalling the public, the task force finally put out a lookout containing the descriptions they had known for at least a week, and the suspects were caught within three hours. It was later revealed that they sympathized with the 9/11 terrorism.

"The FBI profilers were dead wrong, and they misled the public about the nature of the threat," Smith says.[26]

Lest it be accused of discrimination and invite lawsuits in a county already on federal probation for racial profiling, the FBI chased a white ghost up until the last possible second, Smith says. The delay cost at least one life—Johnson the bus driver, who of all things was black.

The same pathological fear of offending minorities and being sued by them also drives the bureau's internal policies, and not just in training agents to be more sensitive toward Muslims. It governs the FBI's employment of Arabic translators, the key to unlocking an encore attack by al-Qaida—or conversely, al-Qaida's key to penetrating the FBI.

16

JEWS NEED NOT APPLY
TO FIGHT TERROR

Trusting Muslims To Investigate Muslims at the FBI

"We sent them a lot of people, and nobody made it to the finish line. Not one person was found eligible for these jobs, which is outrageous."

— DOUG BALIN, director of the Sephardic Bikur Holim
Jewish community center in New York[1]

A few weeks after Islamic terrorists toppled the World Trade Center, two FBI agents from the New York field office paid a visit to a Sephardic Jewish community center in Brooklyn. Their mission: recruit Arabic linguists to help interpret interviews and intercepts of Osama bin Laden's network.

Sephardic Jews have lived in Arab countries like Syria and Egypt and know the language, not to mention the culture and history of the region. And being close to Israel, a main target of Islamic terrorism, they were gung-ho to help the feds fight the war on terrorism here.

It was a good move, or so most involved thought at the time—and long overdue.

Federal investigators had missed clues to both the 2001 and 1993 World Trade Center attacks not because they did not have them, but because they did not know what they had until it was too late. They were buried in a backlog of untranslated wiretaps and documents in Arabic. A chronic shortage of Arabic-speaking translators had resulted in an accumulation of thousands of hours of untranslated audiotapes and written material stored in FBI lockers.

The FBI's New York field office, at least, knew such delays were no longer acceptable after the 9/11 attack. The bureau's translators were the key to preventing another homeland strike, but they had to convert Arabic chatter to English faster. That meant hiring a lot more translators as quickly as possible.

So in October 2001, while rescue workers were still pulling remains from Ground Zero, two agents from the FBI's offices located nearby reached out to local Arabic-speaking Jews to do just that. Agents Carol Motyka and Marsha Parrish met with an official at the Sephardic Bikur Holim, a Jewish social-services agency in Brooklyn.

At the meeting, Yola Haber, who heads the agency's employment division, says she agreed to help recruit Arabic-speaking Jews for the bureau. Most of them applied on-line for the translator jobs. All told, she says she referred some sixty applicants, possibly more, to the FBI. They included retired linguists who had experience working for Israeli radio in Arabic and for the Israeli army.

Remarkably, not one of them was hired.

"We sent them a lot of people, and nobody made it to the finish line," complains Sephardic Bikur Holim Director Doug Balin. "Not one person was found eligible for these jobs, which is outrageous."[2]

Instead, the FBI hired dozens of Arab-American Muslims, as well as Arab Christians, as translators.

The double standard does not sit well with Jewish leaders, who note that Muslim translators hired by the Pentagon to assist in al-Qaida interrogations are under investigation for espionage. And there have been reports of loyalty issues involving Arab and Muslim translators at the FBI.

Since I first broke this story in late 2003, prominent Jewish members of Congress have demanded answers. House Democratic Whip Anthony Weiner of New York, for one, asked FBI Director Robert Mueller to explain, on a case-by-case basis, the reasons for rejecting the Jewish applicants.

"In an attempt to understand why it is that none of the applicants brought to the bureau by Sephardic Bikur Holim were approved for employment, and to ensure that no bias or discrimination exists within the bureau, I request that you provide us with an explanation, on an individual-by-individual basis, of why each applicant was turned down," Weiner said in a November 13, 2003, letter to Mueller, co-signed by Rep. Frank Pallone (D-New Jersey). Weiner is also a House Judiciary Committee member.[3]

In its response to the New York lawmakers, four months later, the FBI confirmed that with the exception of one Jewish applicant—who happened to be hired the same month the story first appeared[4]—none of the Jewish applicants was hired. "One applicant successfully completed each stage of processing and was approved for the Contract Linguist position in October 2003," said Roderick L. Beverly, special agent in charge of the FBI's Office of International Operations, in a March 24, 2004, letter to Pallone. Bottom line: nearly all the Arabic-speaking Jews who applied to help fight terrorism simply did not make the cut.

At the same time lawmakers pressed the FBI for a full accounting, Jewish leaders in New York sent House Government Reform Committee investigators a long list of Sephardic Jews who speak fluent Arabic in an effort to compel the FBI to reconsider Jews for the desperately needed translator jobs. One leader said that the chief of the FBI's language services section in Washington, Margaret Gulotta, then reached out to leaders in the Sephardic community and privately assured them she would reconsider Jewish applicants.[5] Gulotta has told congressional leaders that the FBI has done a good job of recruiting Arabic-speaking translators after 9/11.

Still, why were so many Jewish applicants denied? Beverly says the "vetting process" is rigorous, involving a battery of language proficiency tests, a polygraph exam, and a ten-year scope background investigation—all handled through head-quarters in Washington. The Jewish applicants from New York failed to make the grade, he says.

Off the record, however, the bureau says there were loyalty concerns.

POLITICS, NOT SECURITY

Many of the applicants are dual citizens and were rejected after failing to renounce their Israeli citizenship. Some gave deceptive answers during their polygraph examination, Beverly notes in his letter. The Jonathan Pollard spy case, as well as a more recent one allegedly involving a pro-Israel lobby group at the Pentagon, has heightened security fears. Translators require top secret clearance.

But Caroline Glick, deputy managing editor of the *Jerusalem Post*, is mystified. "There is no reason to worry about the so-called dual loyalties of Sephardic American Jews," she argues. "These loyalties are not in conflict. They are identical."[6]

Others familiar with the FBI's foreign language program say the reason the FBI snubbed the Jewish applicants has more to do with politics than security. They say headquarters did not want to offend Arab Christian and Muslim translators, who would have to work alongside Jews. "There's already tension between the Hebrew and Arabic desks," says Sibel Edmonds, a former FBI translator in Washington. "If they hired Arab Jews to translate Arabic, there would be bloodshed. Arabs would never accept it."[7]

Agreed a U.S. intelligence official: "It's yet another example of us hamstringing ourselves for politically correct reasons."[8]

Glick notes that Mueller has pandered to Muslim-rights groups, even ones that support Hamas and other terrorist groups, and has mandated Muslim-sensitivity classes for agents. "In people such as the Sephardic Arabic speakers whose applications were rejected by the FBI, the U.S. has a valuable store of capital for its war on terror," Glick says. "Better it be used than squandered for the sake of pandering to radical Arab groups."

Shelomo Alfassa, vice president of the Foundation for the Advancement of Sephardic Studies and Culture in New York, agrees: "Unfortunately, it is through the plague of political correctness that the FBI does indeed fear offending the Muslim community by hiring Jews."

"This is crazy," he adds. "Imagine if during the war against Hitler, Franklin D. Roosevelt felt that having Jews fight the Nazis might upset the everyday German?"[9]

Instead of hiring Jews fluent in Arabic to help fight Muslim terrorism in the wake of 9/11, the FBI has turned to the Arab-Muslim community for help, even asking the American Muslim Council and other worrisome Islamist groups to help recruit translators for the bureau. Enlisting such potentially sympathetic groups in the war on Islamic terror is inherently fraught with risk.

But the FBI has compounded the risk by rushing Arab and Muslim applicants through the screening process, in many cases putting them to work translating classified materials before completing their background investigations and approving their classified security clearance. (The bureau, in contrast, did not cut corners on background checks for the Jewish applicants.) As a result, the main language unit in Washington has been plagued with loyalty and security concerns—some so serious that both Congress and the Department of Justice's inspector general have urged Mueller to open espionage investigations.

17

THE MOLE HOUSE

Inside the FBI's Foreign Language Squad

"We have serious problems with the hiring of language specialists. Background investigations are not being conducted properly, and we're giving people top secret clearance who shouldn't have it. And we have espionage cases because of it."
—JOHN M. COLE, former FBI program manager for foreign intelligence investigations covering Afghanistan, India, and Pakistan[1]

FBI special agent John M. Cole was bushed after putting in another twelve-hour shift at the Washington command center set up to investigate the 9/11 suicide hijackings. In early 2002, the case, codenamed PENTTBOM, was still top priority for all agents. But Cole had a stack of files waiting for him at his office at FBI headquarters related to his regular duties with the bureau's counterintelligence division managing the national programs for Afghanistan, India, and Pakistan. Part of those duties required conducting what are called "risk assessments" on applicants for FBI jobs, especially foreign language specialists, to evaluate their propensity for spying on the United States, among other security risks. Several of their personnel files landed on his desk. He was the final step in their background investigation.

The first file he looked at that night after dragging himself back to his office involved a Pakistani American who had applied for a language specialist position translating Urdu and Pashto, tongues critical to the bureau in its battle against al-Qaida. After thumbing through the paperwork, "I felt something was missing in that file," Cole says. "So I put it aside and came in early the next day to take a closer look at it." After rereading the file, he found several items that were troubling.

For starters, he learned that the applicant's father was a retired general from

Pakistan. "I went ahead and ran his name through the Automated Case System and came up with several hits," Cole says in an exclusive interview with me.[2] It turns out he had at one time been the subject of an FBI investigation, an alarming piece of information that was somehow overlooked in the preliminary background check on the applicant. The bureau had opened a case file on her father in the 1980s, when he was the military attaché stationed at Pakistan's embassy in Washington. Having worked that particular target, Cole knew that the military attachés assigned there doubled as intelligence officers. And he also knew that Pakistan's military intelligence was in bed with the Taliban, as well as al-Qaida. In fact, its officers introduced Osama bin Laden to Taliban leaders.[3]

Cole stumbled on another alarming piece of information that gave him great pause about the applicant. Her father, who at the time was not a U.S. citizen, spent six months of the year living in the United States and the other six months living in Pakistan. "He's got a lot of friends that are still there in military intelligence, and he more than likely talks to them frequently, living there as he does six months out of the year," Cole says. It was a major red flag. Working as a translator with top secret clearance, his daughter could covertly listen to his Pakistani friends targeted in U.S. counterintelligence and counterterrorism investigations, presenting a clear conflict of interest and loyalties.

Compounding his concerns, the results of her polygraph exam were inconclusive. "That was troubling also," says Cole, an eighteen-year veteran of the bureau.

So he recommended rejecting her application in his risk-assessment report, while suggesting the counterterrorism division conduct its own review of the applicant to be sure. He delivered his report to the personnel security specialist at the FBI who was handling the applicant's case. She thanked him, then confided, "When I reviewed this, I felt there was something wrong, too."

About a week later, the specialist called Cole to get contact information for the counterterrorism division. After Cole provided it, she sighed, saying, "Not that it matters."

"Not that it matters? What do you mean?" Cole asked.

"Well, they hired the individual, and she reported for duty this morning," the specialist said.

"You gotta be kidding me," Cole said.

"No, she got a TS-SCI clearance, and she's working at the Washington field office." TS-SCI stands for top secret/sensitive compartmented information—the government's highest security clearance short of codeword access.

Cole, 43, would not reveal the translator's name, but bureau sources identify her as Hadia Roberts, a Pakistani immigrant who married a State Department official. Linguists who worked with her in the Washington field office say she frequently boasted that her father was a retired general. Known as a Muslim "zealot" who tries to convert colleagues to Islam, she headed the field office's Muslim awareness program and led prayer groups. At one point, bureau insiders say, she also led an effort to persuade management to install separate bathroom facilities for Muslims.

Roberts, who declined comment, was recently promoted to headquarters. And the FBI has also hired her sons to translate highly classified materials, sources say.

Why would the bureau make short shrift of personnel security on the heels of the embarrassing Robert Hanssen spy scandal, and in the middle of a war on terrorism? In a word, politics.

After 9/11, Cole explains, there was a "big push" in Washington to hire translators to clear backlogs of untranslated materials, mainly in Arabic, that had been collected from surveillance of al-Qaida operatives. The FBI took heat for missing clues to al-Qaida plots buried in the chronic backlogs, he says, and the increased political pressure has led to expedited hiring and shortcuts in security background checks.

"There was a lot of politics going on at the time, and the bureau has become very political. Congress had an issue with the language specialists. A shortage had led to backlogs," Cole explains, "And so [FBI Director Robert] Mueller goes up to the Hill and says we're going to go hire all these language specialists, and promises we're not going to have a problem anymore, so on and so forth. So there's a big push."

As a result, translator applicants like Roberts have been rushed through what normally would be a rigorous security clearance process. "In fact, when I got her file, there was a very short deadline on it," Cole says. "I was supposed to have that risk assessment done within about five days." Normally, he had thirty days to complete such reports.

"So I knew somebody was pushing this," he says. "Everything was a priority to get these language specialists hired."

Cole, who resigned from the FBI last year, says he observed serious security lapses involving the screening and hiring of translators, and the lapses were not just limited to Roberts. He says at least a dozen translators still on the job have major "red flags" in their personnel security files.

"We have serious problems with the hiring of language specialists. Background investigations are not being conducted properly, and we're giving people top secret clearance who shouldn't have it," Cole warns. "And we have espionage cases because of it."

About six months after Hadia Roberts of Pakistan was hired, the FBI's counterintelligence division was handed a spy case involving Pakistan. Someone had leaked highly classified FBI radio frequencies to Islamabad.

The division opened an "unknown subject" case to try to determine who provided the information to the Pakistani Embassy. Agents sent the information to the FBI's engineering research facility down at Quantico to help isolate suspects. It was determined that the only employees who could have known the frequencies were the technical agent and the translators who had access to the codes.

"Boy, wouldn't that be something if it was one of the translators we hired," one of the agents told his unamused supervisor. The leak is still under investigation.

"WE'LL DO THE BACKGROUND CHECKS LATER"

Finding qualified and trustworthy translators has been a special challenge in the war on terrorism, since few native-born Americans speak Middle Eastern and Persian tongues fluently. In what critics call an unfortunate move after the 9/11 attacks, Director Mueller issued a plea for translators among militant Islamic groups, such as the Council on American-Islamic Relations, the Islamic Society of North America, and the American Muslim Council, whose members typically pledge allegiance to Islam over America. Thousands responded to his plea, and many have marched into the FBI's ranks. Mueller thanked American Muslim Council members at their 2002 convention, saying:

> Six days after September 11, some of you may recall, I announced that the FBI was seeking additional Arabic and Farsi language experts. And the response was truly extraordinary. Within hours our switchboard was overwhelmed with calls, and those who came forward included doctors, lawyers, engineers, academics—Muslim- and Arab-Americans from all walks of life who were willing to quit their jobs, come to work for the FBI, and give something back to their country in the fight against terrorism, for which we are grateful, extraordinarily grateful. As a result of that process, we have doubled our numbers of Arabic translators.[4]

"That's absolutely crazy," says retired FBI special agent John Vincent, who says AMC should have been one of the last groups Mueller enlisted to help fight terrorism. But he says the director gullibly thought AMC was the most "mainstream" Muslim group in America at the time. "Of course, they're not mainstream," Vincent says. "Their founder, Alamoudi, has been convicted of plotting terrorism."

As the bureau processed more than thirty thousand translator applicants after 9/11, FBI official Margaret Gulotta joined Mueller in assuring Congress that they were not cutting corners and were maintaining thorough and intensive background investigations. Gulotta is chief of the Language Services Section at FBI headquarters, which employs more than twelve hundred linguists stationed across the U.S. The largest and most important squad is in Washington, home to foreign embassies. She insists the bureau has not loosened its standards one bit: "We have not compromised our standards in terms of language proficiency and security."[5]

But that is simply not the case, say FBI agents and translators, some of whom are still working in the bureau.

"They were going up to the Hill saying that whatever the problems, we're taking care of it. We're hiring all these language specialists, and we're making sure that we're doing extensive background investigations on these individuals," Cole says. "They were telling them all this stuff, but that's not the case."

Sibel Dinez Edmonds, who worked as a Farsi and Turkish translator at the FBI's Washington field office after 9/11, agrees: "It's not true that they conduct tough background checks and have high standards for screening translators." She says she knew of several translators who were hired without undergoing full background checks. Some even started working for the squad months before they were cleared for top secret security access. Citing classified testimony Edmonds gave to its staff, the 9/11 Commission admonished the FBI to "maintain security and proficiency standards with respect to its permanent and contract employees."[6]

Former FBI special agent Emanuel "Manny" Johnson Jr., who worked closely with Farsi translators as a squad supervisor in the Washington field office, says the bureau expedited background checks even before coming under pressure to staff up after the terrorist attacks. For example, he says relatives of applicants who lived overseas were rarely interviewed. The vetting only slackened after the attacks. "After 9/11, they just grabbed a bunch of Arab people off the street and said, 'Oh, we'll do the background checks later,'" Johnson tells me.[7]

GIFTS FOR ENEMY MOLES

The FBI's translator program plays a vital role in interpreting interviews and intercepts of the al-Qaida network. The faster translators can clear backlogs of untranslated materials in Arabic, Urdu, Pashto, Farsi, and other languages critical to counterterrorism investigations, the faster they can uncover terrorist plots. The more translators, the bigger the dent they can make in the backlog.

But many translators pose a grave threat to national security themselves. Some have had relationships with targets of counterterrorism and counterintelligence investigations, raising fears that translators could tip off the terrorists about investigations to help them avoid detection and even reveal the sources and methods federal authorities use to gather intelligence about their activities.

"The language department has just been one problem after another," Johnson says.

Before 9/11, for example, a female translator from Iran who worked in the New York field office was caught having a relationship with one of the Iranian targets of an international terrorism investigation. "She took the information and warned them off that they were targets, and the FBI wiretapped her and found she was talking to the targets," Edmonds says. Cole and other bureau sources confirmed her account. Rather than prosecute the translator and risk bad press, her supervisors asked her to resign, and she quietly left the bureau.

And a few months after 9/11, an Arabic translator working for a Midwest field office of the FBI was found to be romantically involved with an al-Qaida target and was quietly shown the door without any investigation or even formal firing, Edmonds says. "They quickly let her go because she used to be engaged to one of the top al-Qaida targets in the U.S.," she says.[8]

Coleen Rowley, an FBI special agent in Minneapolis, agrees the bureau has seen its share of bad apples in the foreign language program. "We have had some problems with translators going south," she says.[9]

Also after 9/11, a male translator from the Middle East was fired for taking gifts from foreign targets and then lying about it, according to an investigation by the Department of Justice's inspector general. "A Language Specialist was dismissed for unauthorized contacts with foreign officials and intelligence officers, receipt of things of value from them, and a lack of candor in his 'convoluted and contradictory responses' to questions about his contacts," the inspector general found.[10] It is not clear if the bureau opened an espionage investigation or assessed the damage to national security caused by the translator's breaches.

But it would not be the first time security was compromised for greed, in addition to ideology, in the FBI's language squad.

Witness the case of Melek Can Dickerson, who joined other translators in the Washington field office during the flurry of post-9/11 hiring. Like others, she received top secret clearance without a full scrubbing of her background, sources say. Dickerson, who likes to be called "Jan," moved to America from Turkey, where she had met and later married a major in the U.S. Air Force, thereby becoming a U.S. citizen eligible to join the FBI.

The affable Dickerson immediately struck up a friendship with Edmonds, also from Turkey, who had been hired two months earlier.

One day in early December 2001, Dickerson called Edmonds at her home to arrange a meeting with their husbands over tea. "Can we stop by?" she asked. "It was very strange," Edmonds, 35, recalls, but she replied, "Sure."

THE TURKISH TARGET

Dickerson came over with her husband, Douglas, just before noon. And they sat down with Edmonds and her husband, a computer contractor born and raised in Virginia, in the living room of their waterfront townhouse on the Potomac. The major did most of the talking.

"He comments on the large Turkish community in the Washington area and asks me and my husband if we were members of any Turkish organizations," as Edmonds recounts the conversation. Then he suggested they join the American-Turkish Council, a Washington lobbying group that aids U.S. defense contractors doing business in Turkey.

"Don't you need to be in the export-import business to join?" Edmonds asked.

"No, not at all. Just say you're with the FBI and you will get in like that," the major said, snapping his fingers. Edmonds, who had access to top secret intelligence, got the uneasy feeling she was hearing a classic spy pitch.

Then the major brought up the name of a wealthy Turkish man who lived in nearby McLean, Virginia. He was involved with the American-Turkish Council and had access to a lot of U.S. military information. Edmonds's eyes got big as saucers. "I immediately recognized his name from an investigation I was working on," she says. He was the target of an FBI counterintelligence operation.

The major told Edmonds and her husband that if they hitched their fortunes to their Turkish friend, "You could retire early," as Edmonds tells it. The Dickersons intimated that they were so close to the target that they shopped for him and his wife, picking up baked goods from Middle Eastern stores in Alexandria, where they lived at the time.

Scandalized, Edmonds felt compelled by FBI security guidelines to report what she had heard. After all, she had come into receipt of information that a co-worker had inappropriate and undisclosed contacts with the target of an active investigation. That night, she typed up everything that transpired during the afternoon tea, "because I would be liable if I didn't report it," she says. And she gave her report to her supervisor at the Washington field office on December 6, 2001. The supervisor, Michael Feghali, a Lebanese immigrant, did nothing with the information.

Later that month, the Dickersons traveled to Turkey for ten days and did not report the trip, even though they went to the target's home country. Dickerson did not notify the bureau of the trip as required, which should have been grounds for automatic revocation of her top secret clearance under the security guidelines. She also omitted from her FBI security application the fact she worked for Turkish groups under surveillance.[11]

Edmonds says she briefed Dennis Saccher, a special agent in the FBI's Washington field office who was conducting the surveillance on the Turkish target, about her colleague's actions, and he responded, "It looks like espionage to me."

Saccher, who declined comment, discovered that a number of wiretap translations by Dickerson were marked "Not pertinent," and a majority of them suspiciously involved the Turkish target from McLean. So he asked Edmonds to retranslate the recordings to check Dickerson's work. As a contract monitor, Dickerson performed summary, not full, translations of voice recordings and could get away with leaving whole sections untranslated by simply marking them irrelevant to the case. Monitors are typically less fluent and experienced than contract linguists such as Edmonds, who did word-for-word translations and transcriptions.

In reviewing Dickerson's work, Edmonds found she had left out information crucial to the FBI counterspying investigation—information that Edmonds says would have revealed that the Turkish intelligence target had spies working for him inside the Department of State and the Pentagon, who were trying to obtain U.S. military and intelligence secrets. When she heard the tapes, she thought, "Oh s—, that's the guy they named at my house."

Outraged, Saccher asked Feghali, the language unit supervisor, to reprimand Dickerson. But again he did nothing. Dickerson stayed on the job, maintaining her top secret clearance. Meanwhile, the Turkish target unexpectedly and abruptly left the U.S. "He didn't even wait to sell his house. He gave someone else the power of attorney to sell it," Edmonds says. "He took his wife and family and hastily moved in the first week in February" of 2002.

Did Dickerson tip him off? The FBI never investigated to find out.

THINLY VEILED THREAT

Edmonds says Dickerson had instructed her not to translate certain FBI wiretaps involving the Turkish subject, explaining that she knew him personally and was confident that there would be nothing important to translate concerning him. When Edmonds refused, she says Dickerson managed to get ahold of translations meant for Edmonds and forged her signature and initials, rendering the communications useless to the case agent.

Edmonds says in documents filed in federal court that "extremely sensitive and material information was deliberately withheld from translations," and that her supervisor barred her from alerting the case agent about the serious matter. Feghali decided not to send the retranslated information to Saccher who requested it, she says. Instead, Feghali sent him a note stating that the translation was reviewed and the original translation was accurate. He explained to Edmonds that sending the revised translation would only hurt Dickerson and cause problems for the FBI language department.[12]

Here the story takes a bizarre turn.

When Dickerson heard about her tea companion complaining about her translations, she made a thinly veiled threat for her to stop. "Why would you put your life and your family's lives in danger?" she allegedly told Edmonds, a petite brunette. Not long afterward, plainclothes agents with Turkish intelligence showed up at her younger sister's apartment in Istanbul with an interrogation and arrest warrant. Luckily, Edmonds had already brought her sister, employed by a major airline, and mother to Washington in anticipation of such reprisals.

At that point, Edmonds reported Dickerson and her alleged security breach to upper management, but nobody at the FBI wanted to hear about it. She was told, in effect, to let sleeping dogs lie. When she continued to raise a fuss, she was summarily fired.

Two days later, the feisty Edmonds took her grievance to the U.S. Senate. In a March 2002 letter to Sen. Patrick J. Leahy, then chairman of the Senate Judiciary Committee, she warned that Dickerson posed a "significant threat to national security."[13] Alarmed, the committee called FBI officials to the Hill to answer the charges. They disproved none of Edmonds's accusations, committee staffers say.

Nonetheless, Dickerson stayed on the job through July 2002, when she went on maternity leave. "She was never forced out" of the bureau, Edmonds says.

Meanwhile, Edmonds filed a complaint with the Department of Justice inspector general and retained a team of whistleblower lawyers to sue the FBI over her dismissal. Her lawyers served the Dickersons with a subpoena for deposition in August 2002 after learning they planned to leave the country. Astoundingly, the FBI interceded on the couple's behalf. "Two days before their scheduled deposition, the bureau stopped us and gave us signed agreement by both Dickersons stating that they would agree to be brought back by the bureau if necessary," Edmonds tells me.

The Senate stepped in at that point. In an August 13, 2002, letter to then-Attorney General John Ashcroft—which has since been classified by the FBI, retroactively—Leahy and Sen. Charles Grassley warned that Dickerson has dual citizenship abroad and might not return or cooperate with an investigation by the inspector general.

"The FBI currently opposes depositions of the monitor and her husband as part of the investigation into this case," their letter states. "The FBI takes this position despite the fact that the monitor is no longer employed by the FBI, that the monitor's husband never worked at the FBI, and even though the military agency that employs the monitor's husband does not oppose a deposition."

The letter adds, "It is unclear, then, why the FBI is taking this position in the wake of such important allegations bearing on national security."[14]

Frantic that the Dickersons would get away, Edmonds fired off a letter to White House Counsel Alberto Gonzales asking that he look into the matter to prevent the Dickersons from leaving the country "until a thorough investigation has been completed."[15]

The campaign failed. In early September 2002, the Dickersons moved to Belgium, where the major took an assignment with NATO.

Edmonds's first attorney, David K. Colapinto, then appealed directly to the Pentagon to investigate its officer, who he charged had "a substantial financial interest" in Turkey, which made him vulnerable to foreign influence. He further charged that the major could not be considered an "innocent spouse" in his wife's alleged misconduct at the FBI.[16]

MORE THAN A "CAT FIGHT"

Still, the Pentagon never opened a formal investigation into Edmonds's complaint against Dickerson's husband. A preliminary review of "Major Dickerson's relationship with the American-Turkish Council" found "no evidence of any deviation from the scope of his duties," says Col. James N. North, director of the Air Force's office of inquiries.[17]

Edmonds describes the powerful American-Turkish Council as a "semi-legitimate organization," set up for the benefit of "shady arms dealers" who trade on insider government information to secure military aid and contracts for the Turkish government.

The nonprofit lobbying group states on its latest available tax filings, which show $1.2 million in revenue, that its purpose is to "help resolve problems and disputes that affect U.S.-Turkish commercial, defense, and cultural relations." It includes on its board of directors several Turkish officials who list addresses in Istanbul, including military officials such as retired Turkish Vice Admiral Isik Biren, who led NATO naval forces in the 1970s. Its executive committee includes officials from Boeing, Lockheed Martin, Raytheon, and other U.S. defense contractors. And ATC's chairman is retired Gen. Brent Scowcroft, who served as former President Bush's national security adviser. Plainly, the case Edmonds may have stumbled upon has repercussions in both the diplomatic and political worlds.

Interestingly, the same year Edmonds went public with her charges against the Dickersons, the ATC indemnified its directors against attorney's fees and judgments resulting from civil and criminal action against ATC.[18]

Edmonds charges that the wealthy Turkish target tied to ATC dealt weapons to Pakistan and Chechnya, as well as Turkey. "He'll sell to whomever pays," she says. Formerly stationed in Turkey, Major Dickerson at one point worked with the Pentagon in weapons procurement for Central Asia, including Turkey.

Attempts to reach the Dickersons, now in Brussels, were unsuccessful. But an associate wrote off the allegations against Melek Dickerson to a "catfight" between Dickerson and Edmonds. He attributes her failure to translate certain material properly to a lack of training, rather than anything sinister.

Edmonds, a naturalized U.S. citizen from Turkey, says it was nothing personal. She says she blew the whistle on her colleague's alleged security breaches because "it is my duty as an American."

Though her tale may sound like something out of a spy thriller, there's nothing fictional about it, U.S. officials say. Grassley, a leading member of the Senate Judiciary Committee and noted FBI watchdog, calls Edmonds, who recently earned a Ph.D. and holds degrees in both criminal justice and public policy, "very credible. . . . And the reason I feel she's very credible is because the people within the FBI have corroborated a lot of her story" during closed-session hearings on the Hill.[19] And Leahy continues to champion her cause. He recently wrote Mueller to remind him of his "grave concerns about the translator program" and the potential compromise of counterterrorism investigations. (Of course, Leahy's concern is an ironic switch from the past, when he blocked terrorism-fighting reforms at the FBI out of sympathy for Arabs and Muslims. Apparently receiving anthrax in the mail from Arab terrorists praising Allah woke him up to the threat.)

Even the Department of Justice, which oversees the FBI, has not disputed Edmonds's allegations. From day one, she warned Department of Justice Inspector General Glenn A. Fine that terrorist "investigations are being compromised" and demanded an independent probe of the FBI's language department. Last year, finally, Fine issued a report essentially agreeing with her. It criticizes "the FBI's failure to adequately pursue her allegations of espionage." Most of his report remains classified as secret by the FBI, however.[20]

Mueller and Gulotta, for their part, still maintain the FBI's foreign language program is solid and secure.

A battle-weary, but vindicated, Edmonds regrets their stubborn denials. "They have no idea how many other Dickersons are in there," she says. "I mean, it's like a mole house over there." Remarkably, some translators have openly exhibited hostility toward America, she says, and yet they have been allowed to remain on the job, still entrusted to protect the country they hate.

CELEBRATING 9/11

When Edmonds showed up for her first day of work at the Washington field office, a week after the 9/11 attacks, she expected to find a somber atmosphere. Instead, she was offered cookies filled with dates from party bowls set out in the large open room where other Middle Eastern linguists with top-secret security clearance translate terror-related communications. (The highly secure language unit room is walled off from agents, who do not have badge access and must be escorted into the room.)

She knew the dessert is customarily served in the Middle East at weddings, births, and other celebrations and asked what the happy occasion was.

To her shock, she was told the Arabic linguists were celebrating the terrorist attacks on America, as if they were some joyous event. Right in front of a supervisor from the Middle East, one Arabic translator named Osama cheered, "It's about time that they got a taste of what they've been giving to the Middle East!"[21]

Edmonds says her co-workers were not shy about making such hostile comments. "These statements were neither rare nor made in a whisper," she says. "They were open and loud."

She found out later that it was her supervisor Feghali's wife—an Arabic linguist on loan from the National Security Agency—who brought the date filled cookies.

Edmonds was taken aback by the blatant display of anti-Americanism that day. But she soon found that it was more the rule than the exception. The language squad was rife with linguists with questionable loyalties, she says, all with top-secret security clearance.

"There were those who openly divided the fronts as 'Us'—the Middle Easterners who shared certain views—and 'Them'—the Americans who were the outsiders [bristling] with arrogance that was now 'leading to their own destruction,'" she says.[22]

Though all translators working for the FBI must be U.S. citizens, "citizenship doesn't take care of it," she adds, referring to loyalty.

"Wherever there's a conversation about America or Americans, it's always still

'They' or 'Them,' and not 'Us,'" says Edmonds, who is not a practicing Muslim. "Whenever 9/11 is brought up, you know, it happened to *Them*." She estimates that the roughly forty Arabic linguists there account for "easily more than 75 percent of the loyalty problems," and yet they are the most indispensable to investigations of al-Qaida suspects.

A warning in advance of an encore al-Qaida attack more than likely will come in the form of a message or document in Arabic that will have to be translated. That message may go to an Arab or Muslim sympathizer within the language department, and it may never be translated in full, if at all, Edmonds warns.

"The translation of our intelligence is being entrusted to individuals with loyalties to our enemies," she says. "Important [terrorist] chatter is being intentionally blocked."

Another translator who worked in the Washington field office before his recent promotion to headquarters agrees with Edmonds up to a point. Middle Eastern translators on the Arabic desk "did express their displeasure with U.S. policy in the Middle East," he says, "but they never said they wanted to see the U.S. attacked so far as I heard." He doubts their objection to U.S. foreign policy affects their loyalty.[23]

SEPARATE POTTIES

But in another sign of a prevailing Us-versus-Them mindset, several Muslim translators have demanded separate bathroom facilities for Muslims at the Washington field office.

"Certain translators fanatic about Islam were sending e-mails around saying they didn't want to use the same commodes as Christians, because if they touch where a non-Muslim has been they could get dirty," Edmonds says.

The other translator now at headquarters says he is not sure the proposal for separate bathrooms was motivated by religious beliefs. "There were also complaints that agents left the restrooms a mess," he says, insisting on anonymity for fear of reprisals.

But Edmonds says the bathroom initiative was led by Hadia Roberts, the Pakistani translator who also was in charge of Muslim-sensitivity training at the Washington field office after 9/11. "She's an Islamic fanatic," Edmonds says. "She goes around trying to convert all the Christians."

Edmonds says Roberts and other Muslim "zealots" also complained about non-Muslim co-workers "munching and crunching" food near them during the Muslim holy month of Ramadan, when Muslims partake in sunrise-to-sunset fasting.

FBI counterterrorism veteran Donald Lavey agrees that loyalty is a serious issue among Arab and Muslim employees of the FBI. And he argues for stricter background checks on translators from the Middle East to ensure their loyalty to America. "Care needs to be taken at this point in time as to their religious background and political views," he tells me. "Loyalty to the United States is the *sine qua non* for any translator or analyst."

Currently, FBI translators must be U.S. citizens residing in this country for at least three out of the last five years. Besides having to pass a battery of language proficiency tests, they must also pass a ten-year scope background investigation and a polygraph examination, which asks two questions about national security but none about religious extremism. And the questions are vague, agents say, and not even applicable to people with no prior government experience. For example, one question asks, in so many words, "Have you ever passed classified information to a foreign government?" And although those who possess dual citizenship with the U.S. and another country must be willing to renounce their citizenship with the foreign country, renunciation is not enforced.

Lavey, who spent twenty years working counterterrorism cases for the FBI and INTERPOL, says the FBI has to do a better job of screening the people who have access to the information it is trying to protect. At a minimum, he says, personnel security specialists should interview prospective Arab and Muslim translators before hiring them.

Edmonds agrees, adding, "Interviews would help establish a tendency toward zealotry." Saccher, the counterintelligence agent who worked with Edmonds, was so disgusted by the divided loyalties he saw among Arab and Muslim translators that he volunteered to pre-interview translator candidates. He even sent a proposal to headquarters. "Give us some control over translators," he pleaded, to no avail. His proposal "was not well received," Edmonds says. "At least they're not carrying guns," he quipped one day in frustration.

FBI spokesman Ed Cogswell confirmed that though nearly all the Arabic translators the bureau hires are from the Middle East, they are not scrubbed any more than other employees handling classified information. "They go through the same background check as everyone else—full field background investigations," Cogswell said in a recent interview, though he claims their checks might take "a little longer" if investigators travel to their home countries to ask questions.

But Johnson, the former FBI supervisor, says investigators typically just check criminal records with foreign police and nothing more. Of course, police in Saudi Arabia are not going to tell investigators if an applicant supports jihad against America, he says.

Lavey and other agents worry that the religious bonds of Muslim agents may trump their oath to protect and serve America.

In a moment of candor, Ihsan Bagby, a black convert to Islam who has taught at American universities, revealed what many skeptics say is the true sentiment of devout Muslims in America. "Ultimately we can never be full citizens of this country," he said, quoted in a previous chapter, "because there is no way we can be fully committed to the institutions and ideologies of this country."

"YOU CAN'T TRUST THEM"

Even leaders of Muslim groups considered mainstream by Washington are on record saying they hope the U.S. Constitution will one day be replaced by Quranic law.

Lavey recalls a problem with a former Arab translator in the FBI's Detroit office who tried to back out of secretly recording a fellow Muslim suspected of terrorism by claiming the subject had threatened his life. "I know of one case where a translator claimed to have heard the subject speaking about him and making threats against him," Lavey tells me. "Three other translators listened and did not hear any of that information."

There is also the more recent case of FBI agent Gamal Abdel-Hafiz, an immigrant Muslim, who twice refused on religious grounds to tape-record Muslim terrorist suspects, hindering investigations of a bin Laden family-financed bank in New Jersey as well as Florida professor Sami Al-Arian, recently indicted for his ties to the Palestinian Islamic Jihad terrorist group. Former FBI agent Vincent says Abdel-Hafiz, who started out as a linguist translating Arabic for the bureau, finally explained to him that "a Muslim does not record another Muslim," after first claiming he feared for his life. Vincent says he contacted Arab subjects under investigation without disclosing the contacts to the agents running the cases. Despite his divided loyalties, the FBI subsequently promoted Abdel-Hafiz by assigning him to the U.S. Embassy in Saudi Arabia, a critical post for intelligence-gathering. (The full bizarre story will be told in a subsequent chapter.)

Vincent says Edmonds's story rings true from his experience working with Arabic translators at the Chicago field office, which grappled with the same issues of loyalty as the Washington field office. "What she related is not unusual," he says.

He cites a surveillance case he worked on around 1997 involving allegedly one of the top Hamas operatives in America—Sheikh Jamal Said of the Bridgeview mosque in Chicago. Said is a Palestinian schooled in Islam in Saudi Arabia. The Arabic translator assigned to the case was a Muslim from the Middle East.

"We had trouble with him from the beginning," Vincent recalls. "He kept sending over stuff to me, and it would say 'No pertinent information . . . No pertinent information.' And I said to him, listen, you can't do that. I said, it's my job to determine what's pertinent or not. Your job is to translate."

"And he kept doing it, and I had to remove him from my case because he just wouldn't translate the stuff," he adds. "And he wouldn't translate it because he knew he was working against another Muslim."

The reluctant linguist was transferred to the FBI's Milwaukee field office, where he did the same kind of selective translating on a case there. "And the translations he *did* do were slanted in such a way that he continually painted it up like nothing was going on," Vincent says. "And they had to send him back to Chicago."

"Bottom line," says Vincent, "he was refusing to do what he was ordered to do."

Management received a number of complaints about the Muslim linguist but did not fire him. "The FBI was afraid to do anything with him," Vincent says. "They finally suspended him with pay for three years."

"We saw it as yet another example of political correctness on the part of the FBI," he adds. "They don't want to make an issue of Muslim translators who won't do their jobs when they're working against other Muslims."

Around the same time, the Chicago office was shorthanded and put in a request to the Pentagon for Arabic translators. The U.S. Army detailed a couple of them to the office to help clear a backlog of untranslated Arabic material gathered in terrorism cases.

But, "When they found out that they were gonna be translating against Muslims, they refused to do the work," Vincent says. "And we had to send them back."

To be sure, a great many Arabic translators are Arab Christians who do not have the same reservations. But there is a definite pattern of conflicting loyalties involving Arabic linguists who are Muslim, Vincent says. "I personally know of five Muslim translators," he says, "and three out of the five refused to do their work."

"You can't trust them to translate another Muslim. You'd have to have somebody go over it again," Vincent asserts. "Now that's a huge problem, because most of your subjects in terrorism are Muslim."

THE AL-QAIDA APPLICANT

Edmonds notes that "those with questionable loyalties are still" translating al-Qaida and other terrorist wiretaps in the FBI's Washington language squad.

Could al-Qaida use the translator program to penetrate the FBI and learn its sources and methods for uncovering terrorist cells and disrupting terrorist plots? Some U.S. officials wonder.

"We have to watch out that the people who go to apply for the jobs as translators aren't working for al-Qaida," warns U.S. Attorney Patrick Fitzgerald, who prosecuted the U.S. Embassy bombings case. "One of the classic intelligence techniques is to [have] people that come in and pretend to work for you and gather information and feed it back [to the enemy], and we've seen indications that al-Qaida will do that."[24]

In fact, al-Qaida has tried to infiltrate the FBI's translator program in the past.

Take the chilling example of Ali Mohamed. A veteran of the Egyptian military, he helped train the top leadership of al-Qaida on intelligence techniques such as security codes, ciphers, and surveillance. He came to the United States and became a citizen, joining the army. Mohamed later applied for a job as an FBI translator to spy on its anti-terrorism efforts. Luckily, prosecutors got to him first, putting him away for his role in the embassy bombings.

However, Mohamed still managed to obtain a sensitive sealed court document from the trial of Blind Sheikh Omar Abdel Rahman, convicted of plotting to blow up New York landmarks. He faxed the confidential document to a close aide to Osama bin Laden for distribution. Officials shudder to think what secret information he would have been able to feed back to al-Qaida had he been able to penetrate the FBI.

Exacerbating concerns about infiltration is rampant nepotism within the bureau's foreign language department. Relatives of several questionable translators have skated behind them into the high-paying FBI jobs since 9/11.

"The language squad is infested with nepotism and cronyism," Edmonds says. "This kind of corruption is normal in the Middle East. I recognize it and expect it there, but not at the FBI of all places. I mean, this is like the *Twilight Zone*."

As mentioned earlier, the sons of Hadia Roberts, the daughter of the known Pakistani intelligence officer, were hired as translators not long after she got in the door. The bureau even agreed to pay to fly one of her sons down to Washington every weekend while he attended college in Boston, Edmonds says.

Then there is Kevin Taskesen, a Turkish translator who previously worked as a busboy and prep cook for a Middle Eastern restaurant in Washington's DuPont Circle. He was hired even though he scored poorly on FBI language proficiency tests. In fact, he flunked basic, entry-level English, Edmonds says. He was nonetheless assigned to the U.S. military base in Guantanamo Bay, Cuba, for a couple of months to translate interrogations of Turkish-speaking al-Qaida detainees who had been captured after 9/11. "He's working on one of the most sensitive issues there, and he's still there," Edmonds laments. "This is who we've put on the front line in the war on terrorism." How did he make the cut with such poor qualifications? "Because his wife worked at FBI headquarters administering the language proficiency exams," says Edmonds.

Taskesen and his wife, Cynthia, declined to be interviewed. An aide to Gulotta at headquarters acknowledged Taskesen's English is "rough," though he says "he can get across general ideas." He adds that he works as a monitor, not a linguist, which requires a lower level of language proficiency.

Edmonds says Cynthia Taskesen also helped Feghali get several of his family members and friends jobs in the language department. A contract linguist can earn up to thirty-eight dollars an hour.

Another translator currently employed by the FBI recently stepped forward to corroborate Edmonds's charges of favoritism within the language department, prompting Sens. Leahy and Charles Grassley of the Senate Judiciary Committee to ask the inspector general to look into allegations of "backdoor hiring practices" that allow unqualified linguists to land jobs. They said the new whistleblower told them that, despite deficiencies, translators are getting a "passing grade surreptitiously because of personal contacts among the translator staff."[25]

AT THEIR MERCY

Given the severe shortage of translators and mounting backlogs, the FBI is all too willing to let translators recruit relatives. But there is another reason it does not curb the nepotism: appeasement of minorities. Arab Americans have a habit of crying racial discrimination if they do not get their way in the workplace, and the last thing the politically correct FBI wants is to be accused of racism. After 9/11, you will recall, headquarters instated a bureau-wide Muslim-sensitivity training program.

After being passed over for promotion, Feghali, the Lebanese supervisor, threatened to sue the bureau for racial discrimination but dropped the lawsuit once the bureau promoted him to supervising the all-important Arabic language desk serving the FBI's counterterrorism operations. The Beirut-born Feghali was promoted despite a record of previous allegations of misconduct, including overbilling and sexual harassment. Edmonds says Feghali was known to take female translators into his office and lock the door for as long as an hour at a time, in violation of the bureau's open-door policy. "He'd make them sit on his knee and beg for candy and call him 'Daddy,'" she says.

Feghali even started an Arab-rights group within the bureau that acts as a clearinghouse for discrimination complaints. Several Arab linguists have threatened the bureau with lawsuits for alleged discrimination. For example, Bassem Yusuf, an Arabic polygrapher, claims he was marginalized after 9/11 and sued the bureau for discrimination. The FBI quietly settled with him, giving him the promotion and raise he demanded.

"They are ferocious," Edmonds says. "And the bureau is pretty intimidated by them. In fact, they are more afraid of discrimination suits than any possible espionage or terrorist attack."

Their leverage does not stop there.

Most agents working counterterrorism and counterintelligence cases are white guys who do not speak a lick of Arabic. At the end of the day, they rely on the judgment and recommendation of translators as to whether enough probable cause exists to conduct raids on terrorist suspects, based on the activities those translators have told agents they overheard in Arabic from wiretaps. And terrorist suspects under arrest will be kept in custody or kicked based on the judgment of the Arabic translator reviewing documents confiscated in raids. There are no analysts in the middle to work with the translators and evaluate the translations and in turn work with the agents. Agents are at the direct mercy of the translators.

"The translators determine what goes to the agent, what gets to be blocked," Edmonds says. "That's a lot of power. Agents are sitting there totally deaf, dumb, and blind."

Johnson agrees: "There is no question case agents are at the mercy of the Arabic translators, and you've got to be able to trust what they say."

But many times "they fool the agents," Edmonds says. "They tell them, 'Oh, these [remarks or documents] aren't incriminating.'" And the agent isn't the wiser.

Lavey says wiretap translations by Mideast-born agents should have a "second opinion," because their backgrounds may "prejudice" their interpretation and analysis. "We are at war, and we need more than one translator for each subject under electronic surveillance," he says. "We are relying too heavily on single Arab translators for significant information, and worse yet, investigative guidance."

He says translators will often leave out large sections of conversation in surveillance logs because they deem it irrelevant to the investigation. "It's noted as 'personal' or 'family' information with a comment by the translator that there is no substantive investigative information. It is viewed as immaterial to the case," Lavey says.

"But this is often inaccurate," he adds. "Very easily, and too often, something like, 'I am picking up my brother at the station,' is overlooked and never made note of, but it may be very significant."

Bad guys planning an attack do not come right out and say it, even in Arabic.

In fact, terrorist targets know the FBI is listening in now more than ever, and they "make fun of it on the phone," Edmonds says. They throw out terms such as "melon" or "wedding" when they mean something else to try to throw off agents. They also invoke dates and events of special Islamic significance. Unfortunately, very few agents and even analysts in the bureau understand the culture and history of Islam and the Middle East to catch the hidden meanings behind certain words and phrases. They rely almost exclusively on the interpretation of the Arabic linguist from that region, whose loyalties are often suspect.

In response, Cogswell says that case supervisors "try to vet [logs] through two people, if they can," but the shortage of translators makes that next to impossible. An aide to Gulotta at headquarters admits that "there was no quality control before 9/11." But he says they now try to at least do "random sampling" of translations to check for accuracy, and they almost always do retranslations before a case goes to trial.

"There was no cross-checking when I was there," says Johnson, who left the bureau before 9/11. "They don't have enough translators to cross-check even if they wanted to."

The 9/11 Commission determined that to be the case. "We have learned that if a language specialist mishandles a translation, there are few checks to catch the error."[26]

THE HOLE

Making matters worse, agents do not even have direct access to the room inside the Washington field office where Arabic translators work—unbelievable as it sounds.

Housed on the fourth floor of the building, just a few blocks from FBI headquarters, the language unit is officially known by the codename CI-19. But agents have their own name for it—"The Hole." More than two hundred translators, most of them immigrants from some sixty-nine countries around the world, work side-by-side in a large open room. "There were so many people crawling around, it looked like an anthill," Johnson says.

Agents also call it "the United Nations," and tensions between some nationalities can run high. Edmonds recalls an Indian translator and a Pakistani translator almost coming to blows one day over a religious dispute. "They won't go to the coffee room at the same time now," Edmonds says. The same violent hostilities exist between the Hebrew and Arabic desks, she says.

And the room is highly secured. So high that, as previously mentioned, agents are not even allowed to enter the room without an escort. "Agents do not have [security] badge access to the unit," confirms a translator who still works there. "They have to call us to come and open the door for them, and then we let them in." So basically, the translators—many of whom are Middle Eastern immigrants with divided loyalties—rule the roost.

And the FBI will continue to rely on Arabic translators born in the Middle East for the foreseeable future. It is having a hard time recruiting fluent American-born translators because the Arabic language is rarely studied in American colleges. "It's very problematic," acknowledges FBI spokesman Cogswell, although he says the bureau has made recent strides in recruiting. Since 9/11, he notes, the FBI has tripled the number of Arabic language specialists and contract linguists on staff, expanding from 70 to 209. But they have hardly made a dent in the ever-growing backlog of untranslated materials in Arabic.

Since the 9/11 attacks alone, a whopping 123,000 hours of audiotaped recordings associated with counterterrorism (including significant portions related to al-Qaida), along with 370,000 hours of audio related to counterintelligence, have not been translated and reviewed, according to a recent audit by the Department of Justice inspector general. The counterterrorism backlog alone is equivalent to fourteen years.

What's more, the FBI is not meeting Mueller's requirement that all al-Qaida communications collected under the Foreign Intelligence Surveillance Act, or FISA, be reviewed within twelve hours of interception. Last year's shocking audit, requested by Leahy of the Senate Judiciary Committee, found that 36 percent of such communications were not even *received* at FBI headquarters within twelve hours. The audit also found that the FBI still lacks the number of translators needed to clear the backlog, despite tripling the number of Arabic translators.

Compounding the problem, the volume of FBI wiretapping has soared to a record level due in part to the USA Patriot Act, which makes it easier for agents to obtain surveillance warrants under FISA. Surveillance collection in languages related to counterterrorism—Arabic, Farsi, Urdu, and Pashto—has jumped 45 percent in the past two years and is expected to continue to grow at a 15 percent annual clip in coming years, the audit found. So the backlog, like the federal debt, just keeps mounting.

TICKING E-MAILS

"That kind of volume of backlog doesn't surprise me one bit," says Cole, who has firsthand knowledge of just how bad the backlog has gotten. Experienced in putting applications for FISA warrants together, Cole was detailed to the counterterrorism division at headquarters to help with surveillance requests in December

2003. When he first reported to one of the units there to help out, he was floored by what he saw. He retells this jarring exchange with the unit chief that day:

> COLE: All right, what do you have?
> UNIT CHIEF: Well, we have all these FISAs that are up for renewal, about a dozen or so.
> COLE: Okay, let me see what you have.

All the surveillance requests the unit wanted were on e-mail accounts used by terrorist suspects. They were set to expire in two weeks. To justify their renewal, agents had to demonstrate to the FISA court that the previous surveillance—in this instance, e-mail sniffing—had produced information relevant to their case. They also had to show the e-mail accounts were still active and being used by the subjects.

Cole looked at the trail of information generated from the e-mail accounts under surveillance and was impressed with the substance of it.

> COLE: Has anyone even looked at this stuff, because some of it is pretty good.
> UNIT CHIEF: We're sure someone has reviewed it.
> COLE: Well, we just need to fill in some gaps. Because when I'm reading this stuff, there's a lot of dates missing. You know, there's like lapses in time. I'm missing little pieces here and there. Is there any more stuff here?
> UNIT CHIEF: Yeah, we know where we can probably find it.
> COLE: Where?

The unit chief then led Cole to stacks and stacks of cardboard boxes filled with reams of documents. "I mean, there was a ton of them, all full of text cuts" from e-mails, Cole recalls.

> UNIT CHIEF: They're all in those boxes right there.
> COLE: Great. Has anybody gone through those boxes yet?
> UNIT CHIEF: No.
> COLE: What do you mean?
> UNIT CHIEF: We don't have the people to go through and read all the stuff that comes in on these texts. A lot of it is in Arabic, and still has to be translated.
> COLE: Isn't this what got the bureau in trouble in the first place? There

could be an e-mail in there saying they're going to blow up a building tomorrow. And you're telling me that nobody has had a chance to review that stuff?!

The unit chief, equally frustrated, could only nod.

Cole points out that investigators had missed clues to both the 1993 and 2001 World Trade Center attacks because they were buried in a backlog of untranslated wiretaps and documents in Arabic. Months before the first World Trade Center bombing in 1993, he says, one of the plotters of the terrorist attack was heard on tape having a discussion in Arabic that no one at the time knew was about how to make explosives. And he had a manual that no one at the time knew was about how to blow up buildings. No one knew *because none of it was translated until well after the bombing.*

And on September 10, 2001, U.S. intelligence intercepted a message in Arabic that warned, "Tomorrow is zero hour." Again, the taped message went untranslated until *after* tragedy struck—the September 11 attacks on the World Trade Center and Pentagon. An embarrassed intelligence community tried to tell the 9/11 Commission that additional information later came to light that suggested the message was connected with the opening of a Taliban and al-Qaida military offensive in Afghanistan against the Northern Alliance, rather than the 9/11 attacks. But that's political spin, say bureau sources. Fact is, they just plain missed the warning.

Lavey claims that at some FBI field offices, wiretap conversations of Arab terrorist suspects recorded as far back as the 1980s have only "very recently" been translated into English. And frighteningly, the pre-9/11 backlog of untranslated material has not yet been cleared, as new surveillance tapes are added to already-crammed lockers where such untranslated evidence is stored at the Washington field office and other sites.

Johnson worries that key al-Qaida intercepts are being lost, even now, after 9/11. "I'm not convinced we have a handle on it at all." He says "ticking time bombs" are likely buried under the mountain of untranslated materials.

That any backlog at all still exists more than three years after the 9/11 attacks is outrageous, Lavey says. "The bureau can no longer tolerate that situation in a war."

"LET THEM BEG US"

Cogswell, while not excusing the backlog, explains that the FBI does not have a large pool from which to recruit translators to clear the backlog. He fairly notes that the Arabic language is a difficult and demanding one to learn and few Americans are fluent in it.

But Lavey says the FBI was advised years ago to send more agents to learn Arabic at the bureau's language school. It was also told to lengthen the course. "It was pointed out to headquarters that agents leaving language school after one intensive year of Arabic were ill-prepared to use the language effectively, and that, at a minimum, another half year was needed to learn a dialect conversationally," he said. "This information was ignored."

Minneapolis FBI agent Coleen Rowley agrees that the current program is not intense enough to produce native-born Americans who are conversant in Arabic. Very few non-immigrants can score a Level 5 on the Defense Language Proficiency Test—the highest rating. At that level, a linguist is considered an "educated native speaker."

"The bureau has had a hard time training our own because Arabic is such a hard language to learn and be conversant in," Rowley says. "So we have to hire immigrants who are fluent. And trying to ensure their allegiance to the FBI and the United States is dicey business. There's a lot of tension there."

But it only gets worse.

Despite the backlog of untranslated materials, Edmonds says her supervisor, Feghali, told her and other translators to just let the work pile higher. Why? Money. She says Feghali explained to her that Congress would approve an even bigger budget for the department if they could continue to show big backlogs.

"We were told to take long breaks, to slow down translations, and to simply say 'no' to those field agents calling us to beg for speedy translations so that they could go on with their investigations and interrogations of those they had detained," says Edmonds. She claims Feghali actually tampered with her work to slow her down. "He went as far as getting into my work computer and deleting almost completed work so that I had to go back and start all over again."

Edmonds says 9/11 put Feghali and his Arab cronies in the driver's seat, and Feghali even told her he intended to leverage their power. "As he put it: 'This is our time to show those a—holes we are in charge,'" she says. "Just let them beg us." Edmonds officially made the shocking allegations in letters to the Senate Judiciary Committee, 9/11 Commission, and Department of Justice inspector general.

Reached by phone at his Maryland home, Feghali was brusque and refused to talk about the charges. "I'm not at liberty to discuss this thing, okay?" he said before abruptly hanging up. The spokesperson for the FBI's Washington field office, Debbie Weierman, had no comment. At least one other translator confirmed Edmonds's account. But the aide to Gulotta, who wishes to remain anonymous, says her story does not square with the spike in overtime hours billed by translators in the Washington field office since 9/11.

Cole says Feghali is simply borrowing a page from FBI management, which commonly uses such tactics to protect turf. "Supervisors have the mentality that if we don't do the work, then we can justify going to the Hill and asking for more resources so we can get more money," he says. "That happens a lot."

For instance, "One of the units at headquarters I worked in didn't have a damn thing to do, and the supervisor would never say that, because they didn't want to lose the bodies," Cole adds. "Matter of fact, they were trying to get more bodies."

But the rise of an Arab fiefdom within the bureau begs the question: who is in control? Technically, Gulotta has authority over Feghali and his Washington field office operations, but Edmonds says she rarely visits there. "There's no supervision in that office," she says. "Gulotta stays in her headquarters castle and hardly ever steps foot in that office." Others say Gulotta, a former translator herself, is not cut out for the job, which requires hiring, firing, and administrative oversight of the translator program. "She never in my view, and in the view of quite a few others, exhibited sound managerial skills," says a senior FBI official who worked with her at headquarters.

But her aide defends her performance, arguing that she is pushing the use of translation software to summarize recordings and other materials, which will at least give agents a "general idea" of what is in backlogs so they can prioritize the material for further review. He says his boss is also involved in setting up the National Virtual Translation Center, which brings work to translators around the country via secure computer links. The bureau will no longer have to move people around the country to do translation work, which should speed up the process and help clear backlogs.

SHOOTING THE MESSENGER

But, however much good the new technology does for managing backlogs, it does nothing to solve the security problems plaguing the foreign language department, critics say. In that area, the bureau appears to be out to lunch.

Remarkably, headquarters has a tin ear for hearing about security complaints from conscientious and patriotic employees, even after 9/11. And when such employees become frustrated and take their complaints to Congress or the press, headquarters responds by punishing them—proving once again that the FBI is better at protecting itself than the country. Cole is no exception.

"After I started raising the issue with the language specialists and the security, the bureau's response was kill the messenger," Cole says. "They decided to go after me."

He says he sent four letters to Mueller's office in 2002 and 2003 warning the director about the security problems. He never heard back from Mueller. So the longtime agent briefed the Senate Judiciary Committee and the office of the Justice Department inspector general, which promised to open an investigation but never even interviewed him.

After word got back to FBI brass of his whistleblowing activities, Cole was demoted and given negative evaluations, his first in eighteen years of service. "They didn't want to investigate" any of the personnel security and espionage cases he brought to their attention, he says. And then early last year, he was suspended. Cole decided to call it quits three months later.

The FBI went after Edmonds hammer-and-tongs after she reported security breaches and potential espionage to upper management, including Dale Watson, the bureau's counterterrorism chief at the time. She was subjected to a polygraph, which bureau insiders say she passed without a glitch. Headquarters still ignored her allegations and then thanked her with a pink slip. The day of her firing, the petite Edmonds, who hardly poses a threat, was physically escorted out of the building by FBI official Thomas Frields and the head of security. Frields told her "she would never be allowed to set foot on FBI premises again, and that the next time he would meet her would be in jail," according to documents filed in federal court.[27]

Trying to make good on that promise, the FBI seized her home computer and subjected her to a security review. But officials could find nothing incriminating to use against her. Edmonds got her computer back, but not the belongings she kept at her FBI desk, including memos from agents praising her work performance. The FBI also impounded family mementos she holds dear, including two black-and-white photos of her late father, a surgeon who served under the Shah of Iran, and a Farsi-English dictionary her father gave her as a gift.

The bureau, which just months earlier had renewed her contract for another year, gave no reason for her termination. The cause listed on her pink slip stated only that she was "terminated completely for the Government's convenience."[28]

Even the Justice Department's inspector general has concluded that Edmonds's security whistleblowing was a factor in her firing, determining that her allegations "were at least a contributing factor in why the FBI terminated her services."[29]

When Edmonds sued the bureau, it got former Attorney General John Ashcroft to invoke the rarely used "state secrets privilege" to block the lawsuit and prevent the public disclosure of information. State secrets privilege is the neutron bomb of executive privilege claims because it is an absolute privilege that automatically renders the information unavailable in any litigation. Ashcroft argued that airing the facts about the Dickerson case could jeopardize national security and disrupt diplomatic relations with a foreign government—that is, Turkey. While describing the move as "draconian," a federal judge nonetheless agreed with his argument and threw out Edmonds's lawsuit last year.

CIRCLING THE WAGONS

Then Ashcroft dropped another bombshell. He took the highly unusual move of retroactively classifying information about the Edmonds case that was already in the public domain, including letters to the FBI from the Senate Judiciary Committee that were posted on Senate Web sites. The documents have been removed from the sites. The retro-classification, which goes back to 2002, also effectively put "a gag order on Congress," Grassley complains, by hindering further congressional investigation. Facts about the scandal cannot be openly discussed in public hearings now. In effect, he charges, Mueller and Ashcroft initiated a cover-up. "It looks like an attempt to cover up the FBI's problems in translating intelligence," Grassley says. Even Inspector General Fine's report, which urges Mueller to open an internal espionage investigation in at least the Dickerson case, has been classified secret.

So why has the FBI taken such drastic measures to bury the internal security problems that Edmonds exposed?

For one, admitting wiretap translations are shoddy could jeopardize criminal prosecutions. Defense lawyers for the Holy Land Foundation, the Muslim charity indicted for underwriting Hamas terrorists, are already challenging key translations in the FBI's case as inaccurate. If the FBI admits translations are faulty, then lawyers for prosecuted terrorists might have grounds for appeal, as was the case last decade when an internal inquiry revealed that the FBI forensics lab was sloppy in handling evidence.

Holy Land Foundation lawyers have brought a formal complaint to the Department of Justice arguing that the translation of a key Arabic document the FBI used to support its criminal case against the Muslim charity is "distorted" and erroneous. The document, originally obtained by Israeli intelligence, fingers Holy Land Foundation founders as Hamas operatives. Lawyers in their complaint cite sixty-seven alleged discrepancies or errors in the translation of the four-page document.[30]

Naturally, the defense team is now seeking the release of the still-classified sections of the inspector general's 157-page audit of the FBI's translator program, which allegedly details widespread problems, including mistranslations and incompetence. The Justice Department is keeping the report, which could undermine the bureau's terrorism cases, under tight wraps.

Edmonds recognizes that the last thing the FBI wants to do is shake up the department and invite a legal nightmare. "If they acknowledge security and competency problems with the language program, the courts would force them to reopen cases," she says. "They'd have to retranslate everything. It would be a huge liability for the government."

But she says Mueller is also circling the wagons at headquarters to protect the bureau from another embarrassing spy scandal. Indeed, the FBI would be loath to admit a major breach in security so soon after the Hanssen case, which severely damaged the bureau's reputation. The political blow from new revelations of spying would be devastating.

Robert Hanssen, an FBI special agent with a two-decade career, mostly in counterintelligence, was arrested in early 2001 for spying for the Soviet Union and, later, for Russia. It was regarded as the worst known case of foreign penetration of the FBI, and investigators are still assessing the damage to national security.

Yet it could have been prevented. Headquarters turned a blind eye to suspicious security breaches and other signs of treachery by Hanssen. Some lawmakers fear the FBI has not learned from its mistakes.

Leahy and Grassley say every official at the FBI who was notified of the allegations against Dickerson reacted by questioning why Edmonds was "causing trouble," rather than investigating her allegations.

"Even after verifying these allegations, the FBI downplayed the importance of this matter and seemed to imply that it had ceased looking into the complaints as a security matter," they wrote Ashcroft in a now-classified letter. "Anyone who remembers the longtime treachery of former FBI agent Robert Hanssen would be concerned at this reaction."

For years Hanssen's bizarre actions were also written off as minor security breaches and unworthy of serious consideration. "If even routine diligence had been exercised earlier, Hanssen could have been stopped from doing untold damage," they added. "The FBI needs to learn from its mistakes."

Grassley, commenting separately, says he is convinced the FBI's language squad has been penetrated by enemy moles. "I think the FBI is ignoring a very major internal security breach," he says, "and a potential espionage breach."[31]

MISSING LAPTOPS

After the Hanssen spy scandal, Congress ordered the bureau to overhaul security. But many of the regulations have not been put in place, according to Cole, who personally saw lapses in personnel security that continued even after 9/11. The bureau was cutting corners on hiring Middle Eastern linguists at the same time it was telling Congress it was doing everything possible to tighten security.

In addition, tighter procedures for handling classified materials have not been followed. Edmonds, for one, saw several different translators leave the building with secret documents and audiotapes in their gym bags, a major no-no. According to security policy, bureau employees can leave documents classified at the secret level or lower out on their desks, but top secret documents have to be locked in a drawer. And sensitive compartmented information has to be locked in a safe.

But the rules were routinely broken in the language unit, Edmonds says. Many translators, who were handling information as sensitive as the names of informants, did not even know the location of the safe, known as an "SCIF." "Everything is just out there in the open," Edmonds says. Also, she says it is not uncommon to see extra copies of top secret documents left unshredded in the photocopying room.

Johnson observed the same sloppy handling of sensitive national security information. "The translation unit was so cluttered," he says. "There was stuff left out on the desk all the time."

Perhaps most shocking, laptop computers containing classified information routinely have gone missing from the unit. Edmonds says there are eleven laptops assigned to the Washington field office, all loaded with classified information. She remembers seeing a 2002 memo from security stating that "computer No. 6 and computer No. 9" were missing from what should be a secure room outside the language unit. The room is supposed to be locked, but "it's never locked," she says. The laptops are supposed to be logged out, but "no one ever signed out in that log," she adds. The laptops were typically checked out by Arabic and other translators who were assigned to help with interrogations of terrorist suspects, or who took them on other temporary-duty assignments, called "TDYs," outside the office.

Another translator who worked in the field office but now reports to head-quarters confirms Edmonds's account of the missing laptops. "I just assumed they were found, because the e-mails stopped coming," he says. "Apparently they were never found though."

Offering a bizarre defense, the aide to Gulotta says the breach is nothing new. "The bureau is notorious for missing laptops," he says.

Indeed it is. Just between 1999 and 2002, the FBI lost 317 laptop computers, which represents more than 2 percent of the total 15,017 laptops in its inventory, according to an August 2002 report by the Justice Department's inspector general. "It is possible that the missing laptop computers would have been used to process and store national security or sensitive law enforcement information that, if divulged, could harm the public," the report says. More maddening, the report notes that the FBI rarely took disciplinary action against individuals responsible for the lost laptops. And it did not even know the full extent of the loss because it had not taken a full inventory of its computers in ten years.[32]

The FBI's response: don't blame us, everybody loses stuff. "Some property theft and loss, to include guns and laptops, is inevitable for any law enforcement agency," the FBI said in a statement at the time. How comforting.

The following year, the inspector general released more embarrassing findings from an investigation into the lax internal security program at the FBI that allowed a mole like Hanssen to go undetected in its ranks for years. Here is the bureau's progress report, released more than two years after the Hanssen scandal, in August 2003:

> In our review, we observed serious deficiencies in nearly every aspect of the FBI's internal security program—from personnel security, to computer security, document security and security training and compliance. These deficiencies led to the absence of effective deterrence to espionage at the FBI and undermined the FBI's ability to detect an FBI mole. . . . Some of the most serious weaknesses still have not been fully remedied. These weaknesses expose the FBI to the risk of future serious compromises by other moles.[33]

In other words, security is still a mess at the FBI, and the agency is as vulnerable as ever to penetration by enemy moles. "It proves my point that the FBI is still wide open to infiltration," Edmonds says.

She wonders how an agency that cannot even protect itself from internal theft and espionage can protect the country from al-Qaida terrorists. After 9/11, "we are all cautioned to be vigilant, yet the FBI is not vigilant within its own departments," Edmonds says. "How can the FBI possibly help protect us, the citizens of the United States, against terrorist attacks, when it cannot—or will not—even protect itself?"

She has a point, but one the bureau plainly does not want to hear.

18

THE CASE OF THE RELUCTANT AGENT

When Muslims Investigate Fellow Muslims

"A Muslim does not record another Muslim."
—FBI special agent GAMAL ABDEL-HAFIZ

Soliman Biheiri was nervous. It was 1999, and his bookkeeper had just received a federal subpoena ordering his cooperation in an FBI counterterrorism investigation. Biheiri, an Egyptian national, ran an investment banking firm in the Washington area that counted Osama bin Laden's nephew and other wealthy Saudis connected to al-Qaida as investors. The firm, BMI Inc.—which stands for Bait ul-Mal, or House of Money—was the target of the FBI probe. The bureau received a tip that some of the funds that the bookkeeper, Abbas Ebrahim, had transferred overseas on behalf of his boss may have been used to finance the U.S. embassy bombings in Africa.

Biheiri was desperate for advice. "Put me in touch with Gamal Abdel-Hafiz," he told his accountant.

Abdel-Hafiz, also from Egypt, was well known in the local Muslim community and a good friend and college roommate of Ebrahim. He also happened to be the FBI's first Muslim agent, and one Biheiri hoped could shed some light on the case the government was building against him and his company. Over dinner one evening, Ebrahim asked his old pal Abdel-Hafiz if he would be willing to meet with Biheiri privately.

Abdel-Hafiz, in turn, brought the proposal back to the lead investigators in the case, who jumped at the chance to have an agent question the subject of their probe without his attorney present.

"We were excited about the meeting," said former FBI special agent John Vincent, who worked on the case. "And even though we knew he had an

185

attorney, we didn't have to advise him [of the meeting] since the subject came to us."[1]

He and his partner Robert Wright thought it might be a big break in the case. "Let's do it," they told Abdel-Hafiz, who agreed to set up the meeting. They brought in then-Assistant U.S. Attorney Mark Flessner, the prosecutor assigned to the case, and he decided to have the Muslim agent wear a wire to record the conversation with Biheiri, gathering any incriminating evidence.

At that point, Abdel-Hafiz got goosey, according to Vincent and others involved in the discussions. He resisted recording Biheiri, offering up a number of excuses to Flessner to explain his reluctance before finally revealing the true reason:

FLESSNER: We want this meeting recorded.

ABDEL-HAFIZ: Well, I can't use recording devices because Muslims hug each other, and they'll detect them.

FLESSNER: No problem, we'll wire up a hotel room for you.

ABDEL-HAFIZ: Uh, I don't want to do that either.

FLESSNER: Why not?

ABDEL-HAFIZ: Because a Muslim does not record another Muslim.

Vincent and Wright were dumbstruck by what they were hearing from their fellow agent, who wore a badge and a gun just like them. He was refusing to help nail a key target in a major counterterrorism case for religious reasons. As a result, the agents never got Biheiri on tape, and they accused Abdel-Hafiz of disloyalty and insubordination.

Abdel-Hafiz says he remembers it differently. In an exclusive interview with me, he claims he was explaining the view of other Muslims, not necessarily his own, who he feared would threaten him and his family if they found out he betrayed their trust by secretly taping them.

"I told them that this is something that would become discoverable in court. I do a lot of things with the Muslim community. I work a lot of cases where my subjects are Muslims. When this becomes discoverable, every person who meets with me or talks to me will say 'Oh my God, who is this guy? Does he record me every time I talk to him?'" Abdel-Hafiz says. "And this will become a safety issue for me and my family because Muslims would look at it as a betrayal of trust. When they [Flessner and the agents] asked why would it be a betrayal of trust, I said because, in their opinion, they would say a Muslim should not record another Muslim."[2]

But it was not the first time Abdel-Hafiz failed to record a fellow Muslim and friend of a friend under investigation for terrorism.

The prior year, 1998, Abdel-Hafiz met a Muslim activist through a friend at the Dar al-Hijrah Islamic Center outside Washington, a hard-line Wahhabi mosque the agent regularly attended at the time. The two exchanged business cards. Not long afterward, Abdel-Hafiz got a call from one Sami al-Arian in Florida. The Tampa professor said he got the agent's business card from the mutual acquaintance and wanted to know if he would do him a favor and, among other things, poke around the FBI to see if it had ever opened an investigation into alleged death threats against terrorism researcher Steve Emerson. Al-Arian wanted to try to catch the pro-Israel Emerson possibly exaggerating claims he made in congressional testimony about such threats. Abdel-Hafiz agreed to look into the issue for al-Arian, bureau sources tell me.

Hearing of the encounter, the FBI's Tampa field office asked Abdel-Hafiz to follow up by asking al-Arian several questions related to a counterterrorism case they were building against him—and secretly record his answers. Abdel-Hafiz agreed to speak to al-Arian by phone but said he would not record the conversation without al-Arian's knowledge. The lead Tampa agent on the case, Barry Carmody, was scandalized by his refusal, calling it "outrageous."[3]

Then Abdel-Hafiz met, unexpectedly, with al-Arian at an American Muslim Council conference in Washington and wrote a summary of their conversation, which he had not coordinated with Tampa. The report he filed was not well received by Carmody and his team of investigators in Tampa—or by Vincent and Wright, whose Chicago investigation dovetailed with the al-Arian case.

"After Gamal had a conversation with Sami al-Arian, he made a lot of self-serving statements for al-Arian and denigrated the FBI agent [Carmody] who was investigating the case," Vincent says.

"So we knew there was a problem," he adds. "We had suspicions about whether Gamal would write down conversations accurately, and we wanted to know exactly what the conversation was" between him and Biheiri, who is tied to al-Arian.

Even without Abdel-Hafiz's cooperation, investigators were able to gather enough evidence on Biheiri, a member of the notorious Muslim Brotherhood of Egypt, to bring terrorism-related charges against him. He was finally indicted last year. Prosecutors say he falsely denied business relationships with al-Arian and Hamas leader Mousa Abu Marzook.[4] Al-Arian's phone number was found in Biheiri's computer address book.

Biheiri is also accused of conducting financial transactions with al-Qaida financier Yassin Kadi, a businessman from Saudi. After the 9/11 al-Qaida attacks, witnesses observed Biheiri destroying financial records, according to federal court documents.[5]

Abdel-Hafiz, 46, says he does not regret refusing to record Biheiri. "He wouldn't have admitted anything," he says. "Recording him would have been of little value."

Despite the recent charges filed against Biheiri, he says he doubts his pal's former boss is mixed up in terrorism financing and speculates Biheiri used BMI primarily to enrich himself. "Personally, I think he's more a used car salesman than anything," Abdel-Hafiz tells me. "He's in it for personal gain, not religious reasons."

But Vincent says he was bothered by Abdel-Hafiz's close personal ties to the subject. He felt the Muslim agent and Biheiri's bookkeeper Ebrahim were far too cozy, a relationship that he says may have compromised Abdel-Hafiz's integrity.

"There were also complaints that he was meeting with subjects of investigations in Washington without advising the Washington field office," Vincent says. "He would fly up there [from Dallas, where he was worked in the FBI's field office] because his good friend was up there, the bookkeeper at BMI."

Carmody says Abdel-Hafiz hurt the al-Arian probe by refusing to record the professor. Al-Arian even bragged to Abdel-Hafiz that the Tampa office did not have a strong case against him. Asked why he did not record al-Arian at their private meeting, the Muslim agent simply says, "I had no recording equipment with me." In the end, Carmody got his man, however. Al-Arian is now behind bars awaiting trial on charges he raised money for the Palestinian Islamic Jihad, a terrorist group.

While he would not comment on al-Arian's guilt or innocence, Abdel-Hafiz says the Tampa office handled the case clumsily. "These people think Sami al-Arian is an idiot," he says. "But Sami al-Arian is a very smart man."

Abdel-Hafiz, a devout Sunni Muslim whose Egyptian father is known as a Quran memorizer, showed a pattern of pro-Islamist behavior, say agents who worked with him. Yet FBI headquarters overlooked it and even promoted him. Carmody, Vincent, and Wright all complained to headquarters about Abdel-Hafiz twice refusing on religious grounds to tape-record Muslim terrorist suspects. Despite that, he was handpicked in early 2001 by former FBI Director Louis Freeh to become the FBI's deputy legal attaché at the U.S. Embassy in Riyadh, Saudi Arabia—a key post in the battle against al-Qaida, which had hit American military barracks inside Saudi and a warship in neighboring Yemen. After 9/11, when fifteen of the nineteen hijackers turned out to be Saudi nationals, Abdel-Hafiz was in a prime position to run down leads in the Saudi capital.

But agents also complained about his performance there, saying they were not getting answers to the leads they were sending him in Riyadh. Abdel-Hafiz says he was one of only two people manning the office there and was further hobbled by an antiquated computer system. But he and his boss Wilfred Rattigan, a black convert to Islam, had nonetheless found time to fly off to Mecca for the *hajj*.

"Headquarters ignored our complaints, ignored the fact that we wanted to file a dereliction of duty complaint against an agent for not doing his job," Vincent says.

So he and Wright went to the media with their complaint. In 2002, ABC News, Fox News, and others jumped all over the story, and suddenly FBI headquarters took a harder look at Abdel-Hafiz. In early 2003, he was recalled from Saudi Arabia and suspended with pay, while the bureau conducted an internal investigation of him. A few months later, it fired Abdel-Hafiz, citing only his failure to disclose information on his application for a security clearance. They got him on a technicality unrelated to his failure to help investigate terrorism suspects, although bureau sources say his disciplinary file includes statements by Wright and a copy of a news article detailing his refusal to tape-record suspects.

The technicality, however, raises further questions about Abdel-Hafiz's integrity. It stems from an accusation his ex-wife made about him faking a home burglary to fraudulently collect insurance money.

"The reason they fired him is because when we do a five-year personnel reinvestigation, his ex-wife came out and said he put in a claim for twenty-five thousand dollars for stolen property, and she said that it was all set up, that it was fraud," Vincent says. "And she showed insurance investigators some of the property that was claimed to have been stolen. They still owned it." The insurer refused to pay the claim.

"But the bureau didn't fire him for that, either," he continues. "They fired him because he did not put on his new agent application that he was a party to a lawsuit to sue the insurance company after it refused to pay his claim. Which was ridiculous. No one gets fired for that."

Abdel-Hafiz hired a lawyer and appealed the firing, arguing he was wrongfully dismissed. He also threatened to sue the bureau for discrimination.

Last year, the FBI reinstated Abdel-Hafiz, even though he had failed a polygraph when he denied the charges. He got his old job back in the international terrorism squad at the Dallas field office, where he had been reassigned after returning from Saudi, and retained his top secret security clearance.

Then, he tried to clear his name, filing defamation suits against Vincent and Wright, as well as ABC News's Brian Ross and Charlie Gibson and Fox News's Bill O'Reilly for allegedly accusing him of sympathizing with terrorists.

At the same time, he complained he had lost credibility in the Muslim community and was essentially worthless as an undercover agent in counterterrorism cases. He is now working mortgage fraud cases, where he no longer has a conflict with his Muslim brothers.

Vincent says he was floored by the FBI's extraordinary reversal but says he and Wright did the right thing in blowing the whistle on Abdel-Hafiz. He says other agents commended them, noting the New York field office also had concerns with Abdel-Hafiz when he worked as an Arabic translator there in 1994 before becoming an agent. "When we were on TV, they were applauding the fact that we were blowing the whistle on this Muslim agent," he says.

Abdel-Hafiz argues that he received praise for his New York work. He points out that he testified against the Blind Sheikh Omar Abdul Rahman and helped put him behind bars for plotting to blow up New York landmarks. He says he also helped break a Yemeni suspect in the USS *Cole* attack and obtained a crucial confession in a 2002 FBI investigation of an al-Qaida cell based in Lackawanna, New York.

He says Vincent and Wright are simply biased against Muslims and Arabs: "They were motivated by racism and bigotry." Abdel-Hafiz says he wanted Wright, whom he calls "vindictive," to go through Muslim-sensitivity training and write him an apology. Wright did neither, so he sued. He says he will have no mercy on him or Vincent.

Abdel-Hafiz, who still has family in Cairo, where he studied Islam, insists he is not a terrorist sympathizer or traitor and supports the war on terrorism. "There are a lot of beneficial things that take place in mosques, but I am not opposed to the Patriot Act," which authorizes spying on mosques, he says. "I am, however, opposed to the abuse of the Patriot Act."

Before Abdel-Hafiz graduated from the FBI academy in 1995, there were no other Muslim agents in the bureau. Now there are seven, and FBI Director Robert Mueller is busy recruiting more. "We are recruiting Muslims as special agents," he said. "We have been very active in pushing more for Muslim Americans to consider a career with the FBI."[6]

19

THE IRANIAN INFORMANT

Burying a Pre-9/11 Tip at the FBI

"It was a big piece of the puzzle."
—BEHROOZ SARSHAR, former FBI linguist who translated
an informant's tip outlining the 9/11 plot

When he watched the planes hit the Twin Towers on 9/11, former FBI translator Behrooz Sarshar says he "immediately" remembered a sensational tip about an al-Qaida plot the bureau got from an informant more than four months before the terror group attacked America.

In April 2001, a longtime Iranian informant for the FBI signaled to his handlers at the bureau that he had picked up from his sources overseas some urgent information regarding terrorism, and he volunteered to pass it on to them. "The asset," as he is known to his FBI handlers, has been on the bureau's payroll for more than a decade and is considered very reliable. He worked for Iranian intelligence under the shah and still maintains close contact with sources in Iran and neighboring Afghanistan, where Osama bin Laden was based at the time. Though he has lived in America since the shah's fall and speaks some English, the FBI has had trouble understanding the Iranian informant in the past. So his handlers—two case agents in the Washington field office—brought in sixty-seven-year-old Sarshar, then one of the top Farsi translators in the Washington field office, to act as an interpreter.

The four men met at a residence in the Washington area. The asset revealed that his sources back home had heard that al-Qaida was plotting to attack America in a major suicide operation involving airplanes. Europe was also mentioned as a target by the asset. What's more, he said that al-Qaida agents, already in place inside America, were being trained as pilots.

At the time, the tip sounded too sensational to be true. Nonetheless, both FBI agents took notes at the secret meeting, Sarshar says, and one of them—Anthony

"Tony" Orefice—filed a report with his squad supervisor, Thomas Frields, back at the Washington field office. It is not clear if the information was teletyped to headquarters, however. Orefice, who still works at the Washington field office, would not comment on the case.

Frields, now retired from the bureau, says the case is too "sensitive" to discuss, though he did not deny hearing about the tip at the time. "It involves very sensitive matters that took place while I was an on-duty agent, and I have absolutely nothing to say," says Frields, reached at his Washington-area consulting office. The headquarters official in charge of counterterrorism at the time was FBI Assistant Director Dale Watson, also retired and now working at Booz Allen Hamilton, the same consulting firm as Frields. He did not return phone calls.

On 9/11, as soon as the shock of the attacks wore off, Sarshar's mind raced back to the meeting with the informant. "I immediately remembered the source," and wondered if more could have been done to follow up on his warning, he said during a three-hour interview at a coffee shop near his home in Vienna, Virginia.[1] Sarshar, who has since left the bureau, says he has no doubt Orefice and the other case agent were wondering the same thing.

But he did not feel it was the time for second-guessing. "I didn't want to discuss it [with the agents] because I was sure that they had done their job," he says, though he shared his dismay over what in hindsight was a hot tip with other linguists at the Washington field office.

The FBI has maintained it had no advance knowledge of the 9/11 attacks and could not have disrupted the plot.

Speaking on the condition of anonymity, FBI officials explain that the Iranian asset's tip was just too incredible to believe. "At the time it sounded unbelievable," one official says. "People in Afghanistan being trained to fly jumbo jets to attack America just seemed unbelievable. Camels, maybe. But not planes."

Plus, officials say the information they received was too skeletal to act on. The asset did not provide specific targets and did not even mention any cities. Nor was there any indication when the attacks might occur.

While true, Sarshar says it was still "a big piece of the puzzle," and if it had been combined with other pieces the FBI had in hand before the attacks, it could have formed a pretty clear picture of the plot.

Indeed, the bureau had other clues before the attacks that al-Qaida was planning aviation-related terrorism inside America.

In July 2001, for example, an FBI agent in Phoenix warned headquarters that an "inordinate number" of Middle Eastern men sympathetic to al-Qaida were taking local flying lessons. And the following month, a FBI supervisor in Minneapolis told headquarters that he worried a foreign flight student he had in custody on visa violations—Zacarias Moussaoui—might be part of a plot to "take control of a plane and fly it into the World Trade Center."

If those two pieces of information had been combined with the broader tip from the Iranian informant, the FBI might have been able to see the outline of the plot, says Sarshar, a former Iranian police colonel.

"If you put that big piece of the puzzle together with the two smaller pieces that also came into headquarters, you would have seen the whole plot. Those three pieces together make up a big part of the puzzle," he says. "But the pieces were buried at headquarters."

FBI counterintelligence veteran I.C. Smith thinks the FBI had enough information to disrupt the 9/11 plot but failed to act. "They've all said there's nothing we could have done anyway," he said. "Well, that is wrong, wrong, wrong."

He notes that in his July memo, the Phoenix agent had asked headquarters for "authority to obtain visa information on persons seeking to attend flight schools." But supervisors there had closed the matter the next month without taking action. "If FBI agents had been allowed to interview those Middle Eastern students at the flight schools, there is no doubt in my mind they could have disrupted" the hijackers, says Smith, who retired in 1998. "We would have found them overstaying their visas and booted them out of the country."

In light of the pre-9/11 tip, Smith commented, "I'm convinced there's more information in the FBI."

Tom Bloch, another recently retired FBI counterintelligence agent, agrees but says such information was virtually meaningless to the bureau before 9/11 because there was no system in place to put it all together and make any sense of it. Hot tips routinely got buried.

"Back then, in the pre-September 11 world, the analysts didn't work together. Heck, the computers weren't even tied together. It was just hodgepodge," Bloch tells me. "We used to call it the Federal Bureau of Information because we used to gather all sorts of stuff and not do anything with it. There was just too much paper."[2]

Sarshar says he briefed 9/11 Commission investigators about the 9/11 tip in February 2004, providing them the name of the trusted informant. Part of the independent commission's mandate was to investigate leads that U.S. law enforcement may have missed before the terrorist attacks, which killed 2,745 American citizens. Investigators told Sarshar they would call him back to testify with the informant but never did.

It turns out the informant got cold feet when investigators contacted him. "They called him, and he got scared and called his son, and his son told them to leave his father alone," Sarshar says. Investigators then told the son, "Look, it's his civic duty—they don't execute people here." But the informant still refused to brief the commission, which chose not to subpoena him. It also chose not to question FBI Director Mueller about the tip during hearings, which surprised even Mueller, aides say.

Sarshar says the informant, who was "very proud" of the information he provided the FBI, repeated his warning in a follow-up interview with the FBI agents around the summer of 2001. Al-Qaida's plan to attack America at that point was in the final stages. Most of the muscle hijackers began arriving in the U.S. at that time, some traveling through Iran, according to the 9/11 Commission findings.[3]

It is not surprising that the Iranian informant got wind of the 9/11 plot around that time. Listen to this staff statement released last year by the 9/11 Commission:

> Although access to details of the plot was carefully guarded, word started to spread during the summer of 2001 that an attack against the United States was imminent. According to [Khalid Sheikh Mohammed], he was widely known within al-Qaida to be planning some kind of operation against the United States. Many were even aware that he had been preparing operatives to go to the United States, as reported by a CIA source in June 2001. Moreover, that summer bin Laden made several remarks hinting at an upcoming attack, which spawned rumors throughout the jihadist community worldwide. For instance, [Mohammed] claims that, in a speech at the al-Faruq training camp in Afghanistan, bin Laden specifically urged trainees to pray for the success of an upcoming attack involving twenty martyrs.[4]

The Iranian informant was not the first source to warn the FBI about al-Qaida's interest in planes and pilots.

A year earlier, Niaz Khan, a British subject of Pakistani descent, informed the FBI he had learned of a bin Laden plan to hijack a jumbo jet while training at a terrorist camp in Pakistan. He says he and others were trained to seize jetliners in small teams using guns or knives. Khan, who passed a polygraph, says he was instructed to meet a team of about five persons in America, some of them pilots. His story was outlined in the 9/11 congressional report:

> In April 2000, the Intelligence Community obtained information regarding an alleged bin Laden plot to hijack a Boeing 747. The source, a "walk in" to the FBI's Newark [New Jersey] office, claimed he had learned hijacking techniques and received arms training in a Pakistani

194

camp. He also claimed that he was to meet five or six persons in the United States. Some of those persons would be pilots, who had been instructed to take over a plane.[5]

Sarshar, a Sufi Muslim, deeply regrets the puzzle was not solved in time to head off the attacks. After 9/11, when the language unit at the Washington field office was flooded with faxes and other messages from foreign intelligence services, Sarshar pulled twenty-hour shifts to help translate the communications, even sleeping on the floor next to his desk one night.

A political refugee from Iran who joined the FBI in 1995, he says he has testified seven times in federal court against FBI suspects, more than any other translator on the Farsi board. He says his life was threatened once after testimony he gave sealed a drug conviction. He also has worked on terrorism cases related to Mujahedin el-Khalq, or MEK, an Iranian dissident group that has killed Americans.

Sarshar, a short but powerfully built man whose gentle disposition belies his black belt in judo, clearly was a dedicated FBI employee—but one who perhaps knew too much. After seven years of service, he was suspended with pay in 2002 when the bureau opened an internal investigation of him. He initially tried to fight it but then decided to resign. A former investigator for FBI watchdog Sen. Chuck Grassley who consulted with Sarshar says he found his story credible. "We thought he was a pretty credible guy," says Kris Kolesnik, who interviewed Sarshar as an investigator for a Washington public-interest law firm handling federal whistleblower cases.[6]

Sarshar, who memorialized the 9/11 tip and other matters in a ten-page letter to Mueller, says the FBI warned him, "If you talk about these things, you'll be locked up." A former co-worker still with the bureau suspects Sarshar's firsthand knowledge of the tip may have played a role in his disciplinary review. "I don't doubt it was a factor," he says.

20

THE PRISON POWDER KEG

Converting Violent Offenders to a Violent Faith

"Chaplaincy services in the [U.S. Bureau of Prisons] remain vulnerable to infiltration by religious extremists."
—inspector general of the Department of Justice[1]

Imam Warith-Deen Umar was one of the first Muslim chaplains hired to lead prayers and counsel inmates fulltime in American prisons. Based in New York, he reigned as the state's most influential Muslim prison chaplain, responsible for the hiring and firing of all imams in its prison system. He exercised complete control over personnel matters, including doctrinal training, before his recent retirement. Under his twenty-five-year leadership, the New York state prison system added fifty-six Muslim clerics—the most of any state in the country. Early in his career, Umar founded the National Association of Muslim Chaplains, a recruiting operation he still runs from his home in Bethlehem, New York. The U.S. military plucked its first Muslim chaplain from his state prison corps.

Umar and his fifty-six protégés have ministered to some of the most violent members of American society, converting thousands of them to Islam—a trend that is sweeping prisons nationwide and ringing alarm bells at the FBI. Several high-profile al-Qaida suspects have been drawn to Islam while in prison.

But instead of rehabilitating inmates by preaching peace and respect for society, Umar glorified violence and incited prisoners against America. Shockingly, he told them the terrorist attacks on New York and Washington were justified and that the 9/11 hijackers should be remembered as Allah's "martyrs," not murderers.

"Even Muslims who say they are against terrorism secretly admire and applaud" the September 11 hijackers, he said.[2]

Umar argues that the Quran condones violence against oppressors of Muslims and their allies, even if innocent people die. "If there is peace, you don't have to do anything," he says. "But if there is no peace, we need to address and teach and practice the religion and go to [the] extreme sometimes."

"Every person makes his *shahada*, the first pillar in Islam," he explains. "You become a *shaheed*, or a witness to give his life or death for Allah. You'd want to take a plane into the building, too, if there's a great deal of tyranny."[3]

Many of the clerics Umar hired during his tenure echo his sentiments in sermons before New York State's thirteen thousand Muslim inmates.[4]

But his influence does not end there, unfortunately. At the time he made the execrable remarks about 9/11, he was working for the U.S. government as a Muslim contractor for the federal penitentiary in Otisville, New York, having retired in August 2000 as chief Muslim chaplain of the New York state prison system. At Otisville, he led Quranic studies, presided over *Juma* prayers on Fridays, and privately counseled Muslim inmates. When the New York press discovered Umar was an al-Qaida sympathizer and broke the story in 2003, the U.S. government swiftly terminated his $37-an-hour contract.[5] And New York state, for its part, banned him from its prison chapels, while punishing two other imams for espousing pro-al-Qaida views.

But here is what has not been reported in the press:

Federal Bureau of Prisons officials knew well before 2003 that Umar was instilling in prisoners the same kind of militant ideas that drove the 9/11 hijackers to slaughter three thousand people. And yet they did nothing. In fact, prison officials rewarded him with sparkling evaluations.

"BOP [Bureau of Prisons] staff observed Umar repeatedly give sermons that violated BOP security policies but failed to terminate his contract," the Department of Justice's inspector general found in an investigation of Umar and the federal Muslim chaplains program. The embarrassing revelation was buried in a footnote on page forty-eight of the department's 2004 report, part of which is classified.

"Several of his Contractor Progress Reports explain that he 'disparages Judaism and Christianity' and that his sermons are 'sometimes not appropriate,'" the report adds. "Despite this conduct, the same reports provide him with 'Good' or 'Excellent' marks."[6]

Umar, who has a master's degree in Islamic studies and a bachelor's degree in criminal justice, is not an isolated case. A classified addendum to the report documents several cases in which FBI officials assert that authorized Muslim chaplains, contractors, and volunteers leading federal prison prayer sessions may even have ties to terrorist groups. And they suspect these individuals pose a threat to homeland security.[7]

How could this happen?

For starters, some of the prison officials doing the hiring and evaluating of Muslim chaplains are Muslims themselves. Eight of the ten Muslim chaplains employed by the U.S. prisons bureau were interviewed by a Muslim. Some were interviewed by a regional official who happens to be Muslim. And one was interviewed by another Muslim chaplain.[8]

All of them, moreover, are under the supervision of a sweet old nun, who by all accounts is overly trusting of the Islam practiced behind bars. As discussed in an earlier chapter, Sister Susan VanBaalen runs the federal prisons ministries, including the Islam programs. Lax screening of Muslim chaplains and contractors, along with spotty monitoring of their sermons and prayer sessions, have led to the radicalization of inmates on her watch.

Sister Sue, as she is known, and her staff think that if there is an Islamic threat, it comes from the inmates, not the chaplains. Even so, they rely on inmates to inform them of any jihadists in their ranks. "Nearly every BOP staff member we interviewed believed that if a Muslim radical infiltrated a BOP facility and began expressing his views, an inmate would report the conduct," the report says.[9] Confident of that, they have allowed large numbers of Muslim inmates to meet in chapels with no guards present and no remote monitoring to check for militant messages. "Audio monitoring is not currently employed in any BOP chapels to evaluate the messages," the report found. And even if they did monitor the sessions, they might not know what participants were saying. Some prayer sessions are conducted partly in Arabic.[10]

BLACK "REVERTS"

Islam is the fastest-growing religion in American prisons, and the ranks of Muslim inmates at state and federal facilities have swelled to an estimated two hundred thousand. FBI officials now suspect prisons are al-Qaida's recruiting ground of choice in America, surpassing hard-line mosques.

Concerns were heightened after former inmates Richard Reid and Jose Padilla were arrested for allegedly attempting to commit terrorist acts against the U.S. Reid, convicted of trying to blow up an American Airlines flight from Paris to Miami with a shoe bomb, had converted to Islam in a British prison. British officials suspect he was radicalized in part by hard-line Muslim clerics who preached at the prison. Padilla, detained for allegedly planning to detonate a so-called dirty bomb in the U.S., converted to Islam after serving time in a Broward County, Florida, jail on a prior offense.

American inmates are natural targets for al-Qaida recruitment, FBI officials say, because many are predisposed to violence and seek revenge against government authorities who locked them up. Terrorists convicted in the 1993 World Trade Center bombing have radicalized fellow inmates by telling them that violence against the U.S. is sanctioned under Islam. Their pitch also includes overthrowing the government. "Some Islamic extremist inmates told other inmates that if they were going to convert to Islam, they had to overthrow the government because 'Muslims aren't cowards,'" the Department of Justice report says.[11]

The prisoners have become even more valuable to al-Qaida since 9/11. Its leaders now want to use terrorists who are non-Arab Muslims, preferably English-speaking Americans, to lower the group's profile and avoid suspicion in carrying out future strikes on America. All nineteen hijackers on 9/11 were Arab nationals who spoke broken, if any, English. While some of the two hundred thousand Muslim inmates in America are Hispanic, most are black. And they are not as likely to attract the same level of scrutiny at security checkpoints as Arab Muslims.

Umar, himself a black convert and ex-con, has predicted that further attacks may be led by black Muslim converts. He believes "black inmates who converted to Islam in prison were logical recruits for committing future terrorist attacks against the United States," according to the report.[12]

Black Muslim inmates, in turn, may be attracted to al-Qaida because they share the global terror network's hostility toward the U.S. Even outside prison, black Muslims hold alarmingly hostile views toward the U.S. In fact, national polls reveal that even more black Muslims blame U.S. policy in the Middle East for the 9/11 attacks than Arab Muslims. Fully 70 percent of African-American Muslims think it was a major factor, while 68 percent of Arab-American Muslims agree with that view, according to Zogby International. And a whopping 57 percent of African-American Muslims say the U.S. is an "immoral" society, mirroring the half who think the terrorist attacks against it were "inevitable," which suggests they think the U.S. had it coming.[13]

In converting blacks, Muslim leaders try to tap into their anger over slavery and discrimination. In fact, they refer to such conversions as "reversions." "Some African Americans have left Christian affiliations, choosing to revert to the Islamic faith prominent among their West African forebears who were forced into slavery," says Islamophile Paul Findley, author of *Silent No More: Confronting America's False Images of Islam*.[14] Many young black men identify Christianity with white oppression, and Islam appeals to their quest for empowerment. "You have African-American men seeking liberation, and many see Christianity as a white man's religion that continues to oppress,"[15] says black convert Eric Erfan Vickers, who as head of the Washington-based American Muslim Council redefined the brutal terror groups Hamas, Hezbollah, and al-Qaida as mere partners "in a resistance movement."[16] Close to half the Muslim population in America is now black, which makes predictions of a black wave of terrorism all the more frightening.

Muslim prison chaplains defend their program by arguing Muslim inmates are among the most disciplined in the prison system, religiously shunning drugs and other vices.

Still, they have been known to riot over religious matters. Last decade, for instance, a group of Muslim inmates stormed a cellblock at Rikers Island prison in New York over an attack on its religious leader. Nine inmates and thirty-nine correction officers were injured. Two officers were stabbed. Prosecutors charged a Muslim chaplain with inciting the riot by allegedly calling for jihad, or holy war, during a service just before the riot, but he was later acquitted of the charges. Rushing to the chaplain's defense was none other than Umar.[17] More recently, another Muslim chaplain at Rikers was barred from counseling inmates because of his ties to a Brooklyn mosque linked to al-Qaida fundraising.[18]

SISTER SUE'S BLIND FAITH

More scandalous is the way prisons select Muslim chaplains. In the federal system, they are referred by Islamic groups, and officials accept their recommendations on blind faith without applying any religious litmus test of their own to screen out militants. If the Islamic groups certify the clerics as moderate and mainstream, that is good enough for Washington. Their word is gold. Problem is, the pre-approved Islamic groups that accredit and recommend Muslim chaplains to the Federal Bureau of Prisons are not moderate or mainstream themselves. In fact, they have links to Islamists and even terrorists, associations that have completely escaped Sister Sue and her staff, amazingly enough.

The Islamic Society of North America—a "group accused of ties to Islamic extremists," asserts U.S. Senator Jon Kyl[19]—has endorsed three federal chaplains and at least five Muslim contractors and volunteers. Sister Sue insists ISNA is a "moderate" organization. In 2002, she even spoke at its national conference along with ISNA board member Imam Siraj Wahhaj, an unindicted co-conspirator in the 1993 World Trade Center bombing. And she is comfortable recruiting contractors directly from the group's Saudi-backed affiliate, the Muslim Student Association, as discussed earlier in the book.

Though an approved endorsing body, the Graduate School of Islamic and Social Sciences has not endorsed any federal prison chaplains, but one of them did study at the school—along with Umar. GSISS was raided by federal authorities after 9/11 and remains under investigation for supporting terrorism. One of its top officers was named as an unindicted co-conspirator in the Sami al-Arian terror case. Sister Sue thinks the school is a-okay, though, and has maintained a close relationship with it since 1996. "In her opinion, GSISS is a mainstream Islamic organization that has not demonstrated any tendency toward extremism," the Department of Justice report says.[20] She faithfully delivered a commencement address at the Washington-area school's graduation ceremony in 2002.

Even the American Muslim Council, which was founded by confessed terrorist Abdurahman Alamoudi, endorsed one of the prison bureau's ten Muslim chaplains.

Their word was good enough for Sister Sue. She sought no second opinions and did no independent research, such as checking candidates' past sermons for militant statements, before hiring them.

"Currently, the BOP's policy is not to ask chaplain candidates what they believe or require them to provide a statement of faith," the report says. "Rather, the BOP relies on the certification of national endorsers that the candidates are mainstream Muslims and capable of teaching in BOP institutions."[21]

Yet critics say relying on the hardcore Muslims at ISNA and GSISS to certify that other Muslims follow moderate doctrinal beliefs is like asking the ear-biting Mike Tyson to certify that other boxers follow Marquees of Queensberry rules. They just aren't credible endorsers.

Sister Sue, who declined an interview request, also does not mind if candidates for chaplain positions receive training and sponsorship from Saudi Arabia, even though it promotes Wahhabism and husbanded most of the hijackers. "She said that because Saudi Arabia has diplomatic relations with the United States, she did not believe Muslim chaplain candidates who have studied in Saudi Arabia should be excluded from BOP positions," the report says.[22]

Umar took at least four trips to Saudi Arabia to study at Saudi expense.[23]

TERRORIST UNIVERSITY

What's more, Sister Sue has turned a blind eye to the potentially dangerous propaganda that Islamists traffic into prisons. Even after 9/11, she and her staff failed to take inventory of chapel books and videos to see if they pose a threat to security, according to the Justice Department investigation. "Of the institutions we visited, several did not have an inventory of the books currently available to the inmates," the report says. "And none of the collections had been re-screened since the September 11 terrorists attacks."[24]

Yet FBI investigators fear distributors of pro-jihad propaganda are turning prisons into a kind of terrorist university where young men enroll as felons and graduate as terrorists. One supplier of prison library materials is the notorious

Islamic Assembly of North America, which has hosted al-Qaida speakers at its conferences. Not exactly moderate. Nonetheless, the Detroit-based group has donated about 530 packages of Islamic books and tapes to prison libraries across the country.[25] Another source of prison resources is the National Islamic Prison Foundation, a spin-off of the embattled American Muslim Council.

And look who is helping parolees go straight and readjust to life outside prison. Before his recent arrest, confessed terrorist Alamoudi counseled released prisoners through his American Muslim Foundation. Not exactly the best mentor. Since 1993, his National Islamic Prison Foundation also has been helping felons reentering society after incarceration.

Another dubious prison-outreach program is run by the Islamic Foundation of America, also based in the Washington area. According to its tax returns, the nonprofit has spent tens of thousands of dollars on "support [for] Muslim inmates."[26] The foundation, which is the subject of a Senate Finance Committee investigation, is affiliated with the Saudi government and preaches Wahhabism. One of its lecturers is Ali al-Timimi, the imam under indictment for inciting the group of Northern Virginia jihadists, some of whom were black converts.

Officials from the prisons bureau have not seen these red flags in part because they have not been looking for them. They did not even meet with the FBI to discuss terrorism concerns until more than two years after 9/11, and they did so only after the Umar scandal made headlines. No wonder they were surprised to find their two main chaplain-endorsing agencies on the FBI's radar screen.

"The BOP did not screen Islamic organizations through the FBI prior to [October 2003]," the reports says. "As a result, the BOP did not have information from the FBI on the ISNA or the GSISS when public concerns surfaced about those organizations' alleged terrorism connections."[27]

Sister Sue has agreed to suspend hiring of new Muslim chaplains until the FBI can complete its investigation of ISNA and GSISS. She says the prisons bureau needs to add three more chaplains to meet growing demand for Islamic services. It now has ten Muslim chaplains serving more than ninety-six hundred Muslim inmates in the federal penitentiary system. "She said the BOP would not accept ISNA-endorsed candidates until the FBI determined that the organization was not radical and does not have ties to terrorism," the report says.[28]

But that is not enough, it warns. The bureau must take steps to examine the doctrinal beliefs of all Muslim chaplains, contractors, and volunteers to ferret out the militants. And it can start by requiring a "statement of faith" from them.

"It is essential that candidates who have extreme views and pose a security threat not be allowed into the prisons," the report asserts.

Even though prisons top the FBI's list of concerns as it monitors terrorists' efforts to recruit foot soldiers, little has been done by Washington since 9/11 to block terrorist infiltration of the religious programs of its own correction facilities.

"Chaplaincy services in the BOP remain vulnerable to infiltration by religious extremists," the inspector general's report concluded.[29]

And believe it or not, security is not any better at the Pentagon.

V
MILITARY INFILTRATION

21

THE FIFTH COLUMN

Muslim Traitors in the Ranks

"The FBI considers these matters to be potentially serious breaches of national security."
—JOHN PISTOLE, FBI assistant director of counterterrorism, regarding the investigation of a possible Muslim spy ring at the Pentagon's al-Qaida prison camp at Gitmo[1]

After the U.S. military operation in Afghanistan, President Bush praised the estimated ten to twenty thousand Muslims serving in the U.S. armed forces. "Muslim members of our armed forces are serving their fellow Americans with distinction, upholding our nation's ideals," he said in a speech to Muslim leaders at a Washington mosque in 2002.[2]

While that may be true for a good many Muslim-American soldiers, it cannot be said for all of them. Shockingly, a growing number have put their religion before their duty, and several have sold out their country. Some have infiltrated the military in order to undermine it. Others have even killed, or tried to kill, their fellow soldiers.

What follows are the disturbing portraits of some of the traitors, and the accused traitors, who make up what may be just the tip of an Islamist fifth column operating within the ranks of the U.S. military—which is too blinded by political correctness to see the threat.

PORTRAITS

Sgt. Hasan Akbar: On the eve of his Army unit's push into Iraq in early 2003, the black Muslim convert lobbed three grenades into tents housing commanding officers at a military camp in Kuwait. He killed two of them and wounded fifteen others in the treacherous attack from within. Why did Akbar frag his fellow soldiers? Because he opposed the killing of fellow Muslims and the war in Iraq.

"You guys are coming into our countries, and you're going to rape our women and kill our children," he was overheard by soldiers who survived the attack as saying.

Clearly, his loyalties lay with the *ummah,* or world brotherhood of Muslims, and not America. Akbar, who studied Islam at a Saudi-funded mosque in Los Angeles, awaits trial on murder charges.

Jeffrey Leon Battle: The former Army reservist from Oregon pleaded guilty in 2003 to conspiracy to wage war against the U.S. A black convert to Islam like Akbar, Battle tried for months to enter Afghanistan to fight U.S. forces. Federal prosecutors said he enlisted in the reserves "to receive military training to use against America."

Semi Osman: The ethnic-Lebanese immigrant served in both the Army and the Navy reserves before his arrest in 2002 on terrorism-related charges. Osman, who attended a Seattle mosque with suspected al-Qaida recruits, was accused of providing "material support for terrorists." He pleaded guilty to a weapons violation, in a deal in which he agreed to testify against other terror suspects, and has served his sentence.

Abdul Raheem al-Arshad Ali: A former Marine who converted to Islam during the first Gulf war, Ali has been charged with selling a semiautomatic handgun to Osman. He was a leader in the same militant Seattle mosque and trained at a suspected terrorist camp in Oregon.

Sgt. Ali Mohamed: The Egyptian immigrant came to the U.S. in 1985. He joined the U.S. military the next year, rising to the position of sergeant with the Army's Special Forces based at Fort Bragg, North Carolina, where he received secret security clearance. When FBI agents raided the New Jersey home of an Islamic terrorist a few years later, they found secret military documents from—surprise—Fort Bragg.

In 1989, Mohamed moved to Santa Clara, California, where he emerged as a top aide to Osama bin Laden while fronting as a computer technician. He trained some of the 1993 World Trade Center bombers in surveillance and other techniques he learned at Fort Bragg. He helped al-Qaida's second in command, Dr. Ayman al-Zawahiri, a fellow Egyptian, raise money at his Santa Clara mosque.

Mohamed, also known as "Ali the American," was put away for his role in planning the U.S. embassy bombings in Africa. The green beret now sits in prison.

Sgt. Hammad Abdur-Raheem: Another black convert, he was a decorated Gulf war veteran and member of the National Rifle Association before getting caught up in a plot to wage jihad against American troops in Afghanistan. Abdur-Raheem, a Virginian, was convicted last year of terrorism-related offenses and sentenced to eight years in prison.

Spc. Ryan G. Anderson: Yet another Muslim convert, he was convicted last year of aiding and abetting the enemy by trying to leak military intelligence to al-Qaida terrorists. Specifically, he tried to pass highly sensitive information about the vulnerabilities of armored Humvees. Anderson, a white National Guardsman, was stationed at Fort Lewis, an Army base near Tacoma, Washington.

John Allen Muhammad: He joined the Army in 1985—the same year he converted to Islam—and also was stationed at Fort Lewis, where he honed his sharp-shooting skills. The Gulf War veteran is suspected of having thrown a grenade at a fellow soldier. He is now in prison for leading the sniper terrorism spree that killed ten and wounded three in the nation's capital a year after the 9/11 attacks.

Muhammad, who is black, passed out pro-Islamic fliers in the town north of Seattle where he lived and was known to speak sympathetically about the 9/11 hijackers and make anti-American slurs. Before and during the D.C.-area shootings, Muhammad visited with his former wife—a practicing Muslim who wears traditional garb—and their children at her Maryland townhouse. (This is at odds with Mildred Muhammad's story, incidentally. She claimed to be surprised to find her ex-husband in the Washington area and speculated he was hunting her down, motivated more by revenge over their divorce than hatred for non-Muslims and America.)

Muhammad, who is also linked to a shooting at a Tacoma synagogue, followed a strict Muslim diet—so strict, in fact, that he once went off on a relative just for bringing porkchops into his home.

His young protégé and partner in the D.C. killings, Lee Boyd Malvo, is also a black Muslim convert. He drew jailhouse sketches of Osama bin Laden, praising him as a "Servant of Allah." In a self-portrait, he drew himself saying, "Allah Akbar!" or Allah is Great! In a notebook, he wrote, chillingly, "Sept. 11, we will ensure, will look like a picnic to you." He said he was ready to die in jihad against America. "Islam. We will Resist. We will conquer. We will win," he wrote. And he showed no remorse for the victims of his sniper spree: "They all died and they deserved it. We will not stop. This war will not end until you are all destroyed utterly."

While in county jail awaiting trial, Muhammad and Malvo insisted on *halal* meals, such as veggie burgers, and got them. They also got copies of the Quran. Both have been convicted of their heinous crimes and are serving life terms.

Ahmed Fathy Mehalba: A contract Arabic translator at the terrorist prison in Gitmo, he was arrested by U.S. border authorities upon returning from a trip to Egypt, where his family lives. In his luggage, agents found a computer disk with classified information including the names of dozens of al-Qaida operatives, whose names surfaced in interrogations with Gitmo detainees. He denied the disk contained classified information, maintaining they instead contained digital music files and movies. He also had an unidentified FBI document labeled "SECRET." He was arrested and charged with mishandling classified information and lying to investigators. Mehalba has pleaded innocent to the charges.

The FBI is investigating whether he gave the enemy the names of the al-Qaida operatives being exposed. Mehalba's background concerns investigators. For starters, his uncle was an intelligence officer in the Egyptian army, according to an FBI affidavit filed in his case. His brother also served in the army there. Egypt is home to three of the most senior al-Qaida leaders still at large.[3]

Also, it turns out that Mehalba was involved in a previous FBI investigation in 2001, when he was enrolled in the Army's intelligence school at Fort Huachuca, Arizona. His girlfriend, an Army specialist at the school, was under investigation for stealing a classified laptop. Secret counterespionage training materials were also found in her quarters. Mehalba left the Army after his girl-friend's arrest.[4]

Senior Airman Ahmad Al-Halabi: A native of Syria, a designated terrorist state, the Air Force linguist also was assigned to Gitmo to translate Arabic. He made unauthorized contacts with terrorist detainees, including giving them baklava desserts. At the same time, he corresponded with the Syrian Embassy, failing to report the suspicious contacts as required.

Halabi was originally charged with espionage and aiding the enemy, but last year he pleaded guilty to reduced charges of mishandling classified information and lying about it to military investigators. They found in his possession a secret diagram of a new U.S. prison camp that was under construction and a secret list of Gitmo detainees and their cell numbers. He received no jail time.

Remarkably, Halabi had been under investigation for making anti-American statements before he was assigned to the U.S. base in Cuba. Because the Pentagon was desperate for translators, it cut corners on his security check, as it had for Mehalba. What's scary, say terrorism experts, is that al-Qaida knows the military is short of Arabic linguists and may be using the positions as a vehicle for infiltration. (Another Arabic interpreter, Marine Cpl. Wassef Ali Hassoun, faces desertion charges after turning up in Beirut while on duty in Iraq.)

Capt. James "Yousef" Yee: Another convert, he served as the Muslim adviser to the commander of the joint task force at Gitmo, where he had unfettered access to al-Qaida detainees to whom he ministered. He also dined with Halabi at the prison camp. Initially accused of spying for Syria, where he and his wife have spent time, he was formally charged in 2003 with mishandling classified information.

But the military dropped the charges altogether because of "national security concerns that would arise from the release of the evidence" in court proceedings, the Army said in a statement.

Yee was stationed at Fort Lewis, the same base where both Anderson and Muhammad had served, interestingly enough. The base boasts the only Muslim military chaplain on the West Coast. Yee, a Chinese American who graduated from West Point, has resigned in disgrace from the Army.

BIG PICTURE

When news of at least three security breaches at Gitmo first leaked back to Washington, officials feared it represented a monumental security breakdown and a crushing intelligence setback in the war on terrorism. Key information the CIA had collected on al-Qaida more than likely was fed back to the enemy. Others were expected to be charged in the scandal. The FBI was called in to investigate what looked to be a Muslim spy ring. "The FBI considers these matters to be potentially serious breaches of national security," said John Pistole, FBI assistant director of counterterrorism.[5]

But once Congress began amplifying the scandal in hearings, an embarrassed Pentagon went into damage-control mode. Brass quickly tried to downplay the mess. "We have found a couple [of military translators] who were not as trustworthy as we had hoped initially," senior Pentagon official Charles Abell shrugged in one Hill hearing, clearly understating the magnitude of the problem.[6] The Pentagon has opted not to aggressively prosecute the case, arguing that national security secrets could be exposed in court (as if they haven't already been exposed). And the scandal has faded from public view.

Yee was one of more than a dozen active-duty Muslim chaplains serving in the armed forces, alongside roughly one hundred Islamic lay leaders. Each wears the Islamic star and crescent on his uniform. The first chaplain was hired in 1993 after the Gulf war led to a surge in conversions. More than three thousand Army soldiers, possibly as many as five thousand—including Yee—converted to Islam during or right after the war, thanks to intense Saudi government efforts. The Saudis set up tent-side programs on Islam to make their pitch to GIs. The Muslim influence in the military is so strong now that packaged "Meals Ready to Eat" field rations come certified as *halal,* or religiously approved, sans pork or pork byproducts. Muslim soldiers are allowed to pray five times a day and are even given leave to attend the annual Muslim pilgrimage to Mecca in Saudi Arabia.

In fact, the Pentagon has permitted a Saudi charity tied to al-Qaida to fly planeloads of Muslim-American soldiers to Mecca over the past decade. In 2001, for example, a Muslim chaplain led a delegation of about sixty soldiers on a trip to Saudi Arabia that was organized and financed by the Muslim World League, even though the CIA determined years earlier that it was a front for al-Qaida.

Saudi influence does not stop there. In effect, the Saudis are also training the military clerics who counsel Muslim-American troops. Below are the supposedly mainstream Islamic groups the Pentagon relies on to endorse its Muslim chaplains. All of them are influenced by the Saudis, and all espouse Wahhabi dogma. And none of them, with one exception, have been dumped as certifying agencies. Why? Because the Pentagon does not want to be seen as "judging" the Islamic faith.[7]

American Muslim Armed Forces & Veterans Affairs Council: The group is a spin-off of the American Muslim Council, whose founder, Abdurahman Alamoudi, helped place the first Muslim chaplain in 1993. In fact, the criminal Alamoudi created the whole Muslim chaplain corps for the Pentagon, which now includes as many as a hundred Islamic lay ministers in addition to fulltime chaplains. One serving inside the Pentagon building now as its Muslim lay leader is an American Muslim Council board member!

Working in concert with the Saudis during the Gulf war, Alamoudi first set up an organization called the Muslim Military Members to organize Saudi pilgrimages for all the new converts. That was in 1991. Later that year, then-President Bush encouraged religious tolerance by sending Alamoudi's organization a supportive message at the conclusion of its first *hajj* to Mecca.[8] At Alamoudi's request, the Bush administration also granted soldiers permission to watch Saudi television for religious programming and counseling. At the same time, it began distributing pork-free meals for Muslim GIs.

Alamoudi is now in prison serving a twenty-three-year sentence for plotting terrorist acts. Recent IRS tax records I obtained show his veterans affairs council is funded in part by the U.S. branch of the Saudi-based International Islamic Relief Organization—one of bin Laden's favorite charities.[9] The president of the branch, Mohamed S. Omeish, lists his address as 3606 Forest Drive in Alexandria, Virginia—the same address as Alamoudi's office. Alamoudi's wealthy brothers live in Saudi and have also helped fund his organizations.

Several Gitmo detainees granted Alamoudi power of attorney over their affairs, raising even more concern among federal investigators about his connections to terrorists. Some speculate he may have set up the chaplain's program as a spy service for al-Qaida. Alamoudi has made numerous trips to Saudi, Egypt, and Syria.

It was Alamoudi's group that sponsored Yee for his chaplaincy.

Institute for Islamic and Arabic Sciences in America: The Saudi-based and Saudi-funded center trains imams to serve in American mosques and clerics to serve in the American military. Alamoudi worked with the Saudis to set up its military training program.

But last year, federal agents raided the institute's offices in Northern Virginia, virtually shutting it down. Earlier in the year, sixteen Saudi diplomats formally affiliated with the institute had their passports revoked for abusing their diplomatic credentials by secretly propagating anti-Western hate. Essentially, they were engaged in subversive activities under the auspices of the Saudi Embassy. Prince Bandar, the Saudi ambassador to Washington, is the chairman of the institute's board of directors. In fact, he has presided over graduation ceremonies at the institute for dozens of Muslim-American soldiers. All told, the institute has helped train as many as a hundred people as Islamic religious advisers for Muslim-American troops.

The institute also serves as an official Saudi distribution center for Wahhabi propaganda and includes a large prayer hall. It served as a meeting place for the "Virginia jihad network"—the group of young Muslim men who were convicted in a conspiracy to wage holy war against American allies and troops abroad. Abdur-Raheem, the former Army sergeant, was one of the jihadists. The institute featured a number of hardcore Wahhabi lecturers, including the 9/11 imam Anwar Aulaqi.

The Pentagon continued to post job notices for Muslim clerics at the institute after 9/11, including one seen there as late as October 2003. But it now says it no longer uses the school as a recruiting ground for its Muslim chaplain's program.

Graduate School of Islamic Social Sciences: Part of the Saudi-funded Safa group, the school was raided after 9/11 by federal authorities as a suspected terror-financing front. It is located in a nondescript building in an office park at the end of a small airport runway in the middle of Northern Virginia horse country. A state accrediting agency, the Virginia Council on Higher Education, did not think much of its curriculum when it evaluated it several years ago in response to a request by its board to certify it as a legitimate masters program.

In fact, the council official who reviewed GSISS, as it is now known, was more impressed by the board's ties to Islamic extremism. "I looked into the backgrounds of the directors, and it was all shocking information," says Ken Masugi, who in 1999 conducted a preliminary review for the state accrediting body.[10]

GSISS is run by Taha Jaber al-Alwani, a stocky Muslim man who is a key figure in the Safa group scandal, as well as an unindicted co-conspirator in the Sami al-Arian terrorism case. Investigators say the two men share the same jihadist objectives. In a letter to al-Arian citing a donation to his Islamic Jihad front groups, al-Alwani said, "Islam is an ideological and cultural concordance with the same objectives, and all of your institutions are considered by us as ours."[11]

Most of the military's Muslim chaplains were trained at GSISS. Sgt. Akbar's chaplain, Capt. Mohammed Khan, trained there. So did a Navy chaplain by the name of Lt. Abuhena M. Saifulislam, who, like Yee, ministered to al-Qaida detainees at Gitmo.

Islamic Society of North America: This is another Saudi-tied group under FBI investigation for terrorism ties, yet one that still has the approval of the Pentagon. Even more astounding: its past president, Muzammil Siddiqi, opposes Muslims serving in the U.S. military and defending America while it remains a non-Muslim nation. "Islam will not allow a Muslim to be drafted by non-Muslims to defend concepts, ideologies, and values other than those of Islam," asserts Siddiqi, who still serves as an ISNA board member. "A Muslim shall defend non-Muslim lands not."[12]

Given his religious ruling, you really have to wonder what the chaplains ISNA refers to the Pentagon are counseling Muslim soldiers to do—or not to do—in performing their duties to their country.

Nonetheless, in the middle of the Yee scandal last year, the ever-accommodating Pentagon asked ISNA how it could be even more accommodating.

Chief chaplains for the Navy, Army, and Air Force, as well as the executive director of the Chaplaincy Board of the Armed Forces, met with a top ISNA official for a politically correct powwow. The official, Louay Safi, also met with the Pentagon chaplain. During their meeting, Deputy Chief Chaplain Rear

Adm. Robert Burt stressed the need "to educate the military on the Islamic faith and Muslim cultures" to combat "prejudicial acts by military personnel, reflecting a lack of clear understanding of Islam and Muslims." To help increase troops' sensitivity toward Islam, he and other chief chaplains agreed to distribute information on Islam and Muslims provided by ISNA. Burt informed Safi that the Navy was pleased with the track record of the chaplains endorsed by ISNA, according to the group's account, and is interested in hiring more Muslim chaplains. Swell.[13]

It is hard enough to believe that most of these groups are still credentialed to certify Muslim chaplains for the armed forces. But here is the really maddening part: the Pentagon is not directly investigating its other Muslim chaplains in the wake of the Yee scandal. "These are all good chaplains who have represented their faith and other faiths well," says Army spokeswoman Martha Rudd.[14]

The Pentagon has effectively swept the problem under the rug. Infiltration? What infiltration?

But the problem is even worse than infiltration of the armed forces by Islamic terrorists and sympathizers. The enemy's penetration of the military goes even deeper, to the heart of homeland security—the nation's nuclear weapons labs.

22

LOOSE NUKES

Hosting Terror Sponsors at the Weapons Labs

"Every terrorist country was represented at the labs, either as post-doctoral workers and students assigned there, or as visitors. Iran, Syria—you name it, we had them from all of those places."
—RET. COL. EDWARD MCCALLUM, former head of the Department of Energy's Office of Safeguards and Security.[1]

Michael Ray Stubbs worked for about ten years as a heating and air-conditioning technician at the Lawrence Livermore National Laboratory, a major U.S. nuclear-weapons defense lab outside San Francisco. He left the facility a year before 9/11 and traveled to the Philippines. Last year, authorities there deported him to the U.S. after arresting him for suspected ties to al-Qaida-linked groups.

The FBI is now looking into whether Stubbs obtained sensitive information or materials while working at the lab, which stores hundreds of pounds of plutonium and enriched uranium used in nuclear bombs. As a maintenance worker, he was given Q-level security clearance, the highest level granted to employees. That clearance would have allowed him access to classified buildings.

Stubbs was arrested with his brother, a Muslim convert who studied Arabic in the Sudan, where he met in 2003 with the founder of several suspected al-Qaida fronts. His contact there happens to be a close associate of Osama bin Laden's brother-in-law.

Bin Laden, of course, has long sought to obtain a nuclear weapon or radioactive materials to make a so-called dirty bomb. But more recently, he is said to have secured from a Saudi cleric a religious ruling giving him the green light to use nuclear weapons against Americans.

While scary enough, the Stubbs case may be just the tip of the iceberg.

Before 9/11, the labs kicked open their doors to hundreds of foreign nationals from sensitive countries in the Middle East, including known terrorist countries, making the likelihood of infiltration from other al-Qaida sympathizers very high, say U.S. intelligence officials. They did not just come and visit a day or two and turn around and go home. Many got jobs and high-level security clearance and are still assigned to the labs. And the welcome mat is still out, even after 9/11, say U.S. officials—particularly to post-doctoral students from Iran, a terror-sponsoring state which most experts now agree is secretly developing a nuclear weapons program.

Ret. Col. Edward McCallum knows a little something about lab security. Last decade, he headed the safeguards and security office of the Department of Energy, which owns the defense labs. He says he locked horns with former Energy Secretary Hazel O'Leary over security issues. She wanted to open up the labs to more foreigners, including those from Middle Eastern countries that sponsor terrorism, as part of her controversial "openness policy."

McCallum was beside himself over what he described as O'Leary's "disdain for security." He had conducted an internal review of lab personnel and found the facilities to be highly vulnerable to espionage, terrorism, and theft from employees from sensitive Middle Eastern countries, among others. He drew up a list of workers by lab and internal critical facility, including those who had hands-on access to special nuclear materials or highly radioactive materials subject to dispersal. But before he could finish his assessment of suspect individuals, he was steered off the project by headquarters and lab directors who, in the interest of sharing science, did not want foreign access to the labs restricted.

"There was a great deal of resistance, and we weren't able to finish the job. But the initial results were eye-opening to the extreme, if not frightening," McCallum tells me. "Many were Q-cleared, and many others worked on support or maintenance crews with significant access" to classified buildings and nuclear materials.[2]

He says hundreds of students from sensitive Middle Eastern countries worked at the Department of Energy's labs, including Lawrence Livermore, Los Alamos, and Sandia, where America's nuclear weapons are designed and maintained.

"Every terrorist country was represented at the labs, either as post-doctoral workers and students assigned there, or as visitors," he says. "Iran, Syria—you name it, we had them from all of those places."

"And we got hundreds of visits from their intelligence agencies—that we knew about," he adds.[3]

Take Los Alamos, for example, which designed most of the warheads in the U.S. arsenal and stores nuclear materials at its New Mexico facilities. In 1994, the first year after O'Leary, a Clinton appointee, took over the Department of Energy, the number of foreign nationals from sensitive countries working at the lab more than doubled to 107, according to an internal lab report. By 1999, the latest available numbers, the total number of employees had shot up to 182. The sensitive countries include Iran, Iraq, Pakistan, and Syria. Los Alamos also hired foreign students from Jordan, Egypt, and Turkey.[4]

In 1998 alone, the three major labs, plus Oak Ridge in Tennessee, hosted more than 3,100 foreign visitors and academic assignees from sensitive countries, some of whom stayed on site for as long as two years, according to the House Science Committee, which oversees the labs.[5]

"They kicked the doors wide open," McCallum says, despite his protests. "They were encouraging visitation."

He says that in her trade junkets to Pakistan, India, and Africa, O'Leary invited scientists to tour the labs. "When Hazel was on her flying carpet trips in the mid-1990s, one of the pitches she made was, 'Send your scientists. We have technology to share,'" McCallum says.

And she made sure they got into the labs. Under the Reagan and Bush administrations, the Department of Energy required background checks on foreign visitors. But in 1994, O'Leary granted Los Alamos and Sandia exemptions from the rule. As a result, few background checks were conducted at those labs, and the number of foreign visits exploded. Los Alamos, for example, had 2,714 visitors in two years from sensitive countries, but only 139 were checked, according to a 1997 congressional report.[6]

The new policy did not sit well with McCallum, a former green beret. "We raised hell about it all the time," he says. He and other security officials worried that the uncontrolled access to the labs invited not only espionage but also terrorism.

But O'Leary dismissed their warnings.

In one meeting, McCallum recalls, the former Energy secretary pooh-poohed the idea of threats from other countries. "Hazel said to me, and this is a quote, 'Boy, don't you understand that the Cold War is over, and all these people are our friends now?'" McCallum recalls. "And we were talking about security against terrorists and espionage in the same conversation." O'Leary did not respond to requests for comment.

After McCallum told Congress about the security problems at the labs, he was punished by former Energy Secretary Bill Richardson, who is now the Democratic governor of New Mexico. McCallum left the department in 1999.

Although the labs have cut back on the number of visitors from sensitive countries since 9/11, many of the foreign workers are still assigned there. "And believe it or not, they just keep coming," says a former high-level U.S. official involved in counterintelligence operations. He says concerns have been raised specifically about the high number of Iranian students still being assigned to the labs.

"There's no doubt that the number of foreign nationals from the Middle East who got assigned to the labs ballooned in the decade before 9/11," he says. "But there are an awful lot of them out there now.

"In fact, they're letting a lot of Iranians in on post-doc fellowships," he adds, "so they are there three months, six months, a year, sometimes longer."

Another source, an active U.S. counterintelligence official involved in lab security, says a number of warnings have been issued regarding Iranian penetration. "There is a great deal of concern about Iranians throughout the national lab complex," he tells me. "A lot of directives have been issued concerning this issue."

The former senior official, who prefers anonymity, says the new director of Los Alamos "raised all kinds of hell about all the Iranians that they were letting in to all the weapons labs." But instead of addressing his concerns, "the Energy Department just cut him out of the approval process," he says. "This is Iran, right. I mean, these are some of the guys we're really suspicious of."

In terms of developing deployable nuclear weapons, "the Iranians are years ahead of where the Iraqis ever were, and they always have been for a long time," the official adds. "The opportunities they have to collect intelligence from the lab is pretty damn frightening given how leaky that place is. They can do a lot of harm."[7] Iran is also believed to be a transit point, if not a safe haven, for al-Qaida operatives.

Los Alamos, which handles the country's most sensitive nuclear secrets, was ordered to shut down for a month last year after officials discovered that several portable computer devices containing classified information were missing. It was just the latest in a string of embarrassing security lapses at the lab.

And computer devices are not the only thing vanishing at the nuclear labs. Between 1998 and 2003, federal investigators documented more than thirteen hundred disappearances of radioactive materials in the U.S. Some of the losses have not been recovered. Los Alamos investigators concluded in a recent study that, despite tightened security after 9/11, terrorists still have a "very significant" chance of getting their hands on enough radioactive ingredients to make a dirty bomb.[8]

The ex-intelligence official, who still maintains contact with lab officials and is familiar with current lab security procedures, says the Bush administration has "talked a better game" of controlling security at the labs but has failed to live up to its rhetoric.

"When it comes to management in the labs and the security business, I don't see a dime's worth of difference between the Bush administration and the Clinton administration," he says, shockingly enough. Bush appointed Spencer Abraham, an Arab American, to take over responsibility of the labs from Richardson.

After the Chinese nuclear espionage scandal erupted in 1999, Congress barred scientists from sensitive nations seeking nuclear weapons technology from visiting the labs unless they received a waiver from the energy secretary.

The ban was eventually lifted, but while it was in place, former Energy Secretary Spencer Abraham had final authority to approve visitors from sensitive Middle Eastern countries such as Iran, Iraq, Sudan, and Syria. Some assignments from Pakistan also had to be okayed. For the most part, he did not disappoint sensitive visitors, the official says.

Abraham, who is of Lebanese origin, previously represented one of the largest Arab constituencies in the country as senator of Michigan. He received more money from the Arab American Leadership PAC, which counted Abdurahman Alamoudi as one of its top contributors, than any other senator. And the year before the 9/11 attacks, he introduced a bill called the Secret Evidence Repeal Act of 2000 to end the government's use of classified evidence to deport suspected Arab terrorists.

Needless to say, Abraham is not high on the former counterintelligence official's list of favorite guardians of national security. He says he was aloof when it came to security.

"Abraham was as bad as Richardson or O'Leary, if not worse," says the official, who is Republican. "He was completely out of touch with his department and allowed things to be run by the Clintonistas."

Lab security officials are also concerned about visitors from Pakistan, in light of the fact that Pakistani nuclear scientists have met with Taliban and al-Qaida leaders in recent years. The administration has nonetheless invited Pakistani scientists to the labs to review security procedures as part of an effort to help it safeguard its own nuclear arsenal. "We're helping the Pakistanis on control issues," the official says, "which is ironic as hell."

Not to mention potentially dangerous. With al-Qaida terrorists actively seeking nuclear materials for weapons, the threat of theft or sabotage at the labs is now very real, officials note. And that makes the presence there of Pakistanis and other Muslim foreigners all the more worrisome.

"I've always felt that if there were an insider at one of the labs who had access to nuclear materials, it would be tough to stop them," says Troy Wade, former assistant energy secretary for defense programs under the Reagan administration.[9]

Nuclear materials are kept at Los Alamos, Oak Ridge, Sandia, and Livermore, as well as other labs and storage facilities. Having access to the labs would, of course, make it easier for would-be terrorists to steal such materials. It takes less than fifty pounds of weapons-grade plutonium or highly enriched uranium to craft a crude nuclear device.

"But they don't have to steal it," McCallum says. "All they have to do is detonate it right there. It's a one-way trip for an Islamic student or visitor" who wants to die for Allah.

According to Wade, now a consultant, energy headquarters is aware of the potential threat from within and even issued an internal warning to the labs about Middle Eastern visitors after 9/11. The warning actually came from the National Nuclear Security Administration, or NNSA, the semiautonomous energy agency that Congress forced Richardson to create to tighten security at the labs.

"After September 11, the NNSA went out to all locations, including the labs, and told them to be careful about visiting Middle Eastern scientists and [holding] scientific meetings that involve people from the Middle East," Wade tells me.

Los Alamos has responded to 9/11 by tightening its screening of foreign visitors, says Lori Hutchins, project leader of the lab's foreign visits and assignments program. Curiously, she would not provide current numbers for visitors and academic assignees from the Middle East and Pakistan to compare them to pre-9/11 numbers. But she notes that many are still coming to the labs through "international agencies such as the IAEA," and not necessarily through energy headquarters and hosts and sponsors within the labs.[9]

IAEA, which stands for the International Atomic Energy Agency, is a United Nations group that guards against loose nukes around the world. It sponsors foreign nationals—including ones from terrorist-sponsoring states, incredibly—to tour U.S. nuclear sites to learn security procedures. The controversial international-training course, held every other spring at Sandia National Laboratory in Albuquerque, New Mexico, has come under new fire since 9/11.

"The biggest joke is that the IAEA course participants include all the world's bad guys, who promptly collect nuclear information on the facilities that are inspected," says the former U.S. intelligence official.

A Sandia spokesman confirms that sensitive countries have participated in the tours of security operations at U.S. nuclear facilities.

"Over the years, a variety of Sandia projects in support of its national-security and nuclear-nonproliferation roles have involved inviting visitors from foreign countries, including sensitive countries," says Sandia spokesman Rod Geer. "In fact, even people from India and Pakistan have been here at the same time."[11]

Since 1978, Sandia has presented the course more than a dozen times to more than four hundred participants from fifty-seven countries, all of them IAEA members, Geer says. Besides Pakistan, Islamic countries represented include Iran, Saudi Arabia, and Indonesia, adds Sandia's Basil Steele, a course instructor. "We have everybody coming here."

The international security classes, which ordinarily run three weeks, are held at the Marriott Hotel in Albuquerque. They cover sensors, cameras, entry and access controls, response-force communications, and other security methods to protect nuclear facilities and materials from sabotage or theft. The foreign visitors are also taught to identify vulnerabilities and weaknesses in security systems.

After classes, participants are taken on "field trips" to some of the Nuclear Regulatory Commission's facilities, Steele says. "They go out to an NRC site to tour it, to see security there, and understand how they practice security."

He would not say which facilities are toured. But the fact that even one is being inspected by Middle Eastern nationals bothers security experts who worry that al-Qaida could target reactors for attack.

More than twenty nuclear reactors in America are located within five miles of an airport, and almost none were built to withstand attack from even a small plane, notes Edward Markey, a senior member of the House Energy and Commerce Committee and a persistent watchdog on nuclear plant security. Theft of reactor fuel is also a concern. He complains that the Nuclear Regulatory Commission does not know how many Middle Eastern nationals are employed at nuclear reactors and does not require adequate background checks on reactor employees. "Post-9/11, a nuclear safety agency that does not know—and seems little interested in finding out—the nationality of nuclear reactor workers is not doing its job," says Markey, a Democrat from Massachusetts.[12]

The threat is only compounded by the foreign tours of such facilities. A spokeswoman in IAEA's New York office acknowledges the risk of sharing security techniques with potential Arab terrorists, who may be using the U.N. invitation only to scout U.S. nuclear facilities for weak areas to penetrate.

But she says the agency weighs that against the benefit of helping foreign nationals safeguard nuclear materials in their countries from terrorists (even though some of the countries themselves sponsor and harbor terrorists). She says IAEA does not blackball any member from participating and provides rosters of participants to the Department of Energy. "We encourage our member states who host such meetings to allow entry for *all* nationalities," she asserts.[13]

Steele says the Department of Energy does not vet the rosters for suspected terrorists. "It's up to IAEA to screen their participants," he says. The IAEA spokeswoman demurs that the Department of State is the final check, since it grants visas to those on its roster.

Also, Steele says that, to the best of his knowledge, federal authorities have not gone back and scrubbed the roster of four-hundred-plus foreign nationals who have participated in the course over the past twenty-five years to see if any of their names match names of suspects on federal terrorist watch lists.

However, authorities have audited another controversial security-training program, started by the Clinton administration, that teaches Yemenis, among other Arabs, security techniques at Kirtland Air Force Base in Albuquerque, where they interface with security officials at Sandia.

After 9/11, "there was a name-by-name audit done to determine if any foreign students who came through showed up on a terrorist watch list that the intelligence community had," says Frank Martin, an energy security contractor who supervises the program.[14] No known terrorist matches were found, he says, but authorities are still worried about individuals who have gone through the program. "There obviously was a concern, and there remains a lingering concern about individuals who have been here," Martin says, adding that both the Energy and State Departments vet the foreign students before they arrive in Albuquerque.

The foreign security-training courses began in October 1999 under the auspices of the Non-proliferation National Security Institute, which was set up by former energy secretary Richardson. Energy, in partnership with the State Department, teaches basic security to the foreigners with the hope that they will go back to their countries and assist security officers at American embassies "if things get dicey" and Americans are attacked, Martin explains.

He says groups from nearly twenty-five countries, including terrorist hotspots such as Kenya, the Philippines, and Yemen, have gone through the course. The students are mostly young men, who bring along interpreters. Yemen, where terrorists bombed the USS *Cole*, is one of many Arab countries that harbors al-Qaida cells.

The Department of State's Bureau of Diplomatic Security, meanwhile, also trains Saudis and other Middle Easterners at Louisiana State University and at facilities in the Washington area. So does the FBI at its training facilities at Quantico.

The Bush administration has not canceled the programs.

VI
CORPORATE
INFILTRATION

23

WUDU IN THE RESTROOM

Islamizing the Workplace

"Before prayer, Muslims are required to wash their faces, hands, and feet with clean water. This washing is normally performed in a restroom sink. The time it takes to perform the washing and the prayer is usually about fifteen minutes. . . . Employers must work out a reasonable arrangement for those employees to pray."
—CAIR's workplace guide for employers

The Council on American-Islamic Relations has a few minor requests of companies employing Muslims. They are contained in a handy three-dollar booklet the Washington advocacy group has put together for companies called "An Employer's Guide to Islamic Religious Practices." It is designed to assist employers in changing their policies to create a "culturally sensitive" workplace for Muslims, who practice a number of religious customs at odds with American corporate culture. Here are several examples, along with CAIR's recommendations to employers:

- Many Muslim men wear beards for religious reasons. Let them, even if you have a company policy forbidding facial hair. "Should there be safety and health considerations, employers may require employees with beards to use proper covering such as hair nets or masks."

- Some Muslim men wear a head covering called a *kufi*, and some Muslim women wear a headscarf called a *hijab*. Let them, even if you have a policy forbidding the wearing of hats. "This rule may be amended to exempt items such as headscarves and skullcaps."

- Some Muslims will be reluctant to shake the hand of an unrelated person of the opposite sex. "This should not be taken as an insult," even if you are their boss.

- Many Muslims avoid sustained eye contact. Again, don't take it as a sign of disrespect, or "an indication of an unwillingness to communicate."

- Muslims are forbidden from eating pork and pork byproducts, as well as any meat not slaughtered and prepared by Muslim standards. If you have a company cafeteria, you should specially order meats from certified *halal* food providers. "Employees should be given choices that meet Muslim dietary requirement."

- Many Muslims are reluctant to take part in social gatherings celebrating religious holidays of other faiths, or any work-related function where alcohol is served. "These employees should not be penalized for not participating in such functions."

- Because alcohol is taboo in Islam, "a Muslim employee should not be asked to serve or sell religiously offensive products, such as alcoholic beverages." Neither should he be asked to participate in any form of gambling, also forbidden.

- Friday is the Muslim Sabbath. Congregational worship, called *Jumah*, takes place at a mosque during the day. It lasts up to ninety minutes. Let Muslim employees take "an extended lunch break" to attend the service each Friday.

- Muslims observe the holy month of Ramadan by fasting. That means they skip lunch during that month, so "a work shift could be shortened by the length of the lunch break if the break is not taken."[1]

- Muslims pray five times a day, including twice during normal work hours. "Employers must work out a reasonable arrangement for those employees to pray within the prescribed time period." And they should be accommodated with a quiet, dry, and clean place such as a conference room where they can practice their ritual, which involves standing, bowing, and touching their foreheads to the ground while facing Mecca (generally northeast in America). Do not disturb them. "During the prayer, the Muslim is fully engaged. He or she may not respond to a ringing telephone or conversation. Fellow employees should not take offense if the worshipper does not answer their call during the prayer."[2]

- Muslims must also perform a cleansing ritual called *wudu* before each prayer. It involves washing their faces, hands, and feet with clean water. This washing is normally performed in a restroom sink. Allow them time to perform both the washing and the prayer, which "is usually about fifteen minutes."

But it may take longer. *Wudu,* also known as ablution or purification, is a ten-step process that goes something like this:

1. Begin by praising Allah (for no prayer in Islam is valid without *wudu,* and no *wudu* is valid without mentioning the name of Allah). Then wash both hands up to the wrist three times, making sure that water has reached between the fingers. Remove rings so that water can reach the skin underneath them.

2. Using the right hand, the one not used for cleaning private parts, put a handful of water into the mouth and rinse it thoroughly three times.

3. Sniff water into the nostrils from the right hand three times to clean them. Clear the passages of water, dirt, and mucous using the left hand.

4. Wash off the tip of the nose with the left hand.

5. Wash the entire face three times from right ear to left ear.

6. Continue washing from forehead to throat.

7. Wash the right arm and then the left arm thoroughly from the wrist up to the elbow three times, removing watches.

8. Move the wet palms over the head from the top of the forehead to the back of the head.

9. Pass the wet tips of the index fingers into the grooves and holes of both ears and also pass the wet thumbs behind the ears and ear lobes.

10. Finally, wash both feet to the ankles starting with the right foot, including between the toes. Then recite: "*Ash-hadu an la ilaha illal lahu wa ash-hadu anna Muammadan 'abduhu wa rasuluh,*" meaning there is no god but Allah and he has no partners, and Muhammad is his servant and messenger.

CAIR says more and more companies are showing an interest in its work-place-sensitivity booklet. It says more than fifteen thousand corporations and businesses nationwide have ordered copies. And it says they are adopting its recommendations primarily in response to the increasing number of Muslim employees in the workforce.

That may be a part of it, but they are also responding to pressure from CAIR. The Muslim-friendly procedures cited in its booklet are not really requests; they are demands. And judging from the raft of religious-discrimination charges it has filed, CAIR is more vexatious litigant than advocate. Its employer's guide amounts to a subtle threat: do this or be sued.

"CAIR says it's championing Muslim rights, but its real agenda is to Islamize the workplace," says an executive with a Fortune 500 company. He says the group is a cultural "fifth column," and CEOs across America are letting it march right into their boardrooms. Many are so intimidated by CAIR that they have ripped up longstanding company policies against head coverings and beards. UPS, for example, has revised its policy to allow for beards. And many have allowed Muslims to take off for Muslim holidays including the two *Eid* festivals. Some companies have even installed floor-level sink basins in their restrooms to make it easier for Muslim workers to perform *wudu*.

Of course, this is not to suggest that bias against Muslims does not exist in corporate America. But critics argue that CAIR has exploited anti-discrimination laws for political gain. CAIR keeps a full stable of lawyers in its Civil Rights Department who tirelessly solicit discrimination lawsuits on behalf of Muslims. And they have the full backing of the federal government.

As the law is written now, an employer must allow Muslim workers to wear headscarves and other religious head coverings even if they make customers and co-workers uncomfortable. Same goes for beards. The law makes no exception for retailers or service providers who employ Muslims, even if they operate at airports where travelers may be spooked by their appearance, and where their clothing may pose a safety or security risk. "Customer preference is never a justification for a discriminatory practice," the EEOC says.[3]

It is also illegal to deny Muslim employees a place to pray in the workplace. In fact, the EEOC recommends offering them a conference room. Likewise, it is illegal to bar them from leaving work on Fridays to go to mosque. Employers also must permit Muslims to take off work for Islamic holidays. They must accommodate Muslims in all these things unless they can prove undue cost or hardship.

But the government makes that burden of proof very difficult and has usually sided with Muslim complainants. Bottom line: employers are obligated under currently worded civil-rights law to permit Muslim employees to engage in their religious expression on the job.

CAIR knows the law all too well, critics say. It has teed up hundreds of alleged Muslim discrimination cases for the EEOC to pursue against employers. CAIR lawyers initially try to settle cases on behalf of Muslim employees through meetings with company lawyers. If they cannot get them to agree to their demands, they draft formal complaints and file them with the EEOC. In turn, the EEOC usually issues a right-to-sue letter, which is as good as gold in court. CAIR lawyers then provide letters of support to plaintiffs or join their lawsuits directly.

Meantime, CAIR's propaganda arm issues media *fatwas* threatening a boycott of the company allegedly violating the rights of Muslims.

Such pressure tactics have proved highly effective. No company wants to be accused of religious bigotry or racism, especially ones with public shareholders. CAIR has helped aggrieved Muslim employees reach favorable settlements with dozens of publicly traded companies, including JC Penney, McDonalds, Sears, and Office Depot. Such settlements often mandate companywide sensitivity training on the Muslim faith. CAIR executive director Nihad Awad has personally conducted sensitivity training for executives and employees at Nike, DKNY, and other Fortune 500 companies.

The EEOC considers CAIR and other Muslim and Arab grievance groups as "partners" in its efforts to fight employment discrimination. And their legal teams work closely together.[4] The EEOC even ordered a hundred copies of CAIR's employer's guide when it first came out in 1997.

Since 9/11, the EEOC has placed a priority on cases involving discrimination against Arabs and Muslims and has reinvigorated its partnerships with Arab and Muslim groups such as CAIR. The EEOC has been advertising its complaints hotline in Arab yellow pages while translating its employment-discrimination brochures into Arabic. It has even sent its lawyers to mosques to make presentations.[5]

As a result, charges of employment discrimination filed by Muslims and Arabs have ballooned. Over the past three years, EEOC has processed 944 claims against employers alleging discrimination tied to the events of 9/11. And the agency has obtained a total of about $3.2 million for aggrieved workers since 9/11.

EEOC spokesman James Ryan says the agency is unable to determine the exact number of discrimination cases CAIR has referred to the agency, but it is substantial. Muslim-bias complaints filed with the EEOC began to accelerate with CAIR's founding in 1994, soaring from a total of 178 that year to 334 by 2001. CAIR's civil-rights squad went on high alert after the 9/11 attacks, and complaints more than doubled to 726 in 2002. Arab-bias complaints also shot up after 9/11. Almost 700 employees of Middle Eastern origin filed complaints against their bosses in 2002, up from just 18 in 2001 and only 1 in 2000. The number of charges filed by both Muslim and Arab employees dropped off in 2003 and 2004 but are still at historically high levels.

CAIR estimates it has handled more than 1,000 cases of employment discrimination. The Michigan chapter of CAIR alone "defended" in one year more than 76 Muslims whose civil rights allegedly were violated, winning concessions from employers such as Kelly Services and Webasto Roofing Systems, according to the chapter's 2000 tax filings. Here are other recent cases in which CAIR lawyers have badgered employers on behalf of offended Muslims:

- In Minnesota, security guard Abdirisak Abdi Jama was fired after refusing to shave his beard to comply with company policy. Burns International Security Services, which had a strict uniform policy prohibiting beards, warned Jama twice for wearing a beard before he was sacked. CAIR helped him file a formal complaint with the EEOC, which determined Burns International discriminated against Jama.

- Also in Minnesota, thirty-five employees walked off their factory jobs at Advantek Inc. in a protest over prayer breaks. They became upset when a supervisor reprimanded one of them for extending the prayer break longer than fifteen minutes. When they returned to work, they were suspended for three days. In the end, however, Advantek bowed to pressure from CAIR and constructed a "quiet room" for Muslims to pray on the job. It also put managers through sensitivity training.

- A Georgia woman employed by Sears was denied a transfer to the jewelry department because she refused to comply with store policy forbidding head coverings. CAIR filed a complaint with the EEOC on her behalf and won. In a January 24, 2002, press release boasting of the concession, CAIR advised all American employers, "CAIR publishes a booklet, called 'An Employer's Guide to Islamic Religious Practices,' designed to prevent these incidents from occurring."

- CAIR has also assisted several Muslim women battling airline caterer LSG Sky Chefs for the right to wear the *hijab.*

- Sixteen Muslims at a Whirlpool plant in Tennessee complained about company resistance to prayer breaks and headscarves. The company said it tried to accommodate *hijabs* where they do not pose a safety risk and praying in non-hazardous areas of the plant. CAIR is helping the Muslim workers sue.

- A Maryland woman said she was harassed for wearing a *hijab* while working for Best Buy. CAIR has filed a complaint with the EEOC on her behalf and has threatened a Muslim boycott of the consumer electronics retailer.

- An Illinois Muslim complained UPS denied him a promotion to a position driving delivery trucks because of his beard. "UPS has been stubborn in its refusal to offer religious accommodation to Muslim employees," complained Omar Ahmad, chairman of CAIR, which worked with the EEOC on the case. The agency ruled against UPS.

- Six Muslim men in Georgia alleged a Delta Air Lines contractor illegally fired them for refusing to comply with company policy by shaving their beards as other Muslim workers had done to continue working there. The EEOC sided with the Muslim men against Delta. "It is hypocritical for Delta to accept the money of bearded Muslim travelers and at the same time forbid beards for its workers," argued CAIR executive director Nihad Awad. In its October 28, 1998, press release quoting Awad, CAIR again advised employers to heed the demands in its handbook for a Muslim-friendly workplace.

But CAIR won its biggest victory in a case involving aviation security. Working with the EEOC, the group's lawyers in 1999 extracted major concessions from a United Airlines contractor manning security checkpoints at an airport where one of the 9/11 hijackings would later originate.

THE ARGENBRIGHT CASE

The contractor, Argenbright Security Inc., told several female Muslim guards at Washington Dulles International Airport that they would have to give up their headscarves or give up their jobs. The women were screening passengers and flight crews while wearing their *hijabs*.

United had received complaints from passengers and crew members nervous about Middle Easterners still running security after the year-earlier U.S. embassy bombings in Africa. Four of the Muslim screeners were from Sudan, Osama bin Laden's former headquarters and a country on the Department of State's terrorist blacklist. One was from Egypt, and another from Afghanistan. None were U.S. citizens.

They all refused to remove their headscarves, forcing Argenbright, then United's security contractor at its Dulles terminals, to fire them.

The women immediately complained to CAIR, and CAIR in turn complained to United's legal department in Chicago. Within no time, Edmond L. Soliday, United's vice president of security operations, got a phone call from the carrier's lawyers. He recounted in an exclusive interview what took place behind the scenes during the controversy.

"CAIR piggybacked onto every grievance filed by Muslims or Arabs, and we got bit by them back then," he says.[6]

Soliday refused to bow to pressure to keep the screeners on the job. He instead suggested to United's attorneys that they take the Muslim women off the security checkpoint at the airport and give them less visible jobs where they could wear their *hijabs*.

"I said this is nuts, because if we allow contractors to wear their religious garb, then we're going to have to allow it for crew and pilots," he says. Service companies have to maintain a uniform dress code regardless of religious customs, Soliday argued. "I have my strong religious beliefs, too, but I don't walk around with a big cross around my neck."

What's more, he argued that the long headdresses worn by the Muslim screeners "could be used for a thousand hiding places for weapons, so we can't do any kind of quality control." He explained, "Think about how easy it would be to hide a knife or a box cutter under a headscarf and slip it into a bag after it passed through screening."

Finally, he relayed to the front office that the headscarves made passengers and crew "nervous." Just a few months earlier, al-Qaida had blown up two U.S. embassies in Africa, and American travelers were on edge about Islamic terrorism. "It's reality," he told corporate lawyers. "To pretend that it is not a reality is ridiculous."

Soliday called Frank Argenbright Jr., then the head of Argenbright, and said, "This is stupid," and Argenbright agreed but said it could cost him a two-million-dollar lawsuit.

At that, Soliday checked with United's lobbyist on Capitol Hill to see how much clout CAIR had. "They had very few friends on the Hill back then." Then he called the FAA, but the FAA advised him the government would side with CAIR and its clients. "They told us we couldn't tell them they couldn't wear the headscarves." And, he says, "I was called a bigot for wanting to fight them."

Meanwhile, an attorney for CAIR in Washington drafted an EEOC complaint for the Muslim women, and one of its few friends on the Hill took to the floor of the House to denounce their firings as religious bigotry. In his March 1999 speech, David E. Bonior, then a Democratic congressman from the Detroit area, slammed United Airlines and its contractor:

This incident raises a larger issue: that of widespread and systematic discrimination against Muslims and Arab Americans in airports all across the country. If firms cannot even treat their Muslim employees fairly, how are we to believe they will treat Muslim passengers—whom they do not even know—in a fair and courteous manner? This is not the first airport, and this is not the first incident, that leads me to believe that airport security is being contracted out to companies who do not have a commitment to treat all Americans with fairness and dignity. I applaud these women for standing up for their religious beliefs and for their rights on the job.

Bonior also sent a letter to the head of the FAA to draw her attention to the incident. CAIR trotted out the EEOC complainants for the media. "I'm angry," screener Iklas Musa said. "This is my religion." CAIR chairman Omar Ahmad also weighed in: "It is hypocritical of these companies to accept money from Muslim travelers wearing headscarves and at the same time discriminate against Muslim workers who wish to exercise their religious rights."

"Next thing I know," Soliday says, "our general counsel cuts a deal" through Argenbright with the Department of Transportation and the EEOC. And the women were put back on the job.

Argenbright also agreed to give the women back pay and $2,500 in compensation, as well as a written apology. In addition, the Atlanta-based company implemented a Muslim-sensitivity program at all its U.S. locations. Some of the Muslim women, like Rueaia F. Mohammed, did not think the settlement went far enough and wanted to make Argenbright apologize on television.

HIJACKERS GET A PASS

Two years after the incident, five young Muslim men got box cutters through the Dulles security checkpoint and hijacked an American Airlines jumbo jet before crashing it into the Pentagon. All five passed through the main terminal's west security screening checkpoint run by Argenbright Security.[7] A surveillance video showed that the security screeners, who appear to be of Middle Eastern origin, did not question the hijackers about suspicious items they were carrying even after they set off metal detectors. Nawaf al-Hazmi, the lead hijacker, and Majed Moqed, one of the muscle hijackers, set off alarms for both the first and second metal detectors they walked through at the checkpoint. The video footage indicates that al-Hazmi was carrying an unidentified item in his back pocket clipped to its rim. Both Moqed and al-Hazmi were cleared by the screener, even though he never identified the items that triggered the alarms.

The 9/11 Commission said the hijackers should not have been permitted to proceed until the items were located. It found the quality of the screener's work in both cases to have been "marginal at best." "The screener should have 'resolved' what set off the alarm," the panel's final report says. "And in the case of both Moqed and Hazmi, it was clear that he did not." More baffling, Moqed had been pre-selected for additional screening by a United agent at the check-in counter.[8]

Like the hijackers, a great many of the checkpoint screeners at Dulles airport spoke Arabic and little English. In fact, more than 80 percent of them were foreign nationals mostly from the Middle East, North Africa, and Pakistan—non-American citizens just like the female Muslim screeners who sued Argenbright. A number of Dulles airport employees were in the U.S. illegally and were rounded up and deported after 9/11.[9]

Some United pilots say they were always uneasy with Middle Eastern nationals manning the checkpoints at Dulles and suspected they might aid terrorists. They became annoyed by their continued presence at the checkpoints in the months after 9/11 before the government took over airport security and replaced them with U.S. citizens. One pilot experienced a particularly galling incident at a checkpoint before departing on a flight out of Dulles in December 2001. "I was going through security with the captain, who's a fourteen-year United employee and a twenty-year Air Force lieutenant colonel with a top secret clearance, and he was actually patted down by a guy named Muhammad who barely spoke English," he said. "I'll take a good ol' homegrown guy with a felony somewhere in his distant past than Muhammad with a clean record who's been in the U.S. all of two weeks."[10]

Aviation security experts say Argenbright's EEOC settlement explains why so many of its employees were foreign nationals: it was afraid to fire them. After 9/11, amusingly, the federal government investigated Argenbright for failing to properly screen its foreign guards—just two years after it pressured the security firm to rehire Muslim non-citizens. Argenbright also operated security checkpoints at Newark International Airport in New Jersey, site of one of the other 9/11 hijackings.

Former FAA security inspector Steve Elson says if he were the head of Argenbright, he would have told the government, "You want to sue us? Go talk to the damn EEOC. They're the ones who forced these people on us."[11]

He says the airport security contractors could not win. On one hand, the government slammed them for hiring foreigners. But if they did not hire them, or fired them, the government nailed them for discrimination. In the past, the EEOC has ruled that employers can face a three-hundred-thousand-dollar fine if they fire an illegal immigrant with discriminatory malice—even if it is against federal law to hire illegal immigrants in the first place.

Indeed, Argenbright was so gun-shy regarding its hiring practices that it had to check with the EEOC and Department of Transportation to see if it was okay to start limiting the number of foreign screeners it hired. And this was after 9/11.[12]

Elson says the Dulles headscarves case is emblematic of a bureaucracy more interested in protecting the feelings of foreign Muslims against alleged religious discrimination than protecting the lives of Americans. "The only standard government enforces is making every minority happy and comfortable and not offending anybody," he says.

"But the Constitution doesn't say you can't offend anybody, and it doesn't say we can't discriminate against people if they're a threat to our security," Elson adds. "When it comes to our survival, I really don't give a damn about Muslim sensitivities."

Today, all airport screeners must be U.S. citizens and speak fluent English, although the Transportation Security Administration has farmed out ancillary security duties, such as checking tickets and IDs, to security contractors who still employ Middle Easterners, many of them at Dulles and Ronald Reagan National Airport.

But for the most part, the politically correct shenanigans have stopped at the nation's airports after 9/11, right? Guess again.

24

NORMAN "NO PROFILING" MINETA

Making Airlines the Enemy

"Don't have your guy come down there and tell me we can't pull more than three Arab guys out of line for additional security screening, and then tell us after 9/11 that we should have thrown five guys like that off our planes."
— EDMOND L. SOLIDAY, former United Airlines vice president of security operations, referring to the transportation secretary's civil-rights attorney[1]

After TWA Flight 800 went down in 1996, signaling possible terrorism, President Clinton formed a commission on aviation security to strengthen airline defenses against terrorism. When word leaked out that some on the panel might entertain the idea of a profiling system that would take into account passengers' national origin and ethnicity, the Arab and Muslim communities went into high dudgeon. Crying discrimination, they launched an effective lobbying campaign against the FAA, the Department of Justice, and the White House, enlisting friends in Congress such as Democrat David Bonior of Detroit.

In the end, the commission, chaired by Vice President Al Gore, excluded national origin, ethnicity, religion, and even gender in the passenger profiling system it recommended. The result was the Computer-Assisted Passenger Prescreening System, or CAPPS, which omits exactly the human criteria that security experts say predict predisposition to anti-American terrorism.

"CAPPS was developed because the government didn't want to do human profiling, which is the single-biggest deterrent against terrorism in the aviation industry," says former FAA special agent Bogdan Dzakovic, who led the agency's elite Red Team that tested airport security checkpoints for weaknesses.[2]

Instead, CAPPS looks only at sterile indicators involving behavior, such as how passengers pay for tickets. Cash payments and one-way trips, for example, will get you flagged in the system for special security screening. Of course, these are behaviors that Middle Eastern terrorists can easily change. This was the system in place on 9/11, which managed to flag ten out of the nineteen hijackers. Some paid cash for one-way flights, while one of them—Mohamed Atta, the ringleader—was randomly selected by the automated system.

But the only consequence of their selection was that their checked bags were held off the plane until it was confirmed that they had boarded their flights, which shows a fundamental misunderstanding of the threat from Islamic terrorists, who are willing to die with their victims (and bags). CAPPS "only applied to people with checked bags. A number of us questioned that," says Edmond L. Soliday, former United Airlines vice president of security operations. "It doesn't do any good to do positive bag matching because it does nothing to guard against suicidals."[3]

None of the hijackers were questioned by airport authorities about their travel plans or their business that day. Nor were they searched. "If human profiling was conducted on the terrorists who were made selectees, then maybe some or all of this nefarious plot could have been avoided," says Dzakovic, now a special agent with the Transportation Security Administration.

CAPPS is still part of the passenger screening system in place today (although selectees themselves are searched, not just their bags). Three years after nineteen young Arab men hijacked four jetliners, the security system still does not take into account any of the key variables for terrorism—national origin, ethnicity, religion, age, or even gender. It still does not profile young, Arab, Muslim men, who pose the most common terrorist threat (although Chechen women may be the next generation of terrorists, with the common characteristic still being Muslim).

"It still doesn't have anything to do with fighting terrorism," Dzakovic says. "But computers can't be sued for discrimination," which is what seems to drive decisions regarding security policy inside the Beltway.

He says politicians continue to ignore evidence that profiling based on human characteristics is a more effective way of combating terrorism, Dzakovic says.

Witness the federal immigration inspector who turned back a potential 9/11 hijacker as he tried to enter the U.S. The airport inspector, Jose Melendez-Perez, relied on intuitive experience and subjective analysis more than he relied on any computer-generated data in questioning the suspicious traveler.

A month before the 9/11 hijackings, he conducted a secondary inspection of Muhammad al-Kahtani, a twenty-six-year-old from Saudi Arabia, who was referred to his booth at the Orlando International Airport in Florida. He says

Kahtani was "arrogant" and so truculent that he "gave me the chills." So he refused to let him in the country.[4]

It turns out that Atta was upstairs waiting to meet Kahtani, based on a telephone call he made from that location in the airport at that time. Investigators now believe that Kahtani was meant to be the twentieth hijacker assigned to the shorthanded flight that crashed in Pennsylvania before it could reach its intended target of the U.S. Capitol.

So by profiling a young Arab male, Melendez-Perez may have saved Congress.

SCREENING QUOTAS FOR ARABS

Soliday resents the heat that United Airlines has taken for the security situation on 9/11. Two of its jets were hijacked, and one was flown into the World Trade Center. At the time, carriers were responsible for operating airport security checkpoints, but they did so under Department of Transportation regulations, which he says prevented them from profiling Arab passengers.

He recalls how department officials in 1997 asked him and United Airlines to come up with a prototype of the automated profiling system that would be used by the airline industry. At a September 16, 1997, meeting in Chicago, United's headquarters, officials made it clear that they did not want the new system to discriminate against Arab Americans or any other minorities.

Sam Podberesky, assistant general counsel at the Department of Transportation, led the meeting. Soliday says he "told me that if I had more than three people of the same ethnic origin in line for additional screening, our system would be shut down as discriminatory." Podberesky viewed *any* human profiling as discriminatory, even if it is based on statistical probability. Soliday argued that the "terrorist threat, statistically, is from Muslim males under thirty." At least thirteen of the fifteen people on the FAA's own prohibited-passenger list before 9/11 were Islamic extremists. And every one of the suspects on the FBI's list of most-wanted terrorists were, and still are, Muslim, with nearly half of them named Mohammed.

But Podberesky—a University of Maryland-educated civil-rights attorney, whose wife, Rosita, and son are Hispanic—would hear none of it. He and the civil-rights attorneys working for then-Attorney General Janet Reno were on the same page. "They didn't want any minorities seen hassled at checkpoints," Soliday says.

So "we loaded up the system with randoms to make it mathematically impossible to get three ethnics in line at the same time," he tells me. Those "randoms" selected for additional security scrutiny include such low-risk passengers as soccer moms, Girl Scouts, and even little old ladies with walkers. To try to identify actual security risks, they programmed the automated system to score each passenger's profile based on twenty-four secret travel-related factors unrelated to ethnicity, religion, or place of birth, Soliday explains. They gave passengers points for positive travel habits, such as being a frequent flyer or using a credit card to pay for tickets. The points were added up, and passengers who scored above a minimum threshold were not considered high-risk. Those who fell short of it were selected for additional screening. This was the government-approved CAPPS system that was rolled out in early 1998 and run by the airlines on 9/11.

It is still in use today.

Soliday says the controversial Chicago meeting, including the discussion of the ethnic screening quota, was memorialized in a January 1998 letter from Fran Lozito, then the FAA's principal security inspector assigned to United Airlines, to Rich Davis, United Airlines' security chief. The letter has been classified by the Department of Transportation, which claims it contains still-sensitive security information.

Lozito was later promoted to manager of air carrier operations at FAA headquarters. In early 2001, apparently on Podberesky's instructions, she e-mailed principal security inspectors to advise their carriers across the country to stop showing videos of an anti-terrorism TV documentary in their security training. Why? Arabs and Muslims found it offensive. Headquarters considered terror expert Steve Emerson's "Jihad in America" to be "a civil-rights issue," says an airline security official who saw her memo. "When we saw that message, we couldn't believe it," he says.[5] Emerson calls the ban "outrageous."[6] Lozito, now a senior official with the Transportation Security Administration, did not respond to requests for comment.

Soliday is still sore that the Department of Transportation attempted to shift blame for the 9/11 security lapses to the airlines, when it was the department's civil-rights lawyer who tied their hands. "Don't have your guy come down there [to Chicago] and tell me we can't pull more than three Arab guys out of line for additional security screening, and then tell us after 9/11 that we should have thrown five guys like that off our planes," he steamed.

He says that before 9/11, United Airlines brought in a security consultant from Tel Aviv, and he laughed at the politically correct system in which they were forced to operate. "He said, 'You Americans will never change. You can put a high-risk passenger on the plane stark naked. But if you really want to reduce risk, you don't put them on the plane at all.'" Israeli authorities make no bones about profiling Arab-Muslim passengers at airports.

FRISKING GRANNY

Even screening such passengers for weapons is not foolproof, Soliday says. "It's moot. The hijackers brought nothing illegal on the plane," he says (although several knives much larger than box-cutters were found at the Pennsylvania crash site).[7] "It's the passenger you have to focus on. They don't need to bring on weapons." He notes that one of the hijackers, Ziad Jarrah, who piloted United Airlines Flight 93, became so efficient at street fighting while training at a Florida self-defense gym patronized by Miami cops that he was invited to be an instructor. "He could kill a person with a pencil," he says.

But if American air carriers did the kind of profiling Israel does, "CEOs would have Podberesky sitting in their living rooms," Soliday says. "They'd be sued every day."

He says Podberesky, a Clinton holdover, "has continued in his crusade. He's made it very clear he would encourage lawsuits."

And he has the full backing of Transportation Secretary Norman Mineta, another Clinton holdover, who cites his childhood experience at a Japanese relocation camp during World War II as reason to ban Arab and Muslim profiling at airports now. "As one of the 120,000 Americans of Japanese ancestry forcibly interned by the United States government during World War II, I understand how dangerous times such as these can be to civil rights and civil liberties," he says.[8]

In spite of reason and complaints, Mineta has made it very clear that he would rather frisk little old grannies at airport security checkpoints than offend young Muslim men who fit the terrorist profile. Listen to this exchange between Mineta and CBS's *60 Minutes* correspondent Steve Kroft.

> KROFT: Are you saying, at the security screening desks, that a seventy-year-old white woman from Vero Beach, Florida, would receive the same level of scrutiny as a Muslim young man from New Jersey?
>
> MINETA: Basically, I would hope so.
>
> KROFT: If you saw three young Arab men sitting, kneeling, praying, before they boarded a flight, getting on, talking to each other in Arabic, getting on the plane, no reason to stop and ask them any questions?
>
> MINETA: No reason.[9]

Ten days after the 9/11 attacks, as rescue workers were still pulling bodies from the rubble at Ground Zero, Mineta sent a letter to all U.S. airlines forbidding them from singling out Arab and Muslim passengers for additional security scrutiny, a measure that most security officials agree would be the best way to prevent future hijackings. He warned them that they would be breaking the law if they did.[10]

Then he sicced Podberesky on them. "I cannot overemphasize the importance the department places on civil-rights compliance by the airlines. It is the primary focus of my office," Podberesky announced in a briefing to the U.S. Commission on Civil Rights a month later. "We investigate each security-related discrimination complaint we receive as thoroughly and as expeditiously a possible."[11]

When Mineta later formed the Transportation Security Administration, the new agency responsible for screening airport passengers and baggage, he hired a Clinton crony from his days as head of the Department of Commerce to lead personnel security.

The two see eye-to-eye on terrorist profiling. As head of security at Commerce, David Holmes nixed Islamic groups in a Y2K report on terrorist threats. In fact, he excluded every group that was not white, say Commerce security officials who worked on the report. "We gathered information on all the known threat groups from the FBI, CIA, and other law enforcement sources," one official tells me. "It included all types: Islamic, white supremacist, anti-government, militant black, Latino crime syndicates, druggers."

But Holmes, who is black, "made us take out every group that wasn't white— no minority groups allowed," he adds. As it happened, the only millennium threat came from Islamic terrorists—one of whom, an Algerian national, planned to blow up the Los Angeles International Airport. The white militia groups, in contrast, were quiet.[12]

"FLYING WHILE MUSLIM"

In 2003, the Transportation Security Administration moved out from Mineta's department and into the new Department of Homeland Security.

But Mineta and Podberesky still enforce airline industry compliance with civil-rights regulations. And they have come down hard on carriers who have removed threatening Middle Eastern passengers from flights in the wake of 9/11. In fact, they have even slapped huge fines on United Airlines and American Airlines, which lost hundreds of passengers and crew and hundreds of millions of dollars in revenue after Middle Eastern passengers crashed four of their jumbo jets.

There are two competing federal statutes governing aviation security. One says airlines and pilots have the authority to deny any passengers who pose a threat to the safety of their passengers, and another says they cannot refuse service to passengers due to their nationality, color, or creed.

But the Department of Transportation led by Mineta and his civil-rights watchdogs make sure the latter rule always overrides the former, says Soliday, a former United pilot who flew sorties in Vietnam. In fact, Podberesky is on record saying that even if an airline captain removed four Arab men brandishing guns on his aircraft, he would send a letter of warning to the airline saying, "You had grounds to remove the people from the airplane [but] you shouldn't have considered their race or nationality."[13]

Soliday says United has nonetheless decided to put passenger safety first—and paid a big price for it. "How that law has applied to us is that when we have tried to deny boarding—most recently after 9/11, thirty-eight of our captains denied boarding to people they thought were a threat—those people filed complaints with the DOT [Department of Transportation], we were sued, and we were asked not to do it again," he says. United in 2003 was fined $1.5 million and ordered to conduct civil-rights training for pilots and crew by Podberesky's office.

Last year, American Airlines got hit with $1.5 million in fines and an order to put its staff through ethnic-sensitivity training. Delta Airlines and Continental Airlines also were punished last year for removing Middle Eastern passengers who appeared to pose a security threat.

"In a post-9/11 environment, we had situations where our crew members were uncomfortable with passengers on board the airplane, they hauled them off the airplane—I think there were ten or eleven of them—and today we're being sued by the DOT over each one of those cases," says Gerard J. Arpey, chief executive of American Airlines.[14]

Airline pilots have to worry more about lawsuits than protecting passengers, he complains. "Some of this does defy common sense."

Worse than that, it is "politically correct suicide," says retired FAA special agent Brian Sullivan, who headed risk management for the agency's New England region, including Logan International Airport in Boston, site of two of the hijackings. (In a letter he sent to headquarters four months before the 9/11 attacks, he prophetically warned that Logan was vulnerable to a "jihad" suicide operation possibly involving "a coordinated attack.")[15]

Sullivan fears Mineta and his civil-rights "crusaders" are unwittingly giving terrorists political cover to carry out their plans. He cites a case involving two young Arab passengers who were released from custody after accusing the FBI of racism. Hamda al-Shalawi and Muhammed al-Qudhaieen were detained in 1999 after the crew of a cross-country America West flight reported that one of them had tried to open the cockpit door on two occasions. The duo claimed they thought the cockpit was the bathroom and complained they were being singled out for questioning only because of their nationality and religion. The FBI released them and closed the case.

But after 9/11, their names resurfaced. It turns out that Shalawi had trained at an al-Qaida terrorist camp in Afghanistan. Authorities now believe he and his plane mate may have been conducting a dry run for the 9/11 attacks.

Soliday worries that as the painful memory of 9/11 fades, Americans will "lose their resolve" to fight the unyielding political correctness. With each new lawsuit and fine, it becomes more entrenched, even at the nation's airports, which is only good news for the bad guys.

"The issue of PC spans both administrations," he says. "PC is still tying our hands in fighting terrorism. And I think the American people will lose their resolve, and we'll continue to waste billions of dollars on CTX [bomb-scanning] machines and other weapons-screening equipment rather than profile passengers, and the political correctness will win."

Which means the terrorists may ultimately win. And they are getting a lot of help from Muslim activists, who are encouraging Muslim passengers to file discrimination complaints against the government and airlines. They have even coined a new term to discourage post-9/11 profiling: "Flying while Muslim," which is a play on the term "driving while black" used by black activists to combat profiling by highway patrolmen.

Leading the campaign is CAIR, the Council on American-Islamic Relations, which originally lobbied the Gore Commission against airport profiling. It produces a booklet titled, "Know Your Rights Pocket Guide," that directs Muslim passengers to file complaints if they are subjected to additional security scrutiny.

That would be fine if CAIR were a true civil libertarian organization with no other motives. What's galling is CAIR knows something about being subjected to additional security scrutiny, and for good reason. Some of its own officials are behind bars for terrorism, and the entire organization is under federal investigation for supporting terrorism.

25

THE DARK LAIR OF CAIR

Inside Militant Islam's PR Machine

"I challenge anyone in the eight years of CAIR's existence to find one inflammatory statement that we've ever issued. I mean, it's just ridiculous."

—Council on American-Islamic Relations spokesman IBRAHIM "DOUGIE" HOOPER, defending the Washington-based Muslim group against charges of extremism after 9/11[1]

In June 1994, three Muslim activists established what has become the most powerful Islamic pressure group in Washington—the Council on American-Islamic Relations, better known as CAIR. Two of the founders—Omar Ahmad and Nihad Awad—were born in the same Palestinian refugee camp but did not know it until they met years later in America, where they teamed up to start CAIR with an energetic Muslim convert who emigrated from Canada. Awad had befriended Cary D. "Dougie" Hooper, who changed his name to Ibrahim, while attending college in Minneapolis. Hooper was a local TV producer and activist. The two worked together on "relief" projects for Bosnian Muslims.

Armed with a masters degree in journalism and broadcast experience, the forty-nine-year-old Hooper moved to Washington to direct CAIR's muscular communications program, which defends Islam against "negative stereotypes" while attacking critics as "Islamophobes" and "bigots." He was joined there by Awad, 42, who runs CAIR's sprawling national operations as executive director. Meanwhile, Ahmad, 45, stayed in Silicon Valley, continuing his work in the high-tech industry while raising money for the nonprofit lobbying group as chairman of its board.

His efforts have paid off royally. In its first year of operation, CAIR could barely meet its budget of about $100,000. Now it can haul in many times that in a single fundraising dinner. And its annual revenue has grown to $2.6 million,

246

latest tax records show.[2] By 2000, CAIR was able to move out of its cramped office in a modest building on Washington's K Street and into its own multistory building almost in the shadow of the U.S. Capitol. The source of the funding for the building, as well as some of the group's projects, has been shrouded in mystery. CAIR insists it receives no foreign support, but land and financial documents I have uncovered reveal otherwise, as I will detail further on.

From its new national headquarters, CAIR's more than two-dozen fulltime staffers assist chapters operating in more than twenty major cities across the country, from New York to Los Angeles and from Dallas to Chicago. They field complaints from Muslims who feel they have been wronged in the workplace, as you saw in the last chapter. "We have an incredible record of success in defending Muslim rights in the workplace," Hooper says.

But they also act as watchdogs against negative portrayals of Islam in advertising, media, and Hollywood. The most sensational cases are passed up to headquarters, which goes into high dudgeon, issuing action alerts to some half-million Muslim activists in its e-mail and fax databases, who in turn blast the offending advertiser, celebrity, or studio with flame-mail and threats of boycott. The pressure almost always works. For example:

- When Nike designed a line of shoes with script on the heel that looked like the Arabic word for Allah, CAIR deemed it blasphemous and rallied a protest in the Muslim community that forced the sneaker giant to recall the entire production run and remove the offending script. It even got Nike to finance the construction of playgrounds at several Muslim schools and mosques, and make large donations to Islamic charities.

- When *U.S. News and World Report* publisher Mort Zuckerman wrote an editorial about the Muslim prophet Muhammad violating a treaty with Jews centuries ago, CAIR unleashed a protest so ferocious that it paralyzed the offices at his magazine. Zuckerman pleaded for an end to the siege, but CAIR demanded a written apology and only intensified the pressure. In the end, Zuckerman relented and published a personal apology. "Muslims forced a powerful publisher, for the first time, to issue a clear, unequivocal apology to Muslims," Awad crowed at the time.[3]

- When syndicated radio legend Paul Harvey asserted that Islam "encourages killing," CAIR instructed its members to blast both Harvey and his corporate sponsors like General Electric with angry calls, faxes, and e-mails. In response to CAIR's call to "action," several hundred Muslims contacted GE and convinced it to pull its sponsorship of the program. Harvey caved and issued an on-air statement saying Islam is a "religion of peace." GE then restored its advertising.

Not everyone backs down to CAIR, however. Another radio personality, Dr. Laura Schlessinger, stood her ground when CAIR demanded she apologize for what it called an "anti-Muslim tirade" on her national program in 2003. Her remarks came in response to a caller who asked whether her sixteen-year-old daughter should take part in a Catholic high school's class field trip to a local mosque during Ramadan. The visit was part of a "moral themes" class that aimed to help students learn how "Muslims are treated" in America. The feisty Schlessinger replied to the mother:

> This is a class on morals. What is the point of going to a mosque? You're joking of course. . . . I think you ought to stand up against this class and this teacher. This is despicable. You tell him you are willing to go to the mosque only if it is one that has done its best to root out terrorists in its midst, instead of complaining. I am horrified that you would let her go. I am so sick and tired of all the Arab-American groups whining and complaining about some kind of treatment. What culture and what religion were all the murderers of 9/11? They murdered us. That's the culture you want your daughter to learn about?[4]

CAIR accused Schlessinger of "Islamophobic bigotry," but the tactic failed to cow her into submission. Still, she was hammered by CAIR's friends in the press—and it has a lot of them. In fact, the media elite, from CNN to the *New York Times*, tend to report on CAIR uncritically, while giving it an instant forum to debate just about any issue impacting Islam that pops up in the news. "CAIR has become the primary contact for most major national and international media outlets seeking an American Muslim perspective for news stories," Awad boasts.[5]

CHECKERED PASTS

While Ahmad and Awad like to promote themselves romantically as grassroots champions of Muslim civil rights—even fancying their group a "Muslim NAACP"—they are not exactly Martin Luther King and Medgar Evers. They have a checkered past and a hidden agenda.

CAIR is actually the outgrowth of a suspected Hamas front called the Islamic Association for Palestine, which publishes Hamas communiques, distributes Hamas recruitment videos, and hosts conferences raising money for the Palestinian terrorist group, investigators say. Ahmad and Awad were two of its top officials in the early 1990s.

IAP was co-founded by Hamas political leader Mousa Abu Marzook, an officially designated terrorist and fugitive from justice. In an August 2002 court decision regarding the freezing of terrorist assets in the U.S., a federal judge found that "the Islamic Association for Palestine has acted in support of Hamas." The decision was issued in support of President George W. Bush's earlier executive order freezing the assets of the affiliated Holy Land Foundation for Relief and Development, a large American Muslim charity now under indictment for funneling money to Hamas. Although IAP has not been closed or had its officers charged with any crimes, the government has stepped up its scrutiny of the group.[6]

In October 1993, eight months before CAIR was formed, the FBI covertly recorded Ahmad and other IAP officials professing their commitment to Hamas during a key meeting in Philadelphia with five Hamas leaders and three top executives of the Holy Land Foundation, according to federal court records citing an FBI report. At the summit, which took place in a Marriott hotel, IAP allegedly mapped out a strategy to use the U.S. as a fundraising base for Hamas, while agreeing to masquerade the illicit operation under the cloak of charity to avoid U.S. government detection. It was decided, the FBI wiretaps revealed, that most or almost all of the funds collected by Holy Land Foundation in the future would be steered to Hamas. The charity, now shut down, shared officers and funds with IAP, and both groups have kept offices in the same Dallas suburb.[7]

Awad, like Ahmad, does not talk much about his pre-CAIR days. But back when he was an IAP activist, he made his support for Hamas publicly known. At a March 22, 1994, symposium on the Middle East at Barry University in Miami Shores, Florida, Awad said, "After I researched the situation inside and outside Palestine, I am in support of the Hamas movement."[8]

Three months later, he and Ahmad founded CAIR.

They are not the only CAIR officials with links to Hamas. Ghassan Elashi, a founding CAIR board member who is related by marriage to Hamas leader Marzook, has been charged with financing Hamas as the top check-writer for the Holy Land Foundation. He was present at the 1993 Hamas summit in Philadelphia.[9] Another founding director of CAIR—Rafeeq Jaber—took over for Ahmad as president of IAP and is still involved in the terror-sympathizing organization. And CAIR Board Director Nabil Sadoun has served along with CAIR Research Director Mohamed Nimer on the board of the United Association for Studies and Research, which investigators also believe to be a key Hamas front in America. In fact, Sadoun co-founded the Washington-based nonprofit UASR with Marzook, who incidentally has enjoyed the public support of CAIR since fleeing the country.[10]

CAIR has repeatedly denied any association with Hamas. But don't believe it, says recently retired FBI special agent John Vincent, who has worked Hamas cases in Chicago, where IAP is based. "There is no question CAIR supports Hamas," he asserted in a recent interview with me. He says the evidence clearly shows that the group has aided and protected the operations of groups supporting Hamas, such as IAP and the Holy Land Foundation. Vincent argues that CAIR has managed to hide its true agenda of supporting militant Islam under the "cover" of civil-rights advocacy.[11]

Even more disturbing are IAP's links to al-Qaida. In 1989, IAP dedicated its annual convention to the late Abudullah Azzam, the fiery Palestinian cleric and mentor of Osama bin Laden. And even now, newspapers published by the IAP often contain articles that praise Azzam, who called for bloody jihad against Israel and its supporters. The papers also celebrate Hamas suicide attacks on Israelis and publicize Hamas calls for the death of Israel. Awad helped edit the IAP rags before co-founding CAIR.

But that's not all. Up until 2001, a Palestinian by the name of Ghassan Dahduli served as an IAP vice president. His name was listed in the address book of bin Laden's personal secretary, Wadi al-Hage, who is serving a life sentence in prison for his role in the U.S. embassy bombings in Africa. The address book was introduced as evidence at his trial. Dahduli, who refused to cooperate in the 9/11 investigation, was deported to Jordan soon after the attacks.[12] He served under Ahmad when Ahmad was president of IAP from 1991 to 1994, the year he left to start up CAIR. (Though ethnic-Palestinian, Ahmad and Awad were born and raised in Dahduli's Jordan, site of their refugee camp.)

UNDER FEDERAL SCRUTINY

CAIR is now under investigation by Congress, in addition to federal agencies. The Senate Finance Committee, for one, is indirectly investigating the group as part of an audit of twenty-five tax-exempt Muslim charities and foundations in the U.S. that allegedly "finance terrorism and perpetuate violence," according to Republican Sen. Charles Grassley, the committee's chairman. CAIR's forerunner, the IAP, is on the audit list.

The goal of the audit is to document the extent of cross-fertilization among groups within America's terror-support network. Committee investigators say privately that they want to know if it involves so-called legitimate Muslim political groups such as CAIR. They have obtained copies of the charities' donor lists, which the IRS keeps confidential, to see if they are receiving donations from foreign sources in the Middle East, such as Saudi Arabia, or suspect domestic sources such as CAIR, a 501(c)(4) lobbying group. Investigators also want to take a closer look at where their money is going. By law, CAIR, which also maintains a foundation, does not have to publicly disclose where it gets its money, including sources of large gifts and grants. But the audit of Islamist charities provides a backdoor way of finding out—without publicly raising alarms at politically feared CAIR.

"Many of these groups not only enjoy tax-exempt status, but their reputations as charities and foundations often allows them to escape scrutiny, making it easier to hide and move their funds to other groups who threaten our national security," Grassley explained in a letter to the IRS requesting the confidential tax records.[13]

After several months of delays, the IRS finally responded late last year to the Senate's request for the sensitive tax records. Still, some details might never be released. Committee lawyers must analyze the materials to determine what the committee can publicly reveal without violating privacy laws. Donor information on tax returns filed by nonprofits is protected by a privacy provision in the tax code that makes disclosing such information a crime.

So far, however, the donor lists reveal that most of the Islamic charities share common donors tied to Saudi Arabia and terrorist fundraising fronts, a committee investigator tells me. "They all appear to be connected, and not just through interlocking boards of directors," he says, speaking on the condition of anonymity. "These charities make up an entire system." Audit reports turned over by the IRS, moreover, make it plain that the Muslim charities have "abused" U.S. tax laws, the senior staffer says, and the committee plans to expand its investigation. "There's a lot of smoke here, and we'll be following up with other groups including CAIR," he says, which he notes has received thousands of dollars in grants from the al-Qaida-tied International Relief Organization, for example.[14]

Also on the Senate's audit list is the Holy Land Foundation, another close ally of CAIR. Last year, the Dallas-based charity's founders and leaders were charged with funneling millions of dollars to Hamas. Those jailed included CAIR board member Elashi, who headed the Hamas front. The Palestinian native also helped run an Internet service provider that hosted CAIR's Web portal. (Dallas-based InfoCom Corp. also called Al-Jazeera TV a client until the tech firm was raided and shut down by federal authorities for terror ties.) When the Department of Treasury froze the Holy Land Foundation's assets just after 9/11, adding the group to its terrorist blacklist, CAIR decried the action as "unjust" and "disturbing" and demanded the government unfreeze its funds—some of which, it turns out, have come from CAIR.

Federal tax records show CAIR has donated money to the illegal Muslim charity. For example, CAIR's regional office in northern California sent five hundred dollars to the Holy Land Foundation's post-office box in Richardson, Texas, in 1999. Signing off on the transaction was none other than Ahmad, the chairman of CAIR.[15] He is listed as a director of that regional chapter, which is based in Santa Clara, California, where he lives and worships at a mosque that has held numerous fundraisers for the Holy Land Foundation. Ahmad, in fact, is a long-time member and leader of the large Wahhabi mosque, called the Muslim Community Association, or MCA, which last decade also raised money for a special invited guest—Dr. Ayman al-Zawahiri, the second in command to Osama bin Laden.[16] There is evidence that Ahmad has had a personal hand in raising funds for Palestinians in their intifada, or anti-Israel uprising. A week before the 9/11 attacks, for instance, Ahmad urged Muslims gathered at the Islamic Society of North America's convention in Illinois to start supporting two orphaned Palestinian children of martyrs instead of one to counteract what he called U.S.-supported Israeli brutality.[17]

Investigators say contributors to the Holy Land Foundation who personally knew the charity's leaders more than likely also knew their money would end up aiding Hamas. "Those contributors to HLF [Holy Land Foundation] who knew the leaders of Hamas or HLF—and at least some of those who did not—contributed their money to support suicide bombings and terrorism conducted by Hamas," charges David Kane, senior special agent with the U.S. Bureau of Immigration and Customs Enforcement within the Department of Homeland Security.[18] His definition would include both Ahmad and Awad, who have worked not only with Hamas leader Marzook but also with Holy Land Foundation leader Elashi.

The Santa Clara-based chapter of CAIR has also given funds to Muslims in Chechnya, tax records show, a hotbed of al-Qaida-affiliated terrorism. Chechen terrorists last year slaughtered hundreds of children at a school in Russia.

"CAIR, its leaders, and its activities effectively give aid to international terrorist groups," asserts former FBI counterterrorism chief Steven Pomerantz.[19]

TERRORISTS ON THE PAYROLL

CAIR has even employed officials convicted of terrorism in its own ranks. The alarming news of the recent convictions has prompted another congressional investigation led by Republican Sen. Jon Kyl, chairman of the Senate Judiciary

Committee's Subcommittee on Terrorism, Technology, and Homeland Security, who recently announced that CAIR's "terror-related activities are being scrutinized by my subcommittee as well as the federal government."[20]

Awad suggests Kyl is motivated by "bigotry" and is using the investigation to "vilify and defame the American Muslim community."

"By attacking the more established and respected civil-rights organizations within the American Muslim community, these political instigators' hatred and bigotry is, in effect, unraveling a portion of the social fabric of America," he said in a long letter to Kyl, explaining why he has refused invitations to testify before his committee.[21]

Kyl shot back that claiming to be a victim of anti-Muslim bias is no defense against the charges. "Falsely charging 'bigotry' is simply not an acceptable response to serious allegations of criminal activity," the senator said, noting that "three of CAIR's top leaders were arrested on terror-related charges."[22]

And they have all been convicted. Here is a rap sheet on the trio of CAIR convicts.

Ghassan Elashi: As cited earlier, Elashi was indicted last year on charges he knowingly provided financial and material support to Hamas terrorists as chairman of the Holy Land Foundation. One of CAIR's founding directors, he started up the group's Texas chapter, according to state incorporation records. In a separate case, the fifty-year-old Elashi and his four Palestinian brothers were convicted last year of using their Dallas-based InfoCom Corp. to illegally ship high-tech goods to Syria, a state sponsor of terrorism. Elashi's pal Marzook, the fugitive Hamas leader, is believed to be hiding in Syria.

Bassem K. Khafagi: Another CAIR figure, Khafagi was arrested in 2003 while serving as the group's director of community affairs. He pleaded guilty to charges of bank and visa fraud stemming from a federal counterterror probe of his role in the Islamic Assembly of North America, where he was a founding member and president. He was sentenced to ten months in prison and deported to his native Egypt. Khafagi served in a leadership position at Detroit-based IANA during the time senior al-Qaida recruiter Abdelrahman al-Dosari spoke at IANA's 1993, 1994, and 1995 conferences.[23] Khafagi, 42, is also tied to a recently indicted Saudi student who administered IANA Web sites that published material supporting al-Qaida and advocating suicide attacks on America.

Randall Todd "Ismail" Royer: The former communications specialist and civil-rights coordinator at CAIR was also arrested in 2003 on charges of conspiring to wage jihad in Pakistan and Afghanistan while the Pentagon was still smoldering from the 9/11 attack. Royer was the ringleader of the so-called "Virginia jihad network"—a gang of eleven young Muslim men from the Washington area who had broader goals of helping the al-Qaida network. He is now in prison serving a twenty-year sentence.

The thirty-one-year-old Royer first started working for CAIR in 1994 as a college student. He dropped out of school to fight with the *mujahideen* in Bosnia, an issue dear to Hooper, who once worked for the Bosnian Relief Committee with Awad. Not long after returning from violent jihad, Royer rejoined the staff of CAIR as a communications specialist in 1997. A Muslim convert like Hooper, he worked out of Hooper's office where he wrote news releases, spoke with journalists, conducted research, and monitored the media "as part of CAIR's media relations effort," according to a biographical sketch posted on IslamOnline.net.[24] Then he began working for CAIR's Civil Rights Department, fielding complaints from aggrieved Muslims before and after 9/11. "I was the civil rights guy at CAIR," he says, "taking phone calls about women getting spit on, the FBI barging into houses."[25] He continued in that role at least through October 2001, according to media reports quoting him with that title back then.

So even after the horror of 9/11—as CAIR portrayed itself as a peaceful and patriotic voice for Muslims—one of its top officials was secretly training with a group of jihadists to use AK-47s to mow down non-Muslims in Pakistan and Afghanistan, including American soldiers.[26]

SYMPATHY FOR THE DEVIL

CAIR has been uncharacteristically silent about these terrorist convictions, saying only that it cannot be held responsible for the actions of a handful of its employees.

Still, the group gives the strong impression that it sympathizes with terrorists, which might explain why it attracts so many of them.

In 1998, after Osama bin Laden was fingered for blowing up the U.S. embassies, CAIR demanded that Los Angeles-area billboards with bin Laden's picture under the headline, "Sworn Enemy," be taken down. In 2001, when most of the civilized world condemned bin Laden for attacking New York and Washington, CAIR abstained for nearly four months, while demanding a halt to U.S. bombing in Afghanistan, bin Laden's home base. Its leaders, namely Hooper, refused to assign guilt to the evil mastermind, even under direct questioning by members of the press—until, that is, bin Laden incriminated himself in a videotape aired in December 2001. Only after his guilt became undeniably obvious did CAIR join in the country's outrage against him.

In fact, CAIR has a long history of being on the wrong side of anti-American terrorism cases. In a 1996 report it published on anti-Muslim discrimination, it quoted lawyers for Blind Sheikh Omar Abdel Rahman as saying that his trial was unfair. Rahman is now serving a life sentence for plotting to blow up bridges, tunnels, and buildings in New York.

Awad has a blanket response to all charges his group sympathizes with Islamic terrorism—"We condemn all acts of terror"—even as he acknowledges voicing support for Hamas, a group that commits acts of terror.[27] And even as his boss Ahmad, who secretly met with Hamas leaders and who named his young son "Osama," worships and sometimes delivers sermons at the California mosque that raised money for bin Laden's second in command.[28]

ARAB BENEFACTORS

CAIR has desperately tried to project a moderate and patriotic image in the face of growing skepticism. "We are Americans and we are Muslims," is the motto that it runs in the nation's newspapers. Part of that image campaign involves dispelling notions that it is controlled by foreign interests in the Middle East. CAIR emphatically denies receiving any foreign support, including for its new headquarters. It argues that it is a "grassroots organization" largely supported by members who pay dues.

For the record, here is what Hooper insisted in a November 8, 2001, press release: "We do not support directly or indirectly or receive support from any overseas group or government."

But land and tax records tell a different story—if you can find them, that is (and then figure them out). And believe me, it is not easy. The original deed to the property for CAIR's headquarters—located a few blocks from the U.S. Capitol at 453 New Jersey Avenue, S.E.—is kept at the District of Columbia Recorder of Deeds Building. You can access it by computer. Problem is, you cannot read it once you call it up. The copy in the database was scanned from microfilm, not the original, and the resulting blurry type has rendered it illegible (printing the image does not help). The only way to read it is to view it on microfilm, which requires a trip to the third floor of the building.

In room 319, there are four carousels containing microfilm cassettes. Curiously, the cassette with the reel storing the CAIR document is missing. Not checked-out missing, either; but simply gone—as in lost and nowhere to be found. I asked to see a backup tape, and after some initial resistance, a clerk downstairs agreed to retrieve it from a room marked "Authorized Personnel Only."

Finally, I was able to read the original document, and it led me to a tangled web of Islamic financing. It turns out that in acquiring its headquarters, CAIR first entered into a lease-to-purchase agreement with the United Bank of Kuwait, the same bank used by the Kuwaiti Embassy. The bank owned the property and essentially leased it to CAIR. The unconventional five-year deal—recorded as a "Memorandum of Lease and Agreement To Purchase"—was signed by Awad, the executive director of CAIR, on June 24, 1999. The deed remained with the Bank of Kuwait.

Yet oddly, CAIR listed the property as a real estate "asset" valued at more than $2.6 million on a balance sheet filed with the IRS that year, its tax records show. Odder still, it reported a loan of more than $2.1 million from the Bank of Kuwait for a "building purchase."[29]

The lease contract only included an *option* to purchase the property, adding that the "Buyer/Lessee has the right to receive the deed to the property at any time during the term of the lease," which was set to expire last June.

CAIR did not exercise that option until September 2002, when according to another land document, it was granted title and interest to the property by the Bank of Kuwait in a sale totaling a little more than $978,000, based on the recording and transfer taxes stamped on the back of the document. The lease-purchase agreement was terminated.

At the same time, however, CAIR entered into a "Deed of Trust" contract with the Al-Maktoum Foundation of the United Arab Emirates, which put up the $978,000 for the property and now holds the rights to sell it, manage it, and collect rents from other tenants in the multistory building on the property. The document was signed by CAIR chairman Ahmad on September 12, 2002.[30]

The Al-Maktoum Foundation is based in the United Arab Emirates capital of Dubai and is headed by Gen. Sheikh Mohammed Bin Rashid Al-Maktoum, the Dubai crown prince and UAE defense minister. So essentially, the UAE government is CAIR's new benefactor.

As one of only three countries in the world to formally recognize the Taliban, the UAE has an al-Qaida and 9/11 connection. Money for the 9/11 plot was funneled through UAE banks, and two of the 9/11 hijackers were Emiratis. After the attacks, Crown Prince Al-Maktoum was forced to address reports of al-Qaida money-laundering activities in his country, as well as a rumor that Osama bin Laden had been treated for kidney ailments at a Dubai hospital.

And in a surprisingly unsympathetic statement made just two weeks after the attacks, Al-Maktoum warned Washington not to strike Afghanistan and kill "innocent" Muslims. He also advised against confusing "legitimate" acts of resistance against "Zionist oppression" with acts of terrorism, arguing that the only real terrorists are "Israeli terrorists" and that Israelis should be included in any American war on terrorism.

"We should not confuse legitimate resistance with terrorist acts," Al-Maktoum said, referring to Palestinian suicide bombings. "The Arab and Muslim communities have paid dearly for terrorism, especially the state terrorism practiced by the government of [Prime Minister Ariel] Sharon and extremist groups in Israel. Regrettably, the powers in the international community have done nothing but watch the Israeli terrorists, a matter which has angered Arabs and Muslims." He added, "Confrontation of terrorism must cover Israeli terrorism."[31]

Al-Maktoum's foundation, which builds hard-line mosques and schools in other countries, has also held Dubai telethons to support the families of Palestinian suicide bombers as part of a relief campaign called "We Are All Palestinians."

This is CAIR's new foreign partner—and it is not its only troubling source of Middle Eastern funding, either.

In 1999, the group started renovating the suite of offices it occupies on the second floor of the existing red-brick building near the Capitol, judging from an October 1999 lien filed by a local construction company against the property for unpaid services.[32] The remodeling is impressive. Visitors stepping off the second-floor elevator walk into a hallway outside the CAIR lobby bedecked with marble flooring and ornate molding. The walls are adorned with blown-up video stills of Hooper and Awad during TV appearances on CNN and C-SPAN and other networks. They are the media stars of CAIR, and this is their Hall of Fame. Double glass doors lead into a lobby decorated with new furniture and a wall-size aerial photograph of Muslim pilgrims circumambulating the Ka'aba at Mecca. On tables are copies of every major newspaper and periodical in the country. Workers dart in and out of offices and rush down hallways. It is a busy shop indeed.

According to CAIR's tax returns for that year, it spent $50,300 on furniture and equipment alone. It is not clear how much it spent on the renovation work.

But in August 1999, the Saudi-based Islamic Development Bank pledged $250,000 to help finance CAIR's new offices, a grant that was announced at the time by the Saudi Embassy.[33] Awad disputes any characterization of the grant as foreign support, arguing the Islamic Development Bank is "a multinational financial institution similar in nature to the World Bank."[34]

Actually, the Islamic Development Bank is not much at all like the World Bank. For starters, the IDB is based in Jeddah, Saudi Arabia, while the World Bank is based in Washington. And unlike the IDB, the World Bank does not allocate its funds to Islamic terrorists who eviscerate busloads of non-Muslim women and children. That's right, the IDB has distributed more than $250 million to the families of Palestinian "martyrs" from two large intifada funds it manages—the Al-Quds Fund and the Al-Aqsa Fund, which get most of their contributions from the Saudi kingdom.[35]

CAIR has other Saudi-based sugar daddies as well. On a fundraising trip to the Saudi capital of Riyadh in November 2002—just one year after Hooper denied taking foreign money—Awad secured the financial support of the Saudi government-sponsored World Assembly of Muslim Youth in a million-dollar public-relations campaign to put pro-Islamic material in American newspapers and libraries. You'll recall that the U.S. branch of WAMY is under federal investigation, formerly headed by bin Laden's nephew before he fled the country after 9/11. The U.S. propaganda material the questionable charity is sponsoring is decidedly more benign than the content found in its Arabic-language publications. For instance, WAMY's *Islamic Views* book teaches that Islam "is a religion of Jihad" and that jihad "was an answer for the Jews, the liars." It also says, "Teach our children to love taking revenge on the Jews and the oppressors, and teach them that our youngsters will liberate Palestine and al-Quds [Jerusalem] when they go back to Islam and make Jihad for the sake of Allah."[36]

On Awad's 2002 fundraising trip, he also enlisted the help of Saudi Prince Alwaleed bin Talal, who donated $500,000 to CAIR's propaganda project. That comes on top of the at least $12,000 in financing CAIR has received from the U.S. offices of the Saudi-based International Islamic Relief Organization, one of Osama bin Laden's favorite charities. It is the subject of an active terror-financing investigation.[37]

INFLAMMATORY PRONOUNCEMENTS

So much for CAIR's assertion that it receives no foreign support. It also claims to be America's largest "mainstream" Muslim group and boasts of its acceptance in top political circles in Washington. Every chance it gets, CAIR reminds the public that its executive director was invited by the White House after 9/11 to "stand next to President Bush" at his press conference at the Washington mosque. Any suggestion that CAIR represents extremist views or supports terrorism is met with violent objection.

"I challenge anyone in the eight years of CAIR's existence to find one inflammatory statement that we've ever issued," Hooper growls. "I mean, it's just ridiculous."[38]

What's ridiculous is how easy it is to meet such a challenge, starting with the outrageously anti-American comment by CAIR board member Hamza Yusuf, who two days before the Muslim attacks on America, said, "This country is facing a terrible fate, and the reason for that is because this country stands condemned. It stands condemned like Europe stood condemned because of what it did. And lest people forget, Europe suffered two world wars after conquering the Muslim lands."[39]

Then there is CAIR board member Siraj Wahhaj who prays America's "democracy will crumble," clearing the way for an Islamic theocracy. Past board member Abdurahman Alamoudi has shared the same dream but exercises some restraint in how Muslims can realize it. He argues they can only pray "Oh, Allah, destroy America" if they live outside the country. While here, however, Muslims are commissioned to gradually transform the government from within by infiltrating it.

And, of course, Hooper himself has stated the same desire to overturn the U.S. system of government in favor of an "Islamic" state. "I wouldn't want to create the impression that I wouldn't like the government of the United States to be Islamic sometime in the future," he told a Minneapolis newspaper, as detailed in an earlier chapter. His boss Ahmad, finally, has said he wants to replace the U.S. Constitution with the Quran. Apparently Hooper does not view such seditious talk as "inflammatory."

Despite this ugly record, CAIR is still widely accepted in Washington as a mainstream American group. Even leaders in Congress have given it a platform to legitimize militant Islam, conned as they are into buying one of CAIR's biggest lies of all.

VII
POLITICAL INFILTRATION

26

THE MUSLIM CAUCUS

Representing the Faith in D.C.

"Twenty years ago, Muslims in this country felt it was important to build mosques. Now we have thousands of mosques all over the country. Fifteen years ago, we wanted to build schools, and now we have hundreds of Islamic schools where our youth are being educated. Now, the goal of the Muslim community should be to become politically active."

—ASHRAF NUBANI, one of the attorneys on the legal team
of confessed terrorist Abdurahman Alamoudi[1]

Numbers count in politics. Showing the size and growth of a community translates into increased leverage with elected officials. Finding reliable measures for the size of the Muslim community in America is difficult because the Census Bureau does not survey religious affiliation. But the most widely cited number is six million. A "respected scholar" by the name of Ihsan Bagby came up with the figure in a study sponsored by the Council on American-Islamic Relations, a militant Muslim lobbying group that never fails to tout the number in its press releases.

"There are an estimated six million Muslims in this country," it asserts, "and Islam is one of the fastest-growing religions in America." As a result, most media outlets—as well as Congress, the White House, and the Department of State—have parroted the number to describe the size of the nation's Muslim population.

But it is a myth, and one of the biggest ones going in Washington. What CAIR does not tell you is that Professor Bagby is closely affiliated with CAIR, serving as a member of its board of directors, and has an inherent conflict of interest. CAIR's secret agenda is to Islamize America. Bagby himself once said Muslims can "never be full citizens of this country" until it becomes an Islamic state. Inflating the size of the potential Muslim voting bloc would help them achieve their goals, critics assert.

CAIR also neglects to explain how Bagby, who is not a trained demographer, arrived at his number, which even he admits is a "guestimation."[2] Here is his decidedly unscientific methodology:

1. With assistance from CAIR researcher Mohamed Nimer, Bagby called the nation's 1,209 mosques and interviewed leaders at 416 of them, asking them how many people were involved in their mosque in any way. The average response was 1,625 participants. The figure is more than likely high, however, since two imams in the survey estimated that their mosques had 50,000 participants. By comparison, one of the largest mosques in the country, the Dar al-Hijrah Islamic Center just outside Washington, has only about 3,000 participants. Unlike churches, mosques do not customarily keep records of worshippers, so the margin of error in the survey is abnormally large.

2. Undeterred, Bagby then multiplied that fuzzy participation figure by the 1,209 mosques and came up with nearly 2 million "mosqued Muslims" in America.

3. Next, he multiplied that sum by a magical factor of three to capture Muslims who might not participate in mosque activities and arrived at the 6 million guestimate for the size of the Muslim population. Where did he get his magical multiplier of three? It is an educated guess, based on years of observation of the Islamic community, says Bagby, who used to preach in a Saudi-financed mosque. For all we know, however, it is a wild exaggeration.[3]

No wonder his survey results are at odds with so many other surveys, including ones recently conducted by demographers at the University of Chicago, City University of New York, and Encyclopaedia Britannica. They put the number of Muslims in America at between 1.5 million and 4.1 million.

Yet CAIR now claims in its press releases an even *higher* number of 7 million to account for what it says is robust growth in the Muslim population since early 2001, when it officially released Bagby's findings. Conveniently, the number also beats the number of Jews in America, estimated at 6 million. A larger number, even if artificially inflated, offers Muslim groups greater access and clout in Washington, while buttressing their calls for redefining America's heritage as "Judeo-Christian-Muslim."

So next time you hear there are 7 million Muslims in America, don't buy it. Still, there is no dispute that the Muslim population is growing rapidly and may in the not-too-distant future actually reach CAIR's total. Much of the growth is coming from blacks who are converting to Islam—they now make up close to half the Muslim population in America—and from an influx of Muslim immigrants from the Middle East. The Arab population in the U.S. has nearly doubled in the past two decades, thanks to liberalized immigration laws, and the flow of Arab immigrants is not expected to slow much, even after 9/11. By 2010, 1.1 million new immigrants from the Middle East and Pakistan are projected to settle in the United States, bringing the total immigrant population from that region to about 2.5 million, according to the Washington-based Center for Immigration Studies.[4] And helping to boost Muslim political clout, some of the fastest growth will be seen in key election battleground states such as Michigan and Florida.

The vast majority of the new immigrants are Muslim, a switch from the past. In fact, the religious composition of Middle Eastern immigrants has changed dramatically over the past thirty-five years. In 1970, about 15 percent of them were Muslim, while the rest were mostly Arab Christians, says the Center for Immigration Studies. But today the share of Muslims from that region has soared to about 75 percent. (They look upon this country as Muhammad did Medina when he moved there in the *Hijra*, or migration. In fact, many secretly refer to this land as the "American Medina.")

But is Islam really one of the fastest-growing religions in America? Afraid so. In fact, the Muslim population, also fueled by high birth rates, is on its way to outstripping mainline Protestant membership, which is on the decline. Chicago, Los Angeles, and New York already have more than twice as many Muslims as Episcopalians, for example.[5]

And Muslims are now more politically active than ever—more so than the average American, in fact.

"Twenty years ago, Muslims in this country felt it was important to build mosques. Now we have thousands of mosques all over the country. Fifteen years ago, we wanted to build schools, and now we have hundreds of Islamic schools where our youth are being educated," says Ashraf Nubani, one of the lawyers on confessed terrorist Alamoudi's legal team. "Now, the goal of the Muslim community should be to become politically active."

An overwhelming number of American Muslims agree with that goal. A whopping 82 percent of them say political participation is very or somewhat important to them, a Zogby International poll found right after 9/11. And they are not shy about participating, either. Fully half of American Muslims have called or written the media or a politician about issues important to the Muslim community, the Zogby poll also found.[6]

But they are not just vocal. They are also highly organized. In the 2000 presidential election, Muslims for the first time formed a voting bloc and put George W. Bush over the top in a narrow race. And in the process, they came close to repealing the government's use of secret evidence against suspected terrorists in deportation proceedings. CAIR helped awaken the sleeping Muslim giant by leading voter registration drives.

In the 2004 presidential election, it was the Democrats' turn to court the Arab-Muslim vote, which is now organized around repealing the USA Patriot Act, which authorized the FBI to, among other things, spy on hardcore mosques that double as recruiting and fundraising stations for terrorism.

All but one of the eight Democratic presidential candidates attended the Arab American Institute's national leadership conference in Detroit during the primaries. And so did the head of the Democratic Party (as well as the head of the GOP). Teresa Heinz Kerry, who has given thousands of dollars to CAIR through one of her charities, was the keynote speaker at the American-Arab Anti-Discrimination Committee's convention last year. The Democrats' national convention in Boston, moreover, featured an invocation by a Muslim cleric, along with dozens of Muslim delegates.

The courtship was not confined to Democrats though. Independent candidate Ralph Nader, an Arab American, was a regular at Muslim rallies again this campaign, strengthening a very cozy relationship with the Arab and Muslim community. And although Bush lost much of the Muslim vote this election for signing the Patriot Act, among other reasons, the strategic alliances he built with Muslim groups before 9/11 have not been severed—an unsettling issue I will tackle in the next chapter.

But first, let's talk about appeasement at the other end of Pennsylvania Avenue. Let's take a look at the Muslim community's most cherished friends on Capitol Hill, both past and present, starting with Democrats.

DEMOCRAT BOOSTERS

Cynthia McKinney: One of Islam's biggest boosters in Congress, McKinney has been handsomely rewarded by hardcore Islamists. No less than six of the top donors to her 2002 reelection bid were Muslim officers with companies and organizations under federal investigation for ties to terrorism, including Jamal Barzinji and other members of the notorious Safa group, an alleged terror-financing front underwritten by Saudi businessmen. Jailed terror suspects Alamoudi and al-Arian also gave her money. When her cozy ties to Muslim militants were exposed after 9/11, the black Democrat from Georgia suffered a backlash at the polls. She lost her seat in 2002—only to reclaim it in 2004. McKinney is now back in power and has taken up Islamic causes again.

Jim Moran: Another Muslim darling in the House, Moran took cash from many of the same shady Muslim sources as McKinney. The Virginia Democrat, a frequent honorary guest at Islamic conferences, is known for bashing Israel. Voters in his heavily Muslim district reelected him, too, in the last race.

Dennis Kucinich: The Democratic representative from Ohio was the Muslim community's favorite candidate in the last presidential race. The Arab-American Political Action Committee endorsed Kucinich for the Democratic nod, arguing he was the best candidate to represent the community's interests. The campaign cash the PAC previously raised for him ranked among the largest in Congress. CAIR invited Kucinich to be the keynote speaker at its fundraising dinner in 2003, speaking alongside Siraj Wahhaj, an unindicted co-conspirator in the World Trade Center bombing in 1993. The lawmaker employed one of the few Muslim staffers on the Hill.

John Conyers: A tireless champion of Muslim causes, Conyers co-sponsored a House bill to repeal the government's use of secret evidence to deport terrorist suspects from the Middle East. He has also fought FBI outreach efforts in the Arab and Muslim communities. In 2003, the Detroit Democrat hosted the first dinner celebrating the end of Ramadan for American Muslim leaders on Capitol Hill, something he promises to do every year. Conyers is one of the top recipients of donations from the Arab-American Leadership PAC.

David Bonior: Bonior was Conyers's longtime partner in Islamic appeasement before he left the House in a failed bid for the Michigan governor's mansion. They were a one-two punch for Muslim causes in the Detroit area. Both sponsored the bill repealing secret terrorism evidence. Even though Bonior, a Democrat, had fewer Arab and Muslim constituents in his district than Conyers, he was a more forceful advocate for them. And he hauled in more money from them, including some tainted with the blood of terrorism. For example, the ex-congressman kept thirty-two hundred dollars in campaign donations from al-Arian and his wife. Of lawmakers who received money from al-Arian, Bonior got the most. And he hired al-Arian's eldest son, Abdullah, as an intern in his Washington office.

What's more, Bonior in 1998 lobbied to have al-Arian's brother-in-law, Mazen al-Najjar, released from jail. He was later deported for visa violations and alleged terrorist ties. Al-Najjar attended North Carolina A&T State University's engineering school at the same time as Khalid Sheikh Mohammed, the al-Qaida lieutenant and 9/11 mastermind.[7]

Bonior also has been cozy with Muslim activists accused of sympathizing with terrorist groups. The American Muslim Council in 1999 gave Bonior a special service award. The plaque reads: "In appreciation for distinguished political activism on behalf of the Muslim community." He initially refused to refund a thousand-dollar gift from AMC founder Alamoudi after he declared support for the terrorist group Hamas.[8]

Bonior, who supports a Palestinian state, also worked closely with CAIR to secure airport security jobs for Middle Eastern nationals and at the same time joined the group in fighting federal attempts to profile Arab passengers at U.S. airports. "I am working with members of the Muslim community and government officials to end discriminatory profiling at airports. This is terribly wrong," Bonior told Muslims gathered at the American Muslim Alliance convention in 1998, three years before such profiling could have saved three thousand lives.

"I have been in close contact with the Federal Aviation Administration about this policy," he added, "and met last month with FAA Administrator Jane Garvey and leaders of the Arab-American community in Detroit."

Before speaking at the AMA confab, Bonior was introduced as "the most popular congressman among Pakistani Americans," whom homeland security authorities are now scrutinizing as they return from trips to Pakistan, suspecting some may be training at terrorist camps still active there. He returned the love by complimenting Muslims and then expressed a shared dream: "I look forward to the day in the not-too-distant future when I will serve alongside Muslim Americans in the U.S. House."[9] Of course, he did not get that chance, but others just might.

Bonior, who turned down an interview request, is still active in Muslim politics. During the last election, he joined Democratic leaders in calling for an end to Muslim profiling.

Nancy Pelosi: The House Democratic leader last year held a meeting on the Hill with Bonior and CAIR and other Muslim activist groups to call for an end to any Muslim profiling at airports. "Since September 11, many Muslim Americans have been subjected to searches at airports and other locations based upon their religion and national origin," said Pelosi of California. "Racial and religious profiling is fundamentally un-American, and we must make it illegal." Pelosi said she was a "proud" co-sponsor of the End Racial Profiling Act, which would make it illegal for authorities to scrutinize Muslim airline passengers. And she vowed, "We must correct the Patriot Act."

Hillary Rodham Clinton: During her Senate campaign in 2000, Clinton took a thousand dollars from Alamoudi of the American Muslim Council and another fifty thousand from members of the American Muslim Alliance, headed by Alamoudi associate Agha Saeed.

But she was forced to return the donations when news got out that both leaders voiced support for Palestinian terrorists. Clinton apparently thought she could launder Alamoudi's blood money by renaming his group the "American Museum Council" in her donor report to the Federal Election Commission, thereby disguising Alamoudi as a curator rather than a terrorist supporter.

No one was fooled. She ended up remitting the terror-tinged dough two days after the New York press reported that the former first lady had invited Alamoudi to Muslim holiday receptions at the White House, where he argued in support of Hamas, even though it had been officially designated a terrorist group. Alamoudi later boasted, "We are the ones who went to the White House and defended what is called Hamas."[10]

Moreover, Saeed was quoted backing Palestinian suicide attacks on Israel. Yet Hillary attended a five-hundred-dollar-a-ticket fundraiser sponsored by his group, which even gave her a plaque. Embarrassed, she refunded the money the group raised for her along with Alamoudi's check.

Clinton, who has shown a pattern of deception over her career, claims listing Alamoudi's employer as a "museum" was a typographical error.

Yet no other politician who received money from Alamoudi and his group mistook "Muslim" for "Museum" in filing their FEC disclosure form. By camouflaging the identity of Alamoudi and his group, Hillary gave cause to think she knew they were trouble and took the money anyway (not much unlike all the funny Chinese money she and her husband raised for Bill Clinton's 1996 presidential run).

John Bryant: After leaving Congress, the Dallas Democrat threw his full political weight behind the Holy Land Foundation, the large Muslim charity accused of being Hamas's financial arm in America.

According to lobbying disclosure records, Bryant and his partner Randy White made more than one hundred thousand dollars in fees defending the Dallas-based Holy Land Foundation from 1995—when the Department of State first designated Hamas a terrorist group—to 2001. They lobbied the Departments of State, Treasury, and Justice, along with the FBI, to refute what they called "unfounded attacks" against their client, which came under investigation for aiding Hamas. They argued that Holy Land Foundation's dealings in the

West Bank and Gaza were "lawful activities," and that it was merely providing "relief to areas of the world where Muslims are in distress."[11]

However, their arguments wore thin as the government's investigation picked up steam. Shortly after 9/11, the Department of Treasury froze the Holy Land Foundation's assets. And last year, the Department of Justice indicted the charity for funneling more than twelve million dollars to Hamas for payment to suicide bombers and their families between 1995 and 2001. (Some of those suicide bombers have killed Americans in Israel.) As it turns out, many of the clients Bryant defended during those years of lobbying for Holy Land Foundation were actually relatives of Hamas leaders.

Bryant says he does not regret defending them and says he doubts the allegations against them are true.

"I would sleep better if I knew the Holy Land Foundation had deceived me and were guilty and deserved to be shut down and indicted," he tells me. "But I never saw any evidence of it, and I find the allegations to be counterintuitive. In thirty years as a lawyer, I have represented plenty of clients over the years about whom that cannot be said."

He then blamed the law firm Akin Gump, which represented the Holy Land Foundation in Washington. He says it "abandoned" the group in 2001 after the Bush administration took action against it. The firm's top lawyer in the case, George Salem, is a Republican friend of Bush who raised money for his presidential campaigns.

"Akin Gump ran for the hills," Bryant says. "I am embarrassed that a major law firm took Holy Land Foundation's money, agreed to represent them, and then abandoned them as soon as they were accused."

But records show Bryant severed ties with his trusted client around the same time. Why? "My contract with Holy Land Foundation specifically stated that if there was evidence they were involved in hostile activity against Israel, I would cease to represent them," he explains.[12] Apparently, he is not as trusting of his former client as he indicates.

Democrats hardly have a monopoly on shameless lobbying on behalf of Muslims, however. Some of the biggest Islam boosters in Congress have been Republicans.

REPUBLICAN BOOSTERS

Tom Campbell: A liberal Republican, Campbell became a favorite among Muslims when he joined Bonior and Conyers in co-sponsoring the Secret Evidence Repeal Act. The former representative from California, who lost his seat in an unsuccessful Senate race, also opposed the continuation of economic sanctions against Iraq.

Campbell further endeared himself to Muslims by hiring a young Muslim activist from his district, Suhail A. Khan, as his press secretary. Khan, now in the Bush administration, kicked the door open wider to Muslims and their hobby-horses. "Campbell's office was a hive of activity to weaken our counterterrorism laws," says one Hill observer. And pro-terrorist donors rewarded him with thousands of dollars; he even raked in money from Sami al-Arian for his Senate bid.

Spencer Abraham: The former energy secretary is one of only three Arab Americans to serve in the U.S. cabinet. Before joining the Bush administration, Abraham served in the Senate, where he sponsored the Senate version of Campbell's bill to repeal secret evidence against illegal Arab aliens. Likewise, the Republican raked in a lot of campaign cash from pro-terrorist donors during his tenure in the Senate representing Michigan. He hauled in fifty-five hundred dollars alone from Alamoudi, Barzinji, and other Muslim activists implicated in the Safa group investigation. Federal records show he also received funds from Mohamed Omeish of the Success Foundation, a Washington-area Muslim charity linked to Hamas, and Abdelhaleem Ashqar of the Al-Aqsa Educational Fund, another suspected Hamas front. Ashqar, a Palestinian activist, was indicted last year for financing terrorism by Hamas.

Paul Findley: During his twenty-two years in the House, Findley earned a dubious reputation as "Arafat's best friend in Congress." The liberal Republican championed every Muslim cause, including cutting off aid to Israel, as if he were Muslim himself. But he's not—he's Christian. So what motivated him? Generous campaign donations from people with business interests in Saudi Arabia, for starters. And he has cashed in on those Saudi ties since leaving Congress, taking numerous business trips to Saudi.

He also took a trip to South Africa to give a speech with a confederate of Osama bin Laden. Last decade he and the late Ahmed Deedat—a Saudi-backed anti-Semite and ardent backer of bin Laden—headlined a symposium called, "Is Israel Set Up for Destruction?" Over dinner in Cape Town that night, they pondered a world in which the Quran nullified all government contracts, including the U.S. Constitution.[13]

More recently, Findley shared a stage with the imam who counseled some of the 1993 World Trade Center bombers—Siraj Wahhaj—and the imam who counseled some of the 9/11 hijackers—Anwar Aulaqi—at a 2002 joint convention of the Islamic Circle of North American and the Muslim American Society.

He spends most of his time these days bashing Israel and rationalizing Palestinian terrorism as founder of the nonprofit Council for the National Interest in Washington. After 9/11, Findley criticized what he called "the failure of the Bush administration to deal honestly with terrorism" by failing to see what "is vivid to most of the world—[that] the real Ground Zero of terrorism is in Palestine, not Manhattan."[14]

Findley is also an author. In his 2001 book, *Silent No More: Confronting America's False Images of Islam*, he describes Hezbollah—a terrorist group that killed 240 Marines in Beirut—as a "respected, major political organization" that "came into being as a resistance movement provoked by Israel's bloody and destructive invasions of Lebanon."[15] Not surprisingly, his book is high on CAIR's recommended reading list.

Dana Rohrabacher: If you think only bleeding-heart liberals consort with Muslim militants and do their bidding, think again. U.S. Rep. Dana Rohrabacher is a rock-ribbed, flag-waving conservative hawk who has nonetheless joined Alamoudi and his associates in slamming U.S. policy in the Middle East, while accepting their money. In fact, records show he has raked in more than $15,500 in campaign gifts from them over the years.

The California Republican got so attached to Alamoudi's former deputy, in fact, that some of the top members of his staff revolted.

One day not long after 9/11, the deputy, Khaled Saffuri, strolled into Rohrabacher's office on the Hill and made small talk with his press secretary. During their chat, Saffuri expressed his displeasure with Bush's decision to freeze the Holy Land Foundation's assets. He told the aide that he was a financial supporter of the charity and proceeded to sing its praises. Then Saffuri, a Palestinian Muslim by birth, revealed something that made the aide's jaw go slack. He said he sponsors an orphaned child of a Palestinian suicide bomber—a terrorist.

As soon as Saffuri left the office, the aide, Phaedra Baird, fired off a letter to her boss urging him to "sever all ties with Khaled."

"In the wake of the September 11 attacks, it is imperative that you, as a member of Congress, receive your information about the Middle East and the Arab world from a source whom we can be sure has the best interest of the United States at heart," Baird advised Rohrabacher in her December 7, 2001, letter. "I do not believe this is the case with Khaled. I believe that his loyalties are elsewhere."

"I know Khaled is your friend and that you think highly of him," she continued. "I believe that as your friend, if he is a true friend, he will understand the reason that you would not want to receive further counsel from him in light of his financial support for this organization."[16]

But Rohrabacher did not take her advice. He personally endorsed Saffuri at a private gathering of Republicans shortly thereafter and even picked up an award from Alamoudi's group at a conference held a few months later. Baird, whose husband is in the military, resigned. She was joined by Rohrabacher's longtime foreign policy aide, Al Santoli.

The congressman's consorting goes beyond Islamic awards banquets. Between 1998 and 2002, Rohrabacher took four all-expenses-paid trips to the Middle East with the Arab American Institute and the Islamic Institute, a Republican annex to the American Muslim Council started by Saffuri and GOP powerbroker Grover Norquist. One trip really raised eyebrows. Just five months before the 9/11 attacks, Rohrabacher met privately in Qatar with Taliban leaders who wanted to discuss U.S. sanctions and aid—as they were protecting bin Laden. He was escorted on the trip by Saffuri, who helped arrange an interview with Al-Jazeera TV.[17] When the Taliban first took power in 1996, the congressman described it as a "positive development" and called the *mullahs* "devout traditionalists—not terrorists or revolutionaries."[18]

To be fair, Rohrabacher's ties to Islamist groups and leaders dates back to his days in the 1980s supporting the Afghan *mujahideen* fighters against the Soviets. But the cold warrior is adored by Islamists for another reason: he is pro-Palestine. In 2000, for example, Rohrabacher was one of only four lawmakers who spoke out against a popular congressional resolution to "condemn the Palestinian campaign of violence" against Israel.[19]

MUSLIM MEMBERS OF CONGRESS?

But Muslims are not satisfied with just having surrogates like Rohrabacher protecting and advancing Islamism. They want their own in Congress (of course, their ultimate goal is to put a Muslim in the Oval Office, but first things first). While more than a dozen Muslims now work on Capitol Hill for members of Congress, and while several Muslims have sought election, no Muslim has ever been elected to Congress.

Agha Saeed plans to change that through his American Muslim Alliance, which is devoted exclusively to encouraging Muslim participation in politics. And he is thinking big. Saeed has mapped out 521,000 elective offices in the United States. "Muslims presently have been elected only to a handful of these offices," he says. "They need to be awakened to their full potential in the American political system."

He adds, "We need to transform our pent-up frustration, anger, and pain into creative and meaningful steps for self-empowerment."

His strategy, with the help of AMA's seven thousand members and Muslim think tanks, is to get at least two thousand Muslims elected this decade to offices in states with large concentrations of Muslims and Arab Christians (who are more accepting of Muslims) such as Michigan, Illinois, Florida, Virginia, Texas, New York, California, and New Jersey. He sees eight to ten Muslims elected to the U.S. Congress. "Today, no Muslim serves as a member of Congress," he says. "Muslims should have a presence. Being there is important."[20]

If they achieve those numbers, it is not hard to imagine a Congressional Muslim Caucus, working in concert with the Congressional Black Caucus on the Hill (don't laugh—British Muslims have created the Muslim Parliament of Great Britain). It would be a powerful and natural alliance, since their interests align. Polls show both blacks and Muslims believe America is an oppressive force in the world that contributes to vast global inequalities. And both believe, or would like others to believe, that terrorism is rooted in those inequalities, not Islam. "The Afro-American community and the immigrant community are very strong and united on eliminating the image of Islam as fostering terrorism," says Jameel W. Aalim-Johnson, a black convert who serves as chief of staff for U.S. Rep. Gregory Meeks (D-New York).[21]

Knowing now, after 9/11, that Muslim terrorists are hell-bent on destroying the Capitol, the prospect of just one Muslim lawmaker in Congress makes some nervous. Muslim members would have unfettered access to top secret U.S. intelligence without undergoing any FBI background checks. Unlike their staffs and other federal employees, members of Congress are elected and therefore exempt from such investigations (although they must file financial disclosure papers). And unlike the president, they would not even have to be U.S.-born. Hypothetically, a young jihadist from Saudi Arabia who has been a citizen of the U.S. just seven years could get elected to the House, get appointed to a committee responsible for homeland security, and feed critical counterterrorism intelligence back to al-Qaida. It is not farfetched. An aide to former Sen. Carol Mosely-Braun was recently arrested for spying for Iraq. And documents uncovered in recent counterterrorism raids show jihadists have targeted U.S. agencies for espionage operations, as I will detail in a coming chapter.

"A foreign-born Muslim congressman or senator with access to U.S. secrets is a situation we haven't yet faced," says Mark Levin of the Landmark Legal Foundation in Washington. "But it's one that would certainly raise issues of loyalty and trust."

Levin notes that the executive branch cannot investigate the legislative branch, and the constitution says nothing about the legislative branch doing background checks on its own members. The only real requirement relates to age.

But the Senate or the House does have the power to punish members if they leak classified information, he says. Of course, then it would be too late—the information would already be in the hands of the enemy. Could they block a newly elected Muslim member from taking office if there are credible suspicions he is fronting for terrorists? The short answer is yes.

"The Senate and the House have the power to seat new members," says Levin, a constitutional expert and former Reagan official. "They could say, 'Nope, sorry, we're not swearing you in, because you're tied to terrorists, and we don't care how many citizens voted for you.'"

But that is unlikely to happen, he says, "because they would never challenge the electorate."[22]

Who cares about Congress, though, when Muslims have access to the entire federal bureaucracy, courtesy of this White House? If you are a diehard Bush supporter, you might think twice about turning the page. In fact, you might want to skip the next few chapters altogether.

27

UNDUE INFLUENCE AT THE WHITE HOUSE

Exposing a GOP Operative's Pro-Islamist Quest

"George W. Bush was elected president of the United States of America because of the Muslim vote. That's right, the Muslim vote."

—GOP strategist GROVER NORQUIST, founder of the Islamic Institute, after the 2000 election[1]

Sami al-Arian woke up extremely upbeat. This was the day he had waited for. All his hard work getting out the Muslim vote for George W. Bush was finally paying off. In just a few hours, the Florida professor would be patched into the White House for a conference call with the president and eight of his fellow Muslim leaders. He had assurances that by the end of the day, the president would make good on his campaign promise to end the government's use of classified evidence to deport suspected Arab terrorists.

But then tragedy struck. Arab terrorists began slamming airplanes into buildings, and the White House was evacuated. Meanwhile, President Bush was flown to safety thousands of miles away. There would be no meeting that day—September 11, 2001.

Al-Arian was crushed. "For the past four years, I was fighting very hard for the outlaw of secret evidence," he says, which had led to the deportation of his Palestinian brother-in-law on terrorism suspicions. "At 3:30, the president would have announced the end of secret evidence," he laments, by pledging to sign a bill in Congress doing away with it.[2]

Instead of filing into the West Wing that day, the eight Muslim leaders were escorted by a White House official a few blocks uptown to the offices of GOP powerbroker Grover Norquist, a confidant of Bush political adviser Karl Rove who had helped arrange the top-level meeting. A hawkish defense analyst who works in an office next door to Norquist recalls with a degree of satisfaction how the dejected group shuffled into the office suite.

"I watched bemused as Grover and the White House official responsible for Muslim outreach, Suhail Khan, escorted the displaced Islamists into the conference room we share," says Frank Gaffney, a former Pentagon official who now heads the Center for Security Policy, a think tank known for sounding alarms about the Islamic threat.[3] His former aide, Michael Waller, adds, "They went back to Grover's office to do damage control."[4]

It was an embarrassing irony. At the very moment Muslim terrorists struck Washington, the White House was working with militant Muslim activists to deny law enforcement an important anti-terrorism tool. And the strange alliance has not ended.

How could this come to pass? Rewind to 1997.

MUSLIM STRATEGY

That year, Norquist met with Rove in Austin, Texas—where Rove worked for his client, then-Texas Gov. George W. Bush—and the two hatched a plan to bring Muslims, a growing and largely untapped voting bloc, into the Republican fold. Norquist called it the Muslim Strategy.

The next year, he reached out to two Muslim activists to help him establish a Republican lobbying group to court Muslim voters by pressuring the government to embrace issues important to them. One of the activists was Talat Othman, a Saudi-tied friend of Bush who sat on the board of Harken Energy with the former Texas oilman. He became chairman of the newly founded Islamic Institute in Washington. The other activist was Khaled Saffuri, a longtime lieutenant of Abdurahman Alamoudi at the American Muslim Council, or AMC. He became the institute's president, while Norquist served on its board.

Saffuri, now chairman of the institute, worked in the mid-1990s as AMC's director of governmental affairs. According to federal lobbying records filed by AMC, his assistant at the time was one Randall "Ismail" Royer, who is now a convicted terrorist. In 1996, Alamoudi promoted Saffuri to be his deputy director. Alamoudi is also now in prison serving time for facilitating terrorism.

So Norquist's Muslim political partner worked directly with two terrorists—one his boss, the other his assistant.

Saffuri, a Palestinian American, nonetheless got ringing endorsements from prominent Republicans at the time. "The future of the Islamic Institute will no doubt reach new heights under Saffuri's strong leadership," remarked Spencer

Abraham, then a GOP senator from Michigan, who went on to become Bush's first energy secretary.

At the Islamic Institute, Saffuri advanced the same agenda he did at AMC, which lobbying records show was primarily to fight three laws, all enacted in 1996, that made it easier to deport illegal Arab aliens and profile suspected terrorists at airports.

But convincing law-and-order Republicans to abolish such vital law-enforcement tools would take a lot of lobbying, and that would take a lot of money. So Norquist and Saffuri, with the help of Othman, an ethnic-Palestinian, turned to friends in the Middle East, who donated hundreds of thousands of dollars to their nonprofit institute.

According to financial records I have obtained, most of the money they have raised since 1998 has come from foreign governments or companies and individuals writing checks on foreign banks—with the main source of support coming from the Persian Gulf state of Qatar.[5] The purported U.S. ally, home to Osama bin Laden's favorite TV station Al-Jazeera, initially condemned U.S. strikes on Afghanistan after 9/11.

Among domestic sources of funding, the Islamic Institute received at least ten thousand dollars from the Virginia-based Safa Trust, a suspected terror-financing front that is part of the Saudi-funded Safa group based in the Washington area.[6] Othman served on the board of one of the many entities in the Safa conglomerate that were raided by U.S. Customs agents and other federal authorities after 9/11.

After the raid on the Safa Trust, an outraged Othman and Saffuri demanded the White House set up a meeting with then-Treasury Secretary Paul O'Neill, whose agency had authority over the Customs investigation, which was designed to cut off terrorist funding. They got their high-level meeting within just a few weeks of asking, at which they protested the raids as a fishing expedition and accused agents of using McCarthy-like tactics.

Most disturbing, however, is Alamoudi's own underwriting of the Islamic Institute. He personally provided at least $20,000 in seed money in 1999, according to financial records.[7] The original source of the funds is of concern because he is known to have laundered money from terrorist countries. According to documents filed in federal court, Alamoudi recently planned to launder thirty-four bundles of sequentially numbered $100 bills totaling $340,000 through Saudi banks and into U.S. accounts, where they could be distributed to terror-support groups—such as the American Muslim Foundation, an AMC offshoot—which enjoy exemption from taxes. He was caught by authorities trying to smuggle the bundles in his luggage after a trip to Libya, a terrorist state that he first approached for funding in 1997—the year before Norquist's institute was founded. Court documents also indicate that Alamoudi, whose brothers live in Saudi, secured millions of dollars in funding for AMC and other Muslim groups from the Saudi Economic Development Co.[8]

"HE IS OUR BEST BET"

The Islamic Institute played a key role in the 2000 campaign for Bush.

Saffuri, who met regularly with Rove during the campaign, was named the Muslim affairs adviser to Bush. And he convinced the Republicans that the best way to woo Muslim voters was to speak out against the same issues he lobbied against at the AMC—secret deportation evidence and airport profiling. He then arranged a meeting in the governor's mansion between Bush and his old boss Alamoudi, along with several other militant Muslim activists, who presented their wish list to the Republican hopeful. Not surprisingly, secret evidence and airport profiling topped the list.

Later, Saffuri introduced the candidate to prominent Muslims in the battleground state of Michigan, home to the nation's largest concentration of Arabs and Muslims. Saffuri also arranged for the Bush campaign to enlist al-Arian to rally Muslim support for Bush in Florida, another key battleground state. Bush even took photographs with al-Arian and his family during a campaign stop in Tampa, Florida. At the time, counterterrorism agents at the FBI's field office in Tampa were investigating al-Arian, a Palestinian American who in speeches had referred to Jews as "monkeys and pigs" and shouted "Death to Israel!" while raising money for Palestinian jihadists. Rove never bothered to look into his background or that of other Muslim leaders with whom Bush met.

On the advice of Saffuri, Bush even campaigned at mosques, speaking out against secret evidence and airport profiling. It was music to Muslims' ears. To further win them over, Saffuri suggested Bush include mosques in any religious references on the stump, and he did just that. "Ours is a nation formed by churches and synagogues and mosques," he said in one speech. Then at the GOP convention, Bush tapped his old pal Othman, the founding chairman of the Islamic Institute, to give the first Muslim prayer at such an event.

But the pandering did not stop there.

In early October, Bush met in Detroit with several Muslim leaders to address their concerns over secret evidence and airport profiling. They walked away impressed with the Republican, especially after his opponent Al Gore, who picked a Jewish running mate, canceled an appointment with them. On Saffuri's advice, Bush followed up with handouts in Arabic and English elaborating on his views on profiling. He even provided a videotaped message to an AMC official explaining his position. In it, Bush said, "Airline travelers have experienced harassment and delay simply because of their ethnic heritage. Such indiscriminate use of passenger profiling is wrong and must be stopped."[9] (He kept his promise, as discussed in an earlier chapter, by appointing Norman "No Profiling" Mineta secretary of transportation.)

If that were not enough, Bush then announced his accommodating position to all Muslims on national TV. In his second debate with Gore, he condemned the use of secret evidence and profiling, startling Gore, who could only chime in with his own "me too" denunciation. Bush's statement was just forty-two words long, but it turned out to be the most strategically important of his campaign:

> Arab Americans are racially profiled in what's called secret evidence. People are stopped, and we got to do something about that. My friend, Senator Spencer Abraham of Michigan, is pushing a law to make sure that, you know, Arab Americans are treated with respect.

There it was—the money quote the Muslim community had been waiting to hear. The mood among Muslims was electric. But just to be sure they had not missed the extraordinary overture, Rove phoned Norquist at his home twice during the debate to draw his attention to the remark and urge him to put the word out among Muslims.[10] Bush held up his end of the bargain; now it was their turn. Less than two weeks later, eight national Muslim groups held a press conference to announce they were endorsing Bush. "He is our best bet to do away with secret evidence," remarked Ibrahim Hooper of CAIR, one of the leaders.

The Islamic Institute wasted no time taking credit for the chain of events. "Secret evidence is an issue that the Islamic Institute has previously raised with the Bush campaign," the group said in a press release at the time. "We would like to commend Governor Bush for his stand on this issue." The statement then cited the bill Abraham had sponsored in the Senate: the Secret Evidence Repeal Act of 2000.[11] Islamic Institute board member, David Hossein Safavian, now a top White House official, also praised Bush in a *Washington Times* column.

ISLAMISTS AT THE GATE

The plan hatched by Rove, Norquist, and Saffuri (c/o Alamoudi) was coming off without a hitch. Now they just had to make sure Muslims, as energized as they were, actually turned out for Bush at the polls. But they did not disappoint. They came out for the Republican nominee in droves, breaking a longtime Muslim trend of voting Democratic.

Al-Arian was credited with delivering the Muslim vote for Bush in Florida, which in effect provided him the margin of victory in that hotly contested race. A great many of the Muslims in Florida cast ballots for the first time; and all told, Muslims favored Bush over Gore by twenty to one. "The margin of victory for Bush over Gore in the Muslim vote was 46,200—many times greater than his statewide margin of victory," Norquist noted after the election. "The Muslim vote won Florida for Bush," and thus the national election.[12]

Reliable results for Muslim voting nationwide are hard to come by. But among Arab Americans, who tend to track Muslim voting patterns, Bush garnered 45 percent of the vote, compared with just 29 percent for Gore, according to postelection polling by Zogby International. Bush might have attracted even more votes if Green Party candidate Ralph Nader, a Lebanese American, had not been in the race. He got 16 percent of the community's vote.

Other polling by Zogby shows that it was Bush's stand on secret evidence and profiling that won over Muslims, not any sudden affinity for Republicans. Nearly half of all Muslims identify themselves as Democrats, while only 23 percent describe themselves as Republicans, virtually a mirror opposite of the 2000 results for president. And they named "profiling" as the number one issue for the Muslim community.[13]

Regardless, the strategy worked, generating a powerful Muslim tide for Bush. And Norquist, for one, was quite pleased with himself. "George W. Bush was elected president of the United States of America because of the Muslim vote," he crowed after the election. "That's right, the Muslim vote."

The influence he and his Islamist partners had on the campaign continued into the new administration, as Bush, who became the first president to utter the word "mosque" in an inaugural address, quickly racked up another ethnic milestone—appointing more Muslim and Arab Americans to positions of prominence in his administration than any other president. He helped the Islamic Institute carry out its other stated goal of "promoting the appointments of Muslims to positions of influence." Norquist's group managed to place one of its staffers, Suhail Khan, inside the White House as the official gatekeeper for Muslims. It was Khan who set up the ill-fated Islamist summit with Bush on 9/11.

Safavian followed on his heels, landing a high-level job in the White House. And Bush appointed yet another Islamic Institute staffer—Faisal Gill—to a sensitive post at the Department of Homeland Security. Gill also worked at the AMC, raising eyebrows among Islamist hawks, as I will detail in the next chapter.

Once Khan was inside the gates of the White House, he and Norquist put together a blanket list of no less than eighty-three Muslim activists whom they wanted Rove to invite to White House outreach events. The list, submitted in 2001 to the Secret Service for security clearance, reads like a who's who of hard-line Islamists and Wahhabists, some of whom are known terrorist sympathizers and supporters under federal investigation, such as Jamal Barzinji of the Safa group. Norquist's name tops the list, a copy of which I have obtained.[14]

Another Muslim activist cleared for entry was Sami al-Arian, an alleged founder of the Palestinian Islamic Jihad who is now in jail on related terrorism charges. He was invited along with Alamoudi and some 160 other AMC members, to a meeting at the White House on June 22, 2001. The host was none other than Karl Rove, who used the meeting to talk about the White House's efforts to embrace the Muslim community. Al-Arian got a front row seat.

How he even got into the building is a mystery, however. Al-Arian had been under federal investigation for suspected terrorism ties for the previous six years, something that had been reported in both the media and congressional testimony at the time.

And Alamoudi got past White House security despite voicing support for the U.S.-designated terrorist groups Hamas and Hezbollah just eight months earlier. In fact, he *shouted* his support for them during a hostile anti-Israel rally involving thousands of Muslims across from the White House just days before the 2000 election. Here is a transcript of his October 28 remarks in Lafayette Square:

> I have been labeled by the media in New York to be a supporter of Hamas. Anybody support this Hamas here? Anybody's [sic] is a supporter of Hamas here? Anybody's [sic] is a supporter of Hamas here? [cheers] Hear that Bill Clinton? We are all supporters of Hamas! Allah akbar [Allah is great]. I wish to add here I am also a supporter of Hezbollah! Anybody supports Hezbollah here? Anybody supports Hezbollah here? [cheers] I want to send a message . . . My brothers, this is the message that we have to carry to everybody. It's an occupation, and Hamas is fighting to end an occupation. It's a legal fight. Allah akbar! Allah akbar![15]

"SOMETHING ROTTEN IN DENMARK"

Alamoudi was reacting in part to the New York media's reporting of previous statements he had made supporting Hamas. The stories came out earlier that month, pressuring several political campaigns—including Bush's—to return donations from Alamoudi. The Bush campaign refunded a thousand-dollar gift from him. As top adviser to the campaign, Rove must have been aware of the controversy over Alamoudi. Yet he still invited him to his White House powwow.

Meanwhile, Bush kept his promise to at least restrain prosecutors from using classified evidence to deport Middle Easterners suspected of terrorist activities. "Frankly, the president of the United States has expressed his discomfort with this aspect of American immigration," former Attorney General John Ashcroft told Congress in June 2001. "We have not to date during this administration used such evidence."[16]

Three months later—on the eve of the 9/11 attacks—Norquist went to the Hill himself and urged the Senate to formally outlaw the use of secret evidence by passing Senator Abraham's bill. "I think it's important that we move forward on President Bush's commitment to get rid of the secret evidence laws which have been used to discriminate against Muslims and Arabs in this country," Norquist told the Senate Judiciary Committee on September 7, 2001. He also argued for loosening U.S. border controls to let more immigrants into the country, suggesting that policing the border was a "mistake"—a position wildly out of step with the vast majority of polled Americans.[17]

When Arab Muslims attacked America four days later, the political dynamic Islamists enjoyed completely changed, and the administration had to abandon its promise to outlaw secret evidence. Ashcroft aggressively prosecuted Muslims suspected of terrorism, and Bush signed the USA Patriot Act giving the FBI more power to spy on the Muslim community.

But oddly, Norquist has not backed down from his political jihad for Muslim rights. Odder still, Rove and the White House have not disengaged from the Islamists they courted before 9/11.

At the direction of the White House, the FBI officially certified Alamoudi's AMC as moderate—"the most mainstream Muslim group in the United States," in fact. And it enlisted the group in the war on terrorism—even though AMC advised its members following 9/11 not to cooperate with the FBI! That's right; AMC posted on its Web site a link to a "Know Your Rights" advisory that stated:

- DON'T TALK TO THE FBI

- You have the right NOT to open your door to the FBI

- The FBI is looking for information to use against you, your family, and/or your community

- The FBI has a history of harassing and harming minority and immigrant communities. Some people are spending a long time in jail because they or their friends talked to the FBI

The link was taken down only after Gaffney, the national security hawk, drew attention to it. "Alamoudi's American Muslim Council was among the groups invited to the White House" in the wake of 9/11, Gaffney says. "I observed that on the same day its representatives were meeting with the president and his senior subordinates to talk about how Muslims could help with the war on terror, the AMC's Web site featured a statement urging Muslims not to talk to the FBI."[18]

AMC sanitized its site by removing the statement just before Norquist met with Republicans in one of their weekly strategy sessions held in his office. At the October 3, 2001, meeting, he announced that Gaffney was mistaken about the posting on AMC's Web site. He denied it ever existed, even though Gaffney had presented him with evidence in the form of a series of printouts that captured it on the site from September 12 through September 27.

"Grover said it was not on the site, but it had been. It was just taken off the site after Gaffney called attention to it in a *Washington Times* column," says a Republican who was at the meeting. "Grover was dissembling."

The source, a friend of Norquist who has parted ways with him over his association with Islamists, added, "That's when I first noticed something was rotten in Denmark."[19]

"HANGING OUT WITH TERRORISTS"

Several months later, Republican hawks were in for another shock.

As mentioned above, Gaffney leases an office in the same building as Norquist, at 1920 L Street N.W. in Washington. Gaffney's neoconservative think tank is in Suite 210, while Norquist's Islamic Institute is housed in Suite 200, along with his Americans for Tax Reform lobbying group. Gaffney and Norquist share a large conference room, copying room, restrooms, elevator bank, and hallway.

On his way to the men's room on July 17, 2002, Gaffney spotted what he thought was Sami al-Arian outside Norquist's office suite. He recognized his face from TV. Al-Arian had given an interview after 9/11 to Bill O'Reilly of Fox News to clear his name of allegations that he supported terrorism. But he did not acquit himself of the charges. In fact, he did such an unconvincing job of it that the University of South Florida later fired him, even though he was a tenured professor there.

Gaffney was sure it was al-Arian and wondered why Norquist would still have anything to do with him. Agitated, he stormed back to his office and sought out his aide Waller, who recalled their exchange:

GAFFNEY: Hey, you have that picture of Sami al-Arian?

WALLER: Yeah—why?

GAFFNEY: I gotta identify him. He's right outside.

Waller found the photograph on his desk and handed it to Gaffney, who studied it.

GAFFNEY: Yeah, that's the guy. C'mon and look.

The two went out in the hall. "Al-Arian was by the elevator, chatting with somebody, and then they went into Grover's suite," Waller recalls. "He was in there for a good two-and-a-half hours, and then he finally came out with Khaled [Saffuri]."

After Saffuri said goodbye to al-Arian, he headed for the bathroom, and Gaffney followed behind him. As the two stood at the urinals, Gaffney decided to quiz him about al-Arian: "Was that Sami al-Arian I saw getting on the elevator?" He says Saffuri made a choking sound and muttered something unintelligible. Gaffney asked again, and Saffuri finally replied, "No, I don't think so," according to Gaffney.

"He lied," Gaffney says.[20]

It turns out that al-Arian had dropped by after attending a press conference at the National Press Club, which was held to announce the filing of a bizarre lawsuit against Israeli Prime Minister Ariel Sharon and President Bush, as well as defense contractors and American churches and synagogues that have supported settlements in the West Bank. The class-action suit was filed by a number of Palestinian Americans such as al-Arian. Alamoudi also participated in the press conference.

Saffuri later acknowledged al-Arian's visit, Gaffney says, but claims he was just stopping by to drop off some literature—"an action that generally does not take two-and-a-half hours to perform."[21]

Norquist has maintained that he had very limited contact with al-Arian after he worked for Bush's campaign in Florida. In fact, al-Arian gave Norquist an award eleven days after his 2001 office visit. At a Capitol Hill ceremony on July 28, 2001, al-Arian's National Coalition to Protect Political Freedom honored Norquist as one of the "champions of the abolishment movement against secret evidence." He received a plaque.[22] Al-Arian at the time was president of NCPPF, which he helped set up in 1997 to pressure the release of his jailed brother-in-law. Its members include the Council on American Islamic Relations, the Muslim American Society, and the Muslim Public Affairs Council, as well as a couple of Arab-rights groups. Gaffney calls it "a virtual legal aid office for terrorists."

Waller says Norquist's relationship with al-Arian before he landed in jail on terrorism charges was closer than he lets on. Al-Arian even CC'd Norquist when he e-mailed the *Wall Street Journal* a response to an op-ed piece that tied him to the Islamic Jihad.[23]

"Grover was hanging out with known terrorists, and then he takes an award from the guy." Waller says. "I mean, please."

Now a professor at the Institute of World Politics, a graduate school for national security affairs in Washington, Waller has known Norquist since the early 1980s when they were involved in the College Republicans. He recalls how they drove together to GOP strategist Ralph Reed's wedding in Grover's old Ford Fairmont, which blew a tire on the way to the church. Norquist had never changed a flat, so Waller got out and fixed it. Waller says he is at a loss to explain his old acquaintance's sudden interest in militant Islam.

IN BED WITH ISLAMISTS

"As long as I've known Grover, he's never really been interested in national security issues," Waller says. "But this is weird. Even when he knows these guys are bad, he clings to their cause."

And it is not as if Norquist has a chance of duplicating what he did for Republicans in 2000. He essentially has no Muslim constituency to deliver to the GOP now, as the 2004 results proved. Muslim voters switched back to the Democratic side after Bush signed the Patriot Act and invaded Iraq. Many Muslims say they have sworn off Republicans forever. So what could possibly be motivating Norquist to work so hard still for their interests, especially when it is costing him alliances on the right?"

"He usually cuts things loose when they become a liability, but not this time. It's really weird how he's clinging to this," Waller adds. "I mean, you can't even have a pragmatic, reasoned discussion with him. We told him, 'You know, you've got some bad stuff going on over there,' and Grover's response was pretty much, 'Screw you.'"

He cites a recent meeting with conservatives in which Norquist confronted skeptics and defended his Islamist friends. "He's usually quite sure of himself, but his hands visibly trembled as he read from a prepared statement in a cracked voice," Waller says. "He said all the charges are driven by 'racism and bigotry,' which has become almost a robotic response for him."

But something else besides politics may be driving Norquist's newfound passion for Islam.

The forty-eight-year-old bachelor got engaged last year to a Middle Eastern woman by the name of Samah Alrayyes, who works as a public relations special-ist for Middle Eastern affairs at a State Department agency. Alrayyes, 31, also flacks for the Islamic Institute, where she and Norquist became romantically involved. They plan to wed in April 2005, shortly after this book hits the shelves. The relationship gives literal meaning to the notion that Norquist is in bed with Islamists.

But some see a more sinister side to his activities. A former close associate of Norquist, a conservative who regularly attended his Wednesday Group meetings for Washington conservatives, has arrived at the conclusion that he is acting as an "agent of influence" for groups hostile to American interests.

"He clearly has an agenda of getting bad people into the White House," he says. "I'm convinced Grover is some type of agent of influence, in the same vein as Alger Hiss, who is spreading Wahhabi propaganda and making these groups look good." Hiss, a State Department official, was accused of giving military secrets to a Communist spy for the Soviet Union. He was convicted of perjury in 1950. (Ironically, Norquist grew up reading anti-Communist books like *Witness* by Whittaker Chambers, which exposes Hiss's double-dealing.)

Former Justice Department official John Loftus, who lives in Tampa and is intimately familiar with the al-Arian case, takes it one step further and alleges that Norquist has been providing "protection" for accused terrorists like Alamoudi and al-Arian by persuading the White House to stonewall investigations, taking advantage of his close relationship with Rove and also Bush's loyalty to the Saudis, who are the primary source of funding for Alamoudi's and al-Arian's operations. He makes a compelling case:

[In 2002], people in the intelligence community came and said guys like Alamoudi and Sami al-Arian and other terrorists weren't being touched because they'd been ordered not to investigate the cases, not to prosecute them, because they were being funded by the Saudis, and a political deci-sion was being made at the highest levels: Don't do anything that would embarrass the Saudi government. So, of course I immediately volun-teered to do it, and filed a lawsuit against al-Arian charging him with being a major terrorist for Islamic Jihad. Most of his money came from Saudi charities in Virginia. Alamoudi's headquarters were in the same place. An hour after I filed my lawsuit [on March 20, 2002], the U.S. government finally got off its butt and raided these offices. And the stuff that they're taking out of there is absolutely horrendous. Al-Arian has now finally been indicted, along with Alamoudi.

But who was it that fixed the cases? How could these guys operate for more than a decade immune from prosecution? And the answer is coming out in a very strange place. What Alamoudi and al-Arian have in common is Grover Norquist. He's the super lobbyist. He is the guy that was hired by Alamoudi to head up the Islamic Institute, and he's a registered agent for Alamoudi, personally, and for the Islamic Institute. Grover Norquist's best friend is Karl Rove, and apparently Norquist was able to fix things. He got extreme Muslim people to be the gatekeepers in the White House. . . . Norquist had a lot of clients [and] they had an awful lot of protection.[24]

GOP WING OF THE AMC

The Virginia charities Loftus cites are part of the Saudi-funded Safa group, which is connected to Alamoudi's local operations. And it has directly funded al-Arian's Florida-based operations, investigators say. As noted at the start of this chapter, the Safa Trust helped bankroll Norquist's Islamic Institute. Norquist has said the donations from Safa were made before any questions were raised about the group.

But that is not exactly true. Yes, the donations were made before the Safa was raided in 2002. But the network of Muslim groups that make up the Safa group have been under federal investigation since 1990, and many of those groups, including Safa Trust, had been the subject of congressional hearings and articles in the media, including the *Washington Post*.

In fact, investigators allege in a recent federal affidavit that the Safa group set up an offshore shell company in 1997 to hide assets in response to "adverse publicity in papers about connections to terrorism." They add that Safa group leaders worried that the media was "becoming too probing in 1995-1996" regarding the Safa group financing al-Arian's Islamic Jihad front groups in Florida.[25]

That someone as politically astute as Norquist would miss such negative news connected to such a generous donor strains credulity, Waller and other skeptics say.

As for Alamoudi—who prosecutors have connected to Hamas, al-Qaida, and seven known terrorists whose identities were found on his Palm Pilot—Norquist has said the institute stopped working with him as soon as it became aware of his remarks supporting Hamas and Hezbollah at the rowdy anti-Israel rally in October 2000, the largest ever staged by Muslims.

But what he does not say is that his Islamic Institute was one of the rally's sponsors and participants, along with Alamoudi's AMC.[26] Nor does he tell you that the institute publicized the event in e-mails to members. One dated October 13, 2000, alerts them that "there will be a march and rally in front of the White

House to protest Israel's aggression and violence against the Palestinian people." A second alert went out October 20, 2000, as a reminder. The ugly, terror-cheering event took place October 28, 2000.[27]

And instead of distancing itself from Alamoudi's old group, Norquist's institute has practically merged with it. Around the same time that Norquist claims to have excommunicated Alamoudi for pledging his allegiance to overseas terrorists, the institute hired another top official from his group. Former AMC Deputy Director Abdulwahab Alkebsi replaced Saffuri (Alamoudi's former deputy) as institute president when Saffuri was elevated to chairman. Alkebsi, a Yemeni-born activist, also once headed the International Institute of Islamic Thought, one of the Safa group entities raided by authorities after 9/11. IIIT, as it is more commonly known, gave thousands of dollars to the Islamic Institute, as well as Sami al-Arian's alleged terrorist operations in Florida. (Alkebsi, no surprise, has vocally opposed FBI investigations of Muslim groups.) Other institute employees have migrated from AMC, as well, effectively making the institute a GOP wing of the AMC.

There is something else Norquist does not tell you: he co-founded another Washington lobbying group called Janus-Merritt Strategies that counted Alamoudi as a client well into 2001 and long after his pro-Hamas statements made news. In fact, federal lobbying records show Alamoudi paid the firm some forty thousand dollars to press the government for pro-Muslim policies in the Middle East and at home. (I will explore this controversy in-depth in a coming chapter.)

"A FOREIGN INTELLIGENCE OPERATION"

And finally, if Norquist really parted company with his old pal, client, and financier Alamoudi as he says, why did he hold a fundraiser for his lawyer? In 2003, as prosecutors were bringing terror charges against Alamoudi, Norquist held a campaign fundraiser at his Capitol Hill townhouse for Alamoudi's lawyer, Kamal Nawash, who was running for a Virginia state Senate seat.[28] Nawash claims he never represented Alamoudi, who donated ten thousand dollars to his campaign. He explains that although he has defended Alamoudi against terrorism charges in the media, charges that he argued were politically motivated, he was erroneously identified by the Internet magazine IslamOnline.net as his attorney.

Really? Then why is his signature at the bottom of a "Power of Attorney Affidavit" for Alamoudi at the Fairfax County Circuit Court of Virginia? And why does he make the following sworn statement in that 2003 document I obtained: "I am attorney-in-fact for Abdurahman M. Alamoudi"?[29] Also, one of the partners in his law firm, May Shallal Kheder, shows up in court records as a member of Alamoudi's criminal defense team.

(Nawash, a Muslim Palestinian American, also claims to be a patriotic Republican hawk critical of terrorism and Wahhabism. I visited one of the offices his law firm, Hanania Kheder & Nawash, keeps in Falls Church, Virginia, and found it located in the same small, nondescript building as the Saudi-backed Muslim Student Association. The building also used to be the home of the U.S. branch of the Saudi-based World Assembly of Muslim Youth, before it moved down the street to bigger digs. During his failed political campaign, Nawash, who specializes in immigration law, put up signs outside the nearby Dar al-Hijrah Islamic Center, which is a Saudi-controlled Wahhabi mosque popular with Palestinians like Nawash. But he is against Wahhabism. Of course he is.)

Because of its close ties to Alamoudi and the AMC—and in spite of its close ties to powerful Republicans—the Islamic Institute figures prominently in the FBI's matrix of the terror-support network in America. In fact, knowledgeable sources say the group appears on a wall chart posted in the counterterrorism division at headquarters. Though the institute is on the radar screen of investigators, there is no evidence it is under investigation for any crimes.

Waller maintains that the FBI director has been under White House pressure to appease the AMC and Islamic Institute. "Mueller was under orders from Rove," he says, noting that before Mueller spoke at AMC's convention in 2002, some thirty AMC members attending the convention were given a private briefing by White House staff.

He says the AMC–Islamic Institute alliance "looks an awful lot like a foreign intelligence operation," and is a legitimate target not just for counterterrorism but also counterintelligence investigations.

"You've got agents in place where they can have access to key officials in the White House and sensitive information, including an intelligence post at the Department of Homeland Security," where Alamoudi protégé Gill now works, Waller explains. "You've got Alamoudi, who's a known member of the Muslim Brotherhood in Egypt, where he's taken numerous trips, as the lead operative in the organization, a guy who's a bagman for terrorist groups like Hamas. And you've got seed money coming in from Saudi banks."

He says it is a recipe for an espionage disaster, and Norquist is acting as the top chef, wittingly or not.

Norquist, who is famous for his temper, at first agreed to be interviewed for this book (I knew him as a source for tax-policy stories I wrote for *Investor's Business Daily* in the 1990s). But then, when I sent him a list of questions, including the allegations by Loftus, Waller, Gaffney, and others, as he requested, he changed his mind, saying the questions were too "personal." When I urged him to reconsider, I got a long response instead from his spokesperson Chris Butler, who argued that Norquist is not doing the bidding of Muslim leaders and has also reached out to other religious leaders.

"Grover has worked on Republican outreach with Catholics, Mormons, Jews, Hindus, and Evangelicals," Butler says. Maybe so. But he did not start a Catholic Institute or a Mormon Institute. And he certainly did not start a Hebrew Institute. He started an Islamic Institute and even incorporated it into his Americans for Tax Reform office suite.

"THERE'S NO THERE THERE"

Butler called the allegations that Norquist is in bed with Islamists and is allowing them to exercise undue influence at the White House among "a series of lies" peddled by Gaffney. He says Norquist will not lend credibility to "Gaffney's nonsense."

The conservative I quoted earlier who used to be close to Norquist says blaming Gaffney for all his problems is misplaced. "People like Gaffney warned Grover even before 9/11 about associating with these groups, and he'd always blame the messenger, without addressing the specific concerns," he says. "He blamed all his trouble on Gaffney."

Indeed, Norquist has become increasingly bitter toward Gaffney. After they locked horns in 2003 over the Islamic Institute's placement of the son of a Wahhabi mosque leader inside the White House, Norquist banned Gaffney, a respected national security expert, from his prestigious Wednesday Group strategy meetings, which are attended by Republicans from the Hill, K Street, and the White House. Norquist suggested Gaffney was an anti-Muslim bigot for sounding alarms over some of the Muslims he was sponsoring for key federal jobs.

"The conservative movement cannot be associated with racism or bigotry," he wrote Gaffney in a February 5, 2003, letter. "I am afraid that your attendance at the Wednesday meeting at the offices of Americans for Tax Reform can no longer be allowed."

Their interoffice feud got so nasty, sources says, that Norquist, apparently in a fit of paranoia, at one point changed the locks on the doors to his office suite and even reformatted the hard drives to his office computers.

Rove, whose relationship with Norquist dates back to their days in the College Republicans, shrugs off criticism that he is lending undue influence over security policy to Islamist groups hostile to American interests, while giving their agents undue access to sensitive federal agencies. "What's the evidence" of undesirable influence? Rove, 54, says. "There's no there there."[30]

Saffuri, for his part, claims to be a conservative Republican interested chiefly in bringing Muslims into the Republican Party, which he says is a more natural fit for them because of the GOP's focus on family values (although Islam permits polygamy and wife-beating) and free-market capitalism (although Islam forbids paying or collecting interest).[31]

But some question that claim, noting that he has attended Democratic functions, even posing for photographs with Bill Clinton. And federal election records show he has in recent years given thousands of dollars in campaign cash to anti-Israel Democrats such as Jim Moran of Virginia, Nick Rahall of West Virginia, and David Bonior of Michigan.

In truth, the Palestinian-born Saffuri's main interest is promoting Palestinian causes, not the GOP, says a Republican source who has had dealings with him. "Khaled clearly has a hidden agenda of using the GOP to legitimize Islamist groups and place their agents inside the government, which happens to be controlled by Republicans," he says. "And Grover is their ticket into the White House."[32]

Indeed, Saffuri a few months after 9/11 revealed to an aide to U.S. Congressman Dana Rohrabacher, a pro-Islamist Republican from California, that he was a regular donor to the Holy Land Foundation, which is now under indictment for bankrolling Hamas. Then he said something that really frosted the aide, in spite of his friendship with her boss. Saffuri, an ethnic-Palestinian, said that he sponsors an orphaned child of a Palestinian suicide bomber. "He received pictures and reports on this child's progress, thanks to the money Khaled sends," former press secretary Phaedra Baird reported to Rohrabacher in a December 7, 2001, letter I obtained. "He said he sees nothing wrong with his support of these people, that he's helping a child who has no father." But Baird noted that he was basically supporting terrorism, and urged her boss to "sever all ties" with him.[33]

CHILLY RECEPTION

Norquist, a bearded and squat man, is a familiar and well-respected (some would say feared) figure in GOP power circles in Washington. The anti-tax advocate, who works primarily behind the scenes, was toasted for organizing nationwide initiatives to memorialize Ronald Reagan, notably with the naming of one of the capital's airports after the former president. A kind of Rasputin of the right, he is also credited with helping orchestrate last decade's Republican Revolution, which swept conservatives into power in Congress for the first time in forty years. In fact, Norquist helped draft his pal Newt Gingrich's "Contract with America."

But since Alamoudi's conviction, Norquist has lost some of the respect he once commanded. Some Republicans are even starting to keep their distance from him, wary as they are of his ties to militant Muslim activists. Listen to this senior GOP congressional aide, for example, who thought better of getting mixed up with Norquist's Islamist partners when they came knocking:

> My feeling was Grover was legitimizing some of these people. They were doing a lot of sponsoring of congressional people to travel to the Middle East. They were involved with Grover, and Grover had a lot of influence over members of Congress. So the credibility that they had was the fact that they were involved with Grover Norquist. I mean, they were all over Capitol Hill, and even had meetings with the White House. And that was due to the influence of Grover. But with those guys, I just stay away from them. Even when they came by the office, I just had nothing to do with Grover Norquist. If I was doing national security work, I wanted it completely unfettered by those guys.[34]

Even staunch Republican friends and allies have distanced themselves from Norquist since 9/11. Gingrich, who owes his House speakership in large part to him, had endorsed Norquist's Islamic Institute before 9/11. But his old pal's Islamist ties may be more a liability for Gingrich now, especially since he joined the neocon American Enterprise Institute. Witnesses say Gingrich acted icily toward Norquist when Norquist approached him at AEI's annual blacktie dinner in 2002 at the Washington Hilton. After Norquist sought him out and the two exchanged greetings, Gingrich moved away.

"Grover never had to gladhand like that in the past," says a Republican who attended the dinner. "He's lost some people at his Wednesday meetings, too," he adds. "People in the conservative movement are wary of associating with him now." The source, who requested anonymity, has stopped going to the meetings himself.

"It's a tragedy for the movement," he says. "But for me, national security trumps everything, and his actions can't be excused."

In a possible sign (literally) that Norquist may be having some regrets, or at least taking the hint to tone it down, he recently changed the sign outside his office suite identifying the Islamic Institute. The name had been fully spelled out, but now it is abbreviated—"to get rid of the Islamic image that many friends have complained to Grover about," speculates Waller.

But one Republican who has not distanced himself from Norquist is his best pal Rove, the one Republican who matters in terms of controlling access to power in Washington these days. Despite the hand-wringing by Islamist hawks in the party, despite the appearances of influence peddling, despite the arrests of his Islamist friends and partners, despite the continued threat from Islamic terrorists, Norquist is still in good standing with the White House. And the welcome mat is still out for his unpatriotic partners. Saffuri has not only not been denied access to the administration, he has been granted greater access than ever.

- Last year, for example, he was invited by Defense Secretary Donald Rumsfeld to attend briefings at the Pentagon and visit several military bases in the U.S. and abroad.

- Saffuri also met last year with former Attorney General John Ashcroft and officials at the Department of Homeland Security to discuss protecting Muslim civil rights and abandoning the USA Patriot Act.

- And he still meets about once every six months with Mueller at the FBI to complain about the monitoring of mosques under the Patriot Act, as well as investigations, arrests, and detentions of Muslims.

So despite the conviction of Alamoudi, one of Norquist's silent partners, his Islamic Institute—the nerve center for Muslim lobbying in GOP-controlled Washington—has not lost its nerve. It is waging a new jihad against the Patriot Act, a key weapon in the war on terrorism, which helped make al-Arian's arrest possible. The various law enforcement agencies investigating him over the years were finally allowed to share sensitive information they had collected on his Islamic Jihad operations. Of course, don't expect anyone at the Islamic Institute to appreciate that. They no doubt miss cavorting with al-Arian at the office.

And if investigators had been allowed to monitor mosques earlier, as they now can, they may have been able to nab Osama bin Laden's second in command when he raised money at a mosque in California for al-Qaida before 9/11. Of course, don't expect anyone at the Islamic Institute to appreciate that, either—particularly not their former colleague and co-religionist Suhail Khan. His father used to run the mosque, as I'll detail in a coming chapter.

Norquist may or may not be an agent of influence for militant Islamic activists. But it does appear that he is undermining the war on terrorism. And he has placed inside the U.S. government, in security-sensitive positions—from the White House to the Department of Transportation to even the Department of Homeland Security—Arab Americans with associations that are suspect and loyalties that are questionable. And some U.S. intelligence officials fear they may be agents in place for militant Islam.

28

DEPARTMENT OF HOMELAND INSECURITY

Opening the Door to Muslim 'Agents of Influence'

"[Muslim brothers should] infiltrate the sensitive intelligence agencies in order to collect information and build close relationships with the people in charge in these establishments."

—excerpt from secret Islamic charter written by former American professor SAMI AL-ARIAN, now accused of conspiring with terrorists[1]

Aly Abuzaakouk spent a lot of time on Capitol Hill before the 9/11 terrorist attacks. As head of the Washington-based American Muslim Council, he lobbied both the Senate and House of Representatives to repeal the government's use of undisclosed evidence against suspected Middle Eastern terrorists in deportation proceedings. And targeting foreign policy, he lobbied against U.S. sanctions on Iraq, while pushing for the creation of a Palestinian state.[2]

After 9/11, however, Abuzaakouk spent a lot of time defending Islam. He could not have managed the challenging new task without the assistance of his close aide Faisal Gill, who even helped him coax an apology out of former U.S. Rep. John Cooksey for intemperate remarks the Louisiana Republican made about Arab men wearing "diapers" on their heads. The young lawyer, who also lobbied to end the use of secret terror evidence, served as the American Muslim Council's director of governmental affairs at the time.[3]

Today Gill is policy director for the Department of Homeland Security's intelligence division, where he has access to top-secret data concerning the vulnerability of America's seaports, refineries, nuclear plants, and other facilities to terrorist attacks.

In applying for the sensitive post, however, Gill conveniently left out the fact he worked for the American Muslim Council. The Muslim advocacy group has been under scrutiny in the government's investigation of terrorism financing, led by a special agent who reports to a bureau within Homeland Security. AMC was founded by confessed terrorist Abdurahman Alamoudi. At the time Gill worked there, Alamoudi still controlled the organization, investigators say.

The high-level appointment of an Islamic activist at the agency in charge of protecting America from Islamic attack has alarmed security experts, who worry about divided loyalties during the war.

A senior U.S. counterintelligence official, for one, finds Gill's omission of the information on his national security questionnaire "highly suspicious." And given Gill's association with Alamoudi, he is concerned with his having access to highly classified information about the country's critical infrastructure.

"It turns out that when he did his SF-86, which is the form you submit to get your security clearance, he omitted a couple of things, in particular his employment with a Muslim group that has been tied to funding terrorism," the senior official tells me.

"Someone finally called him on it. Only, this guy is still sitting over there at DHS in a very high-level position where he sees *all* the intelligence, including SAPs and black programs and everything," he adds. "It's outrageous."[4] SAPs are special-access programs subject to the Pentagon's most stringent level of security. They are also known as "black programs" because of their secrecy.

The FBI raised concerns with Homeland Security officials early last year after discovering through a tip that Gill had failed to list his 2001 AMC work on his security forms. He was removed from his job, but only briefly. The White House political appointee was reinstated after a flurry of interagency meetings.[15]

Officials familiar with the controversy say Gill has the strong backing of Norquist, the Republican powerbroker and confidant of White House political honcho Karl Rove.

Gill and Norquist are indeed close. Gill doubled in 2001 as director of governmental affairs for Norquist's Islamic Institute, which has a stated goal of "promoting the appointments of Muslims to positions of influence." He is listed under that title in at least two press releases issued by the institute, which was funded by Alamoudi and co-founded by his deputy Khaled Saffuri. One of them, dated May 4, 2001, describes how Gill arranged a meeting between the attorney general of Virginia and Muslim leaders to coordinate efforts to lobby Congress to repeal the use of secret terror evidence.

"In a letter to the Islamic Institute, Mark Earley, attorney general of Virginia and a candidate for the Republican nomination for governor of Virginia, endorsed H.R. 1266, the legislation in Congress that would repeal the use of secret evidence," the Islamic Institute boasts in the 2001 press release. "During a meeting with Muslim leaders in March [2001] at the offices of the Islamic Institute, and at the request of Faisal Gill, director of governmental affairs for the Islamic Institute, Mark Earley made a commitment to send a letter in support of the repeal."[6]

Earley lost the governor's race, despite the backing of Muslims and Norquist's main lobbying group Americans for Tax Reform, which shares offices with the Islamic Institute. Gill and Norquist worked together on local tax issues during the campaign.[7]

Gill is also listed as representing the Islamic Institute on a copy of an early 2001 White House guest list that I obtained. He is one of dozens of Muslim activists invited, some of whom are now under federal investigation for terrorist ties. Norquist's name tops the list. What's more, Gill listed Norquist as a reference on his employment documents.[8]

Officials say the political connection goes a long way to explaining how a thirty-three-year-old lawyer with no apparent experience in intelligence or security policy landed a top intelligence post at Homeland Security. It also may explain why he was reinstated within days of being removed from the job for failing to disclose critical information on his security clearance documents.[9]

"Anybody else would have been tossed out on their ear," argues the U.S. intelligence official, speaking on the condition of anonymity. "But this guy is a buddy of Karl Rove."

It was not the first time the White House appointed Gill to a top government position, however. From October 2001 to August 2003, he served as deputy general counsel for the Office of Personnel Management—which just happens to be the agency responsible for conducting security background investigations on candidates for federal jobs. Among other things, the background investigations examine candidates' loyalty to the United States and contacts with foreign countries and groups, as well as any previous criminal activity. Or at least they are supposed to. Gill's suspect associations apparently were overlooked.

THE SPY CHARTER

Intelligence officials fear Gill's appointment could be part of a scheme by Muslim militants to infiltrate sensitive government agencies by placing friendly agents in key positions. "There is a lot of smoke that this guy is an agent of influence," the senior U.S. official asserts.

Such notions may not be farfetched.

Before they were jailed on terrorism charges, Alamoudi and his friend Sami al-Arian worked feverishly to repeal the use of secret terror evidence that had kept al-Arian's immigrant brother-in-law behind bars. Gill of course joined that effort. Over the past several years, Muslim lobbyists such as Gill have shuffled between Alamoudi's AMC and the Islamic Institute, where they've enlisted the help of key White House ally Norquist in running influence operations against the federal government. Lo and behold, Gill manages to land a position in the heart of the agency controlling secret terror evidence related to deportation of Muslim immigrants. Homeland Security now oversees the old INS operations.

Investigators have even uncovered evidence of an Islamist scheme to infiltrate the U.S. government and collect intelligence. It is outlined in a document seized from al-Arian's Florida home, called the "Charter of the Center of the Studies, the Intelligence and the Information." Handwritten in Arabic, it lays out a comprehensive plan to establish a hostile intelligence operation in the United States, investigators say. The charter states:

> Our presence in North American gives us a unique opportunity to monitor, explore and follow up. . . . We are in the center which leads the conspiracy against our Islamic world. . . . Therefore, we here can monitor and watch the American policies and the activities of those questionable organizations. . . . Therefore, we have the capability to establish a Center for Studies, Intelligence and Information.

The charter, which investigators believe was authored last decade by al-Arian, provides for the establishment of an Intelligence and Monitoring Apparatus, part of which would be set up "to watch the individuals who oppose the Movement and the Islamic actions—to watch them, monitor them, and to make files on them," the document states.

It also says Muslim members of the so-called Group in America should "infiltrate the sensitive intelligence agencies or the embassies in order to collect information and build close relationships with the people in charge in these establishments." They should use every opportunity to "collect information from those relatives and friends who work in sensitive positions in the government."[10]

Of course, just because Gill worked for a group founded by a confessed terrorist does not mean he would spy for terrorists or those who sympathize with them. And there is no evidence to suggest he has compromised intelligence or homeland security.

Gill, whose formal title is special assistant to the undersecretary for the information analysis and infrastructure protection directorate, has declined comment.

But the department insists it thoroughly investigated his background, ensuring there were no potential conflicts or inappropriate activities. "Following a thorough investigation, we found that Mr. Gill exceeded all requirements set forth by the department office of security for access to classified information as prescribed by the intelligence community that allows him to conduct his day-to-day duties for the department," it said in a statement.[11]

Still, at least two U.S. senators are not satisfied with the explanation and have formally asked the department's inspector general to investigate Gill's ties to Alamoudi, AMC, and other Islamic groups. In a letter sent last summer to Homeland Security Inspector General Clark Kent Irvin, Sens. Charles Grassle (R-Iowa) and John Kyl (R-Arizona) questioned why the political appointee was allowed to stay on the job after omitting information during his security background check. They also sought information about Gill's role in setting intelligence goals at the department. As this book was going to press, the inspector general still had not released the findings of his probe.[12]

CULTIVATING AMERICA FOR ISLAM

There is little doubt Gill is a Muslim activist with ties to hard-line groups. And not just the AMC, either. As a senior U.S. official working for the Office of Personnel Management, Gill found time in 2002 to teach Muslim youth the finer points of "political activism" at the Saudi-backed Muslim Student Association's annual conference in Washington. As a workshop speaker, he reminded MSA members that they are in "a critical position" to "cultivate [American] society for Islam," according to a promotional description of the talk he was scheduled to deliver.[13] Also slated to speak at the group's confab were New York imam Siraj Wahhaj, an unindicted co-conspirator in the 1993 World Trade Center bombing, and Ahmad Totonji, a key player in the Saudi-funded Safa group now under federal investigation for terror-related transactions.

And there is little doubt that Gill lobbied to repeal the Department of Justice's use of undisclosed evidence against suspected Middle Eastern terrorists in deportation proceedings, a vital part of counterterrorism efforts since 9/11. Officials wonder how smart it is to have a Muslim activist who lobbied to deny law enforcement the tools it needs to crack down on terrorists helping craft intelligence policy at Homeland Security.

"Does he want to get rid of the Patriot Act now?" asks the senior U.S. official.

"It's just outrageous this guy is still there," he adds. "Every day he looks at the intelligence. He knows what's protected and what isn't. It's just outrageous."

The official maintains that the department is looking the other way to pander to the Muslim community. "Now they know of his ties [to Alamoudi], and they still don't do anything," he says.

"The White House wants to court the Muslim community," he adds, "but they're only courting disaster."

And the courtship goes on. On June 23, 2004, with Gill firmly ensconced at Homeland Security, his alma mater, the Islamic Institute, and other Muslim activists met with Attorney General John Aschroft to assert their civil rights and demand leniency in investigations of Muslims, carrying on the tradition of Alamoudi and al-Arian. Ashcroft agreed not to target Muslims in the war on terrorism. He was joined by representatives from the FBI, the Department of Treasury, the Equal Employment Opportunity Commission, and Gill's new employer, the Department of Homeland Security.[14]

29

PENETRATING THE WHITE HOUSE

Wahhabi Lobbyists as Gatekeepers

"He is from a background that makes him one of a small number of people that will be going into government service at this high level, and I am proud of that."
—U.S. REP. JOHN CONYERS (D-Michigan), commending President Bush's nomination of David Hossein Safavian to a top White House position[1]

On April 29, 2004, David Hossein Safavian took his seat at the witness table in room 342 of the Dirksen Senate Office Building on Capitol Hill. Like most presidential nominees at Senate confirmation hearings, he brought family and friends for support. The Republican appointee for a top White House job was expected to breeze through the Republican-controlled Senate.

Even so, Safavian, a lawyer-lobbyist, had extra support in his corner that morning. Two congressmen—one a liberal Democrat, surprisingly enough—stopped by to cheer him on before the Senate Governmental Affairs Committee. "I think he will do a great job for the American people in this job," testified Rep. Chris Cannon (R-Utah), who had previously employed Safavian as a top aide. "I would like to second what Chris Cannon has said," added Rep. John Conyers (D-Michigan), who brought along his chief of staff and two lawyers to add to his cheering section. "We are joined with his wife and his mom, as well as his family and friends, to underscore how fine a decision has been made for this appointment," Conyers gushed. "We hope that the Senate will agree and get him to work as quickly as possible."

Democratic Sen. Frank Lautenberg of New Jersey was impressed by the VIP endorsements. "When the nominee comes in with a fortification like John Conyers, you know that this is serious business, and we are going to pay a lot of attention. You, too, Mr. Cannon," he said.

Indeed it was serious business. Safavian was up for nomination to a key White House position—administrator for federal procurement policy at the Office of Management of Budget. The Bush political appointee would be acting as the gate-keeper for the government's contracts, in effect controlling some three hundred billion dollars in annual business.

Safavian, an Iranian American from Detroit, sailed through the approval process, with even Democrats singing his praises at the hearing. Sen. Carl Levin (D-Michigan) seemed more interested in his baby daughter, who was ten months old at the time and unable to attend the hearing. "I wonder if you would tell your daughter when she is old enough to know that we missed her being here this morning," Levin cooed.

The toughest question of the confirmation hearing was posed by the committee's Republican chairwoman:

SEN. SUSAN COLLINS: Is there anything you are aware of in your background which might present a conflict of interest with the duties of the office to which you have been nominated?
SAFAVIAN: No, ma'am.

Actually, there is one matter. It comes in the form of an item typewritten on official lobbying registration papers filed on September 18, 2000, with the secretary of the Senate. There, plain as day at the top of page two, it states:

Client Name: Abdurahman Alamoudi
Lobbyist Name: David Safavian

Safavian at the time served as managing partner for Janus-Merritt Strategies LLC, the Washington lobbying firm that filed the disclosure form that year, as required by law. Did he once lobby Congress and federal agencies for a man with ties to terrorism and al-Qaida? Safavian insists it was all a mistake and that Alamoudi, a confessed terrorist now behind bars, was "erroneously listed" on the form.[2]

Janus-Merritt, now known as Williams Mullen Strategies, points to a letter it wrote in 2001 to the secretary of the Senate informing her that the firm had incorrectly listed Alamoudi. "The lobbying registration form processed by your office listed Abdurahman Alamoudi incorrectly as the contact," the letter states. (In fact, the original form had listed Alamoudi as the "client," not the contact.) "The form should have read Dr. Jamal al-Barzinji as the contact," the oddly worded letter continues.[3]

That's still cold comfort. While not a confessed terrorist like Alamoudi,

Barzinji is an associate of Alamoudi who is under federal investigation for allegedly providing material support to terrorists.

"Barzinji is not only closely associated with PIJ [Palestinian Islamic Jihad] but also with Hamas," alleges senior federal agent David Kane in an affidavit used to obtain a search warrant for the Washington-area businesses and homes of Barzinji and his Muslim partners. In addition, Kane alleges he is also directly connected to accused terrorist Sami al-Arian.[4]

And while Barzinji is not behind bars, he has been in jail on unrelated charges. In November 2000, Fairfax County police arrested him at his northern Virginia home and charged him with domestic abuse and resisting arrest.[5]

This all came to light after the letter was written, however. At the time Safavian's firm was claiming Barzinji was the real client, he was considered a pillar of the community and a nationally respected Muslim leader. Alamoudi, on the other hand, was attracting a lot of negative press. He was not accused of any crimes then, but comments he made before 9/11 were coming back to haunt him. In late October 2000, Alamoudi remarked at an anti-Israel rally in Washington that he supported both Hamas and Hezbollah. Reports of those comments resurfaced in the national media in October 2001 in the wake of the terrorist attacks on America. Janus-Merritt filed its amendment replacing Alamoudi with Barzinji on December 17, 2001. The next month, Safavian left Janus-Merritt to work for Republican congressman Cannon.

Were his official lobbying records sanitized? Several things raise suspicions.

For one, Alamoudi's home address in Falls Church, Virginia, is accurately listed in the "CLIENT" section of the original 2000 disclosure form, as you can see from the copy of the three-page document exhibited on the companion Web site to this book, www.SperryFiles.com. And under the part asking for a description of the client's business or activities, it reads, "Client is an area Muslim activist," which fits the type of business and activities of Alamoudi, whose name is cited not once but three times in the document.

So whoever typed up the form at Janus-Merritt was very deliberate. These clearly are not typos. And as a rule, more than one person would likely have signed off on a document in which the managing partner of the firm is listed as a lobbyist. Safavian and his old firm are at a loss to explain how such a mistake could have been made.

Safavian, 37, doesn't just deny representing Alamoudi himself. He claims no one at the firm represented him: "To my knowledge, neither I nor Janus-Merritt did any work for Mr. Alamoudi."[6]

But federal records tell a far different story. The firm subsequently filed lobbying reports in February 2001 and July 2001 which also list Alamoudi as a client.

The reports show that Janus-Merritt had received an estimated forty thousand dollars from Alamoudi for "foreign policy" and "human rights" lobbying over a twelve-month period starting July 1, 2000, and ending June 30, 2001.[7] The period covers the date when the firm registered Alamoudi as a client under Safavian. And a search of Senate records turns up no amendments to *these* records.

All told, Alamoudi is listed three times as a client in Janus-Merritt's lobbying disclosure forms.

Barzinji, on the other hand, does not show up as a regular client. And Safavian himself failed to list him (along with Alamoudi) on his Senate biographical and financial questionnaire, which directed him to "describe any activity during the past ten years in which you have engaged for the purpose of directly or indirectly influencing the passage, defeat, or modification of any legislation, or affecting the administration and execution of law or public policy."[8]

One client Safavian does admit lobbying for is the Islamic Institute in Washington. Records show he registered as the group's chief lobbyist beginning June 1, 1999.[9] They also show that on behalf of his Muslim clients, he lobbied Congress to end the Department of Justice's use of undisclosed evidence against suspected terrorists in deportation proceedings. He pushed that issue in both the House and Senate up until the start of 2001.[10]

He also helped his Islamist clients fight terrorist profiling at airports by penning op-eds in Washington newspapers.

"When I go through security, my bags are usually chosen for scanning by the new bomb-sniffing equipment. While I cannot prove it, it is pretty clear that I am routinely racially profiled at the airport," he complained in the *Washington Times* two weeks before the 2000 election. "People of Arab-American descent or of Muslim faith . . . are the ones who are targeted as potential terrorists, merely because they wear different clothes or have a strange accent." He closed by lauding then-candidate Bush for speaking out against Arab profiling at one of the presidential debates.[11]

Assisting Safavian in the lobbying effort for the Islamic Institute was one Omar Nashashibi, a Palestinian native who also worked for the Saudi-tied Islamic Society of North America.[12] He is now with Williams Mullen, which took over Janus-Merritt. Curiously, Nashashibi's biography has been removed from the Williams Mullen Web site even though a spokeswoman confirms he works there as director of government affairs. He also oversees its research department.

Safavian's ties to the Islamic Institute shed light on the selection process behind his appointment to be the nation's top procurement policy official. The Senate in its biographical questionnaire asked Safavian to name the reasons he believes he was selected by the president for the job. And in response, he cited his education, background, and experience.

But political connections did not hurt. Safavian not only lobbied for the Islamic Institute, he also sat on its board of directors with co-founder Grover Norquist and Khaled Saffuri, who have arranged meetings between Islamic leaders and top Bush officials, and placed Arabs and Muslims in government jobs. (Saffuri previously was a top aide to Alamoudi, who helped finance the Islamic Institute, making it even harder to believe that Safavian had no dealings with Alamoudi.) What's more, Safavian and Norquist at one point were founding partners at all-Republican Janus-Merritt.[13]

A TROUBLING INFLUENCE

The top White House procurement job Safavian landed was actually a promotion. He was already working at the White House as a counselor in the Office of Management and Budget when Bush tapped him for the senior post. And before that, he worked as chief of staff for the head of the General Services Administration, where he says he mastered the procurement process.

Safavian led an effort at GSA to make it easier for small minority businesses—including ones owned by Arab immigrants—to land federal contracts. He distributed easy-to-read packets to small minority firms explaining how to bid on government contracts, including ones involving homeland security.

"We held seminars all over the country and invited small businesses and disadvantaged businesses to participate and learn how to do business with GSA and the Department of Homeland Security," he says.[14]

GSA is the landlord for the federal government. It holds the keys to more than sixteen hundred government-owned buildings. To save costs on employee benefits, GSA contracts out to private firms for not only janitorial and custodial help but also maintenance workers, including those working at utility plants. None of them undergo FBI background checks, and the turnover is high. And because they are not federal employees, they do not have to be U.S. citizens.

So what? For starters, some contract employees work at the giant central heating plant in Washington that feeds federal buildings. There are storage tanks there at that lightly protected plant, located next to the U.S. Bureau of Engraving and Printing, that contain thousands of gallons of fuel oil that if ignited could light up the capital.

Worse, GSA contracts out for security guards at its buildings, and relies on the contractors to conduct background investigations on them. The EEOC, believe it or not, protects guards of Middle Eastern origin from having to undergo extra background checks by their employers.

Yet these private guards supervise the heating, ventilation, and cooling systems of major government buildings in Washington—systems that al-Qaida has targeted.

"We believe al-Qaida remains intent on using chemical or biological agents on the homeland," according to a closely held Department of Homeland Security advisory I obtained. "Terrorists have designed a crude chemical dispersal device fabricated from commonly available materials, which is designed to asphyxiate its victims. The device produces cyanogens chloride (CLCN) gas and/or hydrogen cyanide (HCN) gas."

"The device could be placed near air intakes or ventilation systems, in crowded open spaces or in enclosed spaces," the five-page document continues. "These gases are most effective when released in confined spaces such as subways, buildings, or other crowded indoor facilities."[15]

As White House procurement honcho, will Safavian give Arab contractors the inside track on federal jobs? That remains to be seen.

But this much is known: he is heading a privatization effort to allow contractors to bid on hundreds of thousands of government jobs, and he intends to favor minority vendors. "I hope to open federal contracting for more disadvantaged businesses," he testified at his confirmation hearing. And he plans to start with the Department of Defense: "DoD should look to see if some portions of the work might be suitable for performance by small or disadvantaged businesses."

Safavian, whose wife works on Capitol Hill, also testified that his number one job would be to recruit and train new procurement officers throughout the government to replace the droves of officers expected to retire over the next five years.

Perhaps this explains the special interest Conyers took in Safavian's nomination. It was an odd scene, after all, a liberal Democrat crossing the aisle to give a ringing endorsement to a Republican. Conyers is not exactly fond of Bush. Why would he suddenly do his bidding?

He wasn't. He was doing the bidding of his many Arab and Muslim constituents in Detroit, who want to see one of their own in the White House—and who better than someone dispensing government jobs and contracts. Safavian could be their Trojan horse.

Conyers's closing remarks during his pitch for Safavian were revealing. "This is a great day for our country," he said. "I am aware that he is from a background that makes him a small number of people that will be going into government service at this high level, and I am proud of that. We are happy that this has come to pass."

Indeed. And so is Norquist, who sees the Islamists he has groomed to influence the U.S. government not only cashing in on their preferred White House treatment, but potentially helping other Islamists secure government jobs and contracts.

But Islamist watchers wonder how prudent it is it to invite a registered foreign lobbyist who represented Islamist interests into the White House to formulate new policy making it easier for Arab and Muslim vendors to perform government functions—especially when he lobbied Congress to make it harder for law enforcement to gather evidence against suspected Islamic terrorists.

They cite as a big red flag the case of Ptech Inc., a Muslim-owned software vendor. After 9/11, its Boston offices were raided by federal agents probing the firm for suspected ties to al-Qaida financiers. Authorities are especially concerned about Ptech because the company has provided software and consulting services to eighteen federal agencies. They include the FBI, U.S. Treasury, Secret Service, FAA, U.S. Postal Service, and the Pentagon.

Safavian and those he has associated with at the Islamic Institute and Janus-Merritt have done their best to confound anti-terrorism efforts in this country. They have pressured the government to roll back the Antiterrorism and Effective Death Penalty Act, the Illegal Immigration Reform Act, airport profiling, the use of secret terror evidence, and now the USA Patriot Act. They seem a lot more interested in their interests than America's interests.

Today, Safavian is on the inside operating as the gatekeeper for all the government's contracts. And he joins another crypto-Islamist in the White House by the name of Ali Tulbah.

ALI TULBAH

This young, clean-cut Muslim from Houston is the gatekeeper for the government's Muslim outreach efforts. If you are a Muslim activist and you want to get into the White House, you see Tulbah, who has been coordinating high-level meetings there since 2002.

He is a gracious host. In January 2003, he invited officials from the Council on American-Islamic Relations and Alamoudi's American Muslim Council and other Islamist groups to the White House to complain to senior U.S. officials about the fingerprinting of foreign visitors to the U.S. from two dozen Muslim countries, including Saudi Arabia and Pakistan. Perhaps not coincidentally, the government no longer singles out Muslim travelers for special registration.

In his official role as associate director for Cabinet affairs at the White House, Tulbah is also responsible for liaison with three of the most sensitive federal agencies in the war on terror: the Departments of Defense, State, and Justice, which had originally implemented the fingerprinting program.

The thirty-three-year-old Muslim, a Norquist protégé who formerly headed the Washington office of the Young Republicans, was put into his influential government position despite having some troubling family ties. Namely, his father, Hasan Ali Tulbah, has served as treasurer of a large Wahhabi mosque in Houston.[16]

The White House recently sent Tulbah to Iraq as a goodwill ambassador. He reported back on the progress thusly: "You can walk right outside now and hear all the voices of the imams coming from the mosques. You can hear the call to prayer and the verses of the Quran coming from all around Baghdad. It is very beautiful."[17]

Tulbah, now back at his old job, took over the White House public liaison duties from Suhail Khan, another apparent Islamist hiding in plain sight.

SUHAIL KHAN

Khan was the first White House staffer assigned specifically to reach out to American Muslims. While the new position is a breakthrough for the Muslim community, it is a setback for homeland security, judging from its first two appointees.

A former board member of Norquist's Islamic Institute, Khan helped arrange the busted September 11, 2001, White House meeting discussed earlier. He invited some of the terror-support syndicate's most dubious characters, including Sami al-Arian, to pressure the president into denying authorities the tools they need to catch terrorists.

And like Tulbah, Khan has troubling family ties.

It turns out his late father is one Mahboob Khan, the legendary leader of a San Francisco-area mosque that raised thousands of dollars for Osama bin Laden's second in command—not once, but twice—in the 1990s. Dr. Ayman al-Zawahiri bought satellite phones with the funds. The large Wahhabi mosque also routinely raised money for the Holy Land Foundation, a large Dallas-based charity which is under federal indictment for funding Hamas suicide bombers and their families. Guest speakers at the elder Khan's mosque, known as the Muslim Community Association, have included the head of Pakistan's militant Islamic Party, who has praised Chechen and Palestinian terrorists.[18]

In fact, Suhail Khan's father left quite a legacy of extremism before his death in 1999. Among other things, he was:

- one of the founding members of the Saudi-backed Muslim Student Association and Islamic Society of North America, major players in the Wahhabi lobby;

- founder of the Santa Clara, California-based American Muslims for Global Peace and Justice, whose chairman defended the Taliban even after 9/11;[19]

- co-founder of the Wahhabi mosque in Orange County, California, which converted al-Qaida suspect Adam Gadahn, whose face is now plastered on FBI wanted posters the world over.

Former Pentagon official Frank Gaffney worries about Wahhabists running amok inside the White House.

"It may be that the family ties both Tulbah and Khan have to Wahhabi religious organizations colors their judgment about the inadvisability of favoring the likes of CAIR and the AMC," he cautions.[20]

Khan left the White House to go to work at the Department of Transportation. He is now an aide to the secretary of transportation, which regulates airline passenger profiling. Khan handles governmental affairs for Norman Mineta and is in a position to influence aviation security.[21] He knows his way around Congress, too, having worked as an aide to former Republican congressman Tom Campbell of Santa Clara, one of the several GOP apologists for Islamists cited earlier.

AFTERWORD

The Perfect Enemy and How To Defeat It

"There are a thousand hacking at the branches of evil to one who is striking at the root."

—HENRY DAVID THOREAU

As details about the hijackers rolled in after 9/11, I was most struck by how long some had lived in America before stabbing their gracious host in the back. Hani Hanjour, the pilot of the Pentagon plane, for example, had lived in Arizona on and off since 1991.

Yet he and the others were not seduced by the many charms of America, and went through with their plan anyway. America is a beautiful, fun, and vibrant place. Its people are friendly and hospitable. Why didn't any of the hijackers have second thoughts? Why didn't they say, "You know, this place isn't so bad after all. Osama can go pound sand up his nightgown; we're gonna chill here for a while"?

The short answer is that they didn't do what they did for Osama. They did it for Allah, who according to the Quran promises a reward better than anything even America could offer them. That is the spell their faith has over them. We are not fighting poverty or ignorance. We are fighting a spiritual seduction we have yet to fully grasp and comprehend, hung up as we are on measuring the dreams and happiness of others against our own dreams and happiness. Pleasing their god makes them happy, even if it means killing themselves and others in his name.

But the officials in Washington leading the fight against this enemy still don't get it. They still don't understand the enemy's motivation, or at least won't talk candidly about it. A virtual taboo exists in official circles about Islam's role in terrorism. It is treated as if it comes out of the blue, as if there is no religious pattern. According to the president, we are fighting "evil-doers" and "a bunch of cold-blooded killers." To hear him and the FBI director, terrorism is generic, not Islamic.

Even the 9/11 Commission hearings tap-danced around the issue of why the hijackers did what they did. Witness this exchange during the June 16, 2004, hearing which brought together 9/11 investigators to reconstruct the plot.

VICE CHAIRMAN LEE HAMILTON: What motivated them to do it?

F.B.I. SUPERVISOR JAMES FITZGERALD: Much of it, I believe, originates in rage, and I think when you look at the nineteen hijackers and see where they came from, you can begin to see the seeds of that—that disenfranchisement and anger.

F.B.I. SUPERVISOR ADAM DRUCKER: These guys are young and impressionable, just like any type of, you know—it's akin to a cult-type atmosphere. What motivated people that followed David Koresh to do what they did?

HAMILTON: It's kind of interesting to me that none of you emphasize the religious motivation. . . . Why did they decide to martyr themselves, I guess that's my question. It's an extraordinary thing for an individual to make that kind of decision. It just runs counter to everything that you think about. We hang onto life. We hang onto life with everything we have, but these men give it up. They give it up at the most promising age—nineteen to twenty-eight. Why did they do it? You've given me some ideas, obviously, and I appreciate that, but it's really puzzling.

The first rule of war is know your enemy. You cannot defeat it if you do not know what motivates it.

Yet shockingly few FBI supervisors running counterterrorism cases have ever picked up a copy of the Quran to read it, let alone study it. "Supervisors don't study the Quran. They don't do any independent analysis," says former FBI special agent John Vincent. "And they're supposed to be supervising counterterrorism at headquarters? We need analysts just to interpret what Muslim leaders are telling supervisors there, because in the Muslim rhetoric, they don't mean what they say." The lack of independent analysis is reflected in federal law enforcement briefings on Islam which erroneously state that "violence is against the teachings of the Quran," a reflection of the false rhetoric of Muslim leaders.

"When you're fighting terrorism, you have to know how they think," adds Vincent, who investigated terrorism cases for several years in Chicago. And to do that, you have to study the sacred book of Muslim jihadists. The Quran is their manual of war and governs their moves. "The FBI is not a student of the enemy," he says. "They don't study it. No one takes time to do it."

Unfortunately, the enemy knows us better then we know it. The al-Qaida training manual quotes an old Muslim general: "The nation that wants to achieve victory over its enemy must know that enemy very well." The Islamic terrorists have studied our system inside and out, and they know its weaknesses and how to exploit them. They know about our open society, our civil liberties, our heavy ethnic mix, and our lax immigration enforcement all too well.

America's enemy goes beyond al-Qaida or the violent terrorist. It includes all those who advance the agenda of militant Islam. It includes the highly organized network inside this country that secretly supports violent jihad—from preachers, to fundraisers, to lobbyists, even to apologists. Instead of bombs, they use words and money, but they are no less dangerous in the overall scheme of things.

How do you fight an enemy driven by a foreign faith and language no one understands, not even your secretary of defense, commander in chief, or central intelligence director; an enemy who is adept at exploiting your religious and civil freedoms by recruiting foot soldiers and raising tax-free funds for them while inspiring and preparing them for battle in places of worship you protect as the cornerstone of your constitution; who prides itself on patience, discipline, and deception; who fight for a god, not even family or country, but a god; who welcomes death, relishes death, even beckons death in order to purchase a ticket to Paradise and a never-ending, wine-feted romp with nubile virgins in which the sex is better than anything experienced on earth and the wine does not cause hangovers?

You have heard of the perfect storm. Well, death-loving jihadists and their supporters and facilitators are the perfect enemy, for the following ten reasons.

NO. 1: PATIENCE

Like the Quran, the al-Qaida training manual counsels patience in defeating the infidels. "The member should have plenty of patience," it says. "He should be patient in performing the work, even if it lasts a long time." And as Dr. Ayman al-Zawahiri, the number two al-Qaida leader, has warned us: "We are a nation of patience, and we will continue fighting you until the last hour."[1] Al-Qaida will wait years to act and decades to succeed. The 1998 U.S. embassy bombings in Africa were a telling case study: surveillance of the embassy in Nairobi was first conducted in 1993. So shelf-planning took five years before the actual attack. That is about how long the 9/11 plot was in the works.

This is a determined enemy. Just because an American city hasn't been attacked again in three and a half years is no cause for complacency. December 2004's attack on the U.S. consulate in Saudi Arabia, launched within weeks of Osama bin Laden's videotaped warning, proves al-Qaida can still reach out and hurt America. These Islamic terrorists are patient, disciplined and relentless, and are planning another major attack on the homeland.

The Red Menace that dominated our lives for nearly a half a century is now being replaced by a Green Menace that may haunt us for the next century. "It may be tantamount to a hundred-year war," laments John Pistole, the FBI's executive assistant director for counterterrorism.

NO. 2: LANGUAGE BARRIER

Because the enemy speaks the inscrutable language of Arabic, it has a major advantage over law enforcement. The FBI has hundreds of thousands of hours of backlogged audiotapes waiting to be translated because of a lack of qualified Arabic linguists. Much of it relates to al-Qaida and may hold clues to the next attack. The government characterizes the Arabic tongue as a Level 4 language, on a difficulty scale of 1 to 4, the same as Chinese. It takes roughly twice as long to reach proficiency in Arabic as it does romance languages like Spanish, French or Italian that share the alphabet and Latin root words with English.

In Arabic, words are written right to left in an elaborate script in which many of the twenty-eight letters of its alphabet can take four shapes, depending on where they appear in a word. The letter *ghain*, for instance, takes a different shape when it starts a word, appears in the middle of a word, ends a word and when it stands alone.

Mix in the different regional dialects, and the enemy has a built-in secret code that is next to impossible to decipher. They can plan, plot and scheme against us with virtual impunity—and not just terrorist leaders abroad. Their supporters can preach insurrection right under the American public's nose. For instance, the Al-Hewar Center in Vienna, Virginia, in 2003 held a panel discussion about "The Role of the Arab Community in the United States: Setting Our Priorities." Taha Jaber al-Alwani, one of the leaders of a Virginia group suspected of aiding terrorists, was one of the panelists. What did he say? We don't know. He and the others all spoke in Arabic.

And when mosque leaders preach violent jihad, they switch their sermons from English to Arabic.

In prison chapels, meanwhile, Muslim chaplains preach anti-American hate to inmates in Arabic. Correctional officers don't have the training in Islam to detect militant Islamic messages—even if they regularly monitored Muslim worship services, which they don't. "Not a whole lot of folks are in tune with that kind of stuff," one associate warden understated in a recent interview with federal investigators.[2]

NO. 3: ALL IN THE FAMILY

It took the FBI decades before it could infiltrate the Mafia. That's how long it took to learn the language and recruit Sicilian informants. But cracking the closer-knit Muslim mafia in America will take even longer. "It's ten times harder to infiltrate radical Islamic groups than the mob," Vincent says. "For starters, only trusted family members can get into their inner circles," adding another layer of insulation on top of the Muslim faith that protects them from prosecution.

Prosecutors believe Hamas is operating in the U.S. under the charitable cover of the Holy Land Foundation. One of its founders, Mohammad El-Mezain, is a cousin of Hamas deputy political chief and fugitive terrorist Mousa Abu Marzook. Another founder, Ghassan Elashi, is related by marriage to Marzook. Holy Land Foundation officer Akram Mishal, moreover, is a cousin of Hamas operative and terrorist Khalid Mishal. And Mufid Abdulgader, a top Holy Land fund-raiser, is Khalid Mishal's half-brother.[3] It is a family enterprise in addition to a Muslim enterprise.

The FBI is a long way from penetrating the leadership of the terror-support syndicate in America, to say nothing of al-Qaida cells. Recruits usually don't go to al-Qaida. It finds them through orthodox Wahhabi mosques. Even the CIA has not been able to penetrate al-Qaida's inner circle abroad. We still have no spies on the inside.

Veteran FBI investigators say they have never faced a more disciplined adversary. They are a lot smarter than the mob. They are highly educated. In fact, many of them have Ph.D.'s. They are adroit at manipulating politicians and the media through skillfully parsed propaganda, and at hiding terror funds through a maze of financial fronts and shell companies.

Michael Rolince, former assistant director of the FBI's Washington field office, says the FBI still knows very little about the militant Muslim community in America. On a scale of one to one hundred, he puts the bureau's knowledge of the enemy at about twenty. It has very few spies in the community, and is still playing catch-up.

NO. 4: DIFFERENT CALENDAR

The enemy uses a different calendar which begins with the year 622, when the Muslim prophet Muhammad migrated from Mecca to Medina (the Muslim year is designated A.H., which means in the year of the *Hijra*, or migration). The Islamic calendar is lunar, and based on a year of approximately 354 days. Because changes are based on observation of the moon, a major Muslim holiday such as Ramadan may begin on different days in different places. Also, the Muslim day begins on the previous sundown.

This makes conversion very difficult. Even if U.S. intelligence intercepts terrorist chatter revealing the date of a planned attack, analysts have to convert it and hope they peg it to the western calendar accurately. One way to get a rough western solar date from a Muslim date, and vice versa, is to use this equation:

$$H \text{ (Muslim date)} = 1.013 \text{ (W - 622)}$$

or

$$W \text{ (western date)} = H - H/31 + 622$$

Also, the Islamic months rotate backward through the seasons and are not fixed to the Gregorian calendar. The months of the Islamic year are: Muharram, Safar, Rabi 1, Rabi 2, Jumada 1, Jumada 2, Rajab, Shaban, Ramadan, Shawwal, Dhul Qidah, Dhul Hijjah.

NO. 5: ALIASES

Just trying to match a terrorist suspect's name against federal watchlists is difficult. It's hit or miss to match the name in a database of 70,000 with all the possible aliases.

"Running Arabic names against watchlists is complex as hell," says Ed Soliday, formerly vice president of security operations for United Airlines. "You have to run them backwards and forwards to cover all the permutations."

First off, Islamic terrorists use compound Arab names often running several words long. Arab names consist of:

- the first name, which is their own name

- followed by the father's name

- and the paternal grandfather's name

- then, in some countries, the family name

Here is an example of a western name using this system: John (given name) Paul (father's name) Ross (paternal grandfather) Smith (family name). Now here's an example of an Arab name: Mohamed (given name) Abdulla (father's name) Mohamed (paternal grandfather's name) Awady (family name).

Terrorists can have up to six, seven, eight names, including nicknames, and use them interchangeably. Al-Qaida terrorists often take on nicknames. For example, Abu Eisa al-Hindi means Abu Eisa "the Indian." Al-Britani means "the Brit." Al-Libbi means "the Libyan." Aziz means "the powerful."

Then there is the problem of all the various spellings. Arab names are not consistently transliterated into English at least in part because the Arabic language does not have letters equivalent to our vowels. This lends itself to even more aliases. And because the Department of Homeland Security still has no single convention for transliterating Arabic names, it enables terrorists to vary the spelling of their names to defeat the name-based watchlist systems.

For example, terrorist suspect Soliman Biheiri of Egypt transliterates his Arabic surname in English as Biheiri, while his brother, Ahmed, goes by the spelling Behairy. Also, Abdullah bin Laden, who is on the watchlist, is spelled Abdulla BinLadin on some legal documents.

Last year, authorities were criticized for allowing Yusuf Islam, the singer formerly known as Cat Stevens, to enter the U.S. even though he is on the watchlist. It was a case of mistaken spelling. Islam was allowed to board a flight from London to the U.S., because his first name was spelled "Youssouf" in the no-fly registry used to prescreen passengers. He was detained in the U.S. once authorities realized the spelling error.

To further illustrate the problem, there are more than sixty published spellings of Moammar Gadhafi's surname, ranging from Qadhafi to Khadaffi. You get the picture.

NO. 6: FREEDOM OF RELIGION

Years ago in Philly, the FBI secretly recorded suspected Hamas operatives stating that the United States provides a secure legal base and a perfect haven from which to operate, because they can disguise their activities as religious activities protected by the Constitution and no one will question them because of the politically tolerant culture.

Indeed, Washington prides itself on hands-off religious policy. Even the Pentagon in relying on religious organizations to endorse its Muslim chaplains stays out of the business of approving them in deference to the constitutional separation of church and state—even though a number of those organizations are run by militant Islamists bent on undermining the military and the U.S. system of government.

They know they can advance their cause safely under the First Amendment, which ironically allows their faith the freedom to flourish even though they deny that freedom to other faiths in other countries. They know they can raise funds—

tax free—at local mosques under the protections of religious freedom. Making it easier for them, America is a welcoming nation, and Americans are respectful of all faiths and want to think the best of Muslims.

NO. 7: NOT EASILY BRIBED

Islam's true believers are not materialistic. The FBI for several years has dangled record amounts of reward money in the Muslim world for information leading to the capture of top al-Qaida figures, and it still has no takers. Unlike the Reds and mobsters, the jihadists are spiritually driven. "The mobsters we rolled up were greedy SOBs," Vincent says. "But Muslims don't really care about money except to help finance jihad. So you can't get into most terrorist organizations that way— by appealing to their greed."

NO. 8: TAX-EXEMPT TERRORISM

Saudi-backed Islamists have infiltrated the U.S. charitable sector by masquerading as philanthropists. Religious charities provide the perfect cover for their terror-supporting activities. These Muslim groups not only enjoy tax-exempt status, but their reputations as charities and foundations often allow them to escape scrutiny, making it easier to hide and move their funds to other groups and individuals who threaten national security.

This tax-free support for the machinery of terrorism was planned long ago by Islamists. A document seized last decade in a raid of al-Arian's home bears that out. Translated from Arabic, "The Charter," as it is called, provides for an "Organization/Law Studies Section" whose job it would be to study the legal aspect of establishing charitable organizations in America that would front for jihadi operations, investigators say.

Not coincidentally, al-Arian founded Muslim charities that co-mingled funds with the Saudi-backed Safa group of charities in Virginia. Investigators say the charities have availed themselves of the advantage of exemption from federal-income tax while abusing the requirements for tax-exempt status to avoid scrutiny of terror-tied financial transactions and associations.

NO. 9: SAUDI PROTECTION

With its deep pockets, the kingdom is a major source of funding for the terror-support syndicate in America. And when its leaders get in trouble, the Saudis are ready to provide legal aid and public relations assistance. They also have a powerful friend in the Saudi ambassador in Washington, who, some believe, can at times make investigations go away with a phone call.

NO. 10: THE "RACISM" AND "BIGOTRY" DEFENSE

Most Islamists are not just a religious minority, but a racial minority, and they know how to work it to their advantage. Jamal Barzinji, a key leader of the Safa group, has threatened to sue the U.S. government for unsealing an affidavit supporting a federal warrant to search his home. He has called the investigation "racist." FBI agent Gamal Abdel-Hafiz, who had unauthorized contacts with Muslim targets of investigation, threatened to sue the FBI for discrimination after he was fired. The bureau reinstated him, despite lingering questions about his loyalties.

"This is how they get the government to back off Muslim suspects," Vincent says.

Now here are ten ways to defeat the perfect enemy, as recommended by counterterrorism experts.

NO. 1: NOT IN MY BACKYARD

Average citizens have the power to block the development of new Saudi mosques and Islamic schools in their neighborhood by protesting. It worked in Loudoun County, Virginia. The Saudis planned to build a new 3,500-student campus—complete with a towering minaret—in the county. But school officials scrapped the plan not long after locals warned of a "Saudi invasion," and raised concerns about terrorism. One vocal local pastor who objected to the Islamic school argued that the Saudis should not to be given free reign to promote their religion in America when they will not even allow American Christians and Jews to practice their religion in Saudi Arabia.

The Saudis already operate a school in neighboring Fairfax County. After 9/11, it drew unwanted scrutiny for teaching anti-Western hatred and receiving most of its funding from the kingdom. The state eventually stripped the academy of its accreditation.

The Saudis still lease their school building from Fairfax County, however. Their lease expires in 2007. Concerned locals should exercise their right to lobby the board of supervisors to deny an extension of the lease. This is a school where ideology of hate is taught on religious grounds. It should be treated no differently than a school that practices racial segregation. They should enjoy no tax breaks, and no government support.

Citizens should also find out what kind of mosque is going up in their neighborhood, and who is backing it. I did. I noticed a large mosque under construction not far from my home in Fairfax, Virginia. So I investigated. After pulling the real estate records at the county courthouse, I discovered the trustees were from Pakistan, and even used a notary public registered in Lahore, Pakistan—a major red flag. Pakistan, the cradle of the Taliban movement, was the base of operations for many of the 9/11 plotters, and the country remains a sanctuary for top al-Qaida leaders.

Then I learned that the lead trustee, Mian Muhammad Saeed, is also the imam of the mosque, called the Islamic Center of Northern Virginia. It turns out Saeed was the spiritual adviser to the Pakistani terrorist who last decade fatally gunned down two CIA employees and wounded three others outside the agency's headquarters in nearby Langley, Virginia. After his recent execution, the Pakistani community hailed him as a martyr. Saeed is a hard-line Pakistani cleric. This is information the public should be aware of, especially the Christian church and Jewish school that will be the mosque's neighbors.[4]

Residents have the right to petition local officials who approve construction permits for such hard-line mosques. Know the local zoning ordinances. For example, do the proposed minarets exceed county height limits for such structures? Does the mosque's drainage plan meet environmental regulations? Does it have adequate parking, or will overflow lead to congestion and traffic accidents? Neighbors also have the right to tip off the FBI to any suspicious activity at such mosques.

NO. 2: ENFORCE THE OATH OF ALLEGIANCE

The U.S. still does not enforce its oath of renunciation and allegiance for immigrants who naturalize here. Yes, it asks them at the swearing-in ceremony to renounce their prior nationality and support the U.S. Constitution.

But unlike Germany, Japan and other major countries, the U.S. allows immigrants to retain their dual citizenship. Again, they do not lose their former citizenship. How in the middle of a war on Islamic terrorism is it in America's national security interest to allow a Saudi or a Pakistani or a Sudanese to naturalize but not actually give up their citizenship of birth—and passport—and comply with the oath? Many Muslims who have attained U.S. citizenship as a birthright have refused to join in the pledge of allegiance, because America is not (yet) a Muslim nation. This is a matter of dual loyalties.

Washington must enforce its oath of renunciation and allegiance by confiscating passports at the public citizenship ceremonies. No passport, no citizenship. It should also start enforcing their registration in the Selective Service.

NO. 3: PROFILE MUSLIM TRAVELERS

The Department of Homeland Security knows where the outside terrorist threat is coming from. It's coming from immigrants from thirty-five mostly Muslim countries. (Go to www.SperryFiles.com to view internal U.S. Border Patrol memo listing "Special-Interest Countries.") Yet it is letting them in anyway, pretending border authorities can screen out Muslim terrorists from entering the U.S. by running the occasional "intelligence-driven special operation" to detect, for example, Pakistani travelers exhibiting "rope burns," "bruises," and other signs of having trained at still-active terrorist camps in Pakistan, as a recent sensitive Homeland Security document I obtained reveals (also available online at www.SperryFiles.com).

But all it takes is one terrorist to get through the net. And watchlists are only good for known terrorists. Only two of the nineteen 9/11 hijackers were on any terror watchlist.

Better: Profile young adult males from all the Muslim countries, and authorize immigration inspectors to ask them if they have ever been to a paramilitary training camp in Afghanistan or Pakistan. (They should also be asked the last time they fired a weapon.) It should be a standard question not unlike the Cold War–era question we put to foreign travelers asking them if they have ever been a member of the Communist Party. And if they should come in to the country and lie, if they should make a false statement, then that would give border authorities reason to kick them out of the country.

They should also be asked to provide specific information about the nature of their visit, where they will be staying, who they will be visiting, who they will be working for, what courses they will be taking, and so on. Then they should be required to report back in thirty days to confirm their story, and then again in a year. Such monitoring is critical to disrupting a terrorist plot, but Homeland Security is not doing it. It is no longer specially registering men from Muslim countries. Why? Because Muslim-rights groups complained.

Instead, it is relying on a newfangled computer system called the Automated Targeting System-Passenger, or ATS-P, which selects non-watchlisted foreign travelers for special border screening based on their travel itineraries, ticketing agencies and other sterile factors. The foreign visitor's ethnicity and religion are not considered.

It is a lot like the automated CAPPS system used to select passengers for additional screening at airport security checkpoints. The government still refuses to profile Muslim passengers (and still won't scan the cargo that rides in the belly of passenger jets for explosives). Yet al-Qaida is still interested in planes to carry out terrorism, according to federal security advisories I obtained (see SperryFiles.com).

The 9/11 experience shows that terrorists study and exploit America's vulnerabilities. Currently Americans returning from Canada, Mexico and the Caribbean are not required to carry passports. They can gain entry by showing minimal identification at the ports of entry. This is crazy. Investigators believe Mexico and the Caribbean are attractive staging areas for terrorist attacks against the U.S. And Toronto and Montreal are hotbeds for terrorist activities. As recently as August 2003, Canadian immigration officials arrested nineteen men for possible links to al-Qaida, one of whom had been taking flight lessons over a nuclear power plant in Toronto.

NO. 4: AUDIT MUSLIM CHARITIES AND MOSQUES

In applying for tax-exempt status with the IRS, Muslim charities should be required to submit an additional form certifying that their organization does not promote separatism, terrorism, or violence. The IRS needs to do a better job of policing nonprofit Islamic organizations. In 1999, the American Muslim Foundation listed on its U.S. tax form a $5,000 contribution from Libya, a state sponsor of terrorism. Yet the line item raised no red flags at the IRS. It turns out the foundation's leader, Alamoudi, was illegally laundering money from the country.

To date, the IRS does not collaborate with the FBI to determine whether a Muslim group applying for tax-exempt status is engaged in terrorist activities. Despite the fact the FBI has had WAMY and its former head Abdullah bin Laden under investigation on and off since 1996, and despite last year's raid on its Virginia offices, the IRS continues to treat the Saudi-based group as a charity exempt from federal income tax. According to court documents, this supposed charity's goal is to "arm the Muslim youth with full confidence in the supremacy of the Islamic system over other systems." It also teaches teen-aged Muslim boys to sacrifice their lives in jihad against the infidels. "Are you miserly with your blood?!" it asks them. WAMY also teaches them to "love taking revenge on the Jews," who it calls "humanity's enemies."[5]

And take the case of the terror-tied Safa group of charities. The IRS continued to authorize tax-exempt status for the group after conducting an audit of its finances in 2000 and early 2001. A subsequent investigation by customs agents after 9/11 found that the group had allegedly falsified some of its returns. IRS auditors apparently were out to lunch.

Also, the IRS exempted the Holy Land Foundation from having to pay any income tax on the nearly $60 million in donations it received since 1992—even though U.S. prosecutors say much of the money was funneled to the terrorist group Hamas. It turns out the Muslim charity filed no less than six false tax returns with the IRS, prosecutors say.

In the future, the IRS should require all Islamic charities to conduct basic vetting of foreign recipients of their donations including whether they show up on any terrorist exclusion lists kept by the U.S., UN, or the EU. They should provide the agency the full names in English and dates of birth of the principals of their beneficiary groups. They should also be required to provide information about the banks where the recipients hold their accounts to further ensure that the funds provided by the charity are not ultimately distributed to terrorist organizations.

Investigators say the slightest association with violence or terrorism should be enough grounds to revoke a Muslim charity's tax exemption.

The same standard applies to American mosques. If they cannot be trusted to regulate themselves, the government must step in.

Like Muslim charities, most are funded and controlled by the Saudis, and many of their leaders belong to the dangerous Muslim Brotherhood, which seeks to achieve a global Islamic theocracy. No wonder so many are hotbeds of terrorist activity and magnets for terrorists. No wonder so many raise the banner of jihad during sermons. No wonder so many serve as political headquarters for Palestinian activists who raise money for Hamas and other terrorist groups. This is all happening inside America right now, and Washington is doing next to nothing to shut these mosques down—even ones in its own backyard like Dar al-Arqam, which aided and abetted the Virginia jihad network, and Dar al-Hijrah, which aided, if not abetted, the 9/11 hijackers.

Wahhabi mosques remain safehouses for terrorist and other subversive anti-American activities. The same wartime imperative that existed in previous wars may require that the government shut down all pro-jihadist mosques. Draconian? Would it have allowed pro-Nazi groups to meet publicly and rally the Nazi faithful after Nazi Germany declared war on the U.S.? Of course not. Why then do we continue to allow the supporters of Islamofascists—the new enemy—to meet, organize and rally against us in this country?

"The civil libertarians will not abide by us shutting down these mosques preemptively as of yet," Vincent remarks. "It will take another terrorism attack with many deaths before we overcome their constitutional objections." Perhaps that is how it ought to be. Nearly half of Americans think so. But the other half say the civil liberties of Muslim-Americans should be curtailed right now, before another attack, according to a recent poll by Cornell University.[6]

Shy of shutting militant mosques down, there are several things the government can do to crack down on them.

For starters, the IRS can probe suspect mosques and revoke their tax-exempt status if they are found to support violence, terrorism or anti-U.S. activities. Or if they fail to report donations from specially designated terrorist groups. By law, any U.S. entity that possesses any funds in which any interest is held by a specially designated terrorist or group must report such interest to the proper U.S. authorities. Any dealings in those funds after the designation date, or any attempt to avoid acknowledgment of the funds is unlawful. How many mosques are getting funds from terrorist fronts and not reporting it? More key, how many mosques are facilitating criminal acts that may support terrorism?

The FBI brought down a militant imam at a Wahhabi mosque in New York by setting up a phony weapons deal. Such stings are an effective tool for smoking out the bad guys, and law enforcement should continue to conduct them.

Congress must renew the part of the USA Patriot Act which allows the FBI to spy on mosques. The bureau can crack down on pro-jihad preachers by wiring up cooperating witnesses to record conversations with clerics inciting others to violence. Such charismatic imams are twice as dangerous as terrorists, since they can inspire many followers to martyr themselves. They should not be allowed to remain in the pulpit.

If this snooping bothers you, consider that even mosques in the nation's capital have warned their members not to cooperate with FBI agents. "There is no reason, in general, that anyone should ever, ever, ever talk to law enforcement as Muslims in the United States," Washington immigration and civil-rights lawyer Ashraf Nubani warns Muslims in a recent compact disk distributed to Washington-area mosques. "The FBI is just a tool of whoever is wielding it. And right now, it is very bad, it is very bad, it is very bad."[7] While FBI headquarters insists mosques have been allies in the war on terrorism, field agents say outreach efforts have borne little fruit. Since 9/11, the jihadists have gone deeper underground, making it harder to ferret them out.

Unfortunately, the government has not fully grasped the threat from these spiritual leaders. The Department of Homeland Security still considers religious workers coming into the U.S. on R-2 and R-1 visas to be the least threatening of all visitors to the U.S., according to an internal document I obtained.

Prosecutors must get creative in putting away spiritual leaders who help plot terrorism and insurrection. Blind Sheik Omar Abdel Rahman, for example, was convicted of charges brought under an arcane Civil War statute against "seditious conspiracy." The FBI also needs to infiltrate *hajj* group tours for American

Muslims. American imams often join them as tour guides and reveal their true colors while on Saudi soil and in the company of Saudi clerics.

FBI headquarters, meanwhile, needs to get off the backs of counterterrorism agents in the field who are trying to do their jobs by canvassing mosque-goers. A few years ago, agents in Chicago interviewed people at the notorious Bridgeview mosque whose names were listed in the address book of a convicted terrorist. The Muslim community got up in arms and complained to the FBI. The agents were barred from asking Muslims questions about Middle East politics or religion. "That's ridiculous," Vincent says. "That's all they talk about. That's all they're interested in. They talk about it at the coffee and tea shops, and they talk about it at the mosques. What should we talk to them about? The Chicago Bears? Most Muslims are not like normal Americans. They don't have the same interests. You won't see them at the Bears game."

FBI counterterrorism veteran Don Lavey agrees, arguing that FBI director Mueller and his civil rights team are so sensitive to the concerns of the Muslim community that they have invited complaints and given Muslims a built-in excuse not to cooperate. "There are always people out there you can find to assist you, but you don't go around publicly apologizing or publicly stating your concern and what you want to accomplish," he says. "I wish the FBI would get its head out of the sand."[8]

At the same time, the federal government should freeze its hiring of Sunni Muslim chaplains and contractors at prisons, the number one recruiting ground for al-Qaida. Prison conversion to Islam has exploded, causing a shortage of imams. But the feds are under no legal obligation to cater to the demand. Under prevailing federal case law, inmates are not entitled to a chaplain of their faith group, denomination or sect. Why help al-Qaida expand its recruiting pool?

NO. 5: BREAK OFF OFFICIAL TIES WITH CAIR

It is critical that the U.S. government, as well as state governments, break off official ties with Islamist groups such as CAIR, the Islamic Society of North America, and the American Muslim Council, including its GOP offshoot the Islamic Institute. CAIR has now seen three of its leaders convicted of terrorism. Continuing ties only lends legitimacy and national voice to militant Islam's main PR machine in America. With each meeting, Washington gives the group a bigger foothold in the political system, when they never even deserved a toehold. Aside from its deeply troubling terrorist ties, CAIR's propaganda defends Islamism and misleads Americans about the broader threat.

Also, public libraries, which do not have to accept donated materials, would be well-advised to refuse CAIR's package of books white-washing Islam.

NO. 6: EXPOSE THE SAUDI EMBASSY

The White House should declassify the twenty-seven pages of the congressional report detailing the Saudi government's support of the hijackers and its suspected advance knowledge of the 9/11 plot. The American public has a right to know the truth about all state sponsors of terrorism.

Meanwhile, Washington should continue to revoke the diplomatic visas of Saudi clerics operating out of the Saudi Embassy, as well as its consulates, who are really agents of influence spreading anti-western Wahhabism under the cover of diplomacy. Investigators say much of the material support and training for the terror-support syndicate in America (if not the terrorists themselves) is being directed out of the Saudi Embassy in Washington, which enjoys sovereign immunity, a powerful privilege that protects states and their officials not just from criminal prosecution, but personal lawsuits. (Its ambassador, moreover, enjoys an unusually close personal friendship with the president and his family.)

The FBI should spy on the Saudi Embassy like it spied on the Soviet Embassy during the Cold war. Unless, of course, it's not serious about winning the war on terrorism.

NO. 7: DENY SECURITY CLEARANCE
TO MUSLIM ACTIVISTS

The administration should stop placing Islamists in government jobs where they have access to secrets they can feed back to the enemy. The al-Qaida manual calls spying on the enemy an essential duty. "Winning the battle is dependent on knowing the enemy's secrets," it says.[9] Al-Arian, moreover, was in possession of a document written in Arabic that outlined a plan to infiltrate sensitive government agencies. Like the communists, who placed fellow travelers inside the government, the Islamists are trying to install their own agents of influence and sympathizers in sensitive posts. And they are getting a lot of help from the Islamic Institute, which has well-placed friends inside the White House.

Since 9/11, the administration has hired several Muslim activists who in the past have lobbied to deny law enforcement tools it needs to fight terrorism. And it has put them in highly sensitive posts where they not only have access to top secret information but control over policies related to the war on terrorism. This defies all common sense.

Vetting of any future Arab and Muslim applicants should include disclosure of memberships in Muslim organizations, religious activities and speeches at Islamic conferences. Security adjudicators should carefully evaluate religious activities of such applicants to confirm their loyalty. If it were okay during the Red Scare to ask government workers if they were members of the Communist Party, it should be okay to ask them in the Era of Terror if they are members of Wahhabi groups and mosques.

NO. 8: OFFER SCHOLARSHIPS IN ARABIC

A shortage of Arabic translators (who are both qualified and loyal) remains a major barrier to the FBI's understanding of the terrorist threat. The number of American students enrolled in Arabic courses accounts for less than 1 percent of all the language students across the country. More than twice as many students are taking Russian, the language of the Cold war. Washington should consider offering full-paid college scholarships in Arabic to expand the pool of Arabic translators from which both law enforcement and the military can recruit. It should also look at ways of subsidizing Arabic language programs at public high schools.

NO. 9: FIGHT MUSLIM ACTIVISM IN PUBLIC SCHOOLS

More parents should challenge the Council on Islamic Education's instructional materials in court. They are stealthily promoting Islam in public schools, while denigrating other faiths. The Muslim activist group and its allies in the Ivory Tower have conned the education establishment—including textbook publishers—into accepting a sugar-coated version of Islam that is misleading students and possibly inspiring more John Walker Lindhs, the American Taliban.

CIE, whose research department is headed by a Muslim educator formerly on the Saudi payroll, edited the Houghton Mifflin social studies text Walker used in California and that is now used at schools nationwide. Christians come off bad in the book, but for Muslims the theme is tolerance. They are said to be "extremely tolerant" of Christians and Jews. Jihad is white-washed. In contrast, Christians are never said to be tolerant of other people but have "persecuted" them, a term repeated throughout the unit on Christianity.

Such pro-Islamic propaganda cannot stand. Judeo-Christian scholars and historians should demand equal time with publishers to correct for CIE's bias.

NO. 10: STEP UP COUNTERTERRORISM
TRAINING AT QUANTICO

The FBI is engaged in the most massive domestic intelligence collection since J. Edgar Hoover's spying on suspected communists during the Red scare. Problem is, agents don't know what to make of all the information they're collecting, because they haven't had proper training in counterterrorism and intelligence.

"You get an agent who comes out of Quantico and you assign him to the UBL [Osama bin Laden] unit out of headquarters and he has no idea about UBL. He has no idea how these people operate, how they think, their mentality, nothing," FBI counterintelligence veteran John M. Cole, a former Quantico instructor, tells me. "And he's coming in and getting these headquarters cases and he doesn't know how to run a counterterrorism case. Yet he's in charge of certain cases now. And it gets screwed up because he doesn't know what's important, what's not important. It's crazy."

Intelligence is key to fighting terrorism. FBI counterintelligence veteran Tom Bloch, who worked Soviet espionage cases for twelve years, says the bureau has to get smarter. "If the approach to counterterrorism is not as sophisticated as our effort against the Soviets, then there is cause to be worried—and there is every indication that it is not," he tells me. "There are a lot of problems with the analytical side."[10]

The key to understanding the enemy is understanding their sacred texts. Yet "the FBI doesn't train people to understand where the enemy is coming from," Vincent says, "and there's no one willing to learn it on their own."

For that matter, he says, "most agents don't want to work terrorism" cases. So Mueller is having to throw bodies at the problem. "Most of the manpower in the war on terrorism is coming from new agents fresh out of classes. They have no idea how to investigate a criminal case, and they're going to crack terrorism cases? C'mon," Vincent adds. "Yet that's who we're sticking in our terrorism squads." Indeed, headquarters assigned a green agent to investigate the hijackers of American Airlines Flight 77—the Pentagon cell. The case agent, Jacqueline Maguire, had just graduated from Quantico three months before the attacks!

"No one knows the problem we're in," Vincent says.

Bloch, a thirty-year veteran of the bureau, agrees. "The bureau has traditionally been able to make up for deficiencies just by throwing manpower at a problem. This terrorism problem is going to be too sophisticated for them to do that. They're gonna have to get smarter," he says. "And I don't know if they're going to get smarter. I don't know if Mueller knows what he's doing, or if he's lost. All I know is the CYA culture and the PC culture are still bad there" at headquarters.

In my first book on the war, *Crude Politics*, I made the case that America has not fought a serious and effective war on al-Qaida abroad, distracted as it is by the commercial fronts that opened up after 9/11. But America is not fighting a serious and effective war on terrorism at home, either, still handcuffed as it is by political correctness. And it is inviting another 9/11.

America is fighting a perfect enemy, one protected by religious freedoms and racial sensitivities. And we have a less-than-perfect understanding of what motivates the enemy, and how it is aided and abetted by a religious support network that exploits American culture and tax laws and is patiently infiltrating the American system to overturn it from within.

More than three years after 9/11, we are still hacking at the branches of terrorism rather than striking at its root.

NOTES

INTRODUCTION

1. Transcript of remarks during hearing of Subcommittee on Terrorism, Technology and Homeland Security, Senate Judiciary Committee, 14 October 2003.
2. United States v. Abdurahman Muhammad Alamoudi, criminal complaint filed in United States District Court for the Eastern District of Virginia, 30 September 2003, 11.
3. Transcript of audiotaped sermon by Wahhaj, as quoted by Paul M. Barrett, "One Imam Traces the Path of Islam in Black America," *Wall Street Journal,* 24 October 2003, A1.
4. Lisa Gardiner, "American Muslim Leader Urges Faithful to Spread Word," *San Ramon Valley (California) Herald,* 4 July 1998. The article also ran in a sister publication, *The Argus (Fremont, California).* Ahmad made the remarks on 2 July 1998, at an Islamic conference held at the Flamingo Palace banquet hall in Fremont, California. The conference was sponsored by the Islamic Study School, a local nonprofit, and Ahmad spoke during a session titled, "How Should We as Muslims Live in America?" When the unpatriotic remarks resurfaced after 9/11, CAIR claimed in an April 2003 press release that they "were either reported inaccurately or wrongly attributed by a reporter at a small California newspaper." The group said it had sought a retraction, but editors at *The Argus,* a daily newspaper, deny being contacted by CAIR.
5. Senate hearing, 14 October 2003.
6. Press release, office of Sen. John Kyl, 3 October 2003.
7. Senate hearing, 14 October 2003.
8. "A Review of the Federal Bureau of Prisons' Selection of Muslim Religious Services Providers," Office of the Inspector General, U.S. Department of Justice, unclassified version, April 2004, 48.
9. Senate hearing, 14 October 2003.
10. Press release, 3 October 2003.
11. Letter by Sibel D. Edmonds to Senate Judiciary Committee and The 9/11 Commission, 6 January 2004, 5.
12. Joint Inquiry Into Intelligence Community Activities Before and After the Terrorist Attacks of September 11, 2001, U.S. Senate Select Committee on Intelligence and U.S. House Permanent Select Committee on Intelligence, December 2002, 164, 179. For all future references, "Report of the Joint Inquiry into 9/11."
13. Khalid Duran, "How CAIR Put My Life in Peril," *Middle East Quarterly,* 1 December 2001.
14. *The 9/11 Commission Report* (New York: W.W. Norton, 1994), 535. A highly classified August 2001 presidential briefing the CIA prepared for Bush on the al-Qaida threat cited seventy active investigations. But many should not have been included in the report. In fact, thirteen of them had been closed at the time, leaving fifty-seven, the commission found in its review of the cases.
15. "Reforming Law Enforcement, Counterterrorism and Intelligence Collection in the United States," Staff Statement No. 12, The 9/11 Commission, 14 April 2004.
16. Affidavit in Support of Application for Search Warrant, "In the Matter of Searches Involving 555 Grove Street, Herndon, Virginia, and Related Locations," U.S. District Court for the Eastern District of Virginia, unsealed October 2003, 36. For all future references, "Affidavit in Support of Application for Search Warrant."

17. Ibid., 30.
18. Author interview by phone, 3 October 2004.
19. *The 9/11 Commission Report*, 363.

CHAPTER 1—Don't Pick on Muslims

1. Transcript of Mueller testimony before the Senate Judiciary Committee, 6 June 2002.
2. Paul Sperry, "FBI Invites Muslim Scholars to Preach," WorldNetDaily.com, 30 July 2003.
3. Ibid.
4. Author interview by phone, 12 August 2004.
5. According to a transcript of Mueller's 28 June 2002, speech at AMC's Eleventh Convention, he said among other things: "Sadly, some individuals in this country have questioned the loyalty of some Muslim Americans to this country just because of their religion. . . . It is our understanding that Islam is a religion of peace." As soon as Mueller began to speak, four anti-AMC protestors walked in front of the podium and held up signs that read, "The FBI should protect Americans from terror, not meet with supporters of terror," according to a 29 June 2002, IslamOnline.net article. They were hustled out of the room, and Mueller continued his speech.
6. Timothy Starks, "G-Man Calls Muslim Council 'Mainstream,'" *New York Sun*, 13 June 2002, 1.
7. Federal authorities believe he still controlled AMC, the group he founded, at the time Mueller gave his speech there, according to the 2003 indictment of Alamoudi. He also was on the board of directors, and chaired the conference at which Mueller spoke, according to congressional testimony.
8. Sperry, "FBI Invites Muslim Scholars to Preach."
9. Ibid.
10. Ibid.
11. Transcript of Al-Marayati's remarks at MPAC conference on U.S. counterterrorism policy, Washington, D.C., 9 September 2003. Al-Marayati has met with Bush on at least one occasion—26 September 2001—at the White House, which did not respond to requests for comment about the alleged agreement. The allegation of a deal with MPAC is all the more disturbing considering Al-Marayati was dumped from a congressionally sponsored anti-terrorism commission in 1999 after the press dug up quotes in which he compared Hamas and Hezbollah terrorists favorably with American freedom fighters like Patrick Henry.
12. Author interview by email, 14 March 2003.
13. Author interview by phone, 12 August 2004.
14. Transcript of Mueller testimony before the Senate Judiciary Committee, 6 June 2002.
15. Ibid. Technically, the Phoenix memo was not even proscribed by bureau rules against profiling. It contained specific information about specific people—male flight students visiting the U.S. on visas from the Middle East, with further focus on Sunni Muslims. Arabs and Muslims *in general* were not targeted.
16. "Counterterrorism Policy: American Muslim Critique and Recommendations," *Muslim Public Affairs Council*, September 2003, Appendix H, 97.
17. Elizabeth Kelleher, "FBI Official Pledges More Outreach to Muslim Community Leaders," Bureau of International Information Programs, U.S. Department of State, 10 June 2003.
18. Ibid.
19. Kenneth R. Timmerman, "Saffuri's Ties to Terror Suspects," *Insight*, 15 March 2004, 34.
20. Author interview by phone, 10 September 2004. While many agents feel demoralized by the director's obsequiousness toward Islamists, and question his judgment, they do not doubt his patriotism. Mueller earned a Purple Heart as a marine captain in Vietnam.
21. Author interview by email, 14 March 2003.
22. Author interview by email, 1 September 2004.

CHAPTER 2—Politically Correct Suicide

1. Transcript of remarks by Secretary of State Colin Powell, *Charlie Rose Show*, PBS, 22 September 2003.

2. Mark O'Keefe, "Muslims: Stop Saying 'Judeo-Christian,'" *Religion News Service*, 31 May 2003.

3. Felix Hoover, "'Judeo-Christian' Nation? Muslims Say: Add Us, Too," *Columbus Dispatch (Ohio)*, 4 July 2003, E1.

4. Gilbert T. Sewall, *Islam and the Textbooks* (New York: American Textbook Council, 2003), 5, 6.

5. UPI, 13 June 2004.

6. "Interviewing Violent True Believers," Muster Module: Briefing Notes, For Official Use Only, Department of Homeland Security, January 2004, 1.

7. http://www.islamicinstitute.org/pressr/pr-2004-6-23-2.htm.

8. "A Review of the Federal Bureau of Prisons' Selection of Muslim Religious Services Providers," Office of the Inspector General, Department of Justice, April 2004, 33, 34.

9. Indictment, U.S. v. Sami Amin al-Arian, U.S. District Court for Middle District of Florida, February 2003, 64. GSISS president and al-Arian pal Taha J. al-Alwani is "Unindicted Co-Conspirator Five."

10. http://www.op.org/adrian/storyvanbaalen.html.

11. http://www.sienahts.edu/storys/honorary.htm.

12. http://www.isna.net/news/miniheadlines.asp?dismode=article&artid=296.

13. http://www.isna.net/idf/newsletter/may2004.htm.

14. http://www.isna.net/idf/newsletter/may2004.htm.

15. Eric Lichtblau, "CIA Officer Denounces Agency and September 11 Report," *New York Times*, 17 August 2004.

16. Transcript of remarks by President Clinton, National Museum of Women in the Arts, Washington, D.C., 21 October 1993.

17. Transcripts of remarks by President Clinton, press briefing, White House, 15 November 1994.

18. Transcript of remarks by President Bush, Embassy at Afghanistan, Washington, D.C., 10 September 2002.

19. Transcript of remarks by President Bush, Eisenhower Executive Office Building, Washington, D.C., 11 October 2002.

20. Transcript of remarks by President Bush, press conference, Bali International Airport, Bali, Indonesia, 22 October 2003.

21. Author interview by phone, 23 August 2004.

22. Mark O'Keefe, "Bin Laden's Religious Justification Rejected by Most Muslims Worldwide," Newhouse News Service, 18 September 2001.

23. Transcript of remarks by President Bush, Islamic Center of Washington, D.C., 17 September 2001.

CHAPTER 3—From the White House to the Big House

1. CAIR press release, 28 September 2001, quoting Bush at meeting held two days earlier with CAIR and other Muslim officials in the Roosevelt Room of the White House.

2. Paul M. Barrett, "One Imam Traces the Path of Islam in Black America," *Wall Street Journal*, 24 October 2003, A1.

3. Sarah Downey and Michael Hirsh, "A Safe Haven?" *Newsweek*, 30 September 2002, 30.

4. Transcript of videotaped speech by Siraj Wahhaj, Muslim Community Building in America, International Institute of Islamic Research, Burlington, New Jersey.

5. Solomon Moore, "Fiery Words, Disputed Meaning," *Los Angeles Times*, 3 November 2001, 20. Siddiqi says not all his remarks were wrathful that day, pointing out he also asked for "blessings" for America.

6. "Muslims Participating in the U.S. Local Councils," Fatwa Bank, IslamOnline.net, 1 October 2003.

7. David Reyes, "Police Called to Quell Clash at Mosque," *Los Angeles Times*, 24 August 1992, B2. Siddiqi later claimed in a correction that the disturbance was minor, and no one had to be removed from the mosque.

8. Hanna Rosin, John Mintz, "Muslim Leaders Struggle with Mixed Messages," *Washington Post*, 2 October 2001, A16.
9. Ibid.
10. Stephen Schwartz, "Is Cat Stevens a Terrorist?" *The Weekly Standard*, 22 September 2004.
11. Yvonne Yazbeck Haddad, *The Muslims in America* (New York: University Press, 1991), 115.
12. CAIR press release, 28 September 2001.
13. Lisa Gardiner, "American Muslim Leader Urges Faithful to Spread Word," *San Ramon Valley (California) Herald*, 4 July 1998.
14. CAIR press release, "Islamophobic Smear Campaign Goes Public," 8 November 2001.
15. Lou Gelfand, "Readers Says Use of 'Fundamentalist' Hurting Muslims," *Star Tribune (Minneapolis)*, 4 April 1993, A31.
16. Transcript of NBC *Today Show* interview, 23 August 2002.
17. Transcript of videotaped speech al-Arian gave as honorary guest at the Islamic Mosque in Cleveland on 7 April 1991, referenced in Affidavit in Support of Application for Search Warrant, 36.
18. Ibid., 29, 33. Authorities found the manifesto, along with the wills of three Muslims planning to die as martyrs in jihad, in an earlier search of al-Arian's home computer.
19. Ibid., 33. The undated document was seized in the earlier raid. Al-Arian gave the speech as president of the Florida-based Islamic Committee for Palestine, which prosecutors believe to be a terrorist front.
20. Mary Beth Sheridan, Douglas Farah, "Jailed Muslim Had Made a Name in Washington," *Washington Post*, 1 December 2003, A1.
21. United States v. Abdurahman Muhammad Alamoudi, criminal complaint filed in United States District Court for the Eastern District of Virginia, 30 September 2003, 11.
22. Ibid., 10.
23. AMC's Eleventh Annual Convention.

CHAPTER 4—White Lies
1. Transcript of Alamoudi remarks, "Symposium: American Muslims and U.S. Foreign Policy," Middle East Policy Council, Russell Senate Office Building, 28 January 1999.
2. Reza F. Safa, *Inside Islam* (Lake Mary, Fla.: Charisma House, 1996), 81, 82.
3. Author interview by phone, 13 August 2004.
4. Walid Phares, "Al-Taqiya," *Israel Resource Review*, 10 November 1997.
5. Abd al-Rahman al-Rashed, "Slow Down, Media of 1967," *Al-Sharq Al-Awsat (London)*, 27 March 2003.
6. Serge Trifkovic, *The Sword and the Prophet* (Boston: Regina Orthodox Press, 2002), 266.
7. Irshad Manji, *The Trouble with Islam* (New York: St. Martin's Press), 42, 43.
8. Peronet Despeignes, "Quran Doesn't Call for Beheadings, Islamic Cleric Says," *USA Today*, 21 June 2004, A13.
9. Mohamad Bazzi, "Waging 'Holy War'," *Newsday*, 24 June 2004, A4.
10. "A Review of the Federal Bureau of Prison's Selection of Muslim Religious Services Providers," Office of Inspector General, Department of Justice, April 2004, 35.
11. Affidavit in Support of Application for Search Warrant, 36.
12. Indictment, U.S. v. Holy Land Foundation, U.S. District Court for the Northern District of Texas, 14, 15.
13. Karen Branch-Brioso, "12 Washington-area Muslims Investigated for Alleged Terrorist Ties," *The Tribune (Port St. Lucie/ Fort Pierce, Florida)*, 13 June 2003.

CHAPTER 5—The Top Ten Myths of Islam
1. Abdullah Yusuf Ali, *The Meaning of the Holy Quran* (Beltsville, Md.: Amana Publications, 1999), 436.
2. CNN, 13 October 2001.

NOTES

3. Reza F. Safa, *Inside Islam: Exposing and Reaching the World of Islam* (Lake Mary, Fla.: Charisma House, 1996), 42,43.

4. Ali, footnotes #1234, 431; #1313, 454.

5. Ibid., footnote #591, 207; also, footnote #1270, 442.

6. Ibid., footnote #614, 216.

7. Dr. Ali Sina, "In the Search of the Moderate Muslim," FaithFreedom.org, 7 November 2003.

8. John L. Esposito, *The Islamic Threat* (New York, N.Y.: Oxford University Press, 1999), 31.

9. Transcript of four pages of notes found after the hijackings, *New York Times,* 29 September 2001.

10. Ali, footnote #1251, 438.

11. Paul Findley, *Silent No More* (Beltsville, Md.: Amana Publications, 2001), 178.

12. CNN, 13 October 2001.

13. Ali, footnote #1287, 446.

14. Safa, 70.

15. Ali, footnote #1362, 470.

16. James A. Bill, *Politics of the Middle East* (Boston: Little, Brown and Co., 1983), 138, 139.

17. Safa, 56.

18. Transcript of Q&A with Siddiqi, *Orange County Register,* 2 November 2001.

19. Karen Armstrong, "The True, Peaceful Face of Islam," *Time,* 1 October 2001.

20. CNN, 13 October 2001.

21. Ali, footnote #5,457, 1,467.

22. Ibid., footnote #764, 265.

23. Ibid., footnote #398, 142.

24. Ibid., footnote #607, 213.

25. "The New World of Islamic Legal Studies," *Harvard Law Bulletin,* Spring 2002.

26. CNN, 13 October 2001.

27. Associated Press, 8 October 2001.

28. Knight Ridder/Tribune News Service, 2 August 2004.

29. Transcript of testimony of Dr. K, the 9/11 Commission, Washington, D.C., 16 June 2004.

30. Vinay Menon, "Rise of Islam in Jails a Risk?" *Toronto Star,* 7 July 2004.

31. Transcript of lectured delivered by Farid Esack, Auburn Theological Seminary, New York City, 10 October 2001.

32. Dr. Mohamed Khodr, "Iraq: Gone with the Wind of Lies and Bombs," *The American Muslim,* May 2004, 30-32.

33. "Muslims Participating in the U.S. Local Elections," Dr. Muzammil Siddiqi, Fatwa Bank, IslamOnline.net, 1 October 2003.

34. Ali, footnote #5906, 1588.

35. Ibid., footnote #5240, 1411.

36. Manji, 46.

37. Paul Sperry, "Airline Denied Atta Paradise Wedding Suit," WorldNetDaily.com, 11 September 2002.

38. Transcript of four pages of notes found after the hijackings, *New York Times.*

39. Ellen Goodman, "Deluded Bombers," *Washington Post,* 6 April 2002, A21.

40. Nasra Hassan, "An Arsenal of Believers," *The New Yorker,* 19 November 2001.

41. Transcript of four pages of notes found after the hijackings, *New York Times.*

42. Ali, footnote #2,839, 837.

43. Ibid., footnote #1271, 443.

44. Ibid., footnote #1362, 470.

45. "Questions about Palestine," Fatwah, *The American Muslim,* 1 March 2002.

46. Safa, 41.

47. Ali, footnote #478, 172.

48. Paul Sperry, "The Quran: Suicide Playbook," WorldNetDaily.com, 9 April 2002.

49. Ali, footnote #5,459, 1,468.

50. Ibid., footnote #469, 168.

51. Hesham A. Hassaballa, "Islam's Culture of Death," BeliefNet.com, October 2004.
52. Excerpts from bin Laden tape, Associated Press, 8 April 2003.

CHAPTER 6—The Threat Still among Us
1. Transcript of Mueller testimony, Senate Select Intelligence Committee, Washington D.C., 11 February 2003.
2. Transcript of *Capital Report with Gloria Borger*, CNBC News, 2 November 2004.
3. *The 9/11 Commission Report* (New York: W.W. Norton, 2004), 525-527.
4. Ibid., 514.
5. Transcript of Mueller testimony, 11 February 2003.
6. *The 9/11 Commission Report*, 535.
7. Report of the Joint Inquiry into 9/11, "Appendix: Evolution of the Terrorist Threat and the U.S. Response (1983-2001)," 38.
8. Author interview by phone and email, 1 July 2004.
9. "Possible Indicators of Al-Qaida Surveillance," Information Bulletin 03-004, Department of Homeland Security, 20 March 2003. Contact listed on bulletin is FBI Special Agent Gary Harter of the Washington Field Office.
10. Ibid.
11. "An Everyday Threat at Home: Significant Terrorist Incident Locations During Two Weeks in 2002," Terrorism Job Aids, For Official Use Only, Department of Homeland Security, December 2003. The Department of Homeland Security has distributed this document among law enforcement officials to demonstrate the need for continued vigilance on a daily basis. The map shows a high degree of terrorist incidents in the U.S. during just a two-week period after 9/11.
12. "Terrorist Cells Operating Within the United States," Terrorism Job Aids, For Official Use Only, Department of Homeland Security, December 2003.
13. "Places with 10,000 or More Population and With 1,000 or More Persons of Arab Ancestry: 2000," Census 2000 Demographic Profile prepared for the Department of Homeland Security, Table DP-2, August 2002, December 2003.

CHAPTER 7—The Facilitators
1. Report of the Joint Inquiry into 9/11, 168.
2. Ibid., 169.
3. Ibid., 171.
4. *The 9/11 Commission Report* (New York: W.W. Norton, 2004), 515.
5. Report of the Joint Inquiry into 9/11, 172, 174.
6. Ibid., 177.
7. Report of the Joint Inquiry into 9/11, 180.
8. *The 9/11 Commission Report*, 517.
9. Ibid., 215.
10. Report of the Joint Inquiry into 9/11, 326, 182,183. Also, *The 9/11 Commission Report*, 521.
11. Report of the Joint Inquiry into 9/11, 172.
12. *The 9/11 Commission Report*, 230.
13. Transcript of Mueller testimony, Senate Select Intelligence Committee, Washington D.C., 11 February 2003.
14. James Blitz, "Leaked Papers Warn of al-Qaida Support," *Financial Times*, 31 May 2004.
15. Report of the Joint Inquiry into 9/11, 29.

CHAPTER 8—The Wahhabi Corridor
1. "Skyline Towers the Axis of Evil," Skyline Towers review, www.apartmentratings.com, 17 July 2003.
2. "Don't Move In," Skyline Towers review, www.apartmentratings.com, 28 October 2003. Skyline is located at 5597 (north tower) and 5601 (south tower) Seminary Road, which runs behind Highway 7, also called Leesburg Pike. The 5913 Leesburg Pike address the hijackers

used to obtain their Virginia drivers licenses was fake, the address of a Hispanic male who was part of their scheme to obtain state IDs. The unit at that address is in a small red-brick apartment building occupied primarily by Hispanic immigrants. Skyline Towers is farther down Leesburg Pike toward Alexandria. Though its property borders Leesburg Pike, its main entrance is on Seminary Road behind Leesburg Pike.

3. "Third World Ghetto," Skyline Towers review, www.apartmentratings.com, 25 January 2004.

4. "Giant towing complex with new response!" Skyline Towers review, www.apartmentratings.com, 21 November 2002. Just 1 in 5 tenants have recommended the complex overall, according to Apartment Ratings.

5. "This Place Sucks Big Time," Skyline Towers review, www.apartmentratings.com, 28 May 2003.

6. "Skyline Towers the Axis of Evil," Skyline Towers review, www.apartmentratings.com, 17 July 2003.

7. Posting by Joye in response to, "9/11: Do You Have a Memory to Share?" Moms in Their 20s Discussion Board, www.pregnancytoday.com, 11 September 2003.

8. "Skyline Towers the Axis of Evil," Skyline Towers review.

9. Center for Immigration Studies analysis of public use file of Census 2000 Supplemental Survey.

10. http://www.washingtonislamicacademy.org/about.html.

11. "Places with 10,000 or More Population and With 1,000 or More Persons of Arab Ancestry: 2000," Census 2000 Demographic Profile prepared for the Department of Homeland Security, Table DP-2, August 2002, December 2003. Baileys Crossroads is a Census Designated Place, or CDP.

12. "Supplemental Declaration in Support of Pre-Trial Detention," United States of America v. Soliman S. Biheiri, United States District Court for the Eastern District of Virginia, Alexandria Division, 11 September 2003, 9.

13. The WAMY office at 5134 Leesburg Pike in Alexandria bustled with activity the day I visited it last summer. Muslim women filed in and out, dressed in head-to-toe black *abayas*, and a couple of young, Western-dressed Middle Eastern men pulled up in a fancy sedan. Visitors walking into the foyer are greeted by a big poster hanging on the wall at the foot of the stairs. Titled "What Do Muslims Think about Jesus?" it is part of a Saudi campaign to reach out to Christians. A "Virginia C.O.P.S. 2003" sticker is attached to a pane on the front-door window, something donors get when they give to the Virginia Coalition of Police and Deputy Sheriffs. It must have given FBI and Customs agents a chuckle when they raided the place.

14. Noreen S. Ahmed-Ullah, Kim Barker, Laurie Cohen, Stephen Franklin, Sam Roe, "Struggle for the Soul of Islam," *Chicago Tribune*, 8 February 2004, A1.

15. Five years earlier, the homeowners association for his Walnut Hill subdivision filed a lien against his property for unpaid dues, records also show.

16. The Form 990 tax return that nonprofit International Relief Organization filed with the IRS in 1998 says it spent more than $90,000 on eight computers, a printer, a copy machine, a fax machine, a phone security system, furniture, and, curiously, a "video camera."

17. Declaration in Support of Pre-Trial Detention, U.S. v. Soliman S. Biheiri, U.S. District Court for the Eastern District of Virginia, 14 August 2003, 3-6.

18. IRS Form 990 filed by International Relief Organization, 2000, 2.

19. "Places with 10,000 or More Population and With 1,000 or More Persons of Arab Ancestry: 2000," Census 2000 Demographic Profile.

20. Matthew Barakat, "Saudi in Va. Pleas Guilty to Fraud," Associated Press, 19 August 2002. Also, Bret Ladine, "Saudi Man with Hub Ties Held in Alleged Test-Taking Plot," *Boston Globe*, 29 June 2002, A3. Also, Tim McGlone, "Local Man Sentenced, Deported for Scam," *Virginian-Pilot*, 16 May 2003, A1.

21. Jerry Seper, "Saudi Accused of Taking English Tests for Illegals," *Washington Times*, 26 June 2002, A1.

22. McGlone, "Local Man Sentenced, Deported for Scam."

23. Barakat, "Saudi in Va. Pleas Guilty to Fraud."

24. Author interview with both Neuperts at their home, September 14, 2001.

25. Author interview by phone, September 14, 2001.
26. Author interview with Vienna police detective, 2002.
27. Recent search of Metropolitan Regional Information Systems (MLS) real estate database.
28. Fairfax County land records also show an electrician in 1994 filed a lien against Keshavarznia's property at 502 Orrin Street for unpaid work he did installing an "outdoor hot tub."
29. "Terrorist Cells Operating Within the United States," Terrorism Job Aids, For Official Use Only, Department of Homeland Security, December 2003.
30. Affidavit in Support of Application for Search Warrant, 53.
31. Ibid., 35, 36.
32. Mary Jacoby, "Muslim linked to Al-Arian Trained Military Chaplains," *St. Petersburg Times*, 27 March 2003, A7.
33. A sister think tank to IIIT called the Graduate School of Islamic and Social Sciences, which has endorsed chaplains for the Pentagon, also is still operating, despite being raided by the feds. Its offices are even more secluded. GSISS, run by al-Alwani and Mirza, is located in a generic-looking office park near the end of a small airport runway in the middle of horse country in neighboring Loudoun County. It too is near Highway 7, which turns from Leesburg Pike into Harry Byrd Highway at the Loudoun County-Fairfax County line.
34. Rebecca Carr, Eunice Moscoso, "Safa Group Charities Scrutinized for Alleged Terror Ties," Cox News Service, 13 November 2003. Also, Rebecca Carr, Bill Torpy, "Terror Money Trail Pursued," *Atlanta Journal-Constitution*, 30 June 2004, A1.
35. Susan Schmidt, "Spreading Saudi Fundamentalism in U.S.," *Washington Post*, 2 October 2003, 1.

CHAPTER 9—The Muslim Mafia

1. Author interview by phone, 12 August 2004.
2. Paul Findley, *Silent No More* (Beltsville, Md.: Amana Publications, 2001), 259, 260.
3. "Declaration in Support of Pre-Trial Detention," U.S. vs. Soliman S. Biheiri, U.S. District Court for the Eastern District of Virginia, 14 August 2003, 3.
4. Author interview by email, 13 March 2003.
5. Affidavit in Support of Application for Search Warrant, Appendix. Attached to the affidavit, this law enforcement document shows the matrix of the Safa group entities and officers.
6. U.S. Department of Justice press release, 18 December 2002.
7. "FBI Raids Muslim and Arab Web-Hosting Company," *Arab American News*, 14 September 2001, 2.
8. Supplemental Declaration in Support of Pre-Trial Detention, U.S. v. Soliman S. Biheiri, U.S. District Court for the Eastern District of Virginia, 11 September 2003, 8. WAMY has a Camps and Conferences Unit for Muslim children ages 14-18. The unit publishes a book, *Islamic Camps: Objectives, Program Outlines and Preparatory Steps*, which teaches children to not be "miserly with your blood" in fighting the infidels during jihad.
9. Ahmed Yousef, "Muslim Leadership Under Siege," *The American Muslim*, February 2004, 22.
10. Falasten M. Abdeljabbar, "Alamoudi—What His Case Means to Muslims," *The American Muslim*, February 2004, 21.

CHAPTER 10—Interfaith Phoniness

1. John L. Esposito, *The Islamic Threat* (New York, N.Y.: Oxford University Press, 1999), 238.
2. Ibid., 270.
3. Ibid., 238.
4. Paul Findley, *Silent No More* (Beltsville, Md.: Amana Publications, 2001), 182.
5. Muzammil Siddiqi, "Basic Principles of Involvement in War in Islam," *The Message International*, February 1991.
6. Richard H. Curtiss, "American Muslims Ready to Fight Back Against USA PATRIOT Act," *Washington Report on Middle East Affairs*, November 2003, 29.
7. "Esposito Speaks at CAIR Event," *Washington Report on Middle East Affairs*, 31 December 2001, 56.

8. Mary Beth Sheridan, Douglas Farah, "Jailed Muslim Had Made a Name in Washington," *Washington Post*, 1 December 2003, A1.

9. Press release by The Interfaith Alliance, 7 October 2004.

10. Esposito, 281-283.

11. IRS Form 990, Foundation for Muslim-Christian Understanding, Washington, D.C., attachments, 1997, 1998.

12. Eleanor Kennelly, "Catholic Georgetown Mecca for Islamic Study," *Washington Times*, 7 February 1996, C8.

CHAPTER 11—Sanctuaries of Terror

1. Jennifer Lin, Mark Faziollah, Maria Panaritis, Jeff Shields, "Tracing the Case of the 'Virginia Jihad,'" *Philadelphia Inquirer*, 25 July 2003, A1.

2. "We have overseas suppliers in West Africa, but we do not purchase at all from Saudi Arabia," Sunoco spokesman Gerald Davis told me. Not a drop? "That's correct." Paul Sperry, "Sunoco Pumps Saudi-Free Gas," WorldNetDaily.com, 1 May 2002.

3. Transcript of testimony by Stephen Schwartz, senior fellow, Foundation for Defense of Democracies, before the Terrorism, Technology and Homeland Security Subcommittee of the Senate Judiciary Committee, Dirksen Senate Office Building, Room 226, Washington, D.C., 26 June 2003. Schwartz estimates that the number of places of Islamic worship in the U.S. is closer to six thousand if small prayer centers and Islamic education centers are included with official recognized major mosques.

4. American Muslim Poll, Zogby International, November/December 2001.

5. Ibid. The Zogby results show 57 percent of American Muslims want to be able to express political opinions in the mosque.

6. Indictment, U.S. v. Holy Land Foundation for Relief and Development, U.S. District Court for the Northern District of Texas, 26 July 2004, 13.

7. Clyde Mark, Kenneth Katzman, "Hamas and Palestinian Islamic Jihad: Recent Developments, Sources of Support, and Implications for U.S. Policy," Congressional Research Service, Library of Congress, 12 December 1994.

8. Author interview by phone, 12 August 2004.

9. Author interview by email, 12 March 2003.

10. Author interview by phone, 13 August 2004.

11. Affidavit in Support of Application for Search Warrant, 71, 72, 90.

12. Author interviews by phone, in person, February 2004.

13. Author interviews by phone and email with former FBI Special Agent John Vincent, Chicago Field Office, August 2004. Also, Noreen S. Ahmed-Ullah, Kim Barker, Laurie Cohen, Stephen Franklin, Sam Roe, "Struggle for the Soul of Islam," *Chicago Tribune*, 8 February 2004, C1.

14. Ibid.

15. Paul Sperry, "American al-Qaida Suspect's Imam Headed Probed Group," WorldNetDaily.com, 29 May 2004.

16. *The 9/11 Commission Report* (New York: W.W. Norton, 2004), 220.

17. Indictment, U.S. v. Randall Todd Royer, U.S. District Court for the Eastern District of Virginia, June 2003, 17, 24.

18. Ibid., 23.

19. Lin et al., "Tracing the Case of the 'Virginia Jihad.'"

20. Sarah Downy, Michael Hirsh, "A Safe Haven?" *Newsweek*, 30 September 2002.

21. Author interview by phone, 16 May 2003.

22. Affidavit in Support of Application for Search Warrant, 32.

23. Michael Isikoff, "New Questions about Saudi Money—And Bandar," *Newsweek*, 12 April 2004.

CHAPTER 12—The 9/11 Mosque

1. Author interview with Needham at her home, 2 September 2004.

2. Fairfax County, Virginia, recorded deed agreement between Nina S. Macarow, grantor, and the North American Islamic Trust, grantee, 10 June 1983. The mosque also got financial assistance directly from the Saudi Embassy. "Saudi gave them money from the beginning. It has a Wahhabi influence," says Ali al-Ahmed of the Washington-based Saudi Institute, a leading Wahhabi opposition group, in a 13 February 2004, phone interview.

   The mosque's founders chiseled a rather boorish invitation to non-Muslims into the front wall of its new building. Borrowed from the Quran, it reads: "IN THE NAME OF GOD: Say: O people of the Book! come to common terms as between us and you: that we worship none but Allah; that we associate no partners with Him; that we erect not from among ourselves Lords and patrons other than Allah. If then they turn back say: Bear witness that we at least are Muslims bowing to Allah's will." People of the Book are Jews and Christians. In other words, come to your senses, *kaffirs*, and convert to Islam. After 9/11, Dar al-Hijrah tried to strike up an interfaith dialogue with area churches. The neighboring Church of Christ, for one, was willing to participate—that is, until the mosque wanted its pastor and flock to accept Islam.

3. Author interview with Needham at her home, 2 September 2004.

4. Minutes of meeting on Special Exception Application SE 93-M-022 (Dar al-Hijrah Islamic Center Inc.), Fairfax County Board of Supervisors, 27 September 1993. The board denied the mosque's special-permit application for coordinated parking on the parcel of land adjacent to Needham. But it approved a shared parking agreement with the churches, which allows the mosque to use 120 parking spaces at the Church of Christ and 70 parking spaces at the First Christian Church during Friday afternoon prayer services, giving it nearly 200 additional spaces. Under the agreement, the mosque must provide an off-duty police officer to direct traffic at the intersection of Row Street and Leesburg Pike on Friday afternoons. Permission can be rescinded at any time by the churches.

5. Author interview by phone, 4 August 2003.

6. Fairfax County, Virginia, recorded Deed of Dedication (for subdivision) signed by Dr. Jamal al-Barzinji, Secretary, North American Islamic Trust Inc., 10 December 1986.

7. Affidavit in Support of Application for Search Warrant, 39.

8. Fairfax County land records show several subcontractors filed liens against Hadid Construction Inc. for claims totaling well over $300,000.

9. Associated Press, 9 September 1998.

10. Jonathan Wells, Kevin Wisniewski, "Hub Islamic Leader's Radical Links Run Deep," *Boston Herald*, 14 January 2004, A1. Also, Judith Miller, "U.S. Examines Donations of 2 Saudis to Determine If They Aided Terrorism," *New York Times*, 25 March 2002, A12.

11. Associated Press, 2 July 2002, citing a 1995 memorandum filed in federal court by former U.S. Attorney Mary Jo White.

12. Brendan Lyons, "Imam Retains Local Support," *The Times Union (Albany, N.Y.)*, 14 July 2002, A1.

13. Affidavit in Support of Application for Search Warrant, 26 (which cites FBI memo to the Department of Treasury's Office of Foreign Assets Control, dated 5 November 2001). Also, Lyons, "Imam Retains Local Support."

14. Author interview by phone, 12 August 2003.

15. Ibid.

16. Author interview by email with Mike Tune, pulpit minister, Church of Christ in Falls Church, and director, Amazing Grace International, 13 August 2003.

17. Gayle Reaves, Steve McGonigle, "Paper Trail Leads to Hamas," *Dallas Morning News*, 8 April 1996, A1.

18. Forfeiture Agreement, U.S. v. Ismail S. Elbarasse, U.S. District Court for the District of Maryland, August 2004, 1.

19. Noreen S. Ahmed-Ullah, Sam Roe, Laurie Cohen, "A Rare Look at Secretive Brotherhood in America," *Chicago Tribune*, 19 September 2004, A1. Former Brotherhood leader Ahmed Elkadi, an Egyptian-born surgeon and a former personal physician to Saudi Arabia's King Faisal, is listed as a founding director of the Muslim American Society on the incorporation papers the society filed with the state of Virginia. In a letter to the *Chicago Tribune* editor,

dated 26 September 2004, Muslim American Society President Esam Omeish did not deny links to the Brotherhood.

20. Ashraf Nubani, "Hunger Striking Muslim Activist Honored By His Community," *Washington Report on Middle East Affairs*, December 1998, 104-108.

21. Forfeiture Agreement, U.S. v. Abdelhaleem Hasan Abdelraziq Ashqar, U.S. District Court for the Northern District of Illinois, 28 October 2003.

22. Affidavit in Support of Application for Search Warrant, 26.

23. Dan Eggen, Jerry Markon, "Hamas Leader, 2 Others Indicted," *Washington Post*, 21 August 2004, A4.

24. Valerie Strauss, Emily Wax, "Where Two Worlds Collide" *Washington Post*, 25 February 2002, A1. Dar al-Hijrah also coordinates youth activities with WAMY, a Saudi-based group that teaches Muslim children to hate Jews.

25. Caryle Murphy, "Protesters Seek Release of Saudi Prisoner," *Washington Post*, 18 June 2004, B3.

CHAPTER 13—The 9/11 Imam

1. "Subject: Responding to Potential Terrorists Seeking Entry Into the United States," Customs and Border Protection directive, Department of Homeland Security, 23 February 2004.

2. "Eneral Hajj 2001 Tentative Itinerary Executive Short Program," Dar El-Eiman for Hajj and Umrah, Washington, D.C., 19 March 2001.

3. In a 24 August 2004, interview with me, Holy Land Foundation lawyer John Boyd dismissed the charges as groundless: "If the charges were not so serious and if it were not so easy to convict Arab-Americans of crimes today, the charges would be almost humorous."

4. *The 9/11 Commission Report* (New York: W.W. Norton, 2004), 230.

5. *The 9/11 Commission Report*, 221, 230.

6. Immigration and Naturalization Service, Central Index System, ID#:A29435013, A#:029435013, search conducted 2003; results in data field state, "COB: Aden [Yemen]."

7. New Mexico became a closed-record state after enacting a law making birth and death records secret, ostensibly to prevent identity theft. Such information normally is not available to the general public or press, a fact of which Aulaqi may be acutely aware. The search by state officials for Aulaqi's alleged birth records was conducted at the request of a private investigator working for a law firm in neighboring El Paso, Texas. While Aulaqi does have a Social Security number (which I have but will not reproduce here), it does not necessarily mean he was born in the U.S. He would have had to have obtained a Social Security number to work in the U.S. and report taxes after arriving here in 1990. In fact, law enforcement records show he obtained it that same year. If Aulaqi is a U.S. citizen, he likely received his citizenship through naturalization, not birth.

8. *The 9/11 Commission Report*, 517.

9. *The 9/11 Commission Report*, footnote 33, 517.

10. Aulaqi had still-other ties to extremists. For instance, an individual who attempted to post bond for alleged twentieth hijacker Zacarias Moussaoui's roommate was closely associated with a friend of Aulaqi in San Diego. Abdulqaadir Menepta, a member of the Muslim Brotherhood who recruited for a radical Palestinian group, had been the subject of a full-field FBI international terrorism investigation. He recently served time on weapons charges. And Aulaqi has had run-ins with local police, as well. According to the Copley News Service, he had been a criminal defendant in two separate cases tried in San Diego Municipal Court. In one, he pleaded no contest to charges of soliciting prostitution, and was fined and put on probation.

11. Joe Cantlupe, Dana Wilkie, "Former San Diego Islamic Spiritual Leaders Defends Mosque," Copley News Service, 28 September 2001.

12. Brian Handwerk, Zain Habboo, "Attack on America: An Islamic Scholar's Perspective—Part 1," *National Geographic*, 28 September 2001.

13. Handwerk, Habboo, "Attack on America: An Islamic Scholar's Perspective—Part 2," *National Geographic*, 28 September 2001.

14. Ralph Z. Hallow, Vaishali Honawar, "Muslim Students are Wary of the War," *Washington Times*, 11 October 2001, A1.

15. Cantlupe and Wilkie, "Former San Diego Islamic Spiritual Leaders Defends Mosque."

16. "Understanding Ramadan," Live Online Q&A with Imam Anwar Al-Awlaki, Falls Church Dar Al-Hijrah Islamic Center, WashingtonPost.com, 19 November 2001.

17. Transcript of interview with Aulaqi by Neal Conan, "Muslim-American Viewpoint," *Talk of the Nation*, NPR, 15 November 2001.

18. Ibid.

19. Laurie Goodstein, "Some Muslims Say Tape Removes Previous Doubt," *New York Times*, 15 December 2001, B6.

20. Liza Mundy, "The Politician: Finding the Right Words," *Washington Post Magazine*, 4 November 2001, 24.

21. George Washington University spokesman Andre Fletcher says Aulaqi enrolled in a Ph.D. program in January 2001. He was a candidate for a doctorate in human resources development. His last date of attendance was December 2001. He did not re-enroll, and was not awarded a degree, Fletcher says.

22. The known residences listed for Aulaqi in the government's dossier on him, include three in Fort Collins, Colorado, two in Denver, Colorado, two in San Diego, California, and three in Falls Church, Virginia.

23. TECS II—Person Subject Display, TECS Record ID: P9C38736100CHO, entry 12 July 2002.

24. TECS II—Person Subject Display, TECS Record ID: P9C38736100CDC, entry 12 June 2002.

25. TECS II—Person Subject Display, TECS Record ID: P9C38736100CDC, entry 19 July 2002.

26. TECS II—Incident Log, Incident Report No.: 20034701000079, entry 10 October 2002.

27. *The 9/11 Commission Report*, 557.

28. President Bush—whose family is unusually close to Prince Bandar—censored an entire twenty-seven-page section of the 9/11 congressional report implicating the Saudi government in the attacks.

29. Author interview by phone, 13 February 2004.

30. *The 9/11 Commission Report*, 517. Investigators have not ruled out the possibility that al-Bayoumi lent the hijackers his phone that day (February 4, 2000).

31. http://www.astrolabe.com/products/viewitem.php?id=1449.

32. Attempts to reach Aulaqi were unsuccessful. He did not respond to repeated requests for interviews sent to two email addresses he is known to use: al_aulaqi@yahoo.com and aal-awlaki@al-basheer.com.

33. Report of the Joint Inquiry into 9/11, 179.

34. "Outline of the 9/11 Plot," Staff Statement No. 16, The 9/11 Commission, 16 June 2004, 8.

35. *The 9/11 Commission Report*, 517.

CHAPTER 14—Congress and the FBI

1. Paul Sperry, "Democrat Hampered FBI Probe in Detroit," WorldNetDaily.com, 13 March 2003.

2. Paul Sperry, "Leahy Blocked Key Anti-Terror Reforms," WorldNetDaily.com, 5 June 2002.

3. "Countering the Changing Threat of International Terrorism," National Commission on Terrorism, 5 June 2000.

4. Paul Sperry, "Leahy Blocked Key Anti-Terror Reforms," WorldNetDaily.com, 5 June 2002.

5. Ibid.

6. Ibid.

7. Ibid.

8. Ibid.

9. Sperry, "Democrat Hampered FBI Probe in Detroit."

10. Ibid.

11. Bonior, now a professor at Wayne State University in Detroit, declined comment.

CHAPTER 15—Institutionalized PC

1. Author interview by phone, 17 October 2002.

2. Ibid.

3. "Law Enforcement, Counterterrorism, and Intelligence Collection in the United States Prior to 9/11," Staff Statement No. 9, The 9-11 Commission, April 13, 2004, 4-9.

4. Author interview by email, 14 March 2003.

5. "Law Enforcement, Counterterrorism, and Intelligence Collection in the United States Prior to 9/11."

6. Paul Sperry, "Why FBI Missed Islamic Threat," WorldNetDaily.com, 25 July 2002.

7. Paul Sperry, "FBI bureaucrats got top bonuses," WorldNetDaily.com, 6 June 2002.

8. Paul Sperry, "Freeh: 'Right-wing' Groups Bigger Threat," WorldNetDaily.com, 7 October 2002.

9. Michael Dobbs, "An Obscure Chief in U.S. War on Terror," Washington Post, 2 April 2000, A1. Three months after Y2K, and long before 9/11, Clarke was quoted in the article as saying, prophetically, with respect to al-Qaida, "They will come after our weakness, our Achilles heel, which is largely here in the United States." And referring to bin Laden, he advised: "It's not enough to be in a cat-and-mouse game, warning about his plots. If we keep that up, we will someday fail. We need to seriously think about doing more. Our goal should be to so erode his network of organizations that they no longer pose a serious threat."

10. Richard A. Clarke, Against All Enemies (New York: Free Press, 2004), 217. Also, Michael Isikoff, Mark Hosenball, "How Clarke 'Outsourced' Terror Intel," Newsweek, 31 March 2004.

11. "Domestic Terrorism," Muster Module: Briefing Notes, For Official Use Only, Department of Homeland Security, January 2004. Also, "Domestic Terrorism," Muster Module: Handout #1, January 2004; and "Domestic Terrorism Fact Sheet," Muster Module: Handout #2, January 2004, 1-4.

12. Ibid.

13. http://www.fbi.gov/pressrel/pressrel01/102301.htm.

14. Larry Lipman, "Author Links Anthrax Attacks to Hijackers," Palm Beach Post, 3 October 2003, A7.

15. Steve Fainaru, Ceci Connolly, "Memo on Florida Case Roils Anthrax Probe; Experts Debate Theory Hijacker Was Exposed," Washington Post, 29 March 2002, A3.

16. The 9/11 Commission Report (New York: W.W. Norton, 2004), 51, 490.

17. Curiously, the FBI has not publicly released the test results or disclosed if the testing included rental cars and any personal belongings of the hijackers they recovered.

18. Paul Sperry, "Police Tried to Make Eyewitness Doubt Initial ID," WorldNetDaily.com, 1 April 2003. The Washington Post company confirmed Cribbin's story on pages 15 and 16 of its book, Sniper: Inside the Hunt for the Killers Who Terrorized the Nation, which was released in October 2003.

19. Ibid.

20. Author interview by phone, 27 March 2003.

21. Author interview by phone, 18 March 2003.

22. Transcript of Moose news conference, 15 October 2002.

23. Paul Sperry, "Revealed: Secret Sniper Stakeout," WorldNetDaily.com, 19 March 2003.

24. Author interviews by email and phone with Tim Carter of Vienna, Virginia, 25 October 2002, 29 October 2002, 30 October 2002; and Mark Fanning of Virginia, 30 October 2002.

25. Transcript of interview with Charles Moose, Dateline, NBC News, 14 September 2003.

26. Smith singled out for criticism former FBI profiler Clint Van Zandt, who was one of the famously inaccurate pundits pontificating on TV during the sniper scare. "Clint Van Zandt spent most of his career in a lab at Quantico," he says. "He's probably never been to a crime scene."

CHAPTER 16—Jews Need Not Apply To Fight Terror

1. Paul Sperry, "Jews Need Not Apply to Fight Terror," FrontPageMagazine.com, 26 November 2003.

2. Ibid.

3. Ibid. Also, Letter to FBI Director Mueller from Reps. Weiner and Pallone, 13 November 2003. Separately, Rep. Pallone also fired off a letter to Attorney General John Ashcroft. Dated

20 October 2003, it states: "Arabic translation is a critical component of anti-terrorism investigations and it has been widely reported that the FBI faces a backlog of untranslated Arabic documents and recorded conversations. I find it outrageous that, despite a shortage of Arabic-speaking translators, none of the Jewish applicants met FBI qualifications. . . . It is my worry that the FBI denied their employment solely because of their religion."

4. I first wrote about the controversy on 9 October 2003 for WorldNetDaily.com.
5. A spokeswoman for Gullota did not return phone calls.
6. Sperry, "Jews Need Not Apply to Fight Terror."
7. Ibid.
8. Author interview by email, 1 October 2003.
9. Letter by Alfassa to Balin, and copied to Jim Margolin of the FBI's New York field office, 10 October 2003, 2, 3.

CHAPTER 17—The Mole House
1. Author interview by phone, 3 October 2004.
2. Author interviews by phone, 3 October 2004 and 30 October 2004.
3. *The 9/11 Commission Report* (New York: W.W. Norton, 2004), 64, 134, 503.
4. Transcript of remarks by FBI Director Robert Mueller at the American Muslim Council's 11th Convention, Alexandria, Virginia, 28 June 2002.
5. CNN, 19 June 2002.
6. *The 9/11 Commission Report*, 473.
7. Author interview by phone, 28 October 2003.
8. Edmonds says Stephanie Bryan, a supervisor at the Washington field office at the time, told her and other linguists about the scandal contemporaneously in early 2002. Bryan denies it.
9. Author interview by phone, 30 October 2004.
10. "A Review of Allegations of a Double Standard of Discipline at the FBI," U.S. Department of Justice Office of the Inspector General, 15 November 2002, 24.
11. Letter from Edmonds' attorney David K. Colapinto to Pentagon inspector general Joseph E. Schmitz, 19 September 2002.
12. "Complaint for Declaratory and Injunctive Relief and for Damages," Sibel Edmonds v. U.S. Department of Justice, U.S. District Court for the District of Columbia, 22 July 2002, 5, 6.
13. Edmonds letter to Beryl Howell, Office of Senator Leahy, 28 March 2002.
14. Letter from Leahy and Grassley to then Attorney General Ashcroft, 13 August 2002. Letter notes that the FBI "downplayed the importance" of Edmonds' allegations even after verifying them. Instead of investigating the security breaches, the bureau complained that Edmonds was "causing trouble." The senators also note that Turkish translator Dickerson mistranslated material related to a foreign target with whom the translator had contact. In an unusual move, the Department of Justice, retroactively classified the letter. The suspect translator left the country the following month.
15. Letter from Edmonds to White House Counsel Alberto Gonzales, 3 September 2002.
16. Letter from Colapinto to Pentagon Inspector General Joseph E. Schmitz, 19 September 2002. Edmonds' current attorney is Mark Zaid.
17. Letter from North to Edmonds, 10 September 2002.
18. IRS Form 990, 2002, 14, 15.
19. Transcript of interview with Grassley, *60 Minutes*, CBS News, 13 July 2003.
20. Letter from FBI Director Robert Mueller to Sen. Orrin G. Hatch, chairman, Senate Judiciary Committee, summarizing classified inspector general's report, 21 July 2004. Government redacted portions of the letter.
21. Letter from Sibel D. Edmonds to Senate Judiciary Committee and the 9/11 Commission, 6 January 2004, 5.
22. Ibid.
23. Author interview in person, Falls Church, Virginia, 9 August 2004.

24. Transcript of testimony of U.S. Attorney Patrick Fitzgerald before The 9/11 Commission, 16 June 2004.

25. Letter to Glenn Fine, inspector general, Department of Justice, 8 November 2004.

26. "Reforming Law Enforcement, Counterterrorism, and Intelligence Collection in the United States," Staff Statement No. 12, The 9/11 Commission, 14 April 2003, 5.

27. "Complaint for Declaratory and Injunctive Relief and for Damages," Sibel Edmonds v. U.S. Department of Justice, 17.

28. Letter to Edmonds from FBI contracting officer Cynthia W. Wills, 2 April 2002.

29. Letter from Director Robert Mueller to Sen. Orrin G. Hatch, chairman, Senate Judiciary Committee, 21 July 2004. Letter summarizes hundred-page classified inspector general's report, "A Review of the FBI's Actions in Connection with Allegations Raised by Contract Linguist Sibel Edmonds," 1 July 2004. Government redacted portions of Mueller's letter.

30. Author interview with Holy Land Foundation attorney John Boyd by email, 24 August 2004.

31. Gail Sheehy, "Whistleblower Coming in Cold from the FBI," *New York Observer*, 26 January 2004, A1.

32. "Control Over Weapons and Laptop Computers," Department of Justice, Summary Report, Report No. 02-31, August 2002.

33. "A Review of the FBI's Performance In Deterring, Detecting and Investigating the Espionage Activities of Robert Philip Hanssen," unclassified executive summary, Office of the Inspector General, Department of Justice, August 2003, 21.

CHAPTER 18—The Case of the Reluctant Agent

1. Author interview by phone, 12 August 2004.

2. Author interview by phone, 4 November 2004.

3. Author interview with FBI Special Agent John Vincent by phone, 13 August 2004. Also, Michael Fechter, "FBI Agent Who Refused to Tape al-Arian is Suspended," *Tampa Tribune*, 4 March 2003, A5.

4. UPI, 13 October 2004.

5. "Declaration in Support of Pre-Trial Detention," United States v. Soliman S. Biheiri, U.S. District Court for the Eastern District of Virginia, 14 August 2003, 5, 6, 10.

6. "A Review of U.S. Counterterrorism Policy: American Muslim Critique and Recommendations," Muslim Public Affairs Council, Interview with the FBI Director, 24 April 2003, Appendix H, 97.

CHAPTER 19—The Iranian Informant

1. Paul Sperry, "9-11 Panel to Probe FBI Informant's Tip," WorldNetDaily.com, 6 April 2004. When I first broke this story last spring, which has been confirmed by the mainstream media, it was met with violent reaction at the FBI. I got an unusually angry phone call from Debbie Weierman, the official spokesperson for the FBI's Washington field office. Here is a transcript of the conversation:

WEIERMAN: Mr. Sperry, this is Debbie Weierman of the FBI. I have in front of me your article. You put outright lies in your article.

SPERRY: Like what?

WEIERMAN: I'm talking in generalities. I'm not going to get into a pissing contest with you, Mr. Sperry.

SPERRY: Well, wait a minute. If there's a "lie," as you say—

WEIERMAN:—Mr. Sperry—

SPERRY:—or any factual inaccuracy in the story, we need to correct it.

WEIERMAN: Mr. Sperry, listen to me. I don't like working with you. I don't like your spurious and scurious [sic] complaints. I don't like your misrepresentation of the FBI.

SPERRY: Well, I can't do anything if you can't tell me what—

WEIERMAN: DON'T TRY TO BAIT ME! Because I'm not going to take your bait! I'm just saying you should be ashamed of yourself how you print lies about the FBI! THAT'S

ALL I HAVE TO SAY! [click]

Three months later, the *Chicago Tribune* confirmed my story about the pre-9/11 tip through follow-up interviews with Sarshar and federal law enforcement officials. John Crewdson, "As U.S. Steps Up Investigation, Iran Denies Assisting al-Qaida," *Chicago Tribune*, 21 July 2004, A1.

2. Author interview by phone, 4 April 2004.
3. *The 9/11 Commission Report* (New York: W.W. Norton, 2004), 241.
4. "Outline of 9/11 Plot," Staff Statement No. 16, The 9/11 Commission, 16 June 2004, 19.
5. Report of the Joint Inquiry into 9/11, 211.
6. Author interview by phone, 26 March 2004.

CHAPTER 20—The Prison Powder Keg

1. "A Review of the Federal Bureau of Prisons' Selection of Muslim Religious Services Providers," Office of the Inspector General, U.S. Department of Justice, unclassified version, April 2004, 55.
2. Ibid., 35.
3. James M. Odato, "Cleric Battles for His Credibility," *The Times Union (Albany, New York)*, 7 February 2003, A1.
4. Transcript of remarks by Sen. Charles Schumer, D-NY, Senate Subcommittee on Terrorism, Technology and Homeland Security, 26 June 2003.
5. Umar protested the move, calling it unfair, and is fighting for reinstatement. His defense committee, Bethlehem Neighbors for Peace (www.bethlehemforpeace.org), says he was "attacked" because he is "a person who is black and a Muslim." It also insists he is a victim of "guilt by association," and that some of his comments were "taken out of context." However, he appears unrepentant. "If you want to end terrorism," he says through the group, "you need to look at the real reasons why many people hate and fear the U.S."
6. "Review of the Federal Bureau of Prisons' Selection of Muslim Religious Services Providers," 48.
7. Eric Lichtblau, "Report Warns of Infiltration by al-Qaida in U.S. Prisons," *New York Times*, 5 May 2004.
8. "Review of the Federal Bureau of Prisons' Selection of Muslim Religious Services Providers," 22, 23.
9. Ibid., 42.
10. Ibid., 41.
11. Ibid., 8.
12. Ibid., 35
13. American Muslim Poll, Zogby International, November/December 2001.
14. Paul Findley, *Silent No More* (Beltsville, Md.: Amana Publications, 2001), 49.
15. Rose-Marie Armstrong, "Turning to Islam: African-American Conversion Stories," *The Christian Century*, 12 July 2003, 18.
16. Transcript of interview, *Hardball with Chris Matthews*, MSNBC, 27 June 2002.
17. Paul Moses, "Chaplain Charges Bias in Riot Case," *Newsday*, 16 June 1992, 23.
18. "Muslim Chaplain Relieved of Duties Counseling Rikers Inmates," Associated Press, 21 March 2003.
19. Transcript of Senate Subcommittee on Terrorism, Technology and Homeland Security, 14 October 2003.
20. "Review of the Federal Bureau of Prisons' Selection of Muslim Religious Services Providers," 34.
21. Ibid., 22.
22. Ibid., 23.
23. Kenneth Lovett, Fredric U. Dicker, Eric Lenkowitz, "Jailhouse Crock," *New York Post*, 6 February 2003, 23.
24. "Review of the Federal Bureau of Prisons' Selection of Muslim Religious Services Providers," 50, 55.
25. http://www.iananet.org/inmate.htm.

26. IRS Form 990, 2002, 2.
27. "Review of the Federal Bureau of Prisons' Selection of Muslim Religious Services Providers," 37.
28. Ibid., 36.
29. Ibid., 55.

CHAPTER 21—The Fifth Column
1. Transcript of testimony by John Pistole, FBI assistant director of counterterrorism, Senate Judiciary Committee's Subcommittee on Terrorism, Technology and Homeland Security, 14 October 2003.
2. Transcript of remarks by Bush at Eid Al-Fitr event at the Islamic Center of Washington, 5 December 2002.
3. Criminal Complaint, U.S. v. Ahmed Fathy Mehalba, U.S. District Court for the District of Massachusetts, 29 September 2003.
4. Ibid.
5. Transcript of testimony by John Pistole, FBI assistant director of counterterrorism, Senate Judiciary Committee's Subcommittee on Terrorism, Technology and Homeland Security, 14 October 2003.
6. Ibid.
7. Ibid.
8. Paul Findley, *Silent No More* (Beltsville, Md.: Amana Publications, 2001), 202.
9. IRS Form 990, International Relief Organization Inc., 2000, 11.
10. Author interview by phone, 28 April 2004.
11. Affidavit in Support of Application for Search Warrant, 36.
12. Muzammil Siddiqi, "Basic Principles of Involvement in War in Islam," *The Message International,* February 1991.
13. http://www.isna.net/idf/newsletter/may2004.htm.
14. Mary Jacoby, "Muslim Linked to Al-Arian Trained Military Chaplains," *St. Petersburg Times,* 27 March 2003, A7.

CHAPTER 22—Loose Nukes
1. Paul Sperry, "Clinton Opened Nuclear Labs to Terrorist-State Visitors," WorldNetDaily.com, 13 December 2001.
2. Author interview by phone and email, 5 January 2004.
3. Sperry, "Clinton Opened Nuclear Labs to Terrorist-State Visitors."
4. "International Collaborations at LANL," Los Alamos National Laboratory, 1999, Appendix B, Exhibit 1.
5. Sperry, "Clinton Opened Nuclear Labs to Terrorist-State Visitors."
6. Ibid.
7. Author interview by phone, 4 August 2004.
8. Associated Press, 11 November 2003.
9. Sperry, "Clinton Opened Nuclear Labs to Terrorist-State Visitors."
10. Ibid.
11. Paul Sperry, "UN Sponsors Arab Tours of U.S. Nuclear Reactors," WorldNetDaily.com, 12 December 2001.
12. Markey press release, 25 March 2002.
13. Sperry, "UN Sponsors Arab Tours of U.S. Nuclear Reactors."
14. Paul Sperry, "Feds Checking Foreigners At Security-Training Class," WorldNetDaily.com, 6 December 2001.

CHAPTER 23—Wudu in the Restroom
1. Ramadan dates are based on a lunar calendar and change each year, making it impossible for employers to schedule a regular annual time for them.

2. The times for the midday and mid-afternoon prayers change throughout the year because the prayers follow the sun, making it difficult for employers to schedule a regular daily time for breaks.
3. http://www.eeoc.gov/facts/backlash-employee.html.
4. "The EEOC is proud to call the ADC a friend and partner," EEOC chair Cari M. Dominguez told the American-Arab Anti-Discrimination Committee last year upon receiving the group's distinguished "Friend in Government" award. EEOC press release, 1 October 2004.
5. Ibid.
6. Author interview by phone, 12 August 2004.
7. *The 9/11 Commission Report* (New York: W.W. Norton, 2004), 3.
8. Ibid.
9. Transcript of testimony by Department of Transportation inspector general Kenneth M. Mead, House Appropriations Committee, 13 February 2002.
10. Author interview by email, 7 January 2002.
11. Paul Sperry, "Airport Security Firm at Mercy of Muslims," WorldNetDaily.com, 9 November 2001.
12. Argenbright press release, 9 November 2001.

CHAPTER 24—Norman "No Profiling" Mineta
1. Author interview by phone, 12 August 2004.
2. Author interview by email, 3 March 2002.
3. Author interview by phone, 12 August 2004.
4. Transcript of testimony of Jose Melendez-Perez, The 9/11 Commission, Hart Senate Office Building, Room 216, Washington, D.C., 26 January 2004.
5. Author interviews by email, 2 June 2004, 10 August 2004. The source, who works for a major airline in Seattle, insisted on remaining nameless.
6. Author interview by email, 2 August 2004.
7. Paul Sperry, "'Fighting Knife' Found in Flight 93 Wreckage," WorldNetDaily.com, 22 March 2002.
8. Transcript of proceedings of the U.S. Commission on Civil Rights, 12 October 2001.
9. Transcript of Mineta interview, *60 Minutes*, CBS, 11 August 2002.
10. Transcript of proceedings of the U.S. Commission on Civil Rights, 12 October 2001.
11. Ibid.
12. Paul Sperry, "TSA Honcho Nixed Islamic Groups in Terror Report," WorldNetDaily.com, 23 July 2002.
13. Transcript Podberesky testimony during proceedings of the U.S. Commission on Civil Rights, 12 October 2001.
14. Transcript of Arpey testimony, The 9/11 Commission, Washington, D.C., 27 January 2004.
15. Paul Sperry, "The Warning Kerry Ignored," *New York Post*, 15 March 2004, 25.

CHAPTER 25—The Dark Lair of CAIR
1. Transcript of interview with Hooper by Rita Cosby, Fox News Channel, 29 October 2001.
2. IRS Form 990, Council on American-Islamic Relations Inc., Washington, D.C., 2001, 1.
3. Paul Findley, *Silent No More* (Beltsville, Md.: Amana Publications, 2001), 217.
4. "Dr. Laura: No Apologies to Muslims Needed," WorldNetDaily.com, 22 November 2003.
5. Awad letter to Sen. Jon Kyl, 9 September 2003.
6. Transcript of testimony of attorney and terrorism expert Matthew Epstein, Senate Judiciary Committee's Subcommittee on Terrorism, Technology and Homeland Security, 10 September 2003.
7. Affidavit in Support of Application for Search Warrant, 26. Also, Action Memorandum from Dale Watson, assistant director of the FBI's counterterrorism division, to Richard Newcomb, U.S. Department of Treasury's Office of Foreign Assets Control, 5 November 2001. John Boyd, a Holy Land Foundation lawyer, insisted in a recent interview by email that the government's charges against his client are without merit and based on faulty Arabic translations from the 1993 meeting.
8. Transcript of testimony of attorney and terrorism expert Matthew Epstein, Senate Judiciary

Committee's Subcommittee on Terrorism, Technology and Homeland Security, 10 September 2003.

9. Indictment, U.S. v. Holy Land Foundation for Relief and Development, Ghassan Elashi, et al., U.S. District Court for the Northern District of Texas, 26 July 2004, 7.

10. IRS Form 990, Council on American-Islamic Relations Inc., Washington, D.C., 2001, 4. Also, Richard H. Curtiss, "Rafeeq Jaber: An Energetic Muslim Visionary and Fearless Palestinian-American Political Activist," *Washington Report on Middle East Affairs*," 30 November 1999, 67. Also, Jonathan Wells, Kevin Wisniewski, "Hub Islamic Leader's Radical Links Run Deep," *Boston Herald*, 14 January 2004, A1.

11. Author interview by phone, 13 August 2004.

12. Steve McGonigle, "'They Were Just Students . . . They Didn't Do Anything'" *Dallas Morning News*, 13 January 2002, J1.

13. Grassley letter to IRS Commissioner Mark Everson, 22 December 2003. The twenty-five audited Islamic charities, all of which have been designated by the Department of Treasury's Office of Foreign Assets Control, are listed as follows:

> The SAAR Foundation and all members and related entities
> Global Relief Foundation (GRF)
> Benevolence International Foundation (BIF)
> Muslim Arab Youth Association (MAYA)
> Muslim Student Association
> Islamic Association for Palestine
> Holy Land Foundation for Relief and Development (HLF)
> Muslim World League
> International Islamic Relief Organization (IIRO) or Internal Relief Organization (IRO)
> Al Haramain Foundation
> Alavi Foundation
> Institute of Islamic and Arabic Science in America (IIASA)
> Islamic Assembly of North American
> Help the Needy
> Islamic Circle of North America (ICNA)
> Islamic Foundation of America
> United Association for Studies and Research (USAR)
> Solidarity International and/or Solidarity USA
> Kind Hearts
> Islamic American Relief Agency and/or Islamic African Relief Agency
> Islamic Society of North America
> International Islamic Relief Organization
> World Assembly of Muslim Youth
> Rabita Trust
> Human Appeal International
> CAIR's Hooper pooh-poohed the investigation as "another fishing expedition solely targeting Muslims in America."

14. IRS Form 990, International (Islamic) Relief Organization (IRO), Washington D.C., 1995, 1997.

15. IRS Form 990, Council on American Islamic Relations, Northern California, 1999, Supporting Schedules, 2.

16. Sarah Lubman, Matthai Chakko Kuruvila, Richard Scheinin, "One Mosque, Myriad Voices," *San Jose Mercury News*, 13 January 2002, A1.

17. Mahjabeen Islam, "ISNA's 2001 Convention Celebrates Strength Through Diversity," *Washington Report on Middle East Affairs*, 30 November 2001.

18. Affidavit in Support of Application for Search Warrant, 34.

19. Steven Pomerantz, The Journal of Counterterrorism & Security International, Spring 1998.

20. Press release, office of Sen. Jon Kyl, 3 October 2003.

21. Awad letter to Sen. Jon Kyl, 9 September 2003.

22. Press release, office of Sen. Jon Kyl, 3 October 2003.

23. Testimony of Epstein, U.S. Senate.

24. http://www.islamonline.net/livedialogue/english/Guestcv.asp?hGuestID=605R88.

25. Karen Branch-Brioso, "Area Man Found Path With Islam," *St. Louis Post-Dispatch*, 29 June 2003, A1.

26. Indictment, U.S. v. Randall Todd Royer, et al., U.S. District Court for the Eastern District of Virginia, June 2003, 22, 36.

27. Awad letter to Sen. John Kyl, 9 September 2003.

28. Richard H. Curtiss, "Omar Ahmad: Jordanian-Born Silicon Valley Enterpreneur is Influential Muslim-American Activist," *Washington Report on Middle East Affairs*, 30 June 2000, 35. Also, Lubman et al. "One Mosque, Myriad Voices."

29. IRS Form 990, Council on American-Islamic Relations, Washington, D.C., 1999, 3; also attached schedule, "Mortgages and Other Notes Payable." (Another attachment shows Hooper took out a $7,500 "temporary loan" that year for an unspecified purpose.) CAIR would not comment, and United Bank of Kuwait has since been taken over by a banking conglomerate based in Bahrain.

30. District of Columbia Deed of Trust between CAIR and the Al Maktoum Foundation of Dubai, United Arab Emirates, 12 September 2002. "Purchase money to the extent of $978,031.34." Ahmad's signature appears on page four of document.

31. Statement by Gen. Sheikh Mohammed bin Rashid Al Maktoum issued to Reuters, 27 September 2001 (as posted on al-Maktoum's personal Web site, www.sheikmohammed.ae).

32. "Notice of Mechanic's Lien" filed by Mark Merino Construction and Building Services Inc. against owner/lessee Council on American Islamic Relations (453 New Jersey Ave. S.E., Washington, D.C.) with the District of Columbia's Department of Finance and Revenue, $1,918.10, 14 October 1999.

33. "IDB Approves New Projects Worldwide," Royal Embassy of Saudi Arabia, Washington, D.C., 15 August 1999.

34. Letter to Sen. Kyl.

35. Muhammad Saman, "Almost All Intifada Funds by Arab Donors Has Arrived," *Arab News*, 26 August 2001.

36. *Islamic Views, 13th Ed.* (Saudi Armed Forces Printing Press, 1991).

37. IRS Form 990, International (Islamic) Relief Organization (IRO), Washington D.C., 1995, 1997.

38. Transcript of interview with Hooper by Rita Cosby.

39. Hooper has defended his colleague's incendiary remarks. "Hamza Yusuf is a well-respected, well-known Muslim leader in this country," he said 29 October 2001, on Fox. "He was invited to meet with President Bush." Only, FBI agents were looking for him the same day he was at the White House to ask about his eerily prophetic pox on America, as detailed in an earlier chapter.

CHAPTER 26—The Muslim Caucus

1. Falasten M. Abdeljabbar, "Alamoudi: What His Case Means to Muslims," *The American Muslim*, February 2004, 20.

2. Associated Press, 22 October 2001.

3. "The Mosque in America: A National Portrait," Mosque Study Project, Council on American-Islamic Relations, 26 April 2001.

4. "Immigrants from the Middle East: A Profile of the Foreign-born Population from Pakistan to Morocco," Center for Immigration Studies, August 2002.

5. *Religious Congregations and Membership in the United States: 2000* (Nashville, TN: Glenmary Research Center, 2002.

6. American Muslim Poll, Zogby International, Nov/Dec 2001, 9, 10.

7. Paul Sperry, "Is al-Arian Linked to N.C. Qaida Cell?" WorldNetDaily.com, 27 February 2003.

8. Associated Press, 9 January 2002.

9. Transcript of Bonior speech at third annual national convention of the American Muslim Alliance, Hempstead, N.Y., 3 October 1998.

10. Larry Cohler-Esses, "Israel Foes Give Hillary 50G," *Daily News (New York)*, 25 October 2000, 3.
11. Lobbying Report filed by registrant John W. Bryant with the Secretary of the Senate, 8 November 1998, 2. Also, Lobbying Report, 15 February 1999, 2
12. Author interview by email, 24 August 2004.
13. http://store.yahoo.com/talkislam/v47.html. Also, Paul Findley, *Silent No More* (Beltsville, Md.: Amana Publications, 2001), 114-116.
14. "Public Hearing—The Middle East in Election 2004: Voting Out the Neocons," U.S. Newswire, 27 January 2004.
15. Findley, 83.
16. Memo from Phaedra Baird to U.S. Rep. Dana Rohrabacher, 7 December 2001. "In fact, Khalid [sic] went on to tell me he even sponsors an orphaned child of a [Palestinian] suicide bomber," Baird also wrote in the memo. "He said he sees nothing wrong with his support of these people."
17. R. Scott Moxley, "Mr. Taliban," *OC Weekly*, 26 December 2003, 14.
18. Shirl McArthur, "Congressman Dana Rohrabacher: An Expert on South and Central Asia," *Washington Report on Middle East Affairs*, November/December 1996, 8.
19. Findley, 254.
20. Findley, 118, 209.
21. Transcript of remarks by Jameel W. Aalim-Johnson at Middle East Policy Council conference, Russell Senate office Building, Washington, 1 October 1999.
22. Author interview by phone, 17 June 2002.

CHAPTER 27—Undue Influence at the White House

1. Grover Norquist, "'Natural Conservatives:' Muslims Deliver for the GOP," *The American Spectator*, June 2001.
2. http://www.academicfreespeech.com/fea_oracle_0909.html.
3. Frank Gaffney, "A Troubling Influence," FrontPageMagazine.com, 9 December 2003.
4. Author interview by phone, 23 August 2004.
5. Two canceled checks endorsed to the Islamic Institute totaling $100,000 were drawn in 2001 on a Riggs bank account held by the Qatari Embassy. Two other checks totaling $55,000, dated in 1999, were drawn from United Bank of Kuwait accounts held by the Kuwaiti Embassy. Another check for $5,000 from an individual donor was drawn in 1999 on a Riyad Bank account, while another for $10,000 from a different individual was drawn in 2000 on a Saudi Hollandi Bank account. Copies of checks in author's possession.
6. Safa Trust Inc. check paid to the Islamic Institute for $10,000, drawn on a First Union National Bank account, 24 August 2000. Copy of check in author's possession.
7. Two checks totaling $20,000, drawn on Alamoudi's First Union National Bank account, endorsed to the Islamic Institute, 8 February 1999, 6 April 1999. Copies of checks in author's possession.
8. Criminal Complaint, U.S. v. Abdurahman Muhammad Alamoudi, U.S. District Court for the Eastern District of Virginia, 30 September 2003, 13, 14, 19.
9. Findley, 262.
10. Tom Hamburger, Glenn R. Simpson, "Reaching Out: In Difficult Times, Muslims Count On Unlikely Advocate," *Wall Street Journal*, 11 June 2003, A1.
11. http://www.islamicinstitute.org/fb10-13.htm.
12. Norquist, "Natural Conservatives."
13. American Muslim Poll, Zogby International, November/December 2001.
14. White House-generated list of Muslim- and Arab-American leaders and activists, along with their birthdates and Social Security numbers, used by Secret Service for security screening. The eighty-three activists on the list, generated in April 2001, were invited to the White House—even though some of them, such as Jamal Barzinji and Taha al-Alwani, had come under federal scrutiny in counterterrorism investigations. Topping the four-page list is Norquist. David Hossein Safavian, a former Alamoudi lobbyist and Islamic Institute director who landed a high-ranking position in the White House, is No. 79.

15. U.S. v. Abdurahman Muhammad Alamoudi, 10.
16. Transcript of Ashcroft testimony before House Judiciary Committee, 6 June 2001.
17. Transcript of Norquist testimony before the Senate Judiciary Committee, 7 September 2001.
18. Gaffney, "A Troubling Influence."
19. Author interview by phone, 8 August 2004. Source wishes to remain anonymous.
20. Gaffney, "A Troubling Influence."
21. Ibid.
22. http://www.alif.com/award.htm.
23. Franklin Foer, "Grover Norquist's Strange Alliance with Radical Islam," *New Republic*, 12 November 2001, 22.
24. Transcript of Loftus interview with Keith Olbermann, *Countdown*, MSNBC, 23 October 2003.
25. Affidavit in Support of Application for Search Warrant, 77.
26 http://www.americanmuslim.org/5palestine5b.html.
27. This 13 October 2001 "Friday Brief" press release—which has been removed from the institute's Web site—strongly advised Muslim members to attend the event. It directs questions to the institute and also to Alamoudi's American Muslim Council, which has supplied many of the institute's personnel. See also, John Berlau, "Militant Muslims and the GOP," *Insight*, 9 November 2001.
28. Mary Jacoby, "How Secure Is the Department of Homeland Security?" Salon.com, 22 June 2004.
29. Power of Attorney Affidavit, Fairfax County, Virginia, Circuit Court, 21 August 2003.
30. Hamburger and Simpson, "Reaching Out."
31. Surah 4:3 (caps number of wives at four); Surah 4:34 (permits striking disobedient wives); Surah 2:275 (makes no distinction between reasonable and usurious rates of interest in forbidding it).
32. The source requested anonymity. Saffuri did not respond to a request for comment. But he has been quoted recently saying skeptics like Gaffney are simply jealous they do not enjoy the same degree of access he does to the White House. There is no doubt that Saffuri has a lot of pull in town. He successfully lobbied Republicans to have a postage stamp honoring Eid, the Muslim feast. Reviews for the nation's first Muslim stamp, which debuted the same month as the 9/11 terrorist attacks, were understandably mixed at best.
33. Memo from Phaedra Baird to U.S. Rep. Dana Rohrabacher, 7 December 2001.
34. Author interview by phone, 14 November 2004. Source wishes to remain anonymous.

CHAPTER 28—Department of Homeland Insecurity
1. Affidavit in Support of Application for Search Warrant, 31.
2. Lobbying Report for 2000-2001 filed by the American Muslim Council with the Secretary of the Senate, 3 April 2001.
3. Aziz Haniffa, "U.S. Congressman Apologizes for Racist Remarks Against Sikhs and Muslims," *India Abroad*, 5 October 2001.
4. Author interview by phone, 4 August 2004.
5. Mary Jacoby, "How Secure is the Department of Homeland Security?" Salon.com, 22 June 2004.
6. Islamic Institute press release, 4 May 2001.
7. Lisa Rein, "Sales-Tax Rebellion Rattles Prince William; Activists Pressure Assembly Contingent," *Washington Post*, 13 May 2001.
8. Frank J. Gaffney, "The Faisal Gill Affair," FrontPageMagazine.com, 19 July 2004.
9. Jacoby, "How Secure is the Department of Homeland Security?"
10. Affidavit in Support of Application for Search Warrant, 30, 31.
11. Jacoby, "How Secure is the Department of Homeland Security?" It wouldn't be the first time the department has missed red flags in a high-level applicant's background. In 2003, it hired Laura L. Callahan to manage top secret databases, including ones dealing with emergency first-responders and terrorist watchlists, despite the fact thousands of emails covered by subpoena in the Monica Lewinsky investigation were lost on her watch as a White House computer

manager. Four computer specialists in sworn testimony accused her of trying to cover up the glitch by threatening to jail them if they spoke about it even to their spouses. But that's not the worst of it. The department also failed to catch not one, not two—but *three*—bogus college degrees Callahan listed on her application. It turns out she got her bachelor's degree, master's degree and Ph.D. in computer science from a Wyoming diploma mill, according to a General Accounting Office investigation. Presented with proof of its goof, Homeland Security kept Callahan on the payroll for another ten months. One observer quipped that the Department of Homeland Security may need its own Department of Homeland Security to protect it from itself.

12. "Homeland Official Subject of Probe," *Federal Times*, 16 August 2004.
13. "Muslim Students on the Rise: Standing Tall, Reaching Out," schedule of conference events, 39th Annual MSA Continental Conference 2002, Grand Hyatt Hotel, Washington, D.C., 31 August 2002.
14. "Islamic Free Market Institute Foundation meets with Attorney General Ashcroft," press release, Islamic Free Market Institute Foundation, 23 June 2004.

CHAPTER 29—Penetrating the White House
1. Transcript of Conyers testimony before Senate Governmental Affairs Committee, 29 April 2004.
2. Safavian's written responses to: Pre-Hearing Policy Questions for the Nomination of David Safavian to be Administrator for Federal Procurement Policy, U.S. Senate Governmental Affairs Committee, 16 April 2004, 2
3. Letter to Secretary of the Senate by Mark J. Robertson of Janus-Merritt Strategies LLC, 17 December 2001.
4. Affidavit in Support of Application for Search Warrant, 39.
5. Ibid., 99.
6. Pre-hearing Policy Questions for the Nomination of David Safavian to be Administrator for Federal Procurement Policy, 39.
7. Lobbying Report, Janus-Merritt Strategies LLC, 14 February 2001, 1. Lobbying Report, Janus-Merritt Strategies LLC, 17 July 2001, 1.
8. "This was an inadvertent error," Safavian explains; Pre-hearing Policy Questions for the Nomination of David Safavian to be Administrator for Federal Procurement Policy, 123.
9. Lobbying Registration, Janus-Merritt Strategies LLC, 16 July 1999, 1.
10. Lobbying Report, Janus-Merritt Strategies Inc., 12 February 2001, 2.
11. David Safavian, "Racial profiling, Gore-style," *Washington Times*, 25 October 2000, A15.
12. U.S. Newswire, 26 June 2001.
13. "Safavian Named as GSA Chief of Staff," News Releases, U.S. General Services Administration, 11 July 2002. Also, Piper Fogg, "Hill People," *National Journal*, 17 February 2001. Also, http://www.disinfopedia.org/wiki.phtml?title=Janus-Merritt_Strategies.
14. Transcript of Safavian testimony before Senate Governmental Affairs Committee, 29 April 2004.
15. Advisory: "Continued Al-Qaeda Threats Abroad and in the Homeland," Limited Distribution, For Official Use Only, U.S. Department of Homeland Security, 21 November 2003, 5.
16. http://www.isgh.org/new/about_isgh.htm#22. Norquist has publicly decried charges impugning Tulbah's loyalty as "religious bigotry."
17. Transcript of phone interview with Tulbah from Baghdad, White House press release, 27 October 2003.
18. Sarah Lubman, Matthai Chakko Kuruvila, Richard Scheinin, "One Mosque, Myriad Voices as Group Bridges Radical-Moderate Gap," *Contra Costa Times*, 17 January 2002. Khan has said through associates that lots of Muslims come and go at the large mosque, and that his father was not aware of al-Zawahiri's terrorist connections.
19. Associated Press, 23 December 2001.
20. Frank Gaffney Jr., "Islamists' White House Gatekeeper," *Washington Times*, 11 February 2003, A19.

21. A Department of Transportation spokeswoman says Khan's official title is associate director of governmental affairs for the office of the secretary of transportation.

AFTERWORD

1. Craig Whitlock, "Bin Laden Aide Warns U.S. to Alter Policies," *Washington Post*, 30 November 2004, A14.
2. "A Review of the Federal Bureau of Prisons' Selection of Muslim Religious Services Providers," Office of the Inspector General, U.S. Department of Justice, unclassified version, April 2004, 41.
3. Indictment, U.S. v. Holy Land Foundation, 7.
4. Muhammad Ejaz Khan, "Quetta Mourns Kasi's Execution, *The International News (Pakistan)*, 16 November 2002.
5. Supplemental Declaration in Support of Pre-Trial Detention, U.S. v. Soliman S. Biheiri, 8, 9.
6. Associated Press, 17 December 2004.
7. Compact disk recording featuring Ashraf Nubani, obtained from Washington, D.C.-area mosque, August 2003 (as cited in Epstein prepared written testimony, Senate Judiciary Committee).
8. Author interview by email, 13 March 2003. Lavey publicly warned of the Islamic threat to America as far back as 1995 during a conference on terrorism in Chicago. "The potential threat posed by terrorism is greater than ever before," he said as chairman of the Tenth Annual Terrorism Conference held at the University of Illinois that summer.
9. "Al Qaeda Manual," UK/BM–76, translation, government exhibit 1677-T, May 2000, 80.
10. Author interview by phone, 4 April 2004.

INDEX

INDEX

al-Shannaq, Rasmi, 74
al-Shehri, Waleed M., 83–84
al-Sudais, Shaikh Abdur Rahman, 106
al-Thumairy, Fahad, 68–69
al-Timimi, Ali, 32, 81, 86, 100, 107, 202
Alwan, Suleiman, 46
al-Zawahiri, Dr. Ayman, 44, 208, 252, 308, 312
Amana Publications, 34
Amanpour, Christiane, 35, 45
American Airlines, 49–50, 75, 83, 198, 235, 243–44, 327
American Arab Anti-Discrimination Committee, 3, 12, 87, 266
American Enterprise Institute, 293
American Media Inc., 167
American Muslim Alliance, 12, 87–88, 268–69, 273
American Muslim Armed Forces & Veterans Affairs Council, 91, 212
American Muslim Council, ix, xiv, 4, 8–9,13, 15, 26, 78, 87–88, 97, 154, 158, 187, 199, 201–2, 212, 268–69, 273, 277–84, 288–90, 295–96, 298–99, 307, 309, 324
American Muslim Foundation, 78–79, 115, 202, 278, 321
American Muslim Political Coordination Council
American Muslims for Global Peace and Justice, 87
Americans for Tax Reform, 284, 291, 297
American-Turkish Council, 161, 164
Amerithrax, 144
Ammerman, Wade, 123, 128
Anderson, Spc. Ryan G., 209, 211
Antiterrorism and Effective Death Penalty Act, 307
Arab American Institute, 87, 266, 273
Arafat, Yasir, 98, 271
Argenbright Security Inc., 233–36
Argenbright, Frank, 234
Armstrong, Karen, 42
Arpey, Gerard J., 244
Asali, Dr. Ziad, 3
Ashcroft, John, 13, 163, 180–82
Ashqar, Abdelhaleem, 116–17, 271
Ashqar, Asma, 117
Association of Arab University Graduates, 87
Atta, Mohamed, 7, 38, 49–52, 56, 60, 109, 118, 121, 123, 145, 239–40
Aulaqi, Anwar N., xvii, 7, 70–71, 120–32, 213, 271
Automated Targeting System-Passenger, 320
Awad, Nihad, 16, 27, 96–97, 231, 233, 246–50, 252–58

Awadallah, Osama, 70
Ayah Dawah Prayer Center, 107
Azzam, Abdullah, 105, 250

B

Bagby, Ihsan, 23, 169, 263–64
Baird, Phaedra, 272–73, 292
Baker, Bill, 139
Bakker, Jim, xvii
Balin, Doug, 151–52
Bank al-Taqwa, 112
Barzinji, Jamal, 8–9, 34, 85, 112, 116, 127, 266, 271, 282, 302–4, 318
Bassnan, Osama, 69, 12–24
Battle, Jeffrey Leon, 208
Benevolence International Foundation, 90, 105
Best Buy, 232
Beverly, Roderick L., 152–53
Biheiri, Soliman, 116, 185–88, 316
Bill, James A., 41
bin Laden, Osama, xiii, xix, xxii, 6, 15, 17, 43–47, 50, 56, 59–60, 68–71, 78–79, 82, 85–86, 88, 102, 104–6, 108, 112–13, 115, 123, 125, 129, 143, 151, 156, 169, 171, 185, 191, 194, 208–9, 213, 216, 233, 250, 252, 254–56, 258, 271, 273, 278, 294, 308, 312, 327
bin Sultan, Prince Bandar, 101, 213
bin Talal, Prince Alwaleed,
Binalshibh, Ramzi, 7, 123
Biren, Vice Adm. Isik, 164
Blitzer, Robert M., 88, 102, 135, 139–40
Bloch, Tom, 193, 327
BMI Inc., 91, 188
Bojinka, 141
Bonior, David E., 139–40, 234–35, 238, 267–68, 270, 292
Bosnian Relief Committee, 254
Bray, Mahdi, 92, 97
Bremer, Ambassador L. Paul, 135
Bridgeview Mosque, 104–5, 169, 324
Bryant, John, 269–70
Burns International Security Services, 232
Burt, Rear Adm. Robert, 215
Butler, Chris, 215
Bush, President George W., xvi, xxi, 6, 9, 16–18, 21–22, 24–27, 47–48, 109, 125, 165, 207, 212, 218–19, 223, 249, 258, 266, 270–72, 275–83, 285–87, 301–2, 304–6

C

Campbell, Tom, 270–71, 309
Cannon, U.S. Rep. Chris, 301, 303
Carle, David, 137
Carmody, Barry, 187–88

ACKNOWLEDGMENTS

This book could not have been written without the assistance of many others, although that does not necessarily mean they all agree with its content. My debts start with my family. I would not have been able to pull this ambitious project together without the love, support, and patience of my wife and children. I love them (and missed them during my "hermit crab" days) more than they know. I must also acknowledge the love and support of my mother, the teacher, and father, the engineer, who despite their differences, have always been united in their encouragement of me and my passion for raw, unvarnished journalism. They are both free spirits and thinkers, and have given me the courage to not conform to convention, and to remain intellectually curious even when it is not popular to ask questions.

My agent Andrew Stuart made this book happen and was a constant source of encouragement. My editor Joel Miller never flagged in his patience, despite my serial busting of deadlines.

But the core contributors to this project are the former and active law enforcement agents—in the field and on the front lines in the war on terrorism—who were gracious enough to share their time, experience (including internal documents), and insights with me. Unlike their timid bosses in Washington who are still slaves to political correctness and promotions, these are the gutsy public servants to whom the American people owe a debt of gratitude. Trust me when I say that they care more about your safety and security than most of the politicians in Washington. They include agents (and a few courageous and patriotic language specialists) at the FBI, as well as agents at ICE and CBP. Several members of the U.S. intelligence community also contributed to this project.

I also want to extend special thanks to intrepid whistleblower Sibel Edmonds, Mike Waller, Ali Ahmed, Mike Tune, Hale Smith (formerly Abdul Haleem), Ed Soliday, and ret. Lt. Col. Stephen Franke, among others, for their technical assistance, as well as inspiration. (Of course, knowing God's love is unconditional for all—whether you are Muslim, Jew, or Christian—was also a constant source of inspiration.)

Finally, I have to thank Juan Valdez, Glen Ellen, and Ben & Jerry. I could not have reached the finish line of this marathon without them.